John Charles Dent

The last forty years

Canada since the union of 1841

John Charles Dent

The last forty years
Canada since the union of 1841

ISBN/EAN: 9783742855527

Manufactured in Europe, USA, Canada, Australia, Japa

Cover: Foto ©ninafisch / pixelio.de

Manufactured and distributed by brebook publishing software (www.brebook.com)

John Charles Dent

The last forty years

THE
LAST FORTY YEARS:

CANADA SINCE THE UNION OF 1841.

BY

JOHN CHARLES DENT.

VOL. I.

"No picture, no history, can present us with the whole truth: but those are the best pictures and the best histories which exhibit such parts of the truth as most nearly produce the effect of the whole. History has its foreground and its background; and it is principally in the management of its perspective that one artist differs from another. Some events must be represented on a large scale, others diminished; the great majority will be lost in the dimness of the horizon: and a general idea of their joint effect will be given by a few slight touches." MACAULAY: *Essay on History.*

TORONTO:
PUBLISHED BY GEORGE VIRTUE.

Entered according to Act of Parliament of Canada, in the year Eighteen Hundred and Eighty-one, by GEORGE VIRTUE, in the office of the Minister of Agriculture.

C. B. ROBINSON, PRINTER,
5 Jordan Street, Toronto.

CONTENTS.

CHAPTER I.	PAGE.
LORD DURHAM	9
CHAPTER II.	
THE UNION ACT	35
CHAPTER III.	
LOCUS IN QUO	52
CHAPTER IV.	
THE FIRST MINISTRY	68
CHAPTER V.	
THE ASSEMBLY OF NOTABLES	90
CHAPTER VI.	
THE FIRST TEST OF THE UNION ACT	110
CHAPTER VII.	
EXIT LORD SYDENHAM	140
CHAPTER VIII.	
THE CASE OF ALEXANDER McLEOD	163
CHAPTER IX.	
SIR CHARLES BAGOT	179

Contents.

	Chapter X	PAGE
	THE ASHBURTON TREATY	194
	Chapter XI	
	RECONSTRUCTION	213
	Chapter XII	
	THE SHADOW OF DOWNING STREET	252
	Chapter XIII	
	SIR CHARLES METCALFE	263
	Chapter XIV	
	WHAT IS TO BECOME OF THE GOVERNOR-GENERAL?	278
	Chapter XV	
	ON THE EDGE OF THE STORM	305
	Chapter XVI	
	RESPONSIBLE GOVERNMENT	320
	Chapter XVII	
	CHAOS	342
	Chapter XVIII	
	AN APPEAL TO THE COUNTRY	372

The Last Forty Years.

Canada since the Union of 1841

BY JOHN CHARLES DENT

GEO. VIRTUE
PUBLISHER
TORONTO

THE HON. (AFTERWARDS SIR) FRANCIS HINCKS.

LORD DURHAM.

THE LAST FORTY YEARS.

Chapter I.

LORD DURHAM.

"No episode in our political history is more replete with warning to honest and public-spirited men, who, in seeking to serve their country, forget what is due to their own interests and their own security, than the story of Lord Durham. He accepted the Governorship of Canada during a supreme crisis in the affairs of that colony. . . . . From his political opponents, in the place of generous forbearance, he met with unremitting persecution ; and as for the character of the support which he obtained from those ministers who had themselves placed him in the forefront of the battle, it is more becoming to leave it for Tory historians to recount the tale."— GEORGE OTTO TREVELYAN. *Life and Letters of Macaulay.*

ONE day, towards the end of the month of July, 1840, an English nobleman lay dying at Cowes, in the Isle of Wight. It had long been evident to those about him that his days were numbered. He came of an energetic, yet withal a somewhat short-lived race, and had inherited a feeble constitution, combined with a soaring but capricious ambition, an irritable temper, a morbid egotism, and a fondness for hard work. He had from his boyhood suffered from an ungovernable tendency to fretfulness and worry, and an utter incapacity for possessing his soul in patience whenever his too susceptible nature was wounded. These incongruous conditions had brought about their legitimate results, and the Right Honourable John George Lambton, first Earl of Durham, lay racked with pain of mind and body, with the sands of his life rapidly running themselves out. His physicians had advised him a few weeks before to try the effect of the balmy breezes of southern France. His Lordship well knew what such advice meant in the present instance. It simply meant that his physicians were at the end of their resources, and that his exhausted system would no longer respond to their nostrums. Thenceforth he knew that his length of days would simply depend upon how much more his overstrained nervous organization might be able to endure. He was able to gauge his own powers of endurance pretty accurately, and he felt that his life's work was over. He had resolved, however, to act upon the suggestion of his medical advisers, and, without even paying a farewell visit to his princely home in the north—an abode well fitted, both inside and out, to rank among the stately homes of England—he had set forth from his Town-house in Hill Street, Berkeley Square, for the continent. As matter of fact, he was not fit to travel, even after the luxurious fashion which was his wont. Upon his arrival at Southampton he found himself so weak as scarcely to be able to stand alone. A trembling of the limbs and a fluttering of the heart warned him of his unfitness for any further exertion. A rough and heavy sea came rolling in from the Channel, and it was evident that the passage on that day would be even more than usually trying to a sensitive and debilitated frame. Further progress must for the time be abandoned. As the event proved, the abandonment was final. After resting for a day, the invalid passed over to Cowes, not without hope that there, peradventure, he might regain sufficient strength to enable him to resume his journey.

The hope proved fallacious. His vital forces were exhausted. His petulance—for his Lordship *was* petulant, and had, as has been intimated, a high temper of his own—was never again to disturb the peace of mind of his august father-in-law, nor even of his personal attendants. He never regained sufficient vigour even to berate his valet. On the 26th of the month his physician-in-chief was summoned for the last time, and gave it as his opinion that his Lordship would not live to see the light of another day. "Then," said the dying man, with playful melancholy, "the legend is true, and I shall not die at Lambton."* After a pause, he added in a faint voice: "I would fain hope I have not lived altogether in vain. Whatever the Tories may say, the Canadians will one day do justice to my memory." The remark about his not dying at Lambton had reference to a phase of an old legend which predicted that for an indeterminate number of generations no head of the house of Lambton should die at home. The prophecy had been uttered as far back as the days of the Crusades, and was devoutly believed by the peasantry in the neighbourhood of Lambton during the early years of the present century. It is probably not wholly discredited by them even at the present day, notwithstanding that the historical records of the family establish beyond dispute that some leading representatives of the race have died comfortably at home. We can afford, at this distance of time, to smile at his Lordship's reference to the weird family legend of the Worm of Lambton;† but his allusion to his Canadian mission has an ever-living interest for the people of this Dominion. Canadians of all shades of political conviction—whether Tories, Liberal-Conservatives, Grits or Reformers—have long since done justice to his memory.

The physician's prediction overshot the mark. Lord Durham lingered till the 28th of the month, when he breathed his last. He was only forty-eight years and three months old. He had gained a very high political reputation, and if life and health had been spared

---

*Lambton Castle, the family seat, situated in one of the most picturesque districts in the county of Durham.

† For an interesting account of this queer old-time legend, see Howitt's "Visits to Remarkable Places," Second Series, pp. 162-166.

to him he would doubtless have left a name as widely known to posterity as it was to his contemporaries. "Canada has been the death of him," remarked John Stuart Mill, when intelligence of his Lordship's demise reached London. The saying was in a great measure true. Probably Lord Durham would not under the most favourable conditions have attained to a patriarchal age, but he might well have lived a few years longer than he did if he had kept clear of politics, Lord Brougham, and—above all—Canada.

To keep clear of politics, however, would have been no easy task for the son of William Henry Lambton. This gentleman was in his day a very conspicuous and influential member of the Whig party. He for many years sat in the House of Commons for the city of Durham, and was known to hold very advanced opinions upon many subjects altogether unconnected with politics. He was a personal friend and staunch political ally of Charles James Fox. Trained by such a father, and in such a school, it is not to be wondered at if John George Lambton was a Liberal of the Liberals, not only by right of descent, but by right of conviction. As he grew up to manhood he began to display a keen interest in politics. He developed many statesmanlike qualities, and the breadth of his views seemed to some of his contemporaries almost like inspiration in one of his rank. He sometimes startled even his father by the boldness of his speculations on human equality and popular rights. He was well versed in the literature of politics, and in addition to great natural ability was possessed of much acquired knowledge. Unfortunately, he also displayed qualities which threatened to seriously interfere with his usefulness as a public man. He seems to have had an uncommonly sharp and bright, but rather ill-balanced, intellect. He sometimes did extravagant things, and was slow to admit an error. He was aggressive and pertinacious, strong in his likes and dislikes, and very deficient in tact. With all his faults, however, he was a man of great intellectual vigour, of decided opinions, and honourable ambition. He entered the House of Commons for the county of Durham when he was only twenty-one years of age, and soon made himself a conspicuous figure there by his advanced political views, as well as by his denunciations of the non-progressive party in power. He could make a very scathing speech, and was always ready for attack. The Liberals recognized his abilities, and began to look upon him as their rising hope. He materially strengthened his position with his party by his marriage, in 1816, to the eldest daughter of Earl Grey. His influence from that time forward rapidly grew, until he was one of the foremost men in English public life. He introduced into Parliament various measures of radical reform; among them a Bill which, had it passed, would have left the famous measure of 1832 far behind. In 1828 he was raised to the peerage by the title of Baron Durham. Upon the formation of his father-in-law's Ministry, in 1830, he accepted office as Lord Privy Seal. He had a share in the preparation of the Reform Bill, but owing to ill-health and domestic calamity his part in the ensuing debates was less conspicuous than it would otherwise have been. In 1833 he resigned office, and was created Viscount Lambton and Earl of Durham. As a Cabinet Minister he was not popular with his colleagues, owing to his frequent ebullitions of temper, and the incisive sharpness of his tongue. The private memoirs and correspondence of the period abound with instances of his petulance and want of self-control. Lord Grey was very frequently the object of his attacks, and the decorous, well-meaning Prime Minister was wont to quail at the frown of his impetuous and unconventional son-in-law, who at times seemed to take a positive delight in courting antagonism.* His prominent

---

* "December 4th, 1831.—Dined with Talleyrand yesterday. He complained to me of Durham's return, and of 'sa funeste influence sur Lord Grey.'" *The Greville Memoirs*, Chap. XVI.—"December 11th.—George Bentinck told me this evening of a scene which had been related to him by the Duke of Richmond, that lately took place at a Cabinet

position in the ranks of the Liberal party made him an object of antipathy to Lord Brougham, who could not bear that any other man than himself should be considered of much account there. Lord Durham was ready enough to retort the antipathy, and at a banquet given to Lord Grey by the Reformers of Edinburgh, in 1834, made a speech in reply to his antagonist, which thencefor-

---

dinner; it was very soon after Durham's return from abroad. He was furious at the negotiations and question of compromise (on the subject of the Reform Bill). Lord Grey is always the object of his rage and impertinence, because he is the only person whom he dares attack. After dinner he made a violent *sortie* on Lord Grey (it was at Althorp's), said he would be eternally disgraced if he suffered any alterations to be made in this Bill, that he was a betrayer of the cause, and, among other things, reproached him with having kept him in town on account of this Bill in the summer, 'and thereby having been the cause of the death of his son.' Richmond said in his life he never witnessed so painful a scene, or one which excited such disgust and indignation in every member of the Cabinet. Lord Grey was ready to burst into tears, said he would much rather work in the coal-mines than be subject to such attacks, on which the other muttered, 'and you might do worse,' or some such words. After this Durham got up and left the room. Lord Grey very soon retired too, when the other Ministers discussed this extraordinary scene, and considered what steps they ought to take. They thought at first that they should require Durham to make a public apology (*i.e.*, before all of them) to Lord Grey for his impertinence, which they deemed due to *them* as he was *their* head, and to *Althorp* as having occurred in his house, but as they thought it was quite certain that Durham would resign the next morning, and that Lord Grey might be pained at another scene, they forbore to exact this. However, Durham did not resign; he absented himself for some days from the Cabinet, at last returned as if nothing had happened, and there he goes on as usual. But they are so thoroughly disgusted, and resolved to oppose him, that his influence is greatly impaired. Still, his power of mischief and annoyance is considerable. Lord Grey succumbs to him, and they say in spite of his behaviour is very much attached to him, though so incessantly worried that his health visibly suffers by his presence. There is nothing in which he does not meddle. The Reform Bill he had a principal hand in concocting, and he fancies himself the only man competent to manage our foreign relations. Melbourne, who was present at the scene, said, 'If I had been Lord Grey I would have knocked him down.'"—*Ib.*—"We had a dreadful scene at my Cabinet dinner yesterday, which will probably lead to very detrimental consequences for the moment. Durham made the most brutal attack on Lord Grey I ever heard in my life, and I conclude will certainly resign. He will put this upon alterations in the Bill—most unfairly—because there is no alteration of any consequence in the main principle, and I doubt whether he knows anything about the alterations, as he will not allow any-body to tell him what they are. But if he resigns on this ground it will break up the Government."—*Letter from Viscount Althorp to Earl Spencer, 20th December, 1831*, quoted in Le Marchant's *Memoir of John Charles Viscount Althorp, Third Earl Spencer*, pp. 374, 375. For a further characteristic reference to Lord Durham's violent temper, see *The Greville Memoirs*, Chap. XIX., under date of November 27th, 1832.

ward rendered the enmity between them one of intense and caustic bitterness. Brougham was a savage and unsparing foe, and bided his time, which did not arrive until after the lapse of several years. When it did arrive it was taken eager advantage of, and there can be no reasonable doubt that the fierce opposition to Lord Durham which was set on foot by Lord Brougham had the effect of shortening the former's life.

Brougham's opportunity came to him in connection with the disturbed state of affairs in Canada. The troubles in that colony, which had long been gathering to a head, culminated, in 1837 and 1838, in open rebellion. In the Upper Province, the movement, though by no means so insignificant an affair as it has sometimes been pronounced to have been, was not widespread, and did not long present any obstacle to the local authorities. In Lower Canada the case was otherwise. Mr. Papineau and other popular leaders had roused the unlettered French Canadian population to frenzy. They were not only opposed to the Government, but to the Constitution, as established in 1791. Happily it is not necessary to go very deeply into the merits of this conflict in the present work. A brief outline of the events which produced it would seem, however, to be desirable.

By the Treaty of Paris, concluded on the 10th of February, 1763, all the French possessions in North America, with certain insignificant exceptions, were surrendered to Great Britain, and Canada, with a population of nearly 70,000, became a British colony. It was stipulated on the part of the surrendering power, and assented to on behalf of Great Britain, that the French colonists, who made up nearly the entire population, should enjoy the free exercise of the Roman Catholic religion and all their former religious privileges so far as the laws and constitution of England permitted. A royal proclamation was issued during the same year,* whereby the law of

---

* On the 7th of October.

England, civil as well as criminal, was introduced into the colony in general terms. The purely military rule which had prevailed since the Conquest was somewhat relaxed. By degrees tranquillity was restored throughout the land, although the introduction of the law and language of England was very distasteful to the French Canadians. A tide of immigration, not very strong at first, but steadily increasing, set in from the British Isles. It was not until the passing of the Quebec Act, in 1774, that anything approaching to a constitutional system of government was introduced. By that Act—the merits whereof need not be discussed in these pages[*]— provision was made for the appointment by the Crown of a Council, with power to make ordinances, with the consent of the Governor, for the peace, welfare and good government of the colony. The proclamation of 1763 was revoked, and it was enacted that in all matters relating to civil rights, and the enjoyment of property, customs and usages, the old French law which had been in force before the Conquest should prevail. In criminal proceedings the law of England was retained. The power given to the Governor and Council to alter the law in civil matters was subsequently exercised by the promulgation of divers ordinances, whereby, among other important changes, the Habeas Corpus Act and trial by jury were introduced. The most perfect toleration of the Roman Catholic religion was, as formerly, guaranteed to the French Canadian colonists. The Quebec Act came into operation in the month of October, 1774, and remained in force until the 26th of December, 1791, an interval embracing about seventeen years, during which the American colonies now forming the United States of America threw off the yoke of the mother country, and achieved their independence. One result of that independence was the spread

---

[*] For a critical and readable exposition of the merits and defects of this statute, the reader is referred to the fourth chapter of Mr. S. J. Watson's valuable little work entitled "The Constitutional History of Canada."

of republican and revolutionary ideas, not on this continent alone, but throughout Europe. Another result was the settlement in Canada of a great many loyalist refugees from the revolted colonies. These refugees have gained a conspicuous place in our history under the name of United Empire Loyalists. They were ultra-British in feeling, and French manners and customs were not congenial to them. In no great space of time some thousands of them found their way to what subsequently became Upper Canada, where liberal grants of land were made to them, and where, under their auspices, the country soon began to emerge from the condition of a primitive wilderness into that of a thriving and prosperous domain. Many British immigrants also settled in various parts of Canada. Most of them repaired to the Upper Province, but not a few settled down among the French Canadian population, more especially in the cities of Montreal and Quebec. It was noticeable that the representatives of the two nationalities were as incongruous as oil and water, and would not mix. Eventually a "British Party" arose, the policy and sympathies of which were diametrically opposed to those of the native population. They had as little in common as different races of civilized mankind living in a common neighbourhood very well could have. The Custom of Paris and the Edicts of the French Kings and the colonial Intendants were utterly distasteful to the British colonists. Trial by jury and other regulations peculiar to the law of England were equally repugnant to the French Canadians. The latter were of the Roman Catholic religion, whereas the British were generally Protestants. Thus two hostile elements grew up and were fostered side by side. Various petitions were from time to time presented to the Imperial authorities, with a view to the removal of some of these anomalies, and finally the Constitutional Act of 1791 was passed, whereby the power of legislation previously granted to the Governor and Council was taken away, and the Province of Quebec was divided into the two Provinces of

Upper and Lower Canada, a separate constitution and a representative form of Government being granted to each. To each Province was assigned a Legislature, consisting of a Governor or Lieutenant-Governor, appointed by the Crown, and responsible to the Crown alone; a Legislative Council, the members whereof were also appointed by the Crown for life; and a Legislative Assembly elected by the freeholders. The property qualification for an elector was placed so low as almost to constitute universal suffrage. Thus a simulacrum of the English Constitution was introduced into Canada, the Governor representing the Sovereign, the Council representing the House of Lords,* and the Assembly the House of Commons.

The Constitutional Act of 1791, as will have been understood from the foregoing account, introduced a totally different order of things from that which had prevailed under the Quebec Act; and from this time forward the Provinces were distinct in name, as they had already become in fact.† The object of making the division was

---

* In the case of the Legislative Council the Crown was authorized to make the seats in it hereditary, and to annex hereditary titles to them. The Crown was wise enough not to act upon the authority, and we have thus far had no "hereditary nobility" in Canada since the Conquest. During the discussion of the measure in the House of Commons, Mr. Fox remarked that he saw nothing so good in hereditary powers and honours as to incline the House to introduce them into a country where they were unknown, and by such means distinguish Canada from all the colonies on the other side of the Atlantic. He added that in countries where they made a part of the constitution he did not think it wise to destroy them, but to give birth and life to such principles in countries where they did not already exist appeared to him to be exceedingly unwise.—See the Parliamentary debates of the period.

† "The marvellous political prescience of Charles James Fox was never, perhaps, so truly and so sadly exemplified as in the objections which he raised (in the House of Commons) against the Constitutional Act. The greatest Liberal of his age seemed to stand, as it were, upon the mountain peak of the constitution, and project his vision, clear with the light of political prophecy, forth like an arrow's flight, right into the far and misty Future. Almost everything to which he took exception proved, in the after years of Canadian history, a source of heartburning to the people, and of imminent peril to the State. He opposed a Legislative Council nominated by the Crown; the appropriation of the public lands for ecclesiastical purposes; the division of the Province, and the consequent isolation of the inhabitants of both races. The first two of these questions were destined, for over half a century, to be the political plagues of Canada, and the chronic

to separate the two races, and to prevent their fusion. It was hoped that by this means the Upper Province might be kept wholly British, and the Lower Province wholly French. The hope, so far at least as Lower Canada was concerned, was not realized, for there was a considerable British element in that Province which refused to be denuded of its nationality at the bidding of any Act of Parliament.

In each Province the custom, sanctioned by the Imperial Government, came into vogue of governing by means of a body of men known as the Executive Council. The members of this Council were appointed by the Governor, acting on behalf of the Crown, and were chosen as his judgment, predilection or caprice might direct. They were generally taken from the ranks of the judges, salaried officials, and members of the Legislative Council. Their functions consisted of advising the Governor on all matters as to which he might deem it expedient to ask their advice. They were not supposed to be consulted on mere appointments to office, but only on grave matters, or matters of a quasi-judicial character. In point of fact, however, they practically ruled the land, though they were not responsible either to the Governor or to either branch of the Legislature. They were, in a word, a wholly independent and irresponsible body—a junto of oligarchs who, however odious and tyrannical they might become, could not be punished or brought to account for their conduct.

The population of Canada, at the time of the division of the Provinces, was about 200,000,* whereof Upper Canada contained

---

perplexity of great Britain. The third question is left to Time, the great alchemist who transmutes, in his slow, creative laboratory, the elements of doubt and danger of to-day into forces of safety in the hereafter."—*The Constitutional History of Canada*, by Samuel James Watson, Vol. I., p. 126.

* According to a census of the Province of Quebec taken in 1790 the population was then 224,466, but there is good reason for believing that the enumeration was much too large. See Smith's History of Canada, Vol. II. See also, "A Cry from Quebec" (a pamphlet published at Montreal in 1809), p. 17.

considerably less than one-sixth. In the Lower Province the proportion of British to French inhabitants was very small. The proportion, however, steadily increased, and in 1793 the Home Government appointed an Anglican bishop of Quebec, in the person of Dr. Jacob Mountain. In 1804 an Anglican cathedral, built on the site of the ancient church and convent of the Récollets, was consecrated at Quebec. This aroused a certain amount of jealousy and ill feeling on the part of the Roman Catholic population. There were attempts at proselytism on both sides. Owing, in great measure, to Bishop Mountain's influence, a statute was passed providing for the establishment of free schools throughout the Lower Canadian parishes, to be maintained from the funds of the Jesuits. The carrying out of this project was opposed by the Roman Catholic clergy with such determination that it was almost entirely frustrated. The divergence of feeling between the two elements in the population became wider and wider, and was increased by the mischievous efforts of demagogues on both sides. In the year 1806 the publication of a newspaper in the French language was begun at Quebec, for the express purpose of holding the British population up to contumely. Much frothy bombast was written and spoken, and the irresponsible oligarchy incited the Governor to various unwise and despotic acts against the French Canadians. A so-called "Reign of Terror" set in, and the aspect of affairs was dark and threatening. The American invasion of 1812 interrupted these unseemly squabbles, and both sections of the people united in repelling the invader. The French Canadians fought in defence of their country not less valiantly than the English, Scotch, and Irish, and the name of the gallant hero of Chateauguay will go down to posterity side by side with that of the hero of Queenston Heights. But no sooner was peace restored than the internal troubles reappeared in both Provinces, and erelong began to assume a more serious aspect than before. The French Canadians still retained many of the old-world

customs and notions which had formerly prevailed in France, but
which had been swept away there by the Revolution. They looked
with jealousy and distrust upon all attempts to introduce a different
order of things, and more especially upon attempts to give additional power to the British population. But there were still graver
and more extended sources of disquiet. In both Provinces the representative branch of the Legislature began to be frequently at issue
with the executive. The Canadian constitution was confessedly
modelled upon that of Great Britain, but in Canada the executive
declined to act as its prototype in England would have done upon
finding itself out of harmony with the popular branch of the
Legislature. Here, the placemen who made up the executive refused
to surrender their power, patronage and emoluments at the bidding
of the Assembly, and declined to admit the analogy between their
position and that of the executive at home. When the principle
of executive responsibility was propounded, they scouted and
denounced it as a democratic sophism unworthy of serious consideration. This was the beginning of the discussion, energetically
waged and long maintained, on the vexed question of Responsible
Government. Long impunity, and the countenance of successive
Governors, made the executive very bold, and in process of time
the want of unison between the latter and the Assembly came
to be regarded by those in authority as a very insignificant
matter. This involved constant hostility and irritation between
the Assembly and the Government. The popular leaders in the
Assembly of the Lower Province were driven farther in the direction
of opposition and radicalism than they would otherwise have felt
disposed to travel. By their influence the Assembly was induced
to pass various measures to curtail the prerogative. It was evident
that to such a strife as this an end must come sooner or later, and
what that end would be was not doubtful. The foundations of the
constitution must give way. The Government then appears to have

conceived the idea of interposing the Legislative Council between itself and the Assembly, and in pursuance of this policy appointed to that Council persons who were bitterly hostile to the leaders in the popular body The result was frequent and violent collision between these two branches of the Legislature. The opposition became almost inconceivably factious, and in some instances measures were passed by the Assembly for no other purpose than to induce their rejection by the Council. In 1828 the discontent of the people was expressed in a petition of grievances addressed to the king, to which petition 87,000 names were appended. Many crying evils were pointed out, and a clause was inserted praying that the Legislative Council might be made elective. Delegates were sent across the Atlantic to lay the petition at the feet of His Majesty King George IV. The matter was referred to a Committee, which recommended certain reforms, the carrying out of which did something to temporarily allay public irritation; but the system of appointing Legislative Councillors remained unchanged, and it was not long ere the popular discontent was greater than ever. There were also serious misunderstandings between the two Provinces on financial and other questions. The proportion of import duties to which each Province was justly entitled was a frequent bone of contention. At last the Assembly of Lower Canada resorted to the extreme measure of stopping the supplies. The example was followed, in 1836, by the Assembly of the Upper Province. In each case the Government got over the dilemma by appropriating such public funds as were at the Crown's disposal. Then came the rebellion.

It was evident to the Imperial authorities that some change in the Canadian constitution was imperatively required. Their weak but well-meant efforts to govern the colony in accordance with the popular will had thus far proved wholly ineffectual. The condition of affairs was much more serious in the Lower than in the Upper Province. In the latter the great mass of the people were loyal subjects, and though many of them had been goaded into rebellion by the domination of the Family Compact and the unwise administration of arbitrary Lieutenant-Governors, there had been no widespread desire to throw off the British yoke. The local militia and volunteers had been found fully equal to the task of putting down the attempted insurrection. Very different was the case in Lower Canada, where a large majority of the people had long been disaffected and ripe for revolt. Regular troops were called into requisition. Several conflicts took place which might almost be dignified by the name of pitched battles, and there was considerable effusion of blood. Sir John Colborne, who had charge of the military, was an old Peninsular campaigner who had fought at Waterloo. He did not believe in playing with revolution, and put it down with a considerable degree of severity. It is doubtful if there was ever the remotest prospect of success for the rebels, even in the Lower Province, but the outbreak there was at all events of a character not to be despised. The Imperial authorities found it necessary, in the month of February, 1838, to suspend the constitution of Lower Canada. It was well understood that the crisis was one calling for immediate action. It was even apprehended that the rebellion might not be confined to the two Canadas, for there was much excitement in the Maritime Provinces, and an outbreak there was regarded as among the possibilities of the near future. The plan finally determined upon by the Home Government was to send out a high functionary to Canada armed with extraordinary powers, to report upon the condition and requirements of the country, civil and political. The Government would thus acquire an accurate knowledge of the existing state of affairs, and would be in a position to inaugurate useful legislation—a task by no means easy of accomplishment in the face of such contradictory information as had reached them from Toronto, Quebec, and Montreal.

The statesman fixed upon to undertake this important mission was Lord Durham. His Parliamentary experience and his familiarity with matters of administration, conjoined with his great abilities and his decided opinions in favour of popular rights, eminently fitted him for such an undertaking. His infirmities of temper and want of self-control do not seem to have entered into the calculations of the Ministry.

On the 22nd of January, 1838, Lord John Russell, leader of the Government party in the House of Commons, announced in that chamber that Her Majesty had been pleased to entrust the conduct of the Canadian inquiry and report, with the high powers implied in the appointment, to Lord Durham; and accordingly his Lordship was duly appointed High Commissioner, with very full authority, as well as Governor-General of British North America. His mission was a comprehensive one, but its principal object was the adjustment of "certain important questions depending in the Provinces of Lower and Upper Canada." He proceeded across the Atlantic, and reached Quebec towards the close of May. He addressed himself to the object of his mission with characteristic energy, and spent a little more than five months in Canada. He adopted what Bassanio calls "a swelling port," and travelled about the country in a fashion almost regal. He deemed himself to have been clothed with the powers of a dictator, and conducted himself accordingly. The Canada Bill, however, had been shorn of many of its original features during its passage through Parliament, and the High Commissioner's powers had been considerably curtailed in the process. Lord Durham demeaned himself as though he felt untrammelled by the laws which govern ordinary mortals, and altogether independent of authority, whether Imperial, colonial, or other. It is difficult to draw the line at the precise spot where he overstepped the bounds of the authority wherewith he had been entrusted, but it is impossible to deny that some of his acts were wholly beyond the scope of his

powers. One of the most harassing problems which stared him in
the face was how to dispose of the rebel prisoners, large numbers of
whom lay in gaol at Montreal and elsewhere in the Lower Province
under charges of high treason. These prisoners had not been tried.
To try them in the regular manner would have involved great cost,
long delay, and an ultimate miscarriage of justice. If the ordinary
course of procedure had been resorted to it would have been impossible to secure convictions, inasmuch as the jurymen would have
been chiefly drawn from the ranks of those who sympathized with
the rebellion. Such jurymen would never have found a verdict of
guilty against their unhappy fellow-countrymen, who had done no
more than they themselves had felt inclined to do. True, it would
have been practicable to obtain packed juries—a device not wholly
unknown in Lower Canada under some of Lord Durham's predecessors. But his Lordship, notwithstanding certain defects of temper
and constitution, was a high-minded man. To one so constituted
the packing of juries for any purpose whatever is an odious task, and
in the particular case under consideration such a proceeding would
simply have been judicial murder. It would have been most
impolitic, however, to bid the rebels go free, without any mark
of condemnation. Although they had never been tried, their
connection with the rebellious movement was a matter beyond
dispute. The most effectual remedy seemed to his Lordship to
be the proclamation of a general amnesty, with exceptions in case
of the ringleaders; and this course was finally adopted. By the Imperial Act whereby the colonial constitution had been suspended,
temporary provision for the government of Lower Canada had been
made by the creation of a Special Council, the decrees whereof
were to have the same effect as Legislative enactments ordinarily
have. This Council had been summoned by Sir John Colborne,
Lord Durham's predecessor in the government of Canada, about six
weeks before the latter's arrival in the colony. The Councillors,

however, had been notified by Sir John Colborne that their appointment was merely provisional, and that his successor would enter on the discharge of his duties unfettered as to the choice of Councillors. Immediately after his arrival Lord Durham dissolved this provisional Council, and appointed a new one on his own account, which was largely composed of members of his own staff. This step, which was afterwards made a ground of offence against him by some of his enemies, was in reality a wise proceeding, and tended at the time to inspire additional confidence in his Administration on the part of loyal subjects. Various commissions were then organized, to inquire into the state of education, municipal institutions, Crown lands, and immigration. An accurate return of the rebel prisoners was obtained, and then the great problem was dealt with after a truly original and high-handed fashion. His Excellency opened negotiations with Wolfred Nelson, R. S. M. Bouchette, and other personages who had taken a leading part in the insurrectionary movements, and received from them a communication in which they placed themselves entirely at his Lordship's disposal, and prayed that the peace of the country might not be endangered by a trial. Their prayer was granted. They were without any formula of trial placed on board Her Majesty's steamship *Vestal*, and transported to Bermuda, and the penalty of death was pronounced against them in case of their return to Canada without permission from the Governor or other person administering the Government on behalf of Her Majesty. With respect to Louis Joseph Papineau, Dr. O'Callaghan, George Etienne Cartier, and other persons to the number (in all) of sixteen, who had fled from the Province to avoid the consequences of their treasonable acts, a similar penalty was pronounced in case of their unauthorized return. A general amnesty was pronounced with respect to all other persons who had participated in the movement, with the exception of those who had been concerned in the murder of

Lieutenant Weir and Joseph Chartrand.* These latter were treated as murderers, who had no right to expect the clemency due to mere rebels.

Such was the purport of the ordinance, dated the 28th of June, 1838, which was destined to bring down upon Lord Durham's devoted head the thunders of his enemies on both sides of the Atlantic. Brougham, who, since the Edinburgh banquet, had omitted no opportunity of decrying him, and of speaking with contempt of his jejune statesmanship, girded up his loins for an acrimonious attack in the House of Lords. That the High Commissioner had rendered himself peculiarly open to attack was undoubted. He had acted with an arbitrary independence of the ordinary forms of law such as few persons in his position would have ventured upon. He had, as has been seen, dissolved the Special Council in existence at the time of his arrival in Canada, and had substituted for it a body which was merely the echo of his own voice. He had, in some of his proclamations, adopted a tone which smacked strongly of the autocrat. He had associated himself with, and had even taken into his intimate confidence, persons whose moral reputations were not savoury. He had conducted his mission with a costly ostentation. More than all, he had banished British subjects without any form of trial, and had transported them to a colony over which he had no manner of authority. And he had adjudged that these British subjects, who had not been convicted of any offence, should be punished with death if they

---

* Weir was a young officer of the 32nd Regiment who, on the 22nd of November, 1837, was sent from Montreal with despatches to the officer in command at Sorel. Upon his arrival at his destination he found that the troops had marched to St. Charles. He accordingly started for that place, but was captured on the way by some of Dr. Nelson's scouts, who detained him as a prisoner. He was treated with perfect kindness by the gallant Doctor, but was barbarously slain by his guards upon attempting to make his escape. For full particulars of this transaction, see Christie's "History of Lower Canada," Vol. IV., p. 516 et seq. See also Vol. V., p. 302 et seq. For an account of the murder of Joseph Armand dit Chartrand, see Vol. V. of the same work, pp. 206—212.

ventured to return to Canada without express permission. It will thus be seen that there were abundant technical grounds for arraigning his policy. But Lord Durham was by no means without moral justification, even for the most high-handed of his proceedings. Upon landing in Canada he found himself in a position without precedent, where grave interests were involved, and where much must necessarily be left to his own motion. Under such circumstances, if anything approaching to an average discretion be used, public opinion has no right to hold the person exercising it amenable to strict rules of law. Lord Durham did what he and his advisers honestly believed to be for the best, although he and they well knew that he was going beyond the letter of the authority wherewith he had been invested. And herein lay the weakness of his position. He had, as it was said, knowingly set himself above the law. Brougham, Lyndhurst, Ellenborough, and other prominent members of the House of Lords inveighed mercilessly against him. The Government, for a time, defended him in a weak, half-hearted fashion, but they were not strong enough to stand the pressure brought to bear against them, and gave way. Lord Melbourne, First Minister, on the 10th of August, announced to the House of Lords the Government's determination. He admitted the informality of that part of Lord Durham's ordinance which applied to Bermuda, and stated that as it would be illegal to adopt part of the ordinance and disallow the remainder, he had resolved to advise its total disallowance. A Bill of Indemnity, protecting those who had issued and acted on the disallowed ordinance from any penalty therefor, was then passed through Parliament. In the course of the debates in the Commons, Lord John Russell gave utterance to a few manly words with reference to Lord Durham. He expressed a hope that his Lordship would still consider himself bound to continue his services to his country, in spite of the attacks upon him, and of the obloquy attempted to be thrown upon his conduct. "The treatment he has received," observed Lord John, "is certainly far different from what he was entitled to expect after his appeal to the generous forbearance even of his political opponents. If the Canadian Provinces be happily preserved to us: if Lord Durham be able to restore tranquillity and good order, without infliction of the punishment of death, and to reëstablish a free constitution not only unimpaired but improved, he need care for no violence or invective, for no accumulation of charges, for no refinement of sophistry, for no bitterness of sarcasm accompanied by professions of friendship, attempting to disguise, but not succeeding in disguising the petty and personal feeling at the bottom of all these attacks; for he will have deserved well of his country, well of his Sovereign, and well of posterity."

Lord Durham's first intimation of the disallowance of the ordinance came to him from the columns of an American newspaper. Mr. Charles Buller, his chief secretary, who was present at the time, saw from the expression of his Lordship's face that he had received a violent shock. A few minutes afterwards the latter announced his determination to resign his appointment; and a missive containing an intimation to that effect was accordingly forwarded to England. A few days later he received the official despatch announcing the disallowance of the ordinance. He then determined not to wait for the appointment of his successor, but to abandon his mission and return home without delay. On the 9th of October he issued a proclamation announcing the fate of his ill-starred ordinance, and giving a tolerably full account of the history and objects of his mission. He reflected on the conduct of the Imperial Government in not supporting him. "In these conflicting and painful circumstances"—so ran the proclamation—"it is far better that I should at once and distinctly announce my intention of desisting from the vain attempt to carry my policy and system of administration into effect with such inadequate and restricted means. If the peace of Lower Canada is to be again menaced, it is necessary that its Government should be able to reckon on a more cordial and vigorous support at home than has been accorded to me. No good that may not be expected from any other Government in Lower Canada can be obtained by my continuing to wield extraordinary legal powers of which the moral force and consideration are gone." After thus announcing the abandonment of his mission, the proclamation concluded by an assurance that his Lordship would continue, as a peer of Parliament, to watch over the interests of the Canadian people. The whole tone of the proclamation was unwise, and characteristic of Lord Durham's fiery, insubordinate temper. Some of his replies to addresses presented to him before his departure from Canada were still more imprudent. The London *Times*, shocked by his Lordship's unconventional mode of proceeding, declared, and with truth, that the representative of the Sovereign had appealed to the judgment of a still rebellious colony against the policy of the Sovereign's own advisers. It referred to him as "the Lord High Seditioner." The proclamation was too much, even for the Home Government, and a despatch recalling Lord Durham was sent over to Canada. Lord Durham, however, had not waited for the despatch. Leaving the administration of affairs in the hands of Sir John Colborne, he sailed for England. He had won golden opinions from the British residents of Lower Canada during his five months' sojourn in the country, and left many warm hearts behind him. He declined to accept any pecuniary compensation for his services, and directed the salary which had accrued to him as Governor-General to be appropriated to the repair of the Government Houses at Quebec and Montreal. Prior to and during the homeward voyage the greater part of the report which will ever be associated with his name was prepared.* The Govern-

---

* The respective shares of Lord Durham and Mr. Buller in the preparation of the famous report cannot now be apportioned with any approach to exactness, but there are clauses which are undoubtedly the work of his Lordship alone.

ment marked its disapprobation of his course by giving instructions that he was not to receive the customary salute of artillery accorded to returned colonial Governors upon landing in England. His Lordship resented this as another indignity. The English people, however, received him at Plymouth with loud acclaims, and persisted in regarding him as the beneficent English nobleman who had got into disrepute with the aristocracy for his advocacy of popular rights. He did his utmost to respond to the enthusiasm which greeted him from various parts of the country, but in good sooth his own enthusiasm had almost burned itself out. His heart was broken. He could not but feel that he was regarded by most of those of his own order as having brought upon himself something nearly approaching to disgrace.

The rebellion burst forth afresh in the Lower Provinces after Lord Durham's departure, being chiefly due to the machinations of disaffected persons who had previously fled across the borders from Canada to the United States to avoid the consequences of their treason. The chimerical object of this second movement was to establish a republic on Canadian soil, under the Presidency of Mr. Robert Nelson. The movement was speedily suppressed by Sir John Colborne, who felt himself called upon to exercise a greater severity than before towards the prisoners taken red-handed. Courts martial were called into requisition. A few misguided men suffered the extreme penalty of the law, and others were by express authority transported to New South Wales. And that was the last of the Canadian rebellion.

In due time the famous "Report" was published and presented to Parliament. From that time forward the soundness of Lord Durham's general policy with regard to Canada cannot be said to have stood in need of serious vindication. Enemies and friends concurred in pronouncing it a masterly State document. Its great length, and the wide variety of matters treated of in its pages, render an intelligible summary of its contents a difficult matter. No elaborate summary, however, is necessary for the purposes of this work. It will be sufficient to say that among a host of other matters it gave an account of the animosities between the rival races in the Lower Province, and of the principal defects in the colonial system of government which had prevailed up to that time; drew attention to the evils arising from committing details of government to a colonial department; commented on the desirability of permitting the colonists to govern themselves, so far as internal affairs are concerned, Imperial interference being restricted to matters affecting the colonial relations with the mother country; recommended that all colonial officials except the Governor and his secretary should be made responsible to Parliament; and animadverted on the Clergy Reserve question, and the opposition in Upper Canada to the principle of a dominant Church. It suggested the establishment of a good system of municipal institutions, and concluded by recommending a legislative union * of the two Provinces, as the most effectual means of fusing the hostile races, and healing the manifold disorders from which the country had long suffered.

The important results accruing from the publication of this report will be referred to in a future chapter. For all practical purposes, Lord Durham's life may be said to have then and there ended. He lived long enough to know that his recommendations would in the main be carried out, and that the time spent by him in the administration of Canadian affairs had not been thrown away. During the year and odd months that remained to him he struggled manfully against the ever-increasing debility

---

* Canadian historians represent Lord Durham as having recommended a federal union. A perusal of the report will show that his Lordship, who had at first favoured the idea of such a union, saw good reason for altering his opinion. His arguments are in favour of a legislative, and against a federal union. See p. 96 of the Canadian reprint of the report.

which had taken possession of his frame. But the struggle was a hopeless one. After all his physical and mental sufferings he sank quietly to rest at Cowes, as already recorded, on the 28th of July, 1840. He left no successor in the ranks of the Liberal party in England, but he was quite justified in hoping that he had not lived in vain. His Canada mission marks an important epoch in the history of colonial government, and his name well deserves to be held by ourselves and our descendants as something more than a memory and a tradition. His infirmity of temper was a solitary blot upon an otherwise spotless record, and even that blot has been looked at through a magnifying glass. In estimating Lord Durham's character it should always be borne in mind that he was a man very much in earnest. It is possible that not a little of his so-called irritability was merely the vigorous expression of strong and not unamiable feeling, evoked by the intensity of his convictions. Very earnest men are often supposed to be angry and petulant when they are only injudiciously sincere. A popular contemporary writer —Mr. Justin McCarthy*—thus aptly sums up the more salient points of his Lordship's character and career: "His proud and sensitive spirit could ill bear the contradictions and humiliations that had been forced upon him. His was an eager and a passionate nature, full of that *sava indignatio* which, by his own acknowledgment, tortured the heart of Swift. He wanted to the success of his political career that proud patience which the gods are said to love, and by virtue of which great men live down misappreciation, and hold out until they see themselves justified, and hear the reproaches turn into cheers. But if Lord Durham's personal career was in any way a failure, his policy for the Canadas was a splendid success. It established the principles of colonial government. There were undoubtedly defects in the construction of the actual scheme which Lord Durham initiated, and which Lord Sydenham, who died not

---

* "A History of Our Own Times;" Chap. III.

long after him, instituted. The legislative union of the two Canadas was in itself a makeshift, and was only adopted as such. Lord Durham would have had it otherwise if he might; but he did not see his way then to anything like the complete federation scheme afterwards adopted. But the success of the policy lay in the broad principles it established, and to which other colonial systems as well as that of the Dominion of Canada owe their strength and security to-day. One may say, with little help from the merely fanciful, that the rejoicings of emancipated colonies might have been in his dying ears as he sank into his early grave."

Chapter II.

THE UNION ACT.

"The Queen's Government have no desire to thwart the representative assemblies of British North America in their measures of reform and improvement. They have no wish to make those provinces the resource for patronage at home. They are earnestly intent on giving to the talent and character of leading persons in the colonies, advantages similar to those which talent and character, employed in the public service, obtain in the United Kingdom. Her Majesty has no desire to maintain any system of policy among her North American subjects which opinion condemns."—*Despatch from Lord John Russell to the Governor-General of Canada, dated 14th October, 1839.*

LORD DURHAM'S report was seed sown in good ground. From the time when it became public property it formed a prominent topic of discussion among British statesmen, and added not a little to the reputation of both his Lordship and his secretary, Mr. Charles Buller.* Most people approved of it; a few found fault with some of its clauses; but there was no difference of opinion as to the great ability and industry which had gone to its production as a whole. In Upper Canada the Reform party, who had long been struggling against the Family Compact under great disadvantages, and who had strenuously contended for many of the principles recognized by the report, received it with enthusiasm. The Legislative Assembly of that Province passed a resolution in favour of union. The Conservatives,

---

* Mr. Buller was another distinguished man in his day who was only prevented by his untimely death from achieving permanent fame. He was at one time a pupil of the late Thomas Carlyle, who subsequently became his biographer. In politics he was a philosophic radical, and a man of enlightened and capacious views. In his youth he was the admirer of Miss Jane Welsh, of Haddington, who became the wife of Mr. Carlyle.

however, were very well satisfied with the existing order of things, and were, almost to a man, opposed to any change. The Honourable —afterwards Sir—John Beverley Robinson, Chief Justice of Upper Canada, who had long been the chief guide, philosopher and friend of the dominant faction in the Province, went to England at this time, and during his stay there, towards the close of the year 1839, published what was intended as a counterblast to Lord Durham's report, under the title of "Canada and the Canada Bill." It strove to show that the division of the Provinces in 1791 had worked satisfactorily, and that the carrying out of his Lordship's recommendations would by no means remove existing evils or promote the welfare of the country. Mr. Robinson had sixteen years before been an advocate of such a union as he now opposed, but had subsequently seen reason for changing his views.* His little book was well written, and presented the case from his side with great clearness, but it was like arguing against the doctrine of gravitation. A few fossilized Tories on both sides of the Atlantic complimented the author upon having conducted his argument with mathematical precision, but it produced no more effect upon the British Parliament than erst did King Canute's command upon the foaming brine. The Atlantic was not to be turned back by Mrs. Partington's mop, although the mop in the present instance was of most respectable conformation, and held out hopes of developing into a broom which should sweep with remarkable cleanness. In Lower Canada public opinion was much divided. A large majority of the British population approved of the project of union, but there was a considerable minority on the other side. The French Canadians were almost unanimous in their disapproval of the scheme. It thus seemed probable that there would be no slight

---

* In 1822 there was considerable agitation on the subject of a union of the Provinces, but the opposition to it, both in Canada and in the House of Commons, was overwhelming, and the project was shelved for the time.

difficulty in obtaining general assent to the carrying out of Lord Durham's recommendations.

But, the will being present, a way was soon found. During the session of 1839 a Bill for reuniting the Canadas was introduced into the Imperial Parliament by Lord John Russell. When it came to be dealt with by a committee of the House of Commons it was found that some additional information was needed. It was also thought desirable to obtain the formal concurrence of the Canadians, as expressed through their respective Legislatures. To effect these objects it was necessary to send out some clear-headed man, possessed of a large share of tact, and with a due sense of how much was involved in his enterprise.

The gentleman fixed upon to undertake this important mission was Mr. Charles Poulett Thomson, better known to Canadians by his subsequent title of Lord Sydenham. Mr. Thomson, though still a young man to be entrusted with a matter of such importance, had had large experience as a politician and diplomatist. He was particularly well informed respecting mercantile affairs, having been bred to commercial pursuits, and was an ardent disciple of Free Trade doctrines. He had been an hereditary member of an old established and wealthy mercantile house largely connected with the Russian trade. At the time of his entry into public life most of the leading merchants of London—his own father included—were Tories, and he had been reared amid Tory influences. The particular branch of trade in which his firm were engaged, however, and his own reading and observation, had turned his mind in an opposite direction on all purely economical questions. He had become a disciple of Mill and Ricardo, and the personal friend of Jeremy Bentham and Joseph Hume. Certain family connections, moreover, doubtless had some influence upon the formation of his opinions. He was allied, by the marriage of one of his sisters, to the Barings, and the head of that great house (who subsequently became Lord Ashburton) was at that time an advocate of Free Trade. The connection was politically serviceable to young Mr. Thomson, who, in the year 1826, was returned to the House of Commons in the Whig interest for the constituency of Dover. He distinguished himself during his first Parliamentary session by the part taken by him in a debate on the silk duties. He soon won a reputation, not as an eloquent speaker—though he always spoke fluently and sensibly—but as a shrewd and business-like member of Parliament. Some of his speeches smacked strongly of Radicalism, but his mind was of an essentially practical order, and he cared little for mere speculative theories about liberty, equality, and the natural rights of mankind. He was above all things a *useful* man, and from time to time rendered great services to his party. It was noticed that he was always able to make the best of a complicated and awkward situation, and was not deterred by Quixotic scruples from turning even the slips and weaknesses of others to his own account. Though neither a thorough nor a profound statesman, he was at least a very clever politician, and it is doubtful whether any man could have been found throughout the broad realm of England better fitted, alike by nature and by training, to carry out Lord Durham's policy in Canada than was the Right Honourable Charles Poulett Thomson. He at this time sat in the House of Commons for the important constituency of Manchester, and held the position of President of the Board of Trade in the Ministry of the day.[*] Having been appointed Governor-General of Canada,

---

[*] "I had a great deal of conversation with Poulett Thomson last night after dinner on one subject or another; he is very good-humoured, pleasing, and intelligent, but the greatest coxcomb I ever saw, and the vainest dog, though his vanity is not offensive or arrogant; but he told me that when Lord Grey's Government was formed (at which time he was a junior partner in a mercantile house, and had been at most five years in Parliament), he was averse to take office, but Althorp declared he would not come in unless Thomson did also, and that, knowing the importance of Althorp's accession to the Government, he sacrificed a large income, and took the Board of Trade; that when this was

and having enjoyed the great advantage of frequent personal interviews with Lord Durham on the subject of his mission, he set sail for Quebec on his fortieth birthday—the 13th of September, 1839. He reached his destination on the 17th of October following, and two days afterwards issued a proclamation announcing that he had assumed the reins of Government.

The task before him was one of no ordinary difficulty. It has been seen that the people and the Legislatures were by no means unanimous in approving the proposed measures, and yet it was necessary that he should obtain their consent. Owing to the suspension of the Lower Canadian Constitution, already referred to, there was strictly speaking no Legislature in that Province to be consulted. The body that did duty for a Legislature was the Special Council, and this was summoned to meet at Montreal on the 11th of November. No change whatever was made in its composition. It consisted of eighteen members, nearly all of whom belonged to the British party. It had been nominated (after Lord Durham's departure from Canada) by Sir John Colborne, acting on behalf of the Crown, and the body as a whole did not by any means represent the views generally entertained among the inhabitants of the Lower Province. It was Lord Sydenham's mission, however, to carry out his instructions, and to obtain a formal consent from the existing body which stood in the place of a Legislature. Had a fairly representative body been in existence, it would never have given its consent to a union which for a time blotted out the political influence of the French Canadian popu-

offered to him, he was asked whether he cared if he was President or Vice-President, as they wished to made Lord Auckland President if he (Poulett Thomson) had no objection. He said, provided the President was not in the Cabinet, he did not care ; and accordingly he condescended to be Vice-President, knowing that all the business must be in the House of Commons, and that he must be (as in fact he said he was) the virtual head of the office. All this was told with a good-humoured and smiling complacency, which made me laugh internally."—*The Greville Memoirs*, under date Jan. 30th, 1836.

lation. But no potent opposition was to be dreaded from such a body as the Special Council. The Provincial constitution was suspended, and the factious spirits were either effectually silenced or in exile. After several days' discussion the Council adopted the union resolutions by a majority of twelve to three.* The Governor-General was thus enabled to report to the Secretary of State in England that the assent of the Lower Province had been obtained. He then made his way without loss of time to Toronto, to obtain the concurrence of the Legislature of the Upper Province.

In the Upper Canadian Legislature his Excellency had no Special Council to deal with, but a regularly constituted legislative body, with a due sense of its own importance, and an unequivocal disposition to stand upon its rights. With the Assembly no trouble was to be anticipated, as it had already passed resolutions in favour of union, and was desirous of seeing Responsible Government conceded without delay. In the Legislative Council very different sentiments prevailed. Its members had everything to lose and nothing to gain by the proposed change. A large majority of them belonged to the Family Compact. Their power and patronage would go, and the principles to which they had always opposed themselves would triumph, in the event of a union of the Provinces, and the concession of executive responsibility. They dreaded a coalition between the Liberals of the two Provinces. Their position, however, was such that they could not with any show of consistency refuse their assent to the resolutions proposed by his Excellency. Those resolutions were known to embody the Imperial will, and the members of the Family Compact were nothing if not loyal. For years past, and more especially since the suppression of the recent rebellion, their loyalty had become positively, albeit honestly, effusive. They had proclaimed it through the public prints, at the corners of the

---

* The resolutions were six in number. One of them was voted against by Mr. Neilson only, but the statement in the text is literally correct as to the other five.

streets and—literally—from the housetops. Some of them had talked a great deal of hysterical nonsense, and had propounded theories better suited to the early years of the Restoration than to the times in which they lived. How then could they venture to oppose the Imperial mandate, as proclaimed to them by the Governor-General in person. His Excellency was an adept in the science of finesse, and used all his arts to win them over. He appealed in the strongest terms to their life-long fealty. He materially strengthened his position by the publication in the *Upper Canada Gazette* of a despatch from the Colonial Minister. "You will understand, and will cause it to be generally known," said the despatch, "that hereafter the tenure of colonial offices, held during Her Majesty's pleasure, will not be regarded as equivalent to a tenure during good behaviour; but that not only such officers will be called upon to retire from the public service, as often as any sufficient motives of public policy may suggest the expediency of that measure, but that a change in the person of the Governor will be considered as a sufficient reason for any alterations which his successor may deem it expedient to make in the list of public functionaries—subject, of course, to the future confirmation of the Sovereign. These remarks do not extend to judicial officers, nor are they meant to apply to places which are altogether ministerial, and which do not devolve upon the holders of them duties in the right discharge of which the character and policy of the Government are directly involved. They are intended to apply rather to the heads of departments than to persons serving as clerks or in similar capacities under them; neither do they extend to officers in the service of the Lords Commissioners of the Treasury. The functionaries who will be chiefly, though not exclusively, affected by them, are the Colonial Secretary; the Treasurer, or Receiver-General; the Surveyor-General; the Attorney and Solicitor-General; the Sheriff, or Provost Marshal; and other officers who, under different designations from these, are entrusted with the same or similar duties. To this list must also be added the members of the Council, especially in those colonies in which the Legislative and Executive Councils are distinct bodies." The meaning of this was obvious enough. It meant that for the future the persons indicated would have to merit and enjoy a share of public confidence, or else resign their places. It also meant that the Home Government had set its mind on passing a Union Bill, and that no caprice or obstruction on their part would be allowed to stand in the way of such a consummation. It was evident that they might as well bow to the inevitable with a good grace, as, in the event of their refusal, means would be found to get rid of them and supply their places with more manageable material. They yielded. Resolutions expressive of assent to the union were passed, on condition that there should be an equal representation of each Province in the united Legislature; that a sufficient permanent civil list should be voted to secure the independence of the judges; and that the public debt of Upper Canada should be a charge upon the joint revenue of the united Province. In the Assembly certain conditions were pressed upon the consideration of his Excellency which the latter saw fit to oppose, as being unjust to the French Canadian population in the Lower Province. The Governor's views finally prevailed. On the last day of the year he was able to announce to a correspondent that he had satisfactorily accomplished the objects of his mission, and that nothing further remained but for Parliament to pass the Union Bill, a draft of which, he added, would soon be forwarded from Canada.

The draft of the Union Bill, founded upon the resolutions of the Legislature of Upper Canada and the Special Council of the Lower Province, was chiefly prepared by the Hon. James Stuart, Chief Justice of the Court of Queen's Bench for Lower Canada, who for his great services to Lord Durham and Mr. Thomson was subsequently elevated to the rank of a baronet of the United Kingdom. The successive clauses of the Bill were separately and carefully discussed between the Governor and the Chief Justice before transmission to England. It provided for the union of the two Provinces under the name of the Province of Canada. It further provided that there should be one Legislative Council, and one Assembly, with an equal representation from each of the former Provinces; the Legislative Council to consist of not fewer than twenty life members, appointed by the Crown, and the Assembly to consist of eighty-four members (forty-two from each of the former Provinces), elected by the people. The property qualification for candidates for seats in the Assembly was fixed at five hundred pounds sterling in lands or tenements. The Governor was authorized to fix the time and place of holding Parliaments, and to prorogue or dissolve the latter at his pleasure. The Speaker of the Legislative Council was to be appointed by the Governor, and the Speaker of the Assembly to be elected by its members. A permanent civil list of seventy-five thousand pounds annually was provided for, instead of all territorial and other revenues then at the Crown's disposal; and the judges were made independent of the votes of the Assembly. All writs, proclamations, reports, journals and public documents were to be in the English language only; and it was provided that the public debt of the two Provinces should be assumed by the united Province. Such, in so far as it is now necessary to specify them, were the principal provisions of the Union Bill transmitted to England by Mr. Thomson. The Imperial Parliament was then in session, and the Colonial Secretary, Lord John Russell, lost no time in presenting the measure. It underwent some slight modifications in the course of its passage through the Commons. Certain clauses relating to local municipal institutions were struck out, and left to be dealt with by the Provincial Legislatures, but the Bill, as a whole, commended itself to the wisdom of the House of Commons, and was passed with but little opposition. Some of the Irish members, led by O'Connell, raised their voices against it, on the ground that it sanctioned a disproportionate representation of the French and British races; that the former had not assented to the measure, and that in consequence of the suspension of the Lower Canadian constitution, they had no means of expressing their assent. It was further argued that it was unjust to saddle Lower Canada with a share of liability in respect of the debt of the Upper Province. Opposition from this quarter, however, was regarded by the Ministry very much as a matter of course, and was of no special significance. In the House of Lords the objections to the measure were urged with more vigour than commonly characterizes the debates there, and among those who spoke most strongly against it were Lords Gosford and Seaton, both of whom had been Governors of Canada, and might be supposed to bring special knowledge to bear upon the subject. The Act passed, however, and was to come into operation by virtue of a royal proclamation, to be issued within fifteen calendar months. The issuing of the proclamation was deferred until the 5th of February, 1841, when it appeared under the authority of the Provincial Secretary, the Hon. Dominick Daly. By its terms the Act of Union was to take effect from the 10th of the month; and at that date the Union of the Provinces was accordingly complete.*

The French population of Lower Canada generally, and even some of the British, were much averse to the project of union on the terms proposed, and an impartial critic must confess that their discontent was not wholly groundless. In the first place, the population of the Lower Province was considerably in excess of that of Upper Canada;

---

* The day upon which the Union of the Provinces took effect was the anniversary of two events of some importance in Canadian history; viz., of the signing of the Treaty of 1763, and of the royal assent being accorded to the suspension of the Lower Canadian Constitution in 1838. It was also the (first) anniversary of the marriage of Her Majesty Queen Victoria.

whereas the latter, by the terms of union, were granted an equal Parliamentary representation with the former. The financial condition of the two Provinces was still more unequal than the population. In Lower Canada the public debt was insignificant, and if there was less public enterprise than in the Upper Province, there was no financial embarrassment. The revenue was small, but it was ample for the public requirements. In Upper Canada, on the other hand, for some years past an amount of enterprise had been displayed which was altogether out of proportion to the age and financial condition of the Province. The construction of the great canals and other important public works had involved what for those times must be pronounced to have been an enormous expenditure, and for this there had so far been little or no return. A good deal of the expenditure had been unnecessary—the result of mismanagement and inexperience—and would never produce any return. The public debt was large. Further outlay was imperative, and the exchequer was empty. Some important public enterprises had been temporarily abandoned for want of funds. The Province seemed to be on the verge of bankruptcy. By the imposition of the public debt on the united Province, therefore, Upper Canada was clearly a gainer. But, it was argued, this was only fair, inasmuch as Lower Canada would participate in the advantages derivable from the public works which had given rise to the debt. Lower Canada, moreover, had long reaped an undue advantage in respect of the revenue from imports collected at Montreal and Quebec. That revenue was chiefly paid by the Upper Province, where a majority of the consumers resided; yet Lower Canada had for years received the lion's share of it, and surrendered even the smallest proportion with reluctance. The argument as to the representation of the two Provinces being equal, and therefore disproportionate to the population, was met by the plea that the disproportion would soon disappear, inasmuch as the population of Upper Canada had been largely recruited by immigration; that it was rapidly increasing, and would continue to rapidly increase; whereas immigration to the Lower Province was insignificant in comparison, and the increase of population proportionately slow. The Lower Canadians were not disposed to regard this argument as conclusive. They claimed, with some show of reason, that it would be time enough to equalize the representation when the prediction as to equality of population should be realized. The practical proscription of the French language in all public proceedings, moreover, was keenly felt by the French Canadians, and they never ceased to clamour for the repeal of the clause effecting it—a repeal which was finally accomplished after the accession to power of the second Lafontaine-Baldwin Ministry in 1848. The French Canadians, indeed, looked upon the Union Act as the result of a predetermination to destroy their nationality and their religion. It was evident that if the British representatives from Lower Canada should act in unison with their co-nationalists from the Upper Province, the combination would be all-powerful in the Legislature.

The discontent in the Lower Province over the terms of union made itself felt in various quarters before the passing of the Act. In the districts of Quebec and Three Rivers a petition was set on foot under the auspices of the clergy, and erelong 40,000 signatures were appended to it. Some of the signatories were influential members of the British party. It expressed strong hostility to the proposed union, and prayed that the constitution of 1791 might be maintained.* It was sent over to England and laid before the Imperial Parliament, and doubtless influenced the Government there to the extent of inducing them not to legislate without due deliberation. A large meeting was also held at Montreal, where, on motion

---

* This was not because the Constitutional Act of 1791 was regarded as a perfect, or even as a satisfactory measure, but because its provisions were much more acceptable than were those of the Act of Union.

of Mr. Lafontaine, an address to the Imperial Parliament protesting against the proposed union was adopted; but, owing to a want of concord among its promoters, it was not forwarded to England.

Dissatisfaction, however, was now of no further avail. The Union of the Provinces was an accomplished fact, and it only remained for the representatives of both to accept the situation and make the best of it. The Governor-General, for his arduous and indefatigable services, was in the month of August, 1840, raised to the peerage by the title of Baron Sydenham of Sydenham in Kent and of Toronto in Canada. His exertions had not been without their effect on his physical frame, which was even more weakly than Lord Durham's had been; but he was keenly ambitious, and not disposed to sit down and brood over his maladies. He was authorized by the thirtieth clause of the Union Act to fix the capital of the United Province at such place as he might be advised. He chose to fix it at Kingston, in the Upper Province. This was another step which was keenly felt by the inhabitants of Lower Canada, who had hoped that the capital would be either Montreal or Quebec, both of which, as compared with Kingston, were large towns. The pressure from Upper Canada on this point, however, was overwhelming, and the Governor-General exercised a wise discretion in placing the seat of Government in the centre of a district where the unwavering loyalty of the people was a guarantee for free and undisturbed legislation.

The appointment of an Executive Council was a matter which could no longer be delayed, and which required some deliberation on the part of the Governor-General. On the 13th of February—three days after the Union proclamation took effect—His Excellency, having made his selection, called to his Council eight gentlemen who already occupied the highest offices of State. They consisted of Messrs. Sullivan, Dunn, Daly, Harrison, Ogden, Draper, Baldwin, and Day. A month later—on the 17th of March—Mr. H. H. Killaly was added to the list. As the narrative proceeds we shall become better acquainted with all these personages. The principle of executive responsibility having been conceded, it was necessary that the members of the Council holding seats in the Assembly should be reëlected. This was duly accomplished* at the general elections for members to serve in the first House of Assembly. These elections began on the 8th of March, 1841, and were concluded early in the following month. In the Lower Province they were marked by a violence and acrimony unprecedented at any election which had ever taken place in the colony. The British party and the national party had never been arrayed against each other with such bitterness. The latter smarted under a sense of defeat, while the former did not in all cases attempt to disguise their consciousness of triumph. There was a desire for revenge on the one side, and an ill-concealed complacency or contempt on the other. These sentiments, for some weeks before the elections, found frequent expression through the provincial press, and a large proportion of the lower orders of electors was roused to a condition bordering on ferocity. In some constituencies another Reign of Terror prevailed during the progress of the election, and the ruffianism seems to have been pretty equally apportioned between the representatives of the different nationalities.

Mr. Lafontaine, whose name has already been mentioned, and with whom we shall erelong have occasion to form an intimate acquaintance, offered himself to the electors of Terrebonne. He was opposed by Dr. Michael McCulloch, a member of the British party, who was successful in securing his election. The violence displayed on both sides was disgraceful to the causes which they respectively represented, but there seems to be no reasonable doubt that had the franchise been perfectly free and untrammelled, Mr. Lafontaine's election would have been assured. He himself afterwards admitted, however, that

---

* Duly, except in the case of Mr. Harrison. See *post*, Chapter IV.

a large number of his supporters had set out from their homes armed with cudgels, and that those who had not been so provided at starting had made a detour into a wood on the road in order to supply their deficiencies. Upon nearing the polling-place* they found Dr. McCulloch's supporters (many of whom were canal labourers and navvies who were not entitled to exercise the franchise at all) armed and ready for them, and as the latter had contrived to secure an advantageous position for a hand-to-hand fight, the French Canadians adopted the better part of valour and withdrew from the field without recording their votes. At the election for the county of Montreal the opposing forces came into actual collision, and one man, a member of the British party, was slain on the spot. With regard to the possession of the poll itself, Rob Roy's "good old rule" was the order of the day. Those took who had the power, and those kept who could. The French Canadians kept possession the first day, and it was in the struggle of a British elector to record his vote that he met his doom as above narrated. Next day the British mustered in such force that their opponents abandoned the struggle, and the French candidate retired. The Lower Canadian elections, therefore, did not in all cases represent the voice of the people. The French Canadians were vehement in their denunciations of the Governor-General, who was allied, in their minds, with the British party, and was responsible for all the excesses of the latter. To say that he was not so responsible would, it is to be hoped, be a work of supererogation, but it must be owned that his determination to carry out the object of his mission to Canada was great, and that he was not over-scrupulous as to the means employed to secure that end. His conduct with regard to the

---

* The polling-place for the county of Terrebonne was fixed at an insignificant out-of-the-way village called New Glasgow, described by Mr. Lafontaine as being "dans les bois, à l'extrémité des limites de ce comté."—See his letter published in *Le Canadien*, 2 avril, 1841.

electoral limits of Quebec and Montreal lent some colour to the not unreasonable supposition that his sympathies were entirely with the British party, and that he did not intend to allow any impediment to stand in the way of the accomplishment of his wishes. By the Union Bill, as originally drafted by him and Chief Justice Stuart, only one member was assigned to each of those cities. When the measure was laid before the Commons, Sir Robert Peel suggested that a larger representation was due to the commercial interest, and a clause was accordingly inserted assigning two members to each of the two principal cities of Lower Canada. The Act, as finally passed, authorized the Governor to define the boundaries of the various cities and towns mentioned in the Act. Lord Sydenham's attention was drawn to the fact that if the electoral limits of Montreal and Quebec were made to coincide with their municipal limits, the increased representation contemplated by the Union Act would not take effect, as the numerical superiority of electors in the suburbs would enable them to return both members. The number of French Canadian representatives—and by consequence the number of opponents of the Union—would thus be increased. Lord Sydenham's first object was to make the Union a success, and to have a majority of members returned to Parliament who should be favourable to the Government policy. He accordingly exercised the power granted him by the Act, and by a Proclamation issued from Government House, Montreal, on the 4th of March, 1841, defined the boundaries of Quebec and Montreal in such a manner as to exclude the suburbs, which for electoral purposes were amalgamated with the counties in which they were situated. He by this means practically disfranchised a large number of the inhabitants, and secured the return of members pledged to support his favourite project—an achievement for which the French Canadians have never forgiven him to the present day.

It is believed that at least ten of the members who sat in the

First Parliament were returned either by violence or by corruption. The violence, though chiefly manifested in Lower Canada, was by no means wholly confined to that Province. There were "gentle and joyous" passages of arms in all parts of the country. One life was lost in Toronto, and another in the county of Durham. Intelligence of broken heads and arms was received from various quarters. It was even feared lest the published accounts of the innumerable election riots would disseminate such an impression of the lawless state of affairs as to check immigration to Canada. Happily the fear proved not to be well grounded. During the second week in April the returns were tolerably well known, and the Governor made up his accounts. Twenty-four out of the eighty-four members were pledged supporters of his policy. Only twenty French members—French in spirit, as well as in nationality—appeared on the list. Of the remainder, twenty were classed as moderate and five as ultra Reformers. Only seven members of the Compact had found seats. All things considered, the two opposing parties of Conservatives and Reformers were divided not far from equally, and it seemed not improbable that the French party would thus be able to hold the balance of power in their hands. His Excellency, however, felt pretty certain of being able to hold his ground in the Assembly, which was to meet at Kingston in the following June.

Chapter III.

LOCUS IN QUO.

"Les deux provinces étaient en général prospères. Le sol, qui y est d'une grande richesse, est propre à produire les grains de toutes sortes et une grande variété de fruits, malgré un climat un peu sévère pendant les froids de son long hiver, climat qui est cependant des plus salubres et des plus agréables dans la saison tempérée."—Turcotte. *Le Canada Sous l'Union*, pp. 43, 44.

SOME further account of the condition of the two Provinces at the time when the Union Act came into operation would seem to be desirable, with a view to imparting additional clearness to the narrative which is to follow.

Notwithstanding the internal strife and other drawbacks which had prevailed for years past, the country, more especially that part of it comprehended within the limits of the Upper Province, had steadily advanced in population and material prosperity. In the Upper Province, indeed, the advance had been rapid. The population cannot be arrived at with exactitude, the various censuses having been taken at different times in different parts of the country; but according to an approximately correct estimate, the combined population of the two Provinces at the Union was nearly or quite 1,100,000. About 630,000 belonged to Lower Canada, and 470,000 to the Upper Province. The inhabitants of French origin in both Provinces could not have fallen far short of half a million. Of the other nationalities represented, at least half a million were British, the remainder being made up of representatives of various European states, and of immigrants from the neighbouring republic. The Roman Catholics in both Provinces formed rather more than a moiety of the combined population.

In Lower Canada the rural population, composed almost exclusively of French Canadians, were in a condition of intellectual stagnation, if not of positive retrogression. They occupied themselves chiefly with agriculture, which was carried on after the primitive fashion that had been in vogue ever since the original settlement of the country. Most of the farms were situated along the banks of the rivers, and consisted of narrow strips forming rectangles nearly a mile and a half in length, with a frontage of only a few yards. These "ribbons of land," as they have been called, with "the land all longitude," were held under the old feudal seignorial tenure, and generally involved the performance of certain antiquated and more or less absurd services on the part of the occupants. The farmhouses of course, were built on the front of the lots, on the edge of the road, and facing the river, with uplands rising in the far distance behind. They were generally small, unpretentious, but neatly whitewashed cottages, and presented a pleasant and picturesque aspect to the passer-by, who, if not to the manner born, fancied himself to be travelling through the street of an endless village. The habitans, generally speaking, led dreamy, unambitious, satisfied lives, and took little thought for the morrow. They fulfilled the injunction to increase and multiply, but were less assiduous in replenishing the earth. Of moral or intellectual progress there was little or none. What the habitant was at the date of the Conquest, such was he at the time of the Union of 1841. Rotation of crops was a thing unknown to or unheeded by him. He was illiterate, superstitious, and wholly insensible to the value of education. In 1828, as mentioned on a former page, a petition of grievances, to which 87,000 names were appended, was forwarded from the Lower Province to the king, praying, among other things, that the Legislative Council of the Province might be made elective.

Of the 87,000 persons whose names were affixed, about 78,000 were unable to write, and were compelled to make their marks. The remaining 9,000, a goodly number of whom were of British origin, wrote their signatures. Six years later (in 1834) two grand juries were summoned from the most prosperous farmers in the neighbourhood of Montreal, and it was found that only one or two of them could write their names. Even school trustees were permitted by law to attach their marks to their reports. The habitant, indeed, was not merely indifferent to education. He was opposed to it on principle; and he was generally encouraged in this opposition by his parish priest. His children were seldom taught even to read or write. He and his family contrived to get a living out of their holdings without much effort, and there was apparently no disposition to obtain anything beyond. The grain products of the country, under such a system—or no system—of farming, were very precarious. Occasionally a British settler was to be found cultivating the land, and his crops were a marvel, showing clearly the capability of the soil under favourable conditions, notwithstanding the length of the winter and the rigour of the climate.

In the cities and towns of the Lower Province there was a considerable British population, and a fair share of enterprise was to be found. In this enterprise many of the French Canadian citizens participated. Some of the latter were gentlemen of learning and good birth, with a polish and suavity of manner seldom acquired by those whose culture does not begin at the cradle. Under the old *régime* they would have scorned to engage in trade or manufacture of any kind, but those halcyon days were over, and a state of things prevailed more in accordance with the economical and social necessities of the country. Manufactures were carried on to a limited extent. Montreal, with a population of about 40,000, was then much more than now the commercial metropolis of Canada.

A spirit of local improvement had long been afoot there, and the city contained many fine public and private buildings. Of late years many changes for the better had been effected in the aspect of the principal thoroughfares, some of which would have done no discredit to more pretentious towns in the old world. The harbour was good, though not large. Ships drawing two-and-a-half fathoms of water could lie alongside the wharfs where the floating palaces of the Messrs. Allan are now moored. The city contained a more mixed population than any other spot in the Province. Sir Richard Bonnycastle, who visited it in the year before the Union, remarked: "In this city one is amused by seeing the never-changing lineaments, the long queue, the bonnet-rouge, and the incessant garrulity of Jean Baptiste, mingling with the sober demeanour, the equally unchanging feature, and the national plaid, of the Highlander; whilst the untutored sons of labour, from the Green Isle of the ocean, are here as thoughtless, as ragged, and as numerous, as at Quebec. Amongst all these, the shrewd and calculating citizen from the neighbouring republic drives his hard bargain with all his wonted zeal and industry, amid the fumes of Jamaica and gin-sling. These remarks, of course, apply to the streets only. In the counting-houses, although the races remain the same, the advantages of situation and of education make the same differences as in other countries. I cannot, however, help thinking that the descendant of the Gaul has not gained by being transplanted; and the vastly absurd notions which a few turbulent spirits have of late years engendered, and endeavoured to instil into the unsophisticated and naturally good mind of the Canadian tiller of the soil, have tended to restrict the exercise of that inborn urbanity and suavity which are the Frenchman's proudest boast after those of l'amour et la gloire." * Quebec, with its picturesque surroundings and historic associations, was somewhat less populous than Montreal.

---

* "The Canadas in 1841," by Sir Richard H. Bonnycastle, Vol. I. pp. 76, 77.

Its population was almost exclusively French, and it had never been very progressive, but it enjoyed a recognized status as the whilome capital of the Province, and the key to a vast region embracing half a continent. It was then, as it is now, one of the most interesting spots in the world. It was moreover the one important harbour and point of export and import. It contained about 35,000 inhabitants. These two were the only really important centres of population in Lower Canada. Three Rivers, situated at the confluence of the St. Maurice and St. Lawrence, had a population of about 2,500, and was the third town in point of population and commerce. Whatever importance it enjoyed was derived from its age and history (it having been founded in 1618, ten years after the founding of Quebec by Champlain), and from its still being a principal dépôt of the adventurous traders of the North-West.

The exports and imports, though restricted by the commercial policy then in vogue, showed a steady yearly increase. The exports consisted chiefly of lumber and grain. It will be borne in mind that the old system of colonial monopoly was still in vogue. The navigation of the St. Lawrence by foreign vessels was not permitted. Importation from the United States was only permitted under costly and harassing restrictions. Canadian vessels, on the other hand, were not allowed to enter any foreign port. As a recompense for these disabilities Canada enjoyed the exclusive privilege of furnishing lumber and provisions to the West India Islands—a privilege which, while it conferred some advantage upon Canadian merchants, bore hardly and unjustly upon the West Indian colonists. The principal manufacturing enterprise of the Lower Province was shipbuilding, which was largely carried on at Quebec. It was one of the earliest branches of industry set on foot in Canada, and had attained to considerable dimensions within a few years after the Conquest. In 1841—the Union year—no fewer than sixty-four seagoing vessels, with an aggregate of 23,122 tons burden, were built at

FORTY YEARS.

CANADA since THE UNION OF 1841.

By John Charles Dent

Geo. Virtue

THE HON. ROBERT BALDWIN.

THE HON

THE HON ROBERT HAMPTON

THE HON. (AFTERWARDS SIR) L. H. LAFONTAINE.

LORD METCALFE.

A CANADIAN SUNSET.

Quebec. The lumber trade was also a very important branch of industry, though, considering the almost boundless resources of the country, it had developed very slowly. During the French domination the fur-trade had almost monopolized public attention, and had dwarfed every other branch of industry. While the forests of Maine were supplying Great Britain with the means of maintaining her naval supremacy, the forests of Canada were not pressed into requisition for the service of France. Even so late as the year 1752 the French Canadians were accustomed to buy the vessels required for their local trade from their New England neighbours. "With the finest forests in the world for ship-building, unequalled facilities for bringing lumber to the seaboard, and the encouragement of a liberal bounty, French enterprise in Canada, toward the middle of the last century, was not equal to the task of seizing upon the only industry which would tend to secure to them the peaceable possession of the colony in the event of a war with their great and industrious rival, Britain, besides encouraging immigration, amassing wealth, and establishing a political importance."* The year before the Conquest the total lumber exports of the country amounted to only $31,250. Less than a century later they had increased to eleven-and-a-half millions.

Notwithstanding the backward condition of rural Lower Canada from an educational point of view, for fifteen years prior to the Union there had been frequent large money grants by the House of Assembly of that Province for educational purposes. At Montreal, Quebec, Three Rivers, St. Hyacinthe, Nicolet and elsewhere, seats of learning had been established, at which it was possible for any youth so inclined to obtain a liberal education. Learned societies had also been established in the two chief cities. Elementary schools, however, were few, and their management had not been reduced to anything deserving the name of a system. The first

---

* See "Eighty Years' Progress of British North America," p. 285.

general elementary School Act had been passed in 1829. It provided for the establishment of schools by trustees elected for the purpose by the landholders of the different parishes, but it contained no provision for visitation or inspection, and was seriously defective in various particulars. By an amendment Act passed in 1831, some of its most flagrant defects had been remedied, but it had, after trial, been found inefficacious, and in 1832 a new School Act had been passed which was far in advance of its predecessor. The curse of the existing system, however, was that it was not permanent, and was made subservient to the machinations of politicians. Lord Durham's Commissioner, Mr. Arthur Buller, had drawn attention to this great evil in his report on the state of education in Lower Canada, and had sketched the outlines of a system whereby many of the existing drawbacks might be obviated. Up to this time, however, it had not been possible to do anything in furtherance of the recommendations contained in the report, and the question of education was one of the earliest calling for attention at the hands of the united Parliament. How it was dealt with by that body will form the subject of future consideration.

The fur-trade was still an important branch of industry, though the profits arising from it had shrunk greatly since the palmy days of the Hudson's Bay Company. There were likewise a few iron mines, the development of which was not conducted with much vigour. Considerable sums had been expended on public works, but the most important still remained unfinished, and the splendid natural advantages of the country had not been turned to adequate account.

The provincial revenue, unlike like that of Upper Canada, was in a satisfactory condition. That is to say, there was a surplus in the provincial exchequer. The revenue for 1840 was £184,000, whereas the expenditure was only £143,000. The public debt was small, and taxation was light. It is not to be wondered at that the Lower

Canadians, even on this ground alone, should have objected to unite with the sister Province, the financial condition whereof, as has already been seen, and as will presently appear more in detail, was far from healthy.

In Upper Canada, while agriculture was the mainstay of the Province, it was by no means the sole occupation, even of the rustic population. It was moreover carried on after the most modern and approved system then known. While the French Canadian habitant ploughed and harrowed his ground, when he ploughed and harrowed it at all, with implements the very appearance whereof recalled mediæval times, the Scottish, English, German or Irish yeoman of Upper Canada was supplied with the latest fashion which the inventive genius of England or the United States could devise. He had to contend with such difficulties as his Lower Canadian contemporary had never known; yet he managed to raise crops of grain and fruits which were the astonishment of visitors to the primitive agricultural shows of the period. It was not alone, however, that his appliances were better than those of the habitant, but his thrift and enterprise were greater. He had emigrated from his native land, not merely to gain a livelihood, but to better his condition, and to make some provision for the future. In his way, he was ambitious. Upper Canada, indeed, absorbed much of the surplus energy of the British Isles. "In 1828, when the whole population of Upper Canada amounted to 185,500 inhabitants, the number of acres under agricultural improvement was 570,000, or about $3\tfrac{1}{5}$ for each individual; in 1851 the average for each inhabitant was very nearly four acres. The comparative progress of Upper and Lower Canada, in bringing the forest-clad wilderness into cultivation, may be inferred from the following table·

Year.	LOWER CANADA. No. acres cultivated.	UPPER CANADA. No. acres cultivated.
1831,	2,065,913	813,432
1844,	2,802,317	2,166,101
1851,	3,605,076	3,702,783
1861,	4,678,900	6,051,619

Hence, in a period of twenty years, Lower Canada increased her cultivated acres by 1.9 and Upper Canada by 4.5."* The statistics quoted overlap the period when the Union was inaugurated, but they are characteristic of the different influences at work in the two Provinces, and speak louder than any mere words could do. In Lower Canada there were thriftlessness and isolation. In Upper Canada there were energy and coöperation. County and township agricultural societies were formed from time to time, at which farmers living remote from each other met and compared notes on matters of common agricultural interest. In 1830 an Act was passed whereby the Governor was authorized to pay a hundred pounds sterling to any District Agricultural Society which raised half that sum by subscription, to enable the society to import grain, implements, and valuable live stock. Subsequent legislation afforded further encouragement to the formation of these useful societies. It was not till the Union had been five years in operation that a Provincial Agricultural Association was formed; but meanwhile the District Societies proved of incalculable benefit to the farming interest generally. The better class of farmers began to take a pride in their calling. In several parts of Upper Canada there were properties which were conducted as model farms. Such farms would not now be regarded as models, but they were far in advance of what was commonly to be seen, and had a good effect in stimulating a desire for agricultural improvement in the community. At the time when the Union Act came into operation Upper Canada was far behind its present condition, but even then there were parts of the Province where some of the farms approximated much more nearly to those of the best agricultural districts of Great Britain than could have been believed possible. In some districts, too, fruit-growing had become a separate branch of husbandry, and Canadian apples were not unknown in foreign markets.

---

* See "Eighty Years' Progress of British North America," p. 41.

The chief grain product of the country was wheat. Oats, barley, rye, Indian corn and peas were grown to only a limited extent. This arose from the fact that for many years wheat was the only farm-product that could be relied upon with certainty to sell for ready money. Wheat, alone among grains, was always "a cash article." Other crops, as a general rule, could only be bartered for other commodities. As a consequence, there was a general disposition among the farming community to cultivate wheat almost exclusively, without regard to the rotation of crops. This improvident system has left its traces behind it to the present day, in the premature exhaustion of the soil in some townships which once yielded bounteous harvests. The circumstance which first led Canadian farmers to pause in this unwise course was the appearance of the wheat midge, the first visitation of which occurred in the Lower Province in 1829. Five years later it invaded the neighbourhood of Montreal, and in 1835 and 1836 it caused great destruction to the wheat crops in the valley of the St. Lawrence. A strict attention to the recognized principles of husbandry has rendered the periodical visitations of these and other insect depredators less formidable than of old, and among the most effectual means employed against them the rotation of crops is entitled to high rank. The entire wheat crop of Upper Canada in the Union year was about three millions of bushels. The number of bushels per acre varied greatly in different localities, and even in the same localities in different years. Twenty bushels of winter wheat and eighteen bushels of spring wheat were considered a fair yield. The actual number of acres of land under cultivation, or quasi-cultivation, in all parts of the Province, was 1,740,664. Milling and various fairly productive manufactures were carried on, not only in the centres of population, but to some extent in the rural districts.

The towns of Upper Canada, as compared with Montreal and Quebec, were small and sparsely populated. Toronto, the Provincial capital, was first in importance. It was less than half a century old, and only seven years had elapsed since its incorporation. It contained little of architectural beauty, but its excellent harbour gave it certain advantages for purposes of navigation and commerce. It was the judicial, educational and social, as well as the political capital of the Province, and was the point from which the chief intellectual activity radiated. It had long been the headquarters of the Family Compact, who maintained an exclusive social caste, and aped to the utmost of their capacity the manners and fashions of the English aristocracy. Their efforts exhibited much resolution, but not very adequate fulfilment. The town had made considerable progress since its incorporation in 1834, and at this time had a population of about 15,000. Kingston, the newly-appointed capital of United Canada, had the advantage of Toronto in point of age, but in no other respect whatever. Its population was under 6,000. Hamilton, at the western extremity of Lake Ontario, contained a population of about 3,000. Bytown—now Ottawa—was merely a remote village in the wilderness. London, situated in the midst of perhaps the finest agricultural region in Upper Canada, was the military station and chief town of the western part of the Province. Its population was under 3,000.

In respect of education, Upper Canada was very far in advance of the sister Province. Its educational history may be said to be coeval with the history of the Province itself, for a classical school was opened at Cataraqui (Kingston) by the Reverend Dr. Stuart as early as the year 1785. This, so far as is known to the present writer, was the first school in Upper Canada. Four years later a school was opened on the shore of Lake Erie, near the present site of Port Rowan, by one Deacon Trayer. In 1792 the Reverend Mr. Addison opened a school at Newark (Niagara), and another was opened there in 1794 by the Reverend Mr. Burns. In 1796 Mr. Richard Cockerel, who afterwards became well known as an instructor of youth, opened his first school at Newark; and in 1798 Mr. William Cooper opened one at York (Toronto). Dr. (afterwards Bishop) Strachan's labours in the cause of education, first at Kingston, afterwards at Cornwall, and finally at York, are well known. In 1807 legislative provision was made for the establishment of Grammar or High Schools; but no Common School Act was passed until 1816, when an annual grant of twenty-four thousand dollars a year was provided for. It is not necessary to trace minutely the course of subsequent legislation on the subject. Early in 1830 Upper Canada College was opened at York, and in 1836 the Upper Canada Academy, which has since developed into the University of Victoria College, was opened at Cobourg, under the auspices of the Wesleyan Methodist Conference. Various other less important denominational institutions were founded. The charter granted to King's College University will call for more extended remark on a future page. In 1839 the District Schools were converted into Grammar Schools, and 250,000 acres of Crown lands were set apart for their support.

As was the case in the Lower Province, considerable difficulty was encountered in procuring capable teachers of elementary schools. The people of Upper Canada, however, were keenly alive to the advantages of education, and not only sent their children to the common schools, but in many cases made special exertions to place them at more advanced seats of learning. Intelligence was widely diffused, and it was the exception, rather than the rule, to find an adult inhabitant unable to read, or even to write. The Upper Canadian farmer, too, regarded himself in the light of a citizen, and took a strong interest in the politics and institutions of his country. He was actuated by a spirit of inquiry. He could discuss the leading public questions of the day, and could criticise the conduct of the local member with some degree of intelligence. He was, as a rule, devotedly loyal to the Crown of Great Britain, and felt that Britain's fame and glory was a part of his own and his children's inheritance. Such, at the time of the Union, was the condition of the average Upper Canadian yeoman.

The revenue of the Upper Province, as has been explained in the preceding chapter, was in anything but a satisfactory condition. The public expenditure had been far in advance of the times. The construction of the Welland Canal and other important public works had not only swallowed up all available funds, but had plunged the Province in a heavy debt. Further expenditure was absolutely necessary if the canals were to be made serviceable. Not only was the exchequer empty, but there were various unsatisfied claims upon it. Loan after loan had been effected, and the public debt of the Province had rolled up to about five-and-a-half millions of dollars. The annual interest payable thereon almost swallowed up the entire provincial revenue, leaving scarcely anything for the permanent expenses of government. A choice between the two evils of a national bankruptcy and direct taxation loomed before the public eye. From the making of such a choice Upper Canada was saved by the Union. And in this there was no such grievous injustice to the Lower Province as at first sight appears. It was legitimate and reasonable that she should be made to pay a proportionate part of the cost of works which enured to her benefit equally with that of her neighbour.

At this point the question suggests itself: How far was the forcing of the Union measure upon a hostile majority justifiable? For there is nothing to be gained at this distance of time by blinding our eyes to the simple and undoubted fact that the Union was forced upon the French Canadian population of the Lower Province. It is not a sufficient answer to say, as has been said by more than one writer, that the latter had forfeited all claims to consideration by their recent disaffection. Disaffection had not been universal among the French Canadians; or at any rate its open manifestation had not been universal. Moreover, the mere stigma of treason has lost much of its opprobrium in these latter days, and the fact of a man's being found with arms in his hands against an existing Government is no longer to be regarded as conclusive proof of his being unworthy of any human consideration. There is treason and treason, and even the blackest of traitors has certain rights. It may as well be conceded, too, that the Canadian rebels of 1837 and '38 were not without some show of justification for their rebellion. A good many of them might truthfully have echoed the declaration of Dr. Nelson and his fellow-prisoners in the new gaol at Montreal, as expressed in a letter to Lord Durham on the 18th of June, 1838:—"We rebelled neither against Her Majesty's person nor her Government, but against Colonial misgovernment. . . . We remonstrated; we were derided. The press assailed us with calumny and contumely; invective was exhausted; we were goaded on to madness, and were compelled to show we had the spirit of resistance to repel injuries, or to be deemed a captive, degraded and recreant people. We took up arms not to attack others, but to defend ourselves." The true justification for the Union is to be found in the fact that it promoted the true interests, not only of the British who favoured, but even of the French who opposed it. It substituted progress for retrogression, enterprise for stagnation, modern ideas for those which were worn out or effete. It was not a perfect measure, but it served a good purpose for the time. It raised a burden from the shoulders of our grandfathers, to be reimposed upon the shoulders of our fathers and ourselves. Well for us that the latter had meanwhile gained strength to bear it.

Before bringing this chapter to a close, it should be mentioned that during the same session of the Imperial Parliament which was signalized by the passing of the Act of Union, an Act was passed (3 and 4 Victoria, chapter 78,) whereby provision was made for the sale and distribution of the proceeds of the Clergy Reserves in Canada. In a future part of this work the important question of the Clergy Reserves will necessarily occupy a conspicuous place. At present it will be sufficient to say that they had long been the most fruitful source of dissension between rival parties and factions, political and ecclesiastical, in Upper Canada, and that they had largely contributed to produce the rebellion in that Province. Mr. Thomson had been desirous of bringing about some pacific solution of the question before the Union Act should come into force, and had procured the assent of the local Assembly and Council to an Act for the proportionate distribution of the Reserves among the religious communities recognized by law. The English judges, however, decided that the Act was beyond the legislative authority of the colonial Parliament, and it was accordingly disallowed. The Act above named was then initiated by the Home Government, and received the royal assent on the 7th of August, 1840. It empowered the Governor to sell certain of the Reserves, and to apply the proceeds for the benefit of the Churches of England and Scotland. The measure was far from being satisfactory to Upper Canadians generally, but various other important questions engrossed public attention, and the great dispute respecting the Clergy Reserves was shelved—only to be renewed with increased vehemence in the next generation, when a final disposition was made of it, and when the partial domination of a State Church in Upper Canada was forever swept away.

In the foregoing chapter no attempt has been made to reproduce elaborate statistics, or to tabulate facts for the maintenance of any economical theory. The only desire has been to impart such a general knowledge of the condition of the country at large as to enable the reader to face the ensuing Parliamentary debates with some degree of appreciation of the various interests involved. It will probably by this time have been perceived that the Union Act, notwithstanding the beneficent intentions of its authors, was after all, a measure which, in the very nature of things, could only be of temporary utility. It attempted to do what it was beyond the power of any mere legislation to accomplish—viz., to wipe out the memory of the past, to obliterate life-long sympathies and prejudices, and to politically unite elements which were intrinsically and geographically distinct.

Chapter IV.

THE FIRST MINISTRY.

"The members of the Administration, all of whom were heads of departments, distinctly avowed their responsibility to Parliament for the measures of Government. . . Whatever political differences there may have been in the House, it was felt by every one that there was an ADMINISTRATION, and that its existence depended upon the support of a Parliamentary majority."—MR. HINCKS, in *The Examiner.*

THE first Parliament of United Canada assembled at Kingston, where the General Hospital had been fitted up for its accommodation, on Monday, the 14th of June, 1841.* The Legislative Council consisted of twenty-four members, all of whom had been appointed by His Excellency only five days before, but only fourteen out of the twenty-four presented themselves on the opening day. In accordance with the terms of the Union Act, the Legislative Assembly consisted of eighty-four members, forty-two from each of the former Provinces. Of these eighty-four, seventy-nine were present at the opening of the session.†

It will not be uninteresting to glance at the *personnel* of this

---

* MacMullen, Miles, Jeffers, Tuttle, and several other compilers of Canadian history, represent this First Parliament as having been convened for the 13th of June. A little investigation would have disclosed the fact that the 13th fell on a Sunday. As matter of fact Parliament was, by a proclamation dated the 15th of February, 1841, convened for the 8th of the following April. By a subsequent proclamation, dated the 6th of April, the date was fixed for the 26th of May. Finally, by a proclamation dated the 30th of April, the date was fixed for the 14th of June, which was the actual date of assembling "for the despatch of business."

† See *post*, Chap. VI.

First Parliament, for it was, in fact as well as in name, a genuine Representative Body. That is to say, it was representative of the best intellect and culture of both sections of the Province. It contained an unusual number of really capable men, and there were members of each House whose abilities would have made them conspicuous in any country where their lot might have been cast.

Seniores priores. It is fitting that the Ministry should receive earliest attention; and it should be premised that the Ministry was the result of a practical coalition,* skilfully brought about by the Governor-General. Up to the day of the opening of the session, it consisted of nine members, six of whom belonged to the western, and the remaining three to the eastern section of the united Province.

The Attorney-General for Upper Canada was William Henry Draper, a gentleman who for a brief period shared the leadership of the Ministerial party in the Upper Province with Mr. Harrison. Mr. Draper has stamped his name very distinctly upon the political and judicial history of his time in this country. His career had been a somewhat eventful one. He was born in London, England, in 1801. His father was a clergyman, and rector of one of the city churches there. During his early boyhood, being a high-spirited youth, he ran away to sea, and served for some time as a cadet on board an East Indiaman. In his twentieth year, having passed through his full share of adventure, he arrived in Upper Canada, and obtained a situation as teacher of a school at Port Hope. He subsequently studied law, and was in due time called to the bar. He settled at Little York, afterwards Toronto, and devoted himself assiduously to his profession. He was endowed with high natural abilities, and soon achieved success. He possessed a voice of great flexibility and sweetness, and his manner proved

---

* As will hereafter be seen, Mr. Baldwin did not regard it in the light of a coalition, but as a mere temporary arrangement to enable the Governor-General to carry out his purposes.

very effective before juries. No lawyer of his time in Canada excelled him in the subtle art of persuasion, and his silver-tongued eloquence procured for him the sobriquet of "Sweet William." In 1836 he was returned to the Upper Canadian Assembly by the city of Toronto, and at the request of the Lieutenant-Governor, Sir Francis Bond Head, he accepted a place in the Executive Council of that day, but without any portfolio. During the rebellion he served as an aide-de-camp to the Lieutenant-Governor. In March, 1837, he became Solicitor-General, and he retained that office until 1840, when he succeeded the Hon. Christopher A. Hagerman as Attorney-General. At Lord Sydenham's request he had consented to retain that office in the present Ministry.

In politics he was a Conservative of a very pronounced cast. He was an upholder of Church and State doctrines, and had not got beyond the theories prevalent during the reign of George III.; but he could upon occasion simulate a positive enthusiasm for liberal sentiments, and could declaim about the sacred rights of a free people in a manner highly edifying. A newspaper of the day described him as "the most plausible of mortals, bland, insinuating, persuasive, eloquent." He had little or nothing in common with some of his colleagues, and it was impossible that any Ministry containing such incongruous elements should long hold together. As matter of fact, as will presently be seen, one of its most conspicuous members retired from office at the opening of the session. Mr. Draper, however, continued to hold the Attorney-General's portfolio, and we shall meet him frequently in the course of the following narrative. He at this time represented the county of Russell in the Assembly. Many readers of these pages are familiar with his face and figure, for he survived until about four years since, and only died on the 3rd of November, 1877. As known to the present generation he was a man of singularly kindly and venerable appearance, upon whom, nevertheless, the infirmities of age had left an ineffaceable mark. During the days of his Attorney-Generalship, on the contrary, he was in the prime and vigour of a lusty manhood. His figure was muscular and graceful, his gestures were striking, and his language was wonderfully impressive and convincing. His flow of words was smooth and easy, and his elocution almost perfect. His voice was such as fully to justify the sobriquet already mentioned, and his countenance, when lighted up with the animation of debate, was bright and attractive. His tact, adroitness and dexterity in passing executive measures through the House were unrivalled. His Parliamentary influence was long fully commensurate with his abilities. We are not, however, able to approve, or even to sympathize with much of his political career, for we are perforce led to the conclusion that his views were not consonant with the best interests of his adopted country. From any but an extreme high Tory point of view, William Henry Draper, as the Minister of Sir Charles Metcalfe, must appear in the light of a mere party politician and obstructionist, rather than in that of a statesman. It is not as a politician that those who are most careful for his fame wish to remember him. Fortunately he has left a judicial record which all persons, of whatsoever shade of political opinion, must unite in admiring. For more than thirty years he adorned the judicial bench, and when he died he left behind him a reputation for judicial learning and acumen of which his descendants may justly feel proud.

One of the ablest and most influential members of the Executive Council, and in many respects one of the most estimable men known to Canadian political history, was Robert Baldwin.

It has been intimated that one of the most conspicuous members of the Council resigned office at the opening of the session. That member was Mr. Baldwin, and his doing so has been made a reproach against him by Lord Sydenham's biographer, upon the ground that his resignation was calculated to embarrass the Governor. As a good deal of absurdity has been spoken and written on this subject, and as the facts are not widely known, it is desirable that existing misapprehension should be removed, and that a just appreciation of Mr. Baldwin's position should be arrived at.

Mr. Baldwin entered political life in the year 1829, as the successor of the Hon. John Beverley Robinson in the representation of the town of York. A brief account of his previous career will tend to the elucidation of his character and position before the country at the time of his taking office under Lord Sydenham. He was the eldest son of Dr. William Warren Baldwin, a gentleman of high social and political standing, and was born at Little York in 1804. He studied law, and upon completing his studies entered upon the practice of his profession in his native town, in partnership with his father. The latter was a gentleman of very liberal and enlightened views, and brought up his son with political ideas in advance of his time and surroundings. Robert was from his boyhood conspicuous, not so much for brilliant abilities as for a very unusual degree of prudence and good sense. All his actions were dictated by a high sense of duty and responsibility to his Maker. He was scrupulously, almost morbidly conscientious, insomuch that he was in some degree unfitted for the exigencies of party warfare in those days. The writer of these pages cannot better express his estimate of the character and aims of Robert Baldwin than by repeating, in effect, what he has said elsewhere:—' The twenty and odd years which have elapsed since he was laid in his grave have witnessed many and important changes in our Constitution, as well as in our habits of thought; but his name is still regarded by the great mass of the Canadian people with feelings of respect and veneration. We can still point to him with the admiration due to a man who, during a time of the grossest political corruption, took a foremost part in our public affairs, and who yet preserved his integrity untarnished. We can point to him as the man who, if not the actual author of Responsible Government in Canada, yet spent the best years of his life in contending for it, and who contributed more than any other person to make that project an accomplished fact. We can point to him as one who, though a politician by predilection and by profession, never stooped to disreputable practices, either to win votes or to maintain himself in office. Robert Baldwin was a man who was not only incapable of falsehood or meanness to gain his ends, but who was to the last degree intolerant of such practices on the part of his warmest supporters. If intellectual greatness cannot be claimed for him, moral greatness was most indisputably his. Every action of his life was marked by sincerity and good faith, alike towards friend and foe. He was not only true to others, but was from first to last true to himself. His useful career, and the high reputation which he left behind him, furnish an apt commentary upon the advice which Polonius gives to his son Laërtes:—

> " 'This above all: to thine own self be true;
> And it must follow, as the night the day,
> Thou canst not then be false to any man.'

. . . No unprejudiced man can doubt that he was a sincere patriot, or that he was induced to enter public life chiefly by a desire to promote the general good. His frequent sacrifices of personal advantages when required by adherence to his principles are sufficient proof of this; and he will long be remembered in Canada as possessing singular purity of motive, and freedom from the lower influences which operate upon politicians. Our country has perhaps produced greater men, but she has produced none better, and there is no name in our annals to which we can point with more unfeigned respect and admiration than his."*

Reared amid such influences, it was to be expected that he would,

---

* See "The Canadian Portrait Gallery," Vol. I., pp. 17, 45.

upon attaining his manhood, take a pronounced stand on the Liberal side in matters political. From the time when he was old enough to have any decided opinions of his own he was a firm adherent of the principles involved in the theory of Responsible Government. It was as the advocate of those principles that he was returned for the town of York in 1829. Upon the opening of the session in January, 1830, he took his seat in the Assembly. His first Parliamentary experience was very brief. The death of King George IV. in the following June rendered a dissolution necessary, and at the ensuing election Mr. Baldwin's candidature was unsuccessful. His influence in the Reform party, however, continued to grow, although he scrupulously abstained from taking part in the faction disputes of the period. His position would seem to have been a singularly enviable one in all respects. He occupied a high rank at the bar, and had a large and lucrative professional business. He was possessed of considerable pecuniary means, and was the heir to large and valuable estates. His personal character may almost be said to have stood upon a pedestal. Dishonour or crooked dealing had never attached, even in the remotest degree, to the name of Robert Baldwin. The members of the Family Compact, whose policy he and his father had spent much of their lives in opposing, united in bearing testimony to the sincerity and loftiness of his aims, and to the unspotted purity of his character.

When Sir Francis Bond Head arrived in the Province to assume the Lieutenant-Governorship, in January, 1836, there were three vacancies in the Executive Council, owing to the recent dismissal of three of the old members. These vacancies it was necessary to fill without delay. The Lieutenant-Governor found, upon inquiry, that if Mr. Baldwin could be induced to accept office the Government would be very greatly strengthened, as his name inspired more confidence and esteem than that of any other person in the Province. On this point it is sufficient to quote the Governor's own despatch to Lord

Glenelg, the Colonial Secretary, under date of February 22nd, 1836. "After making every inquiry in my power," says the despatch, "I became of opinion that Mr. Robert Baldwin, advocate, a gentleman already recommended to your Lordship by Sir John Colborne for a seat in the Legislative Council, was the first individual I should select, being highly respected for his moral character, being moderate in his politics, and possessing the esteem and confidence of all parties. Having come to this conclusion I deemed it prudent to consult the Chief Justice, who is Speaker of the Legislative Council; Mr. Bidwell, the Speaker of the House of Assembly; and the members of the Executive Council; and as all of these gentlemen unreservedly approved of his selection to the office, I sent for Mr. R. Baldwin, and proposed to him to accept the same."* The Chief Justice here referred to was the Hon. John Beverley Robinson, Mr. Baldwin's predecessor in the representation of the town of York. Mr. Robinson's politics and those of Mr. Baldwin were wide as the poles asunder, and the former's approval of the latter's appointment to office affords a convincing proof of the high estimation in which Mr. Baldwin was held, by opponents as well as by friends.

Mr. Baldwin's reception of the Lieutenant-Governor's overtures was not enthusiastic. He asked time to answer, and to consult with his friends, which was granted him. Several interviews took place between him and the Lieutenant-Governor. He was disposed to insist on certain conditions which the Governor was not advised to concede. The latter, by way of bringing influence to bear upon Mr. Baldwin, sent for his father, Dr. W. W. Baldwin, but for some time found father and son equally unmanageable. One of the chief points of discussion was the responsibility of the Executive Council to the Assembly. The Baldwins contended that by the Constitutional Act of 1791 such responsibility already existed, and that when a Ministry ceased to command a majority of votes in the Assembly it was

---

* Head's "Narrative," Chap. IV.

bound to resign office. This was a question which the Lieutenant-Governor was not very competent to discuss. He had probably never heard of the Constitutional Act of 1791 until his appointment to his present position, and he was not, either by nature or training, fitted to grasp the principles involved in grave constitutional questions. On the occasion under consideration he seems to have fenced with the question of executive responsibility until he could derive inspiration from the Chief Justice. After consultation with that functionary he took a somewhat more determined stand with Mr. Baldwin, but nevertheless made certain concessions which seemed to imply a sincere desire on his part to conduct his Administration in accordance with popular views. Mr. Baldwin's friends urged him to accept office, alleging that he could serve the popular cause better in office than out. After a good deal of diplomacy and negotiation, Mr. Baldwin entered the Administration, two of his friends and political colleagues—Dr. John Rolph and John Henry Dunn—accepting office at the same time. They remained in office only about three weeks. They found that they were treated as mere figureheads, and that the Governor had no intention of permitting them to have any real voice in carrying on the Government. They were thus made to seem responsible, in the public eye, for acts over which they had no manner of control. Remonstrances proving unavailing, they resigned office, and Mr. Baldwin did not again take any part in public life until 1840, the year preceding the consummation of the Union.

Upon the close of the session of the Upper Canadian Parliament in February, 1840, the Governor-General, Mr. Thomson, offered the post of Solicitor-General, which had just become vacant, to Mr. Baldwin. That gentleman's reputation had rather gained than lost during the four years which had elapsed since his retirement, and there could be no doubt that he would add much strength to the Government if he could be induced to join it. He could not, however, see his way

very clearly to accepting a place in a Government with Mr. Draper,
the Attorney-General, whose great abilities he respected, but whose
political views were utterly antagonistic to his own. But the Governor-General, who possessed an abundant degree of *savoir faire*,
was very urgent, and brought not only the weight of his own influence to bear, but also that of several of Mr. Baldwin's friends, with
whom he had established amicable relations. It was represented
to Mr. Baldwin that the Governor-General had been sent over to
Canada to inaugurate Responsible Government, and that neither
the views of Mr. Draper nor those of any other high Tory would be
permitted to stand in the way of such a consummation. It was in
his power, he was informed, to promote this desirable end by lending
his countenance to the Governor; whereas by keeping aloof he would
render the Governor's task, already sufficiently difficult, more arduous
still. To such arguments he was not likely to be insensible. To
see Responsible Government established—the "one idea" with which
his name is inseparably associated—was one of the prime objects of
his life. He finally consented to accept the vacant Solicitor-Generalship, but without a seat in the Executive Council. In order, however, that there should be no misapprehension as to the motives by
which he was actuated, he wrote and published a letter containing
the following announcement:—"I distinctly avow that in accepting office I consider myself to have given a public pledge that I
have a reasonably well grounded confidence that the Government
of my country is to be carried on in accordance with the principles
of Responsible Government which I have ever held. My position
politically is certainly peculiar, but its peculiarity has arisen out
of the position in which the present Parliament placed the Governor-General, themselves and the country by the course they chose
to adopt during the last session, and it is therefore right that it
should be distinctly understood that I have not come into office by
means of any coalition with the Attorney-General or with any

others now in the public service, but have done so under the Governor-General, and expressly from my confidence in him."

For some months after this time nothing occurred to bring the members of the Council into direct collision, although their official relations were not always marked by perfect harmony. Various correspondence took place between the leading Liberals in the two Provinces, with a view to ascertaining how much there was in common between them, and how far they would be able to harmonize after the Union should be accomplished. The French Canadians, as has been seen, were averse to the project of Union altogether, and could not support the Government views. The Upper Canadian Reformers, on the other hand, and even many of the moderate Conservatives, accepted the Union with cordiality. There were also radical points of difference between the inhabitants of the two Provinces on other questions, and perfect harmony was not to be looked for. The Liberals in each Province, however, were desirous of strengthening their hands by an alliance with each other, and communications passed to and fro between their leaders with a view to bringing about such a result. Such was the state of affairs when Lord Sydenham, in February, 1841, immediately after the Union Act came into operation, found himself called upon to form a Ministry for the United Province. He resolved to form it from the principal officers of State in each of the old Provinces, and notified Mr. Baldwin that he had included his name in the list. Now, the list contained the names of only three persons—John Henry Dunn, Samuel Bealey Harrison, and Dominick Daly—with whom Mr. Baldwin felt that he had much political affinity. Of the others, the two Upper Canadian members at least were antagonistic. As to the Lower Canadian members, he had not sufficient acquaintance with them to know precisely how far he could assimilate with them, but he knew from their past careers that there could not be a great deal in common between them and himself. In the very nature of things, however, a Ministry formed under such circumstances could only be expected to be temporary. A reconstruction would become necessary upon the meeting of the Legislature, if not before. So argued Mr. Baldwin. He did not wish to appear factious, or to embarrass the Governor-General in his attempt to make the Union a success. He placed the utmost reliance upon Lord Sydenham's good faith, and desired to assist rather than oppose him. He accordingly accepted office as Solicitor-General; but in order that there should be no misunderstanding on the subject he at once wrote to four of his colleagues—Messrs. Draper, Sullivan, Ogden and Day—apprising them of his entire want of political confidence in them. He wrote to the Governor to the same effect, and announced to His Excellency his opinion that such an arrangement of the Administration would not command the support of Parliament. "Such language," says Sir Francis Hincks,* "could admit of but one construction—Mr. Baldwin plainly indicated his intention, when the proper time came, to require a reconstruction of the Cabinet; but, pending the meeting of the Legislature, was unwilling to create embarrassment to the Governor by any premature action. He, however, did not conceal from his colleagues his want of political confidence in them. If the Governor or his colleagues had been of opinion that Mr. Baldwin's retention of his seat in the Council, under the circumstances, was objectionable, they could have required his immediate resignation. His own opinion was that the assembling together of the newly-elected representatives of the reünited Provinces, on the occasion of the meeting of Parliament, was the proper time for action; and that had he taken any more energetic step than he did, he would have laid himself open to the charge of causing unnecessary embarrassment to the Governor-General." Such is a very plausible, and, as the

* In a lecture on "The Political History of Canada," delivered at Montreal in October, 1877.

present writer believes, a perfectly correct account of Mr. Baldwin's views and motives at the time of his acceptance of office in Lord Sydenham's Government, in February, 1841. It moreover agrees, in spirit and substance, with Mr. Baldwin's own explanation, as subsequently given on the floor of Parliament, when taunted with inconsistency.

After accepting office, Mr. Baldwin was elected for two different constituencies—Hastings and the Fourth Riding of York. He eventually decided to serve for the first-named constituency, but at the period at which the narrative has now arrived he had not expressed his decision. In the month of April he repaired to Montreal, and was sworn in as a member of the Council. Nothing further of importance occurred until just before the opening of Parliament in June. Agreeably to a preconcerted arrangement, the leading members of the Liberal party from both sections of the Province reached Kingston several days before the opening of the session, in order that a conference might be held respecting the political situation. Many members who afterwards fought side by side in Parliament then met for the first time. Mr. Baldwin was present at the meeting; and indeed he had been the instrument used for calling it together. The members were frank and explicit in stating their views. It appeared very clearly that, owing to the presence in the Ministry of Messrs. Sullivan, Draper, Ogden and Day, the Reform party generally were not disposed to support it; although there was, even on the part of the Lower Canadian members, an almost unanimous expression of confidence in Mr. Baldwin. The French Canadian members also, as was natural enough, insisted upon being represented in the Cabinet, and their claims in this respect were recognized by the general voice of the Liberal party. This was made so indisputably clear that Mr. Baldwin felt himself bound to insist upon a reconstruction. He could not retain office in a Ministry which did not enjoy the confidence of his party. The alternative of reconstruction or resignation stared him in the face.

Mr. Baldwin accordingly wrote to His Excellency on Saturday, the 12th of June, explaining his views, and advising such a reconstruction of the Ministry as should include several French Canadian members. His Excellency was apprised that the Reformers from Eastern and Western Canada had formed themselves into a united party which represented the political views of a great majority of the people; that the members of that party had no confidence in the Administration as then constituted—though, it was added, the want of confidence did not extend to the Head of the Government—and that before it would be possible for them to support the Administration Mr. Sullivan, Mr. Draper, Mr. Ogden and Mr. Day must cease to be members of it. Mr. Baldwin added that in the faithful discharge of the sacred duty imposed upon him by his oath of office he felt bound respectfully to tender to His Excellency his humble advice that the reconstruction of the Administration upon the basis suggested was a measure essential to the successful and happy conduct of public affairs.

The reconstruction of the Ministry suggested by Mr. Baldwin at this time would have involved no constitutional irregularity. A very similar reconstruction, indeed, took place in the summer of 1842, during the Administration of Sir Charles Bagot. The Governor-General, however, refused to be dictated to, and declined the overture in no very even frame of mind. The French Canadians, he said, had opposed the Union, and their hostility to that measure had suffered no diminution. He had several months before offered Mr. Lafontaine a place in the Government, and that gentleman had thought proper to refuse the offer. His Excellency's rejection of Mr. Baldwin's proposal left the latter no alternative but to resign, which he did on the evening of the same day, less than forty-eight hours before the opening of the session.* Such are the facts with reference to this matter, which have been garbled to suit the views of two generations of political partisans, and have been made a ground of censure against Mr. Baldwin by Lord Sydenham's biographer,† and others who have followed in his wake.

We have now brought Mr. Baldwin's life down to the point at which the narrative has arrived—the opening of the session of 1841. In personal appearance he was less robust than Mr. Draper, and his address was by no means so ingratiating. He was slightly above the medium height, and though he had scarcely reached middle age there was a perceptible stoop in his shoulders. His countenance was wanting in colour, and its expression was rather stolid. His eyes, unless when lighted up by the excitement of debate, were deficient in animation, and there was nothing about him to proclaim that he was intellectually above the average of his fellow-men. His ideas did not come to him quickly, and as a speaker he was neither fluent nor brilliant. His sentences were ill constructed, and he often paused for want of a word; but his clear common-sense, keen love of justice, and perfect honesty of purpose sometimes made his speeches more effective than the more florid and finished orations of some of his contemporaries. Whether in or out of Parliament, he always commanded an attentive audience.

Robert Baldwin Sullivan, the President of the Council, was probably the most brilliant man known to the Canadian history of his time. He was one of the Crown appointees to the Legislative Council; was Irish by birth and parentage, and had emigrated to Canada in his youth. His mother was a sister of the Dr. W. W.

---

*Mr. Baldwin's resignation was not formally accepted until the evening of Monday, the 14th; so that it did not actually take effect until that date.

†See "Memoir of the Life of the Right Honourable Charles Lord Sydenham, G.C.B., with a Narrative of his Administration in Canada," edited by his brother, G. Poulett Scrope, M.P.; pp. 230-233.

Baldwin already mentioned, so that he was a first cousin of Robert
Baldwin himself. He studied law in the office of Dr. Baldwin,
who, after the manner of those primitive times, united the legal
with the medical profession in his practice. After his call to the
bar he entered into partnership with his cousin, at York, and
speedily attained high professional rank. Notwithstanding this
connection, and the Liberal influences among which his youth was
passed, he allied himself with the Conservative party upon his
entry into public life. It is difficult to believe that he had any
strong political convictions on either side. Indeed, in after years
he was known to say to his colleagues in the Ministry: "Settle
your policy among you as you please. Whatever policy you deter-
mine to adopt, I engage to furnish you with good reasons for its
adoption." He held enlightened views, but they were views merely,
and not convictions. It so happened that when he first began to
take an interest in public affairs, in 1834, various circumstances
combined to alienate him from his Liberal connections. His uncle
and cousin had ceased, for the time, to take an active part in
politics. William Lyon Mackenzie had forced himself upon the
notice of the more advanced wing of the Reform party, and was
besides a conspicuous factor in municipal affairs. He had been
returned as first mayor of the newly-incorporated town of Toronto.
Mr. Sullivan was also an aspirant to municipal honours, and found
himself opposed to Mr. Mackenzie on various questions of local
policy. At a subsequent municipal election he successfully opposed
Mr. Mackenzie in St. David's Ward, and was afterwards elected to
the mayoralty. There was a marked antagonism between him and
Mackenzie, which erelong extended itself beyond the confines of
municipal affairs. Sullivan denounced Mackenzie as a noisy demagogue. Mackenzie retorted by characterizing Sullivan as an oily-
tongued lawyer who would lie the loudest for the client who had
the longest purse. Those who espoused Mackenzie's side were

members of the Reform party, while Sullivan's supporters were Conservatives. Mr. Sullivan's social predilections also threw him among Conservative society. When Sir Francis Head appeared on the scene he fraternized with Mr. Sullivan, and offered him a seat in the Executive Council, which offer was accepted. Four ultra-Conservatives were admitted into the Council at the same time, and erelong the popular branch of the Legislature passed a vote of want of confidence in all the five. Mr. Sullivan's fortunes were thus completely identified with the Conservative party, and he soon became the Lieutenant-Governor's most trusted Councillor. Thenceforward he held office continuously until after the date at which the narrative has arrived.

An impartial historian is bound to give Mr. Sullivan credit for very high intellectual powers. As an orator he certainly had no rival among his contemporaries. He had a brilliant imagination, and wonderful power of expression. He possessed a wide and various knowledge of men and things. He could always be depended upon to make an effective plea either for or against any measure that engaged his attention, and he could feel the pulse of the House while he was speaking. The great defects of his character were want of sincerity and want of genuine earnestness of purpose. Though devoid of strong political convictions, he had the faculty of personating them with wonderful cleverness. He could, when occasion required, make a telling speech in which he would seem to be carried away by a whirlwind of passion. At its close he would sometimes ask his neighbour if he had not played his part well; and on one occasion he added: "My own opinion is all the other way, but there is no one on that side of the House sharp enough to see the weakness of my argument." He spoke with a strong Irish provincial accent, which was sometimes ludicrous, but always musical and effective. He was fond of display, and inordinately vain of his talents. Sir John William Kaye, the biographer of Sir Charles Metcalfe, is not always felicitous in his characterization of Canadian public men, but his pen-portraiture of Mr. Sullivan is near enough to accuracy to be worth quoting. He describes the President of the Council as "an Irishman by birth and a lawyer by profession; a man who, if he had united consistency of political conduct and weight of personal character with the great and original talents which he unquestionably possessed, might have taken a conspicuous part in the public affairs of any country. To Sir Charles Metcalfe he was described as the best writer and the best speaker in the colony—but there the commendation ceased."*

Samuel Bealey Harrison was a less conspicuous figure than those members of the Council already mentioned, but he was leader of the Reform element in the Ministerial party in Upper Canada, and was a man of some mark in his day. It has been said of him that he was "a person very difficult to describe, from want of salient points in his character." He was an English lawyer who had emigrated to Canada a few years before this time with a view to engaging in agriculture. He had, however, drifted into other pursuits, and had become private secretary to Sir George Arthur, the last Lieutenant-Governor of Upper Canada. He subsequently engaged in politics, and at this period held the portfolio of Provincial Secretary for Upper Canada. For some months, indeed, he was the actual Premier. At the time of the opening of the session he was without a seat in the Assembly, having been defeated in Hamilton by Sir Allan MacNab, and in the county of Kent by Mr. Joseph Woods; but he was soon afterwards returned for Kingston, in place of Mr. Anthony Manahan, who resigned his seat and accepted the post of Collector of Customs at Toronto.† With

* Kaye's "Life and Correspondence of Charles, Lord Metcalfe," Vol. II., p. 339. Revised edition, 1858.

† It was said at the time that Mr. Harrison's return for Kingston was largely due to a fear on the part of the inhabitants lest Lord Sydenham might take umbrage at the defeat of one of the most useful of his ministers, and might mark his disapprobation by removing the seat of Government.

no pretence to brilliant parts, Mr. Harrison was a man of strong sense, and was a useful member of the Ministry. In politics he was a moderate Reformer. "His qualities," says Kaye, "were for the most part of a negative description. Unassuming and unaffected, making no display of his talents, he still got through his business in such a manner as to justify a belief in their existence. But although his character was not clearly defined, his political opinions were; and his Liberalism was at least undoubted."* In personal appearance he was above the medium size, ruddy, and of a cheerful countenance. His speeches were short and practical, and had about them an air of candour and sincerity.

A somewhat conspicuous figure in his day and generation was Dominick Daly, who held the post of Provincial Secretary for the Lower Province. He has been aptly called "the permanent secretary, the Vicar of Bray of Canadian politics." A good deal of harsh criticism has been passed upon Mr. Daly's political career in Canada. That career is certainly not one to be held up to unbounded admiration, but those who have censured it the loudest seem to ignore the incidents of his previous life and training. He belonged to an order of things which passed away with the inaguration of the Union. He was an Irishman and a Roman Catholic, who had come out to Canada with Lieutenant-Governor Sir Francis Burton, in 1823. When Sir Francis returned to England his secretary accompanied him, but afterwards returned to Quebec to take the post of Provincial Secretary. He continued in the public service for a continuous period of about a quarter of a century thereafter. He attained some measure of popularity with the French Canadians—owing doubtless in large measure to his religion—and seems to have been a good deal trusted by successive Governors. He was a placeman—"the last of the old bureaucracy"—

---

* Kaye's "Life and Correspondence of Charles, Lord Metcalfe," Vol. II., p. 340. Revised edition, 1858.

and deemed it to be his duty to support the Government policy, whatever that policy might happen to be. Of politics he knew little. He never allied himself with any party, had no aptitude for political life, and was almost devoid of political sympathy. He was a member of Lord Durham's Executive, and seems to have been highly esteemed by that nobleman. Lord Sydenham found in him a man who might be implicitly depended upon to carry out his (the Governor's) will, and accordingly retained him in his post of Provinicial Secretary for Lower Canada. It would have been well if he had been pensioned as an old public servant, and thus disposed of, for his subsequent political career was not an unmixed success. He continued to hold office through repeated changes of Government for a period of seven years, and could never be made to see that he ought to resign merely because his colleagues found it necessary to do so. He regarded his office in the light of a permanent appointment, which he was quite justified in retaining so long as he enjoyed the countenance of the Governor. For the rest, he was a fair specimen of the Irish gentleman. His manners were pleasing, and his heart kindly. Socially he was a Conservative, and, unless when his temper was unduly ruffled, he had a fair share of tact and good judgment. He did not possess the national gift of eloquence, and was but an indifferent speaker. He represented the constituency of Megantic in the Assembly. In the House he exerted little influence, but his experience was useful in Council, and he was generally popular with all classes. "The verdict on him," says a contemporary writer, "ought perhaps to be that at a transition period he fulfilled a useful purpose, though it is impossible to regard him with any warmer feeling than one of criticism, which is baulked for want of a standard."* He was the only Roman Catholic member of the Government.

Charles Richard Ogden, Attorney-General for Lower Canada,

---

* See "The Irishman in Canada," p. 431.

was another old public servant, and sat in the Assembly for the town of Three Rivers. He was a lawyer of ability and experience, who had been loyal to the British interest in the Lower Province, and had successively held the offices of Solicitor-General and Attorney-General there, at a time when those offices yielded about as much trouble as emolument. During Sir John Colborne's administration of affairs in Lower Canada, the task of preparing all the legislative ordinances of the Special Council had devolved upon Mr. Ogden in his capacity of Attorney-General, and he had been very serviceable to the Governor. He was not, and could not have expected to be, regarded with much confidence by the French Canadians, to whose policy he had always been opposed. His connection with the Government was not of long duration. His acceptance of office was a mere temporary expedient, and he soon afterwards withdrew from public life in Canada to become Attorney-General in the Isle of Man, to which position he was appointed by the Imperial Government. Charles Dewey Day, Solicitor-General for Lower Canada, and member for Ottawa County, also held office through only one session, when he retired from public life to accept a seat on the judicial bench. Of all the members of this first Ministry under the Union, Mr. Day is the only one who now survives. John Henry Dunn, Receiver-General, had no very salient points in his character. He had held office in both the Executive and Legislative Councils of Upper Canada, was a trusted member of the Reform party, and now represented the city of Toronto in the Assembly. He is referred to by Lord Metcalfe's biographer as " an Englishman of no great acuteness of perception or ardour of patriotism, equally wanting in the steadier qualities of order and precision."

The only member of the Government still to be mentioned was Hamilton Hartley Killaly, who had entered the Government about five weeks later than his colleagues, and who sat in the Assembly for the town of London. Mr. Killaly was an Irish gentleman of the old school—a man who neither knew nor cared much about politics, and could not be said to belong to any political party, but who was a highly efficient engineer, and eventually made a capable head of a department. For the present he merely held office as an Executive Councillor, without portfolio.*

Such was the many-hued complexion of the first Ministry of United Canada. Lord Sydenham had certainly succeeded in getting together a lot of incongruous material. It might have been said of him, as was long before said of Lord Chatham, that he had made "an Administration so checkered and speckled—had put together a piece of joinery so crossly indented and whimsically dovetailed—a cabinet so variously inlaid—such a piece of diversified mosaic—such a tesselated pavement without cement, here a bit of black stone and there a bit of white—patriots and courtiers, Whigs and Tories, treacherous friends and enemies—that it was indeed a curious show, but utterly unsafe to touch and unsure to stand on." Such as it was, however, it served Lord Sydenham's purpose. It tided him over the only session he was destined to see. Under its auspices the new order of things was ushered in.

* For a humorous and somewhat exaggerated portraiture of Mr. Killaly, see the account of "The Commissioner," in Dr. W. A. Adamson's "Salmon Fishing in Canada," pp. 118, 119.

CHAPTER V.

THE ASSEMBLY OF NOTABLES.

"Meanwhile, suppose we two, good reader, should, as even without miracle Muse Clio enables us, take our station on some coign of vantage, and glance momentarily over this Procession." CARLYLE's *French Revolution*; Book IV., Chap. IV.

VARIOUS men of mark, in addition to the members of the Ministry, were returned to the first Legislative Assembly under the Union.

Conspicuous among the representatives from the Lower Province was Thomas Cushing Aylwin, a lawyer, and a man of shrewd intellect, considerable learning, and great powers of debate. He was a Canadian by birth, having been born in the city of Quebec in 1806. His youth had been one of exceptional brightness and promise, and though still somewhat short of middle age, he had won high distinction in his profession, and was accounted one of the highest authorities in Canada on the subject of criminal jurisprudence. He had shown strong Liberal predilections from his boyhood, and ten years before the time of his appearance in this history he had won considerable reputation as a caustic and slashing writer of newspaper articles. During Lord Gosford's administration of affairs Mr. Aylwin had distinguished himself by his championship of the French Canadians, and by his journalistic and oratorical onslaughts upon the policy pursued by that nobleman. He was one of the original founders of the Constitutional Association of Quebec, and was the friend and coadjutor of John Neilson, the veteran editor of the *Quebec Gazette*.

He now sat in Parliament for the first time, and represented the constituency of Portneuf. He was destined to remain in the House for seven years, during which period he won the deserved reputation of being the keenest Parliamentary debater of his time in Canada. His subsequent career on the judicial bench was of more than average mark, so long as health and vigour were vouchsafed to him ; but it can hardly be said that the performance of his mature age kept pace with the brilliant promise of his youth and middle life. He paid the penalty of precocity, and was an old man, both in mind and body, before his time. When he first took his seat in the First Parliament, however, the prime of his manhood was upon him, and he still, in the words of the poet, felt his days before him. He had a rasping and incisive tongue, combined with great powers of vituperation, by the exercise of which he on more than one occasion brought down upon his head bloodthirsty threats of vengeance from those whom he so mercilessly assailed. He was near-sighted and wore spectacles, and was rather below the medium size. When he chose, he could display most ingratiating manners, and be an exceedingly agreeable companion. Lord Metcalfe's biographer describes him as he appeared two years later—"a man of infinite adroitness and lawyer-like sagacity, skilled in making the worse appear the better reason, and exposing the weakness of an adversary's cause."

Another notable personage was the above-mentioned John Neilson, one of the most energetic and hard-working men who have ever taken part in Canadian public life. Mr. Neilson was Scotch by birth and descent, but had emigrated from Scotland to Canada in 1790, when he was about fourteen years of age. One of his paternal uncles was then proprietor of the *Quebec Gazette*, the first newspaper ever published in Canada, and the nephew seems to have been employed upon the paper in some capacity from the time of his first arrival in the country. Upon attaining his majority, he took the entire direction of the *Gazette*, which was published both in French and in English, and under his active management attained what for those days was accounted as a large circulation and influence. He had been engaged in public life for more than twenty-two years at the time of the consummation of the Union, having been first returned to the Provincial Assembly of Lower Canada in 1818, for the county of Quebec. He identified himself with the interests of his Province, and took a leading part in discussing the many important public questions of the time. He devoted particular attention to the subjects of education and agriculture, and advocated many useful reforms. He was endowed with a large and practical mind, was honest and well-meaning, and of high personal character. He called himself, and doubtless conscientiously believed himself to be, a Liberal, but the cast of his mind was by no means that of an agitator. His zeal for reform was restricted within constitutional bounds. There was about him nothing of the mere demagogue. He fought the battles of the French Canadians, and was highly regarded by them in turn. He advocated the preservation of many of their laws and customs, and stigmatized certain acts of successive Governors as arbitrary encroachments on the rights of the native population. He was opposed to unnecessary changes, and was slow to approve of radical reforms the benefits of which were not clearly demonstrable. In 1822 he accompanied Louis Joseph Papineau to England to oppose the scheme for the uniting of the two Provinces which was then contemplated by the Imperial Government. He was one of the delegates chosen in 1828 to present the "monster petition" of 87,000 French Canadians to the Imperial Parliament. In 1834 he was despatched on a third mission to England on behalf of the people of the Lower Province. During all these years he had exercised a certain supervision over the management of the *Gazette*, and a year or two before the breaking out of the rebellion he had been compelled, in consequence of the death of his son, to resume the entire direction of that journal. He condemned the rebellion, but sympathized with many of the inciting causes which led to it, and put forth the weight of his influence to save many misguided men who took part in the outbreak. To the scheme of union he was vehemently opposed, and as a member of the Special Council voted against it. When the project became an accomplished fact he was not a whit reconciled to it, and now took his seat in the Assembly determined to oppose the Government's policy to the utmost, in so far as the Union was concerned. He was by this time an old man of sixty-five,* but his eye was undimmed, and his natural force almost unabated. He was not an eloquent or even an effective speaker, but the vigour of his intellect was constantly making itself apparent, and he was an invaluable member of select committees. He sat in the House for his old constituency of Quebec County, where he had been returned without opposition.

Etienne Parent, the member for Saguenay, was another conspicuous figure in the Assembly. He was a French Canadian, born at Beauport, near Quebec, in 1801. Though only forty years old at this time he was a veteran journalist, and had done very effective work in the columns of *Le Canadien*. He had received a good education, and had studied law, but had erelong abandoned that profession for journalism. He had at one time held the post of French translator in the Lower Canadian Assembly. As editor of *Le Canadien* he was one of the best known men in his native Province, and made his paper the leading exponent of French Canadian sentiment and views. He was a polished and vigorous writer, well versed in the national politics, but somewhat deficient in prudence, and had on

---

* "The venerable John Neilson, of Quebec, is the Dean Swift of the House. He says what he pleases; is witty, waggish, impudent or polite as he pleases. He is tolerated at all times, out of order as well as in it. He is judicious, and displays a great knowledge of Parliamentary usage." C. C. W., a Kingston correspondent of the *Brockville Statesman*.

several occasions exposed himself to the censure of the Government by his fierce diatribes against the abuses of the times. During the troubled period immediately following the rebellion he had undergone a term of imprisonment in the Quebec gaol for some more than usually rabid utterances in *Le Canadien*. During his confinement he suffered much from cold, and upon his release in the spring of 1838 he found that his sufferings had affected his hearing to such an extent that he was for the time unfit to pursue his career as a lawyer. He resumed his labours as a journalist, having learned wisdom in the school of experience. He now sat in the Assembly as the mouthpiece of a large and influential body of his countrymen, who looked up to him as a heaven-born legislator and patriot, who would guard their interests against the ever-recurring encroachments to which they believed themselves to be subjected.

Robert Christie is better known at the present day by his literary productions than by his Parliamentary career, but the latter extended over a long period, and he was, in his way, a man of mark. He was a Nova Scotian by birth and education, but had long resided at Quebec, and had become somewhat notorious throughout the Lower Province. He had studied law at Quebec, and had been called to the Provincial Bar, but never distinguished himself by his forensic attainments. Neither did he appear to remarkable advantage as a politician. He was eccentric and erratic, hot headed and impulsive, crotchetty and unpractical. He had been a fellow-labourer with John Neilson on the columns of the Quebec *Gazette*. His writing was not without spirit and vigour, and he possessed great political knowledge, though many of his ideas were visionary, fanciful, and unsuited to the times. He had represented Gaspé in the Assembly of the Lower Province, but had been expelled from the House in 1829 for having advised the dismissal of a number of magistrates from the Commission of the Peace on account of their votes and speeches in the Assembly. His advice had been acted upon, and the dismissal had caused great scandal and much strong language. His expulsion was a popular measure at the time, and he himself was visited with a tremendous storm of obloquy. His constituents, however, sustained him, and returned him again to the Assembly. His return was followed by a second expulsion, and he did not again obtain a seat in Parliament until the period at which the narrative has arrived. He now sat in the united Assembly for his old constituency of Gaspé,* which he thenceforth continued to represent until the general elections of 1854, when he was defeated, and finally withdrew from political life. The work by which he is best known is the series of annals called " A History of the Late Province of Lower Canada," in six volumes—a work which is of great value to the student of Canadian history, but which is marred by a heavy and cumbrous style, and by an utter want of system in its arrangement.

Augustus Norbert Morin, a French Canadian advocate of middle age, had already made his mark in the Provincial Legislature, but had not yet gathered all the fame which was in store for him. He came of a middle-class family, and won an honourable place in his profession while he was still a very young man. He was first returned to Parliament in 1830, when he was twenty-eight years of age, and though diffident in his manner, he soon became known as a man of considerable political insight and power. He took part in all the conspicuous debates of the period, and in 1834 was deputed by the Assembly to repair to England as the colleague of Mr. D. B. Viger, who had preceded him thither to present certain petitions and lay certain facts before the British Ministry. His personal character stood very high, and he was respected as a thoroughly upright and honourable man. At this period he did not speak the English language with great fluency, and did not

* Mr. Christie was not present at the opening of the session, and did not actually take his seat until several days after.

often address the House, but his great influence among his compatriots was undoubted. He was a man, too, who wore well. He was undemonstrative, and the reverse of self-asserting. One might know him for years without recognizing the force and genuine depth of manliness that were in him. Lord Metcalfe's biographer, writing of him two years later, says:—"His character, as described to Metcalfe, would have fitted well the hero of a romance. With administrative abilities of the highest class, vast powers of application, and an extreme love of order, he united a rare conscientiousness and a noble self-devotion which in old times would have carried him cheerfully to the stake. His patriotism was of the purest water. He was utterly without selfishness and guile. And he was of so sensitive a nature, and so confiding a disposition, that it was said of him, he was as tender-hearted as a woman and as simple as a child. But for these—the infirmities only of noble minds—he might have been a great statesman." He now sat in the Assembly for Nicolet.

Denis Benjamin Viger, Richelieu's representative, was one of the best known public men of his day in his native Province. He was a lawyer of high standing, well read in his profession and out of it, and of irreproachable personal character. He had been long in public life; had sat in both the Council and the Assembly of Lower Canada, and was loved and trusted by his constituents. The nature of his mission to England in 1834 has been glanced at in the preceding paragraph. He had been the bosom friend and co-worker of Mr. Papineau, and had suffered imprisonment for his complicity in the rebellion. Such an experience was well calculated to endear him to his fellow-countrymen, who returned him to Parliament the first opportunity. His subsequent public career, as will hereafter be seen, was somewhat at variance with his past record. Though considerably past middle life he was of very winning appearance. He was somewhat short of stature, but well made, and of a fine, intellectual, and withal refined cast of countenance.

Several other Lower Canadian members must be passed over with mere mention. Dr.—afterwards Colonel, and finally Sir Etienne Pascal—Taché, a gentleman who subsequently rose to high position in political life in Canada, now took his seat in Parliament for the first time, and represented the constituency of L'Islet. The Hon. George Moffatt, who had been appointed Legislative Councillor under Lord Aylmer in 1831, and in 1838 had been appointed by Sir John Colborne to the Special Council, now sat in the Assembly as the colleague of Benjamin Holmes in the representation of the city of Montreal. Mr. Moffatt was English by birth, but had long resided in Montreal, where he had made a considerable fortune in commerce. He was a man of much local influence, and had been leader of the British party in the Legislative Council. He was a very distinctly pronounced Conservative in his views, but did not make a specially distinguished figure in public life subsequent to the Union. Mr. Holmes was much more advanced in his political opinions than his colleague, and the divergence between them increased with time. Mr. Holmes was known for a man of sturdy independence of spirit, who communicated his ideas in few words, and was no dealer in prosy speeches. Austin Cuvillier, the member for Huntingdon, was chiefly conspicuous for his knowledge of the finances of the country, and of the law and practice of Parliament.

One of the most noteworthy representatives from the Upper Province was undoubtedly Francis Hincks, a gentleman whose political life was then just beginning, and who after a long, useful, and very active career, is happily still spared to us. Mr. Hincks is an Irishman by birth and education. He was born at Cork, in 1807. His father, the Rev. Dr. T. D. Hincks, was a learned divine of the Irish Presbyterian Church. He himself was bred to commercial pursuits. He emigrated from Ireland in 1832, and settled at Little York, in Upper Canada, where he engaged in business as a wholesale merchant. He formed an intimate friendship with the Baldwin family, and attached himself to the Reform party. He soon gave up commercial life, and became the manager of a bank promoted chiefly by the Reformers in and near Toronto, and became known as a man of much shrewdness and good judgment. He first came conspicuously before the public in 1835, in connection with a Parliamentary investigation into the affairs of the Welland Canal, in which he unearthed various abuses, and proved incontestably that there had been great mismanagement in the conduct of affairs. In 1838, having formally allied himself with the Reform party, he established *The Toronto Examiner*, a weekly paper published in the interests of that party, and having for its motto: "Responsible Government and the Voluntary Principle." Mr. Hincks proved himself to be a vigorous and versatile writer, and the *Examiner* did good work for the popular cause. Alone among Upper Canadian journalists, he upheld the doctrines enunciated in Lord Durham's report. The paper obtained a wide circulation for those times, and made the editor's name known throughout the land. At the first general election under the Union he was invited to stand as the Reform candidate for the county of Oxford. He assented, and was returned to the Assembly, where he erelong, as will be seen, became one of the most conspicuous figures. He was a master of accounts, and a fluent and incisive speaker, and he had a thorough grasp of the main points at issue in the country. On questions respecting the trade and currency of Canada his knowledge was greater than that of any man in the Assembly. He was destined to hold an important office in the Government, and to play an important part in our Parliamentary history.

John Sandfield Macdonald, who was destined to play an almost equally prominent part in political life, also took his seat in

Parliament for the first time in 1841. He was in his twenty-ninth year, and sat in the Assembly for his native county of Glengarry. By what insignificant events is the future of some men's lives determined! After several boyish escapades, young Macdonald had begun life as a clerk in a general "store" at Cornwall. He was small of stature, and when carrying parcels home for his employer's customers was sometimes treated with ignominy by the street Arabs, who pelted him with snowballs and called him unsavoury names. In after years the wear and tear of an exceptionally combative political life rendered him case-hardened, but at this time the epithet of "counter-hopper" proved too much for his sensitive organization. One day, after being subjected to greater contumely than usual, he threw up the "counter-hopping" business in profound disgust, and entered upon the study of the law. Some persons might be disposed to pronounce this sudden change of occupation a leap from the frying-pan into the fire. In his case it did not prove so. Notwithstanding the drawbacks inseparable from a constitution far from robust, he studied diligently, and early in 1840 was admitted as an attorney. He settled down to the practice of his profession at Cornwall, and soon gained both money and fame. He was a representative Roman Catholic Gael, and as the population of the country thereabouts was largely made up of persons of the same religion and nationality, he had no lack of clients. He throve apace, and became the idol of the Celtic population. Six months after his admission as an attorney he was called to the Bar, and at the general election of 1841 he was returned to the Assembly, where, as will in due course be seen, he was not long in making his presence felt. He was presumed to have been elected in the Conservative interest, but it was some years before his constituents made any attempt to dictate to him as to his political conduct. It was sufficient for them that he was "the Macdonald," and that he could make a rattling speech to them in their native Gaelic tongue. As for himself, his political views were of a decidedly composite order. He finally determined to cast in his lot with the Upper Canadian Conservatives and the Lower Canadian Frenchmen who opposed the Government, but it cannot be said that he ever acted very cordially with them. He was, as he in after years described himself to be, a political Ishmaelite.

Sir Allan Napier MacNab was more conspicuous by reason of his prominent position in the Conservative party than from his inherent abilities, though he afterwards proved that he possessed one of the most important qualifications for the mere politician —the ability to bow to the inevitable, and to make concessions with a good grace when concessions could no longer be avoided. He had a somewhat chequered history. Like many others of his race and lineage, he suffered from chronic impecuniosity. He was born at Newark (Niagara) in 1798. His father had been a soldier in the Revolutionary War, and afterwards a member of the staff of Lieutenant-Governor Simcoe. The son inherited a fondness for a military life, and notwithstanding his tender age, saw some active service during the war of 1812-'15. He was subsequently employed as a copying clerk in transcribing the journals of the Upper Canadian Assembly. He studied law at York, and while so engaged he was compelled to resort to all kinds of devices to save himself from arrest for debt. On more than one occasion he was in that harassing state of existence known in technical parlance as "on the limits," and was compelled to restrict his perambulations within the charmed circles of the blue posts which in those times marked the boundary that must not be passed by a bailed debtor. He had, however, a robust constitution and a powerful frame, and his pecuniary troubles never seemed to check the hilarious flow of his spirits. In 1825 he was called to the bar, and some years later began legal practice in Hamilton. A more than average measure of professional success attended him there, but he never learned the secret of restricting his expenditure within the limits of his income, and was always in pecuniary straits. In 1829 he appeared as a witness before a committee of the House of Assembly at Little York, to testify concerning his knowledge of an outrage which had been committed at Hamilton a short time previously, when the Lieutenant-Governor, Sir John Colborne, had been burned in effigy. For declining to answer certain compromising questions put by Dr. Rolph, he was declared guilty of contempt and breach of privilege, and was committed to gaol during the pleasure of the House. This made a political martyr of him in the estimation of the Tory party, and at the following general election he was returned to the Assembly in the Tory interest by the electors of the county of Wentworth. He represented that constituency through the three next Parliaments, and in 1837 was elected Speaker of the Assembly. During the rebellion he took the command of the Provincial militia, and distinguished himself on the Niagara frontier by directing the cutting out of the steamer *Caroline* from the American side of the Niagara River, and starting her adrift to float over the terrible cataract several miles below. In recognition of this achievement, and of his military services generally, he afterwards received the honour of knighthood. At the general election for members of the First Parliament under the Union he offered himself to the electors of Hamilton, in opposition to Samuel Bealey Harrison, the Provincial Secretary. As the nominee of the Administration this gentleman was a formidable opponent, but Sir Allan was personally popular, and his services during the rebellion were still fresh in the public memory. The Provincial Secretary was beaten, and, after being again beaten in Kent, was finally compelled to take refuge in Kingston, where, as has been seen, Mr. Anthony Manahan made way for him. Sir Allan took his seat in the Assembly as the avowed leader of the Conservative party, a position which he retained for many years. His Conservatism was the legitimate result of his training and associations. There was nothing of the statesman about him, but his position as leader of a party, his Parliamentary knowledge and experience, and his personal popularity made him a prominent figure in the Assembly. For the rest, he was a man of average capacity and good presence, who could make a fairly effective speech on any subject which he had much at heart. He always seemed to be somewhat weighted by the rank which had been conferred upon him by his grateful Sovereign, but was affable and courteous, and bore himself with a tolerably good grace.

William Hamilton Merritt sat for the North Riding of Lincoln. He was the son of a U. E. Loyalist, and had himself taken part in defending the Canadian frontier during the war of 1812-'15. He was the founder of St. Catharines, but was more widely known from his connection with the Welland Canal—an enterprise as to which a Canadian writer well observes that "the canals of Languedoc, or those which have made memorable the title of Bridgewater and the name of DeWitt Clinton, are mere puny shreds and ribbon-like rills of water, small in themselves, and insignificant in their uses, as compared with the magnificent work that William Hamilton Merritt projected; for the Welland Canal connects the inland seas of North America, and for the purposes of commerce unites in one basin half the fresh water on our globe."* Whether Mr. Merritt originated the idea of connecting Lakes Erie and Ontario by means of a canal may perhaps be open to question; but it is certain that his indefatigable exertions hastened its construction, and that to him, more than to any other man, Canada is indebted for its existence. It is even probable that it would have been constructed through the territory of the United States instead of in Canada had it not been that Mr. Merritt gave up the best part of many years of his life to urging the project upon the Upper Canadian Parliament and people. He was not a particularly brilliant man, but he possessed a large fund of good sense, a high personal character, and a sincere desire for the country's welfare.

* See Mr. Fennings Taylor's "Portraits of British Americans," Vol. II., p. 295.

Before the Union he had sat in the Provincial Assembly for the county of Haldimand. He was moderate in his politics, and acted with the Reform party.

Malcolm Cameron represented the county of Lanark. He was of humble parentage, and was born at Three Rivers, in Lower Canada, in 1808. His father had been hospital sergeant of a Highland regiment stationed in Canada, and was afterwards a tavern-keeper at Perth, in the Ottawa District. The degrading bar-room scenes he was compelled to witness in his early boyhood, added to his mother's wise admonitions, made him a zealous apostle of the temperance cause throughout the whole of his after life. He had been compelled to make his own way in the world, and had devoted his attention to mercantile pursuits, in which he had been fairly successful. He was a Radical in politics, and first entered public life in 1836, when he was returned to the Upper Canadian Assembly as member for Lanark. He made himself conspicuous by his opposition to the Governor, Sir Francis Bond Head, and by his virulent denunciations of the Family Compact. He was an honest, earnest, and upon the whole a well-meaning man, who did a great deal of useful work in his day, and attained much reputation as a member of Parliament; but he was not always easy to manage, and was restive under discipline. Though attached to the advanced wing of the Reform party, he declined to follow Mr. Baldwin's lead when that gentleman declared his want of confidence in, and withdrew from, the Administration. He soon announced himself as a supporter of the Government policy. He was small of stature and insignificant in appearance, and his oratory was marred by want of education and an unmusical voice. At the time of the Union, however, he was still young, and his best days were yet to come.

James Edward Small was a practising barrister in Toronto, and represented the Third Riding of the county of York. He was of English descent, and belonged to one of the old families resident at the Upper Canadian capital. A certain notoriety had at one time attached to his name in consequence of his having taken part as second in a duel whereby a son of Surveyor-General Ridout had lost his life. The other principal in the affair was Mr. Samuel Peters Jarvis, a son of Mr. William Jarvis, a gentleman who had been Secretary to several of the early Lieutenant-Governors of Upper Canada. The seconds were Mr. Small and Mr. Henry John Boulton. The surviving principal had been tried and acquitted, but no proceedings had at that time been instituted against the seconds. The duel took place in July, 1817, and had well nigh passed out of the public mind, when its memory was revived, in 1828, by Mr. Francis Collins, editor of *The Canadian Freeman*, a newspaper published at Little York. Collins had been imprisoned and fined for libel, on account of his having made certain statements in his paper reflecting on the character of the Attorney-General, the Hon. John Beverley Robinson. The prosecution was an unwise and tyrannical proceeding, but was sympathized with by all the leading Tory families of Little York. Collins retaliated on two of these families by indicting Mr. Small and the Hon. Henry John Boulton—who had by that time become Solicitor-General—for their share in the duel fought thirteen years before. The trial lasted two days, and resulted in an acquittal. The prosecution, as well as that which gave rise to it, reflected little credit on any of those concerned, but the notoriety induced thereby is said to have given an impetus to Mr. Small's professional and political fortunes. His views on public questions were more liberal than might have been expected from his social surroundings, and he was a great admirer of Robert Baldwin, whose lead he for the most part followed. His voice was weak, and his constitution delicate. He was not a frequent speaker in the House, but when he did speak his language was well chosen, and he was listened to with attention and respect.

Isaac Buchanan, a gentleman of Scottish birth and descent, and one of the leading merchants of the country, was the colleague of John Henry Dunn in the representation of the city of Toronto. He

LORD SYDENHAM.

LORD SYDENHAM

BRACEBRIDGE, MUSKOKA.

SIR CHARLES BAGOT.

KINGFISHER'S HAUNT, RIVER ST. ANNE, BELOW QUEBEC.

subsequently removed to, and still resides at Hamilton, and is one
of the few prominent men now living who took part in public
affairs in the old ante-Union days. He was an energetic and
public-spirited man, and one of the most strenuous advocates of the
secularization of the Clergy Reserves. In 1835 he had published a
proposition for the settlement of that vexed question. Several
years later he had drawn up and headed a petition to Her Majesty
deprecating the appointment of Mr. Thomson as Governor-General,
alleging that that gentleman was a man chiefly known as connected
with Russia and the interests of the Baltic, and as an enemy of the
colonies. The petition prayed that Her Majesty would reconsider the
appointment, and "select for this important dependency a Governor
not known to be inimical to the great interests which he is sent to
protect and promote." When his Excellency arrived in Upper
Canada he very soon made Mr. Buchanan's acquaintance, but never
succeeded in convincing him that the allegations in the petition
were unfounded. Mr. Buchanan, however, never offered a factious
opposition to the Governor-General. Throughout his career he has
paid special attention to questions of finance and political economy,
and has been a persistent opponent of the doctrines of Free Trade.
His views on the subject of paper currency have long been well
known to the Canadian public. At the time of the Union he
was only in his thirty-first year, and was possessed of a super-
abundant vitality which left its impress upon every enterprise
wherewith he connected himself. He was essentially a man of
business, and made a very useful member of Parliament. He was an
uncompromising advocate of the doctrine of Responsible Government, on which he from time to time spoke and wrote with much
judgment and acuteness. In politics he called himself a Conservative
Reformer.*

* In his address to the Toronto electors, published in January, 1841, we find the following confession of his political faith: "I do not mean to impugn the private character of

James Morris, member for Leeds, was also a man of some mark, and in after days held high public offices of trust. He had had some Parliamentary experience, having sat for Leeds in the Legislative Assembly of the Upper Province throughout the last Parliament before the Union. Without possessing any remarkable vigour of understanding, he exerted a good deal of influence, and was highly respected as a thoroughly upright and well-intentioned man. His political reputation, such as it was, was still to be made. Colonel John Prince was an English barrister who had emigrated to Western Canada about eight years before the consummation of the Union, and settled on an estate in the county of Essex, which county he now represented in the Assembly. He also practised his profession with much success, and in the month of August, 1841, was appointed a Queen's Counsel. During the troubled days following the outbreak of December, 1837, he had taken an active part in repelling the incursions of filibustering parties of American "sympathizers" upon Canadian territory. Upon one occasion he had captured five of these marauders near Windsor, and had ordered four of them to be shot without any form of trial. And, to use his own concise phrase, "they were shot accordingly." This high-handed proceeding had made some noise at the time, and an official investigation had been held, which had resulted in Colonel Prince's acquittal.* He was a frank and genial, but impetuous man, with

---

the old Government Tory party, but as an independent man I shall ever raise my voice against their selfish and exclusive political creed. However respectable or amiable some of them may be, as individuals, I must view them, as a Compact, to be the worst enemies of their country, and blind enough not to see that they are thus the enemies of themselves and their children. . . . I object to the old official party, because they never had, nor would their principles ever permit their possessing the confidence of the people of Upper Canada. And confidence in ourselves must precede the confidence of the people of England in our stability, without which we cannot expect, nor could we honestly advise, emigration to Canada, without which this cannot long remain a British Province. . . . If elected by you, I shall be found a great conservator of our principles, and an unwearied and fearless reformer of details. The perpetuation of the connection between the Colony and the Mother Country I view to be at once the glory and advantage of both."

* It ought to be mentioned that the marauders had murdered an army-surgeon—a Mr.

a fine presence and excellent intentions, but with no particular capacity or taste for politics. In England he had been a Whig. In Canada he acted with the Conservatives, but called himself a moderate Reformer. He was not always amenable to party discipline, and voted in an independent, not to say erratic fashion. He had a pleasant voice and a smooth accent, and his elocution—it could scarcely be called oratory—was listened to with an interest not always accorded to more powerful speakers. George Morss Boswell, who represented the South Riding of Northumberland, was an active politician in those days, and took a prominent part in some of the debates on constitutional questions. He acted with the moderate Reformers. Mr. Boswell is still living, and has long occupied the position of Judge of the County Court of the United Counties of Northumberland and Durham. Among other more or less conspicuous Upper Canadian members may be mentioned Edward Clarke Campbell, member for the town of Niagara; David Thorburn, representing the South Riding of Lincoln; John S. Cartwright, representing Lennox and Addington; James Hervey Price, representing the First Riding of York; and George Sherwood, representing the town of Brockville. Mr. Sherwood is the sole survivor of the four or five Upper Canadian members who represented ultra-Conservative principles in the First Parliament under the Union. He is, and has long been, Judge of the County Court of the County of Hastings.

In the Legislative Council, in addition to Mr. Sullivan, already referred to as a member of the Government, there were several men of some note. Réné Edouard Caron, a Quebec advocate of high character, and father of the present Minister of Militia, had sat in the Legislative Council of Lower Canada before the Union. He

---

Hume—in cold blood, and had burned two other British subjects to death. The Colonel's act was high-handed and legally unjustifiable, but it was committed in a season of intense excitement, and the provocation was great.

was a man of moderation and high principle. His was the first French Canadian name on the roll of the Legislative Council of United Canada. His name is identified with certain correspondence of which some account will be given on a subsequent page. Peter McGill, a sagacious and benevolent citizen of Montreal, was connected with some of the leading banking and commercial institutions of Lower Canada. He did not make any specially conspicuous figure in political life, though six years later, in the early days of Lord Elgin's Administration, he accepted a seat in the Executive Council. He was a shrewd and useful man, popular, and highly respected by his fellow-citizens. He generally acted with the Conservatives, but was no hard and fast party man, and did not hesitate to support Liberal measures when they commended themselves to his judgment. William Morris, a brother of the above mentioned James, is chiefly remembered from his having been the mover, in 1820, of an address to the King, asserting the claims of the Church of Scotland to a share of the Clergy Reserves. With the subsequent agitation on that long-debated question, in all its phases, his name is inseparably bound up. He lived to see his strenuous exertions crowned with even a more complete success than he had at first permitted himself to count upon, for the claim was originally made on behalf of the Church of Scotland alone. During Sir Charles Metcalfe's tenure of office he became Receiver-General, and—later—President of the Executive Council. His eldest son, the Hon. Alexander Morris, is well known to the present generation of Canadians, having from 1872 to 1877 been Lieutenant-Governor of the Province of Manitoba. He is the present representative of East Toronto in the Local Assembly of Ontario. Robert Sympson Jameson, who four days before the opening of the session was appointed to the post of Speaker of the Legislative Council, is partly remembered by reason of his subsequent tenure of office as Vice-Chancellor of Upper Canada, but chiefly from the fact that he was the husband of the clever, brilliant sketcher and art critic, Anna Jameson. Adam Fergusson, James Crooks, Adam Ferrie and Peter Boyle De Blaquière are also names which are more or less suggestive to persons in this country whose memories extend back over the last forty years.*

---

*Of the twenty-four members comprising the Legislative Council, eight were members of the Church of England, eight of the Kirk of Scotland, and the remaining eight of the Church of Rome. The Church of England members were R. B. Sullivan, R. S. Jameson, P. B. De Blaquière, George Pemberton, Augustus Baldwin, John Macaulay, Adam Fergusson, and P. H. Knowlton. The Scottish Kirk was represented by Peter McGill, William Morris, James Crooks, John Fraser, John Hamilton, John McDonald, Adam Ferrie, and Thomas McKay; and the Church of Rome by R. E. Caron, Jules Quesnel, Barthelemi Joliette, Etienne Mayrand, F. B. Bruneau, Olivier Berthelet, J. B. Taché, and Alexander Fraser. The Methodist, Baptist and other dissenting bodies were totally unrepresented in the Council.

Chapter VI.

THE FIRST TEST OF THE UNION ACT.

"It may be satisfactory to you to know that the first *test* of the Union Act has more than answered my expectations. I always considered the first start of the Union Parliament as the touchstone of the plan. The entire want of acquaintance with each other's feelings, character, political history, or state of parties, which prevails between the inhabitants of Lower and Upper Canada respectively, always made me feel that the opening was the crisis of the great work."—*Letter of Lord Sydenham, dated 27th June, 1841.*

FOR some weeks prior to the opening of the First Parliament, the inhabitants of the historic old town of Kingston were in a state of considerable expectation. The hopes of half a century before were about to become realities. At the time of the division of the Provinces in 1791, the little military post at the foot of Lake Ontario had indulged the ambition of becoming the capital of Upper Canada, and Lord Dorchester, the Governor-General, had favoured this idea. Lieutenant-Governor Simcoe, however, had refused to be dictated to in so important a matter as the choice of a capital for his provincial domain, and after spending a season at Newark had (literally) pitched his tent* near the mouth of the Don River, on the site where Little York subsequently emerged from the eternal swamp and scrub. Kingston's hopes were blasted for the time, and she

---

* The allusion here is to the historic canvas tent used by Captain Cook during his travels among the islands of the southern seas, and afterwards purchased in London by Colonel Simcoe before his departure for Canada. On taking up his quarters at York, this tent, or "movable house," was frequently called into requisition, and the Lieutenant-Governor not only used it as his general private and official residence, but sometimes dispensed viceregal hospitalities within its canvas walls.

never again permitted herself to indulge in visions of metropolitan greatness until the project of Union was fairly under way. Upper Canadians would not assent to, or even seriously entertain the scheme of a union of the Provinces, unless upon the express understanding that the capital should be in Upper Canada. This being conceded, it was desirable to place the seat of Government as near to the Lower Province as possible, and Kingston was the nearest town affording anything like suitable accommodation. Kingston was accordingly named by Lord Sydenham, and many of the inhabitants believed it probable that their town would be the permanent capital of Canada, and permitted themselves to look forward to a great and prosperous future. Extensive preparations were made, and the place was victualled as though for a siege. Real estate rose greatly in value, and house-rents attained to what in those days were accounted as phenomenal figures.

The selection of Kingston for the capital of the united Province was more acceptable to the Lower Canadians than that of any other town in Upper Canada would have been. The spot had been well known to the pioneers of France in the New World, and was hallowed for French Canadians by the names of De Courcelles, Count Frontenac, and La Salle. They would of course have preferred the retention of the capital at Montreal or Quebec, or indeed at any point in Lower Canada, but as the matter rested entirely with the Governor-General, and as he had chosen Kingston, there was nothing for it but submission. For some days before the time fixed for the opening of Parliament the members began to arrive. On the morning of the appointed day, seventy-nine out of the eighty-four required to make up the full membership of the Assembly were in attendance. Of the other five, two were absent, and three of the constituencies were left vacant. One of the vacancies was caused by the fact of Mr. Baldwin having had a double return for the county of Hastings and the Fourth Riding of York. He elected, after the session had been some time in progress, to sit for the former. For the county of Kent there was no return, owing to alleged corrupt conduct on the part of the Returning Officer. Mr. Parke, member for Middlesex, had accepted the office of Surveyor-General two or three days before, so that Kent, Middlesex, and the Fourth Riding of York were unrepresented in the Assembly.

The building provided for the temporary accommodation of the Legislature was situated beyond the limits of the town, on the Penitentiary Road, on what was known as Lot Twenty-four. It was a full mile westward of the commercial centre of the town, and, as already intimated, had been erected for a General Hospital. It was a spacious structure, built of Kingston limestone, four stories high, and having a frontage of about 150 feet. Its depth was fifty feet, and it contained twenty rooms. Its interior arrangements were interfered with as little as possible, in order that it might be restored to its original uses as soon as a permanent House of Parliament should be built. Its situation was described by the Kingston correspondent of the *Montreal Gazette* as being so delightful and salubrious that the votaries of faction could not generate sufficient bile to make themselves discontented anywhere within its precincts.* Alwington

---

* This correspondent, under date of May 19th—somewhat less than a month before the opening of the session—gives the following description of the two chambers in which the legislative business of the country was soon to be carried on : "On walking out, the other day, to the building designed as a General Hospital, I had the curiosity to measure the room which is to be occupied by the Legislative Council. It is forty-seven feet long, twenty-two feet wide, and twelve feet high. The Assembly room is of the same size. The latter room is now furnished with the eighty-four seats for the members. They are handsome stuffed arm-chairs, of black walnut, covered with green moreen, with a small projection on the side to write upon. The members may not possess such facilities for transacting their private business as in the House at Toronto, but they will have the necessary accommodation for transacting that of the public. The space below the bar is very small, and I observe no conveniences for the reporters. This defect will, no doubt, be remedied." He adds, towards the end of his letter : "All the necessaries of life continue to be sold at reasonable rates. The only expense of housekeeping which has risen in price is rent ; but new houses are springing up in every direction, and, fortunately for all new-comers, Kingston has large and healthy suburbs, where people may live as they please, under their own vine and fig tree, and still be within a few minutes' walk of the public offices."

House, the abode of the Governor-General, was situated a short distance beyond, near the lake shore.

At noon on Monday, the 14th of the month—that being the hour named for administering the oath to members, by the Commissioners appointed for that purpose—the Assembly Chamber was filled to overflowing. The Commissioners were the Hon. Levius P. Sherwood, William Hepburn and Thomas Kirkpatrick. In addition to the members of the two Houses, various persons of influence from all parts of the country attended to witness the ceremonies. Among them, occupying a seat within the bar, was the Hon. Joseph Howe, who was then Speaker of the Provincial House of Assembly of Nova Scotia. Contrary to general expectation, the Governor-General was not present, and the session was not formally opened until the following day. His Excellency's absence was much commented on, as being contrary to Parliamentary usage.[*]

The seventy-nine members present having been sworn in, and having taken their seats, the Clerk, Mr. William Burns Lindsay, read the Governor-General's Proclamation convening the Parliament. The next matter requiring attention was the election of a Speaker. It was considered politic to elect a Lower Canadian to that position, and, in accordance with a preconcerted arrangement, Mr. Morin, representative of the county of Nicolet, moved that Mr. Austin Cuvillier, the member for Huntingdon, be Speaker. The discussion to which this, the first motion made in the United Parliament, gave rise, was ominous of the fierce faction fights to come in after days, when matters of graver import should form the subject of debate. The mover, in a few well-chosen words, paid a tribute to Mr. Cuvillier's knowledge

---

[*] "Cette manière d'ouvrir un parlement était absolument contraire aux règles parlementaires ; car la présence du représentant de la reine y était obligatoire, ainsi que celle des autres branches de la législature "—LE CANADA SOUS L'UNION. Par Louis P. Turcotte. Première Partie, p. 72.

and experience of Parliamentary business, and expressed a hope that all former differences would be buried, and the business of the country amicably proceeded with. Mr. Merritt, of North Lincoln, seconded the motion, and added a few words to the effect that his support of Mr. Cuvillier was due to that gentleman's being an advocate of Responsible Government. Colonel Prince, member for Essex, then made a few remarks in support of the motion. He said that Mr. Cuvillier, like himself, was a moderate reformer, and that by voting for that gentleman, he, the speaker, was paying his own constituents a compliment, many of them being Lower Canadians. He trusted that members from the Lower Province would hold out the hand of friendship, and evince a desire to pull together by throwing aside party feelings. After paying a tribute of respect to the talents and deportment of Sir Allan MacNab, the late Speaker of the Upper Canadian Assembly, the Colonel took his seat, and it seemed, for the moment, as though the motion was about to pass without debate or wrangling. For a moment only. Scarcely had the echo of Colonel Prince's voice ceased to be heard when Mr. Hincks, Oxford's representative, rose to his feet. He said that in order to prevent being misunderstood, and to do what he deemed his duty to his constituents, he would briefly state the reasons why he should vote for Mr. Cuvillier as Speaker. So soon as the elections were over, he had taken the best means of ascertaining who the most competent person would be to fill the Chair, and the conclusion at which he arrived had led him to support Mr. Cuvillier. He was well assured, he added, that Mr. Cuvillier was firmly opposed to the Civil List being withdrawn from the people, and that he had no confidence whatever in the Administration, being entirely opposed to its Lower Canadian policy. As Mr. Hincks sat down, Mr. Cartwright, the member for Lennox and Addington, arose, and with much warmth said that he had not intended to oppose the motion, but that after the speech made by the member for Oxford he felt it his duty to move, in amendment, that Sir Allan MacNab be Speaker. Mr. Johnston, of Carleton, remarked that he did not believe Mr. Cuvillier entertained the views attributed to him by Mr. Hincks. Mr. Price, member for the First Division of York, concurred with Mr. Hincks in thinking that Mr. Cuvillier could not have any confidence in the Administration, as it was composed of materials that could not possibly work together. Mr. Cuvillier, he said, was a supporter of Lord Durham's policy, which was not carried out by the Administration. Mr. J. P. Roblin, of Prince Edward, regretted that such remarks as those to which he had just listened should have fallen from Mr. Hincks. He considered such remarks as unsuited to the occasion. He would support Mr. Cuvillier for Speaker, and he thought that any expression of Mr. Cuvillier's views was uncalled for. Mr. Thorburn (South Lincoln) concurred in the sentiments expressed by Mr. Roblin, and said that the body of the people in Upper Canada desired moderation. "If there is a time to bury distinctions, and present a peace-offering to the country," said Mr. Thorburn, "now is that time." He thought Mr. Cuvillier every way qualified, and after paying a compliment to Sir Allan MacNab, concluded by hoping that the honourable member for Lennox and Addington would withdraw his amendment. Mr. Hincks explained his previous remarks by saying that he had not given utterance to any desire for an expression of opinion from Mr. Cuvillier; but he claimed a right to state on what ground he supported that gentleman. Mr. Cameron, of Lanark, trusted that the discussion was at an end. He thought the Speaker should be able to speak both the French and English languages, and it was chiefly for this reason that he should support Mr. Cuvillier. Sir Allan MacNab then requested the honourable member for Lennox and Addington to withdraw his motion of amendment; adding that he thought Mr. Hincks justified in giving his reasons for supporting Mr. Cuvillier, and that in his opinion every member ought to do the same.

Mr. Cartwright accordingly withdrew the amendment, whereupon Captain Elmes Steele, of Simcoe, expressed regret that Mr. Hincks should have disturbed the unanimity that prevailed with regard to Mr. Cuvillier. Then followed some pointed remarks from Mr. Aylwin, member for Portneuf. He said that he entirely agreed with what had fallen from Mr. Hincks. For his part he deemed it his duty to declare why he supported Mr. Cuvillier; and for one, he would certainly not support that gentleman if he had not confidence in him. He thought it necessary that the Speaker should be a gentleman possessing the confidence of the whole house. He, however, would prefer Mr. Viger, but would yield to the disposition of the Upper Canadians, and vote for Mr. Cuvillier; it still being on the express understanding that Mr. Cuvillier had really no confidence in the Government. If he, Mr. Aylwin, thought otherwise, he would rather vote for Sir Allan MacNab, or any other Tory, than for the honourable member for Huntingdon. He was convinced, however, that Mr. Cuvillier was opposed to the Administration, and to make the matter certain, he considered it desirable that that gentleman should give an expression of his views. Although he was extremely desirous that unanimity should exist, he could not, he said, sacrifice his principles to preserve it. He thought that an expression of opinion on the part of Mr. Cuvillier was necessary, not only in order that the people of Canada should clearly understand the position of members, but that the people of England, if indeed they took any interest in Canadian affairs, should also comprehend it. Mr. Aylwin repeated that although he would desire to see that true martyr to his country, Mr. Viger, placed in the Chair, still, to preserve cordiality he should vote for Mr. Cuvillier. Mr. Morin concurred with some of the sentiments uttered by Mr. Aylwin, but would consider it extremely wrong to press for an expression of Mr. Cuvillier's opinion at that time, and thought such a course on the part of Mr. Cuvillier would be out of place, and would expose the House to embarrassment and contention, without doing any good whatever. Mr. Morin concluded by recommending Mr. Cuvillier not to state his political views at that time. Mr. Smith (of Frontenac) rose and said that for his part he had entire confidence in the Administration, and thought the remarks of Mr. Hincks in bad taste at that particular time. Mr. Smith thought it would be imprudent in Mr. Cuvillier to state his political views, and in fact the proceedings of the honourable member for Oxford would, if carried out, be equal to a declaration of want of confidence in the Government—a course that would lead to a dissolution of Parliament. This statement brought Mr. Draper, the Attorney-General for Upper Canada, to his feet. He said he had not intended to take any part in the discussion, but he could not remain silent after what had fallen from the last speaker. When he, the Attorney-General, heard the House threatened with a dissolution, because it expressed, in accordance with the constitution, its views on any question, he must repudiate the idea that such sentiments were held by the Government. He highly approved of Mr. Cuvillier as Speaker, on account of his speaking the French language, and in consequence of his high Parliamentary qualifications. Mr. Buchanan, of Toronto, differed from the honourable member for Oxford as to bringing up any thing likely to recall the past. The present Administration, he said, as yet had *no character*—it had no confidence in itself. When the laughter evoked by this dry sally had subsided, Mr. Durand, of West Halton, rose and said that he supported Mr. Cuvillier in consequence of his being an impartial and dignified gentleman, who would give a tone to the House, and he was satisfied that Mr. Cuvillier could never fill the Chair were he not supported by the Reformers present. He believed Mr. Cuvillier was a Reformer, and would only support the Government when it acted in accordance with the expressed wishes of the people. After unimportant remarks by several other members, the motion was put, that Mr. Cuvillier be Speaker of the House. It was carried without a dissenting voice; whereupon Mr. Morin and Mr. Merritt conducted Mr. Cuvillier to the Chair. Mr. Cuvillier begged that the House would re-consider its vote, and choose some more competent person to be its Speaker, but on the House persisting in its choice, he said that he could not express his feelings of sincere and heartfelt gratitude for the high dignity they had conferred upon him. It fell to the lot of few, he said, to adequately fill the office. He, however, would do his best to discharge satisfactorily the important trust conferred upon him. Then, turning to the Lower Canadian members, he repeated his remark in French; after which he took formal possession of the Chair. The royal mace having been laid on the table, Sir Allan MacNab then moved that the House adjourn. This caused a warm and animated debate, in the course of which much ability and research was displayed by the principal speakers. The adjournment was warmly and vigorously opposed by Messieurs Viger, Aylwin, and Morin, who took the ground that they had not the power to adjourn, as they were not an organized body. They argued that it was altogether contrary to Parliamentary usage to adjourn under such circumstances; and not only without precedent, and in opposition to the common law of England, but unsupported by statute law. Mr. Aylwin and Mr. Viger contended with great ability for this, insisting that Parliament could not be said to have assembled until the three estates had met. Messieurs Draper, Ogden and Day supported the motion for adjournment, and argued that the Union Act, having done away with the necessity for obtaining the sanction of the royal authority to the choice of the Speaker, the House, after that officer's election, stood in the same position as the British House of Commons after a Speaker has been chosen. The discussion continued until five o'clock, when the motion was put by the Chair, and carried by a majority of twenty.* The House accordingly adjourned to two o'clock in

---

* Four of the members, besides the Speaker, would seem not to have voted on the motion. The vote stood 47 to 27. The debate was regarded by many people as unnecessary and

the afternoon of the day following. It was noticed that Mr. Baldwin maintained a solemn silence throughout the debate. His reason for so doing was the fact that he had sent in his resignation to the Governor-General, and that he had not received notice of its acceptance, and had consequently felt his mouth closed, though he voted against the adjournment.

And thus ended the first encounter between hostile parties in the United Assembly. Even those who had not taken active part in the discussion had plainly signified, by their demeanour, and by their cheers of the respective speakers, where their own sympathies lay. The want of confidence of a large and influential wing of the Reform party in the Administration no longer admitted of doubt, and before Mr. Baldwin retired to rest that night he was congratulated by some of his friends upon his having resigned office.

The next day (the 15th), at two o'clock in the afternoon, his Excellency, attended by a numerous civil and military staff, repaired in state to the Legislative Council Chamber, for the purpose of formally opening the session. He found the fourteen members of the Upper House already in their places. He commanded the attendance of the members of the Assembly, who were awaiting the summons in their own Chamber. The latter forthwith presented themselves before his Excellency, and Mr. Cuvillier announced that he had on the previous day been chosen as Speaker by the Assembly. His Excellency bowed his acquiescence; whereupon the Speaker demanded the customary privileges. The representative of Majesty was pleased to assent to the demand; after which he proceeded to open the session with the speech from the throne. His voice was clear, and he read his speech from manuscript notes with

---

factious. "I am sorry to see the Reformers disagree on small points. The question about an adjournment, I think, was not worth debating on. It tended to weaken the party. To try the reality of the men, the question must be something that the country has more interest in."—Letter from Richard Woodruff to W. H. Merritt, June 28th, 1841. See "Biography of the Hon. W. H. Merritt," by his Son, J. P. Merritt; p. 233.

ease and fluency, though his bearing was somewhat languid, and it was evident that his labours during the last few months had impaired his health.

The Speech, which touched upon every leading topic of public interest, was marked by a tone of moderation and practical good sense. After a few introductory remarks on the great and important duties imposed upon the Legislature by the Union Act, his Excellency referred to the case of Alexander McLeod, a British subject detained in custody in the United States, on a charge of having been concerned in the cutting-out and burning of the steamboat *Caroline*, in the Niagara River, on the night of the 29th of December, 1837. An account of this *cause célèbre* will be found in a subsequent chapter.* The Speech referred to McLeod's forcible detention, and stated that a demand had been made by Her Majesty's representative at Washington for his release. The Houses were next informed that arrangements had been completed for greatly reducing the rates of postage between Canada and the United Kingdom, and that a more speedy and regular conveyance of letters between different parts of the Province had been provided for. Further improvements in the postal system, it was said, were likely to accrue from the labours of a commission which had been appointed to inquire into and report upon the whole post-office system of British North America. The Speech next adverted to the importance of adopting measures for developing the resources of the Province by well-considered and extensive public works. It was conceded that a great outlay would be needed in order to carry out such works successfully, and that the financial condition of the Province was not such as to encourage the attempt; but his Excellency stated that the Home Government had consented to pledge the credit of the mother country to a loan of a million and a half sterling, to aid the Province in diminishing the pressure of the

---

* See *ante*, p. 101, and *post*, Chapter VIII.

interest on the public debt, and to enable it to proceed with the public works which had been interrupted by the financial difficulties. On the important subject of immigration, the Houses were informed that the Home Government would afford assistance to convey immigrants from the port of debarkation to the place where their labour might be made available. The utility of establishing a general system of local self-government was pointed out, as well as the establishment of a comprehensive and efficient system of education. Reference was then made to the intention of the Home Government to devote a large sum annually to the military defences of the Province, and to Her Majesty's determination to maintain her North American possessions at all hazards as part of her Empire.* His Excellency concluded by an earnest and eloquent invocation to peace, union and progress.

Upon the conclusion of the Speech, the Governor-General left for Alwington House, his departure from the Parliament House being signalized, as his arrival had been, by a salute of the royal artillery. The members of the Assembly then returned to their own Chamber, where the usual formalities relating to the Speech from the Throne were gone through with. The remainder of the afternoon was taken up by motions of members relative to the introduction of Bills and Petitions. On motion of Mr. John Simpson, member for Vaudreuil, a committee was appointed by the Speaker to prepare a set of rules and orders for the guidance of the House, and it was decided that, until the report of the Committee should be received, the rules of the late House of Assembly for Lower Canada should be observed. The subject of the Speech from the Throne was made

---

* This assurance was not altogether beside the purpose, as there was much blustering about the McLeod affair. That cause of dispute greatly aggravated the controversy which had long existed between Great Britain and the United States respecting the right of search on the high seas, and more particularly respecting the boundary-line between New Brunswick and the State of Maine. For some months it seemed not unlikely that there might be war between the two countries.

9

the order of the day for the following Friday, which was the 18th of the month.

The test vote on the Address in reply to the Speech was looked forward to with eager expectation, and even with anxiety, for the Assembly was divided into so many parties that it was impossible to predict the result of the vote with entire confidence. Nightly caucuses were held, and something was accomplished in the way of organization. The strictly Parliamentary business transacted in the interval was formal and unimportant. Early on the appointed Friday the Address, couched in the conventional terms, was adopted in Committee by the Legislative Council, where there were only two dissentient voices. Mr. Sullivan made a powerful speech in support of the Government and its policy, and waxed eloquent over the personal characteristics of Lord Sydenham. He deprecated the national and party animosities of past times, and besought the French Canadian members to join hands cordially with those among whom their lot had been cast. In the Assembly the debate was long, and extended into the middle of the following week.

It may be worth while to glance at the arrangement of members in the Assembly. To the right of the Speaker sat the supporters of the Government, including a majority of the Upper Canadian representatives and nearly all the British representatives from the Lower Province. The lower benches were appropriated to the members of the Administration. Beyond, to the extreme right, sat the members of the old Conservative party of Upper Canada, with Sir Allan MacNab at their head. To the Speaker's left sat the Opposition, including the French Canadian members, several British Lower Canadian members who acted with them, and the most advanced of the Upper Canadian Reformers. On the extreme left sat Robert Baldwin, Francis Hincks, John Neilson, D. B. Viger, A. N. Morin, T. C. Aylwin, J. H. Price and J. E. Small. It would be a great mistake to suppose, however, that an arbitrary line divided the members to the right of the Speaker from those on his left. There were some points in common between members who sat on opposite sides, and there were strong points of divergence between those who sat on the same side. Nothing is more misleading than to mentally divide the members of the first House of Assembly under the Union into two hostile camps of Ministerialists and Opposition. Any one who does so will find himself in a state of utter confusion when he comes to analyze the votes from week to week, as the session drew its slow length along. The fact is that there was as yet so little organization that no well-defined line could be drawn, and the party boundaries were changing almost from day to day. The points of agreement prevailing in 1841 had almost entirely disappeared before the close of the session of 1842; and this elasticity of party lines must be constantly borne in mind by anyone who wishes to clearly understand the motives which gave birth to the somewhat complicated Parliamentary tactics of the period.*

The forenoon of the 18th was spent by the Assembly in adopting rules and orders for their guidance, pursuant to the report of the Committee which had been appointed three days before. The debate on the order of the day did not begin until three o'clock in the afternoon, when Mr. Malcolm Cameron, the member for Lanark, brought up the resolutions on which the Address—an echo of the Speech from the Throne—was to be founded. As the debate was of

---

* "There were at least five if not six parties in the House, three from each Province. In Upper Canada there were, 1st, the old Conservative party led by Sir Allan MacNab; 2nd, the Ministerial party, comprised chiefly of Reformers, with a few moderate Conservatives, under the leadership of Mr. Attorney-General Draper and Mr. Secretary Harrison; 3rd, the Reformers who followed the lead of Mr. Baldwin, numbering six to eight. In Lower Canada there were, 1st, the Reformers of French and Irish origin, with their allies of the British party, led by Mr. Morin, Mr. Neilson, and Mr. Aylwin; 2nd, the British party, including the Conservative French Canadians and Irish elected to support Lord Sydenham's policy, and almost uniformly doing so that session, although several of them had a decided bias in favour of a Liberal policy, while others were as decidedly Conservative."—See Sir Francis Hincks's lecture on "The Political History of Canada," pp. 22, 23.

such importance that it may properly be characterized as an epoch in the constitutional history of Canada, the author considers it desirable to give a tolerably full account of that portion of it relating to Responsible Government.

Mr. Cameron, in proposing the resolutions, stated that he was not desirous at that moment to press their discussion, and would, if the House wished, lay them on the table; but holding the conviction which he did in regard to them, he felt bound to make some prefatory remarks. "A new experiment," said he, "is about to be made in the Government of Canada, and one under the operation of which a greater responsibility devolves upon the Head of that Government. The dry and parched soil is not more eager for the coming shower than are the people of this country for the establishment of the Administration of the Government of this Province upon such a basis as will ensure its tranquillity, and consequently the extension of trade, and the happiness of all classes of Her Majesty's subjects." The speaker then went on to say that the general course of procedure adopted by his Excellency met with his (the speaker's) approbation. He had come to that House prepared to support the Governor-General, and had been elected as a friend of the Administration. He expressed regret that the Government were not then prepared with a Bill for promoting education, which he hoped would have become one of the important features of the session.* He then alluded to the satisfactory declaration respecting the detention of Mr. McLeod; to the improved postal regulations; and to the probability of Canada being able to avail herself of British capital. He concluded by moving, as an introductory resolution, that the House humbly thank his Excellency the Govenor-General for the Speech delivered from the Throne.

The motion having been seconded by Captain Elmes Steele,

---

* As will hereafter be seen, the Elementary School Bill was brought down and passed later on in the session.

the discussion upon it began. Several members on the left complained that they had not had time to examine the resolutions, and that they wished them to be printed. Colonel Prince stated that he saw no reason for further delay. The resolutions, he said, were a mere reiteration of the Speech, and as it was the custom to take up the consideration of the Address at as early a day as possible, it would be discourteous to the Executive to postpone the matter. Members had had abundance of time to consider. After some time spent in discussion, Mr. Buchanan brought matters to a crisis by calling upon the Government for important information, adding that the giving of the information ought, in his opinion, to precede any discussion on the Address. He, in a word, formally called upon the gentlemen occupying the Treasury benches to state for the information of the House the principles upon which it was intended that the Government should be carried on. "Do the members of the Executive Government"—asked Mr. Buchanan—"acknowledge their responsibility to Canadian public opinion, as expressed by a majority of this House, for the advice which they give to the Head of the Government, so far as not to remain connected with an Administration against which a vote of want of confidence has passed in the Assembly, unless in case of an immediate dissolution of Parliament? In other words, will the Ministry in this Province recognize the principle of retaining office when they cannot command a majority in the House of Assembly?"

Such a question as this it was manifestly impossible for the Government to ignore; yet it was a most embarrassing one for them to answer. There was not perfect unanimity of opinion on the subject among them. There were at least two of them who would probably have been hard put to it if required to give an intelligent exposition of their personal views on Responsible Government. There were others who, while professing to approve of Responsible Government, construed the doctrine after a fashion which they well knew not to be in accordance with the popular theories. The task of replying to Mr. Buchanan's pertinent query devolved upon Mr. Attorney-General Draper, and certainly there was no member of the Government more capable of adroitly fencing with it. He was shrewd enough to see that a crisis had arrived, and he addressed himself to his task with all the acumen for which he was preëminently distinguished. He began his remarks by saying that he was very happy to have the opportunity (which was now afforded him for the first time) of entering into an exposition of the views which would guide the conduct of himself and those whose duty it was to advise his Excellency. And in the first place he would declare for the information of those who acted with him and those who acted against him, that so long only as he could give a conscientious support to those measures which the Head of the Government might deem it his duty to submit to that House, so long only would he continue to hold office under the Government. He desired to be understood as explaining the views in which every one of his colleagues entirely concurred. They were such as had been discussed and determined on among themselves without reference to any other persons whatever, for they had felt it to be due to themselves and the country, in the first place, to understand each other. He would next state the views which he entertained respecting the duties of his Excellency. He looked upon the Governor as having a mixed character—firstly, as being the representative of Royalty; and secondly, as being one of the Ministers of Her Majesty's Government, and responsible to the mother country for the faithful discharge of the duties of his station; a responsibility which he cannot avoid by saying that he took the advice of this man or of that man. He, the Attorney-General, looked upon it as a necessary consequence of this doctrine that where there is responsibility, there shall power be also, for he could not admit the idea that one man should possess the power and another be liable to the responsibility. In a matter of such importance he craved the indulgence of the House in referring to notes, in order that he might speak with the greater correctness. He then read from a despatch of Lord Glenelg, dated the 5th of December, 1835, and also read extracts from two of Lord John Russell's despatches. After referring to a proceeding of the House of Assembly of Nova Scotia, he proceeded to the effect following: "The next question that naturally arises in my division of the subject is that which relates more particularly to those who are the Ministers of the Crown. Honourable gentlemen will do me the favour to bear in mind that the principle which I have laid down, that responsibility and power must go hand in hand, is one which cannot be contravened, and that when a man is called upon to answer for the exercise of the power which has been entrusted to him in a particular manner, he cannot and dare not transfer the responsibility into other hands. When I consented to become an Executive Councillor I took upon myself the responsibility of advocating those opinions and those measures which the Head of the Government might think it his duty to recommend to the country; and so long as I continue a member of the Government and of this House, I shall consider it my bounden duty to follow the same course; and whenever I find the Head of the Government and the Ministers of the Crown desirous of propounding measures which I cannot conscientiously support, honour and duty point out but one path, and that is resignation. But there is another important principle to be considered. The Government should take on itself the preparing and bringing forward of such measures as the wants of the country seem to require. It is to be desired above all things that between the Government and the people there should be the greatest possible harmony and mutual good understanding. There can be no good government where the Government is at war with the people, and in this view I will submit in a few words the conclusions at which I have arrived. It is the duty of the Head of the Government to preserve that harmony by all the means in his power, because it is for that officer to account to the Home Government. If he find that he has been led astray by incapable or dishonest advisers, he may relieve himself of them by their dismissal. But unavoidable difficulties may arise. It not unfrequently happens that the Government are unable to carry out the views which they believe to be for the benefit of the public. It may happen that measures carefully digested and well calculated may be defeated by causes over which the Government have no control; and this brings me to speak of another mode of restoring harmony, which is by dissolution of Parliament. And lastly, there is another course to be taken. When it occurs that harmony is broken by something emanating from the Head of the Government himself, the course to be taken is one which rests with Royalty. This much I have thought it necessary to say in reference to the views entertained by myself and those who act with me as the advisers of his Excellency, and I would at the same time disavow any degree of responsibility other than I have now expressed."

The Attorney-General was frequently applauded in the course of his remarks, which, on the surface, sounded so fair and reasonable. But Mr. Baldwin, Mr. Hincks, and their confreres, were sharp enough to see that the Attorney-General—who had doubtless spoken under inspiration from Lord Sydenham*—had skilfully evaded the very

---

* That the Governor-General's views on the question of Responsible Government in the colonies differed widely from those of the Upper Canadian advocates of the doctrine is rendered obvious enough by a private letter written by him to one of his friends in England, under date of December 12th, 1839. "I am not a bit afraid," he writes, "of the Responsible Government cry. I have already done much to put it down in its inadmissible sense, namely, that the Council shall be responsible to the Assembly, and that the Government shall take their advice, and be bound by it. In fact, this demand has been made much more *for* the people than *by* them. And I have not met with any one who has not at once admitted the absurdity of claiming to put the Council over the head of the Governor. It is but fair, too, to say that everything has in past times been done by the different Governors to excite the feelings of the people on this question. First, the Executive Council has generally been composed of the persons most obnoxious to the majority of the

root and essence of the matter. Then or never was the time for removing all misapprehension as to the meaning attached by the Administration to the term "Responsible Government." That their construction varied from that of Mr. Baldwin and his fellow-workers had already become sufficiently apparent, but how far the variance extended was not so clear. Lord Sydenham had been sent over to Canada expressly to introduce Responsible Government. What sort of Responsible Government? How far was the responsibility to extend? It was deemed advisable to force an explicit declaration on the subject from the Government, and no time could possibly be more propitious for carrying out such a design than the present.

Mr. Baldwin rose to his feet. He said that he had certainly listened to the speech of the honourable gentleman with a great deal of attention and pleasure, although the pleasure had not been altogether unalloyed. But he could discover from the speech of the honourable and learned gentleman that a new principle had been applied with reference to the administration of affairs, in which that honourable and learned gentleman had borne so conspicuous a part. The great and important principle involved in the subject under discussion, Mr. Baldwin remarked, had occupied the attention of the country for a number of years, and on the faithful carrying

---

Assembly; and next, the Governor has taken extreme care to make every act of his own go forth to the public on *the responsibility* of the Executive Council. So the people have been carefully taught to believe that the Governor is nobody, and the Executive Council the real power, and that by the Governor himself. At the same time they have seen that power placed in the hands of their opponents. Under such a system it is not to be wondered at if one argument founded on the responsibility of the Governor to the Home Government falls to the ground. I have told the people plainly that, as I cannot get rid of my responsibility to the Home Government, I will place no responsibility on the Council; that they are a *Council* for the Governor to consult, but no more. And I have yet met with no 'Responsible Government' man who was not satisfied with the doctrine. In fact, there is no other theory which has common sense. Either the Governor is the Sovereign or the Minister. If the first, he may have ministers, but he cannot be responsible to the Government at home, and all colonial government becomes impossible. He must, therefore, be the Minister, in which case he cannot be under the control of men in the colony."—See Scrope's "Life of Sydenham," p. 143.

out of that principle the continuation of the connection with the mother country in a great measure depended. The speaker agreed with the Attorney-General that the functions of the Head of the Government are of a mixed character, and that he is responsible to the Home Government for the proper administration of the Government in the colony. He would admit that in the administration of the Government questions might arise in which the Government might not be prepared to adopt the advice which might be tendered them. But if he (Mr. Baldwin) understood the honourable and learned gentleman right, that the Council of his Excellency should offer their advice only when it might be demanded of them, and on all other occasions remain mere passive observers of the measures adopted by the Government, he (Mr. Baldwin) would beg leave from such a system entirely to dissent. That all measures must necessarily receive the Governor's assent he would readily admit, but that those gentlemen whom he called to his Council should never open their lips except when he particularly and expressly called upon them to do so, was what he (Mr. Baldwin) could neither acquiesce in nor approve of. In fact such a Council as that would be no Council at all. To advocate such a course would be, in his opinion, acting in direct violation of the oath which as Executive Councillors they were called on to take. They were commanded to advise his Excellency on all matters connected with the public good. Mr. Baldwin then read the oath prescribed to be taken by Executive Councillors, and then continued. In his understanding of this oath, a Council was necessarily bound to bring under the notice of the Head of the Government those measures which, in their estimation, the country required. If this responsibility was not to lead to the carrying out of what the country required it would be a dead letter. He (Mr. Baldwin) believed, however, that, so much having been conceded, they would be enabled to enforce upon both the Provincial and Home Government a due attention to the wishes of the country.

He concluded his observations by adding a remark to the effect that he could have wished that the representative of Royalty in Canada had made some reference to this matter in the Speech which had been delivered to the Legislative Council and Assembly, and that it had not been left to the honourable member for Russell (Mr. Draper) to announce so important a circumstance to the representatives of the people from his place on the floor of the House.

Mr. Merritt expressed his regret that the advisers of the Government had not come out more distinctly. He did not, he said, approve of mystifying the matter; he believed the Governor-General was fully prepared to carry out the principle of Responsible Government as understood by Lord Durham, and that this was the cause of his Excellency's popularity. The distinction he (Mr. Merritt) would draw was broad and obvious. He believed the power of the Executive, as a Minister of the Crown, could not be delegated; but he believed that his Executive Council, chosen from the people of this country, were responsible to the people for the advice given on internal affairs, and that they were bound to resign when they did not enjoy public confidence. In the old order of affairs no one placed any confidence in the Council, for they were beyond the control of the people. He considered that Canada had now Responsible Government, or that she had nothing at all.

Mr. Cameron said he felt it necessary to express his opinion upon the subject. He felt that the members of the Government had not made any distinct avowal of their intention to act upon the principles of Responsible Government. If such were really their intention it was very easy to declare it. He felt it to be an important point, because it was upon a conviction that such was to be the case that he had taken his determination to support the Administration of Lord Sydenham.

Captain Steele said that as he was the seconder of the resolutions he would explain the views which he entertained with regard to the course of policy to be pursued by the Government. He, the speaker, had also come to that House with a determination to give support to the Administration of the Governor-General, provided he acted up to the professions which had been advanced on his behalf with respect to Responsible Government. But he had come to that House unshackled by pledges, free to act according to the dictates of his judgment, elected by a constitutency which had imposed no conditions and laid down no rule for the guidance of his conduct, other than that broad principle which all the representatives of a free people should strive to obtain—the advancement of the interests of their constituents and of the country generally. He would acknowledge that the explanation which had been given was entirely to his satisfaction, and he would come frankly forward and support the Administration of the Governor-General as long as the conduct of the Executive corresponded with the professions they had heard. But he would desire to see the Administration supported by a frank and honest vote, founded upon conviction and in honesty, and not produced by cabal and faction. When the Head of the Government was seen in this House delivering his speech with painful effort, owing to his declining health, was there a man present who did not say within himself, " I will throw myself in the breach, and prevent any faction from disturbing his nightly sleep."

Mr. Thorburn said that although the discussion had been brought up rather prematurely, still, as the members of the Executive Government were now in their places, and as the question was not altogether new, they might be prepared, he thought, to give a plain answer, and that answer would do more good than 100,000 bayonets would do at that moment. He alluded to New Brunswick, where, in consequence of the principles of Responsible Government being carried out, the late gallant Governor[*] of that Province had received

---

[*] Sir John Harvey.

the unanimous thanks of the House of Assembly, and a substantial mark of their esteem, and had departed with the blessings of the inhabitants. He begged the advisers of the Executive to come out manfully and declare themselves. If they admitted the principle for which the people of the country had struggled for so many years, they should have his hearty support. He hoped they would at once see their way to doing so, and the joyful news would spread like lightning over the country.

Mr. George M. Boswell, member for the South Riding of Northumberland, said he hoped before the Committee should rise, those honourable gentlemen belonging to his Excellency's Council would be fully prepared to answer this important question in a categorical manner, for they might depend upon it the eyes of the country were upon them. He would inform them that it would be impossible to carry on any Government, except a despotism, without the confidence of the people, and without the admission of the principle contended for on that day.

Mr. Baldwin explained with reference to his former remarks that he believed that the present Head of the Government was desirous of carrying out the principle of Responsible Government; and he wished to see it carried out as it had recently been in Nova Scotia. He (Mr. Baldwin) hoped the people of Canada would not be treated with less regard than the people of Nova Scotia.

Mr. Draper said that the question having been put to him as to what course the advisers of his Excellency would take in the event of the majority of the House of Assembly opposing those measures which might be proposed to the Government, he desired no mystification, and that the honourable gentleman (Mr. Merritt) who used the term had found mystification to exist only in his own imagination. After expressing what his views were of the character and degree of responsibility resting upon the different branches of the Government, he had stated that there was an absolute necessity for the preservation of harmony between the Government and the people, and he had pointed out causes on the occurrence of which he would not resign, but would appeal to the country, and ascertain whether he would not be sustained by the people. The responsibility in such cases as he had before stated would rest with the Governor himself. Should his Excellency find that he could not act with the Council, he might call upon them to resign.

Mr. Boswell desired to be informed if he had rightly understood the honourable gentleman to mean that he would be contented to remain a Minister of the Government as long as the Governor desired him to do so, whether a majority of the House of Assembly were with him or not.

Mr. Draper replied that he had said that he would retain office so long as harmony existed between the representatives of the people and the Government. But it could not be considered that harmony existed as long as there was continual opposition maintained from different sides of the House. The distinction which he understood as having been drawn was that the responsibility rested entirely with the Government.

The Attorney-General's sophistry, however, was of no avail. Mr. Boswell once more got upon his feet, and spoke as follows:—" The honourable gentleman has said that he would not resign unless required to do so by the Head of the Government. He has not said that he entertains the slightest respect for the opinion of the representatives of the people. He desires harmony, but he wishes the whole responsibility to be thrown upon the shoulders of his Excellency. I can put no other interpretation upon his language."

Mr. Hincks said it was very much to be regretted that so important a subject should have been so much mystified; at the same time he thought there should be great allowance made for the honourable and learned gentleman. He no doubt felt himself in a very awkward situation. He had come down to the House and avowed principles upon which a few years ago he had said he would "make war to the knife."

Mr. Draper said that what the honourable gentleman had stated was unfounded in fact. The speaker was here called to order.

Mr. Hincks proceeded. He was extremely happy, he said, to be corrected, if he had fallen into an error.

Mr. Draper again requested permission to explain, which, having been granted, he proceeded to observe that he was unwilling to remain under an unjust imputation, which might, with few words, be entirely removed. There were those in the House who could do him the justice to say that long before this discussion was contemplated he had drawn a distinction between those who were discontented and those who were disaffected. The complaints of the former might be remedied, but as for the others he cared not how soon they sought any country which would be more congenial to their feelings.

Mr. Hincks said he was happy to hear the explanation of the honourable gentleman. It appeared that it was not the principle advocated by the majority of the House of Assembly, but the opinions of certain individuals, against which he would make war to the knife. The principles which were then advocated by a majority of the House of Assembly were the same as those which he at present advocated—the principles of Responsible Government—those principles which would be found laid down in Lord Durham's report. Every honourable member of that House must be fully aware that the great mass of the country had been convinced that the Head of the Government had intended this to be the principle upon which the Government should be conducted. "It matters little,"—continued Mr. Hincks,—" who are responsible here if we are constantly to have our laws which we have passed at great trouble and expense set at naught and sent back to us annulled and void. The honourable and learned gentleman, in order to point out the degree of responsibility under which he considers the Government as standing, has quoted from documents which have been always held and acknowledged by those gentlemen with whom he acts as going entirely against the principle for which we are contending. What the country wishes to know is whether the Provincial Government is to be conducted according to the principles of the British constitution. Those are the principles to which a majority of the people of this Province are attached."

Mr. Boswell said the honourable and learned gentleman must excuse him for again pressing the question, because it was of very great importance to him that it should be distinctly answered, as upon that answer would depend his future course of conduct within that House, and he would put it in such a shape as that it might be replied to by a single affirmative or negative. "Does the honourable gentleman mean to say," pursued Mr. Boswell, "that if the Government cannot command a majority of this House, so that its measures may be carried on harmoniously; if they do not find by the whole proceedings of the House that they have the confidence of a majority of its members, that then a dissolution of the House shall follow, or that the Government will resign?"

"Yes, yes," replied Mr. Draper, fairly brought to bay.

"Then," said Mr. Boswell, "I am satisfied." And he added that it was an unfortunate circumstance that the honourable gentleman could not long ago have stated it explicitly to the House, and thus have prevented the necessity for so long a discussion.

So far as Responsible Government was concerned, this important debate ended there and then, not to be renewed with much vigour until after the arrival in Canada of Sir Charles Metcalfe as Governor-General, nearly two years later. The admissions of the Attorney-General, though dragged out of him sorely against his will, had been tolerably explicit, and the true principle of Responsible Government seemed to have been conceded. Still, the evident reluctance of the spokesman of the Administration to commit himself, and his well-known hostility to the popular doctrine in times past, led many of his hearers to doubt the sincerity of his professions. There were not a few who even doubted the sincerity of the Governor-General ; and, notwithstanding all that had been conceded, there was an uneasy feeling of insecurity as regarded the future.*

The debate on the Address, however, had only fairly begun. It was continued at intervals until the following Wednesday (the 23rd), when an Address, founded on the previously-debated resolutions, was submitted to the House to be voted upon. Mr. Neilson, who well knew that he was fighting for a lost cause, but who could not allow such an opportunity to pass unimproved, moved an address in amendment, the penultimate clause whereof was directly condemnatory of the Union. "In conformity to our obligations as subjects of the British Crown,"—ran the clause,—"and bound to fidelity by the most sacred ties, we have assembled in obedience to an Act of the Imperial Parliament and Her Majesty's writs, to advise and consent to such laws as may be deemed necessary for the peace, welfare, and good government of Canada : although we cannot but regret that the most populous portion of the Province heretofore constituted under the Act of Parliament of 1791, as the Province of Lower Canada, has not been consulted on the Constitution of the Government which is now substituted for that which prevailed under the said Act ; and there are features in the Act now constituting the Government of Canada which are inconsistent with justice and the common rights of British subjects." Mr. Neilson made an argumentative and not ineffective speech in support of his motion. When

---

* "The opinions of reflecting men differ widely as to the probable result. While some look upon the enunciation of the new policy as a political advent promising a long course of prosperity and greatness, others look upon it with sincere despondency, and with melancholy forebodings that it is the first step towards those encroachments upon Executive authority which must terminate in colonial independence." Correspondence of the *Montreal Gazette*.

the division was taken there were seventy-five members in the House, in addition to the Speaker. The majority against the amendment was exactly two to one, the vote standing fifty to twenty-five. Nineteen of the minority were French Canadian members, or representatives of French Canadian constituencies. The other six consisted of Mr. Baldwin and his staunchest Upper Canadian followers, including Messieurs Hincks, Price, Small, Durand and Hopkins.*

A subsequent amendment moved by Mr. Hincks and seconded by Mr. Price was defeated by a vote of fifty-four to twenty-one. The Government party was hugely predominant. The Address was carried and presented in due form. During the progress of this long debate Mr. Baldwin, on the 21st, having been attacked with much asperity for resigning office, explained the motives which had impelled him to that course. His explanation was in effect the same as has been set down in a previous chapter.† There were sharp passages of arms during the discussion that ensued, and some acrimonious remarks were indulged in, more especially by Colonel Prince and Solicitor-General Day. The ex-Minister was accused by the latter of having secretly intrigued with a hostile faction to overturn the Government of which he himself was at the time a member. Mr. Baldwin was not always happy at extempore reply, but he felt confident that he had acted rightly, and presented his side of the

---

* It may be interesting to the reader to examine the complete division-list on this representative motion. The vote on the amendment stood as follows:—

Yeas—Armstrong, Aylwin, Baldwin, Barthe, Berthelot, Boutillier, Christie, Desrivières, Durand, Hamilton, Hincks, Hopkins, Kimber, Morin, Neilson, Noel, Parent, Price, Quesnel, Raymond, Ruel, Small, Taschereau, Turcotte, Viger—25.

Nays—Black, Boswell, Buchanan, Burnet, Cameron, Campbell, Cartwright, Chesley, Cook, Crane, Daly, Day, Delisle, Derbishire, De Salaberry, Draper, Dunn, Dunscomb, Duggan, Foster, Gilchrist, Hale, Holmes, Johnston, Jones, Killaly, McCulloch, McDonald (Prescott), Macdonald (Glengarry), McLean, MacNab, Merritt, Moffatt, Moore, Morris, Ogden, Powell, Prince, Robertson, Roblin, Simpson, Smith, Sherwood, Steele, Strachan, Thompson, Watts, Williams, Woods, Yule—50.

† See ante, pp. 76-82.

argument with much felicity and power of expression. It may safely be said that he came out of the controversy with the public respect for him increased.*

What Lord Sydenham had characterized as the first test of the Union Act was over, and, from his point of view, well over. There could no longer be any doubt as to the (at least) temporary success of his undertaking. His policy was sustained by a large majority, and United Canada was fairly launched on her career.

* "Baldwin was at this time the darling of the people, and therefore the object of the hatred of the hateful, and [of] the petty insults of envious mediocrity. Men like Prince and the whole Family Compact saw him take a leading part with the same feelings [as those with which] the Barons watched Gaveston carry the Confessor's Crown." See "The Irishman in Canada," p. 453.

Chapter VII.

EXIT LORD SYDENHAM.

"Lord Sydenham belongs essentially to Canada. His nobility was fairly earned in her service; the ripest fruits of his experience and acquirements are embodied in her institutions; his warmest and latest sympathies are blended with her interests; his mortal remains repose, by choice, among her dead."—*The Rev. Egerton Ryerson, in the Christian Guardian.*

"Canada has had the best of him. His last parting energies were exerted in her cause, his last breath [was] yielded for her. It is not three months since that he told Colonel Prince he would die in harness, and in carrying out those measures which he deemed essential to the salvation of this country. Canada should remember this. It should be recorded on his tomb—on the monuments that we should raise to his memory, now that he has departed from amongst us."—*Montreal Courier.*

HAVING seen the United Province fairly embarked on her course under the new constitution, it is not necessary, nor is it compatible with the limits of this work, that the progress of legislation throughout the session should be traced minutely from day to day. Many of the members then sat in Parliament for the first time, and had still to learn the amenities of a grave deliberative assembly. A good deal of time was wasted in frivolous discussion. The measures passed, however, were for the most part of a practical and useful character, tending to the development of the resources of the country, and to the welfare and due regulation of society. There was a good deal of friction, consequent upon the diverse interests and sympathies of the members of the Assembly. There were frequent exhibitions of personal and party feeling not entirely becoming to a Legislative

body. The French Canadians continued to cherish their grievances, and were especially incensed at the apparently persistent determination to exclude them from the Ministry unless they were content to enter it upon conditions the acceptance whereof would belie the record of their past lives. Some of the Quebec and Montreal papers, published in the French language, and known to be the exponents of French Canadian feeling, from week to week contained articles overweighted with the hate which is bred in a certain order of mind by the consciousness of injury and the inability to obtain any redress. The hate was generally indiscriminate, and there was little apparent recognition of the fact that many persons of British stock sympathized with the legitimate aspirations of their French Canadian fellow-countrymen. Several of the conductors of British papers were little disposed to sit down quietly under such sweeping condemnation, and the want of judgment displayed by the press had much to do with keeping alive the ill-feeling which, it must be confessed, was not altogether without excuse.* It was not till the month of September, 1842,

---

*The following extract from a (British) Montreal paper of the period gives an apt illustration of the state of affairs described in the text:—"It is but a few weeks since the olive branch has been frankly and honestly extended—since several English journals earnestly advocated an oblivion of the past and a reconciliation of the future. We must own that, however much we respected the attempt, we never anticipated that it would be successful, and we daily find in the pages of the *Canadien*, the *French Gazette*, the *Aurore*, and the other small fry, the proof of our prognostications. It is a truth—a truth boldly and continually proclaimed by the above-mentioned public journals, printed in the French language, that the Canadian leaders, and all those who aspire to lead this class of the population, now, as heretofore, must base their only pretensions to popular support on their utter and entire abhorrence of everything that is English. The word 'anti-British' is the type of their political existence—the only true passport to the affections of a French constituency. They hate us—not because we are Unionists or anti-Unionists, Whigs, Tories, Radicals or Conservatives—but because we are British. They hate us—not because we are Catholics, Protestants, Presbyterians or Methodists—but because we are British. They hate us because we speak English—because we love English laws—because we admire English institutions—because we would introduce English improvements—because we have given them two or three good English drubbings, and are ready to give them again if provoked. First, they hate the Briton; secondly, the American,

that a French Canadian—in the person of Mr. Lafontaine—obtained a seat in the Cabinet.

There was, however, nothing absolutely tumultuous in the proceedings during the session; nothing, for instance, which for unseemly violence could be compared to some of the ante-Rebellion disputes in the Lower Canadian Assembly. There was nothing, indeed, comparable to the scenes which had been witnessed in the Assembly of the Upper Province during the old times when William Lyon Mackenzie had been subjected to periodical expulsions. Nor was there any marked disloyalty in the speeches even of the most dissatisfied French Canadians,* who could not reasonably have been expected to bow their heads with a very good grace beneath the yoke that had been imposed upon them.

It soon became apparent that the anxiety which had been felt on the part of certain of the British population lest the French Canadian members would be able to hold the balance of power in their hands had not been well grounded. So far from the latter's holding the balance of power, they commanded, during the first session, not a single avenue to power. Owing to the fact that the elections had not been fairly conducted, the French districts of Lower Canada were inadequately represented in the Assembly; and the French Canadian members were potent as obstructionists only from the fact of their having coalesced with the advanced Reformers from the Upper Province. The real balance of power throughout the session

---

and, lastly, their seigniors and clergy are included in the same category; and if they could only accomplish what they never will—get rid of the Briton—they would be rapidly 'used up' by the Americans, who would rob their seigniors, discard their priests, and 'improve' the *Nation Canadienne* off the face of the earth."

* "The late session displayed little or nothing of this disloyal and disreputable feeling; and if there were men present—and we know there were—who entertained those feelings, they felt abashed in the presence of men who felt differently, in the face of their country, and by a new order of things calculated to preserve, at all hazards, the integrity of the Empire, and secure the true happiness of the inhabitants of the Province."—*Montreal Gazette's* review of the state of affairs at the end of the session.

was held by the moderate Reformers of Upper Canada, who generally voted with the Government.* Mr. Baldwin and his most trusted followers acted with the French members, and the union thus formed was more formidable by reason of the talents and character of its adherents than from its numbers. Mr. Baldwin himself, both in and out of Parliament, frequently spoke up on behalf of his Lower Canadian allies, and showed an active sympathy with their complaints of injustice. In this way he endeared himself greatly to them, and the result of his sympathy brought forth much fruit in its season.

A matter which caused not a little embarrassment to the Government was the strong censure pronounced by some of the members on the manner in which the recent elections had been conducted. The Houses had not long been in session when an inquiry was projected into the origin of the riots which had occurred at some of the elections in the Lower Province. Mr. Lafontaine, Mr. L. M. Viger, and others who had been defeated, as they alleged, by corrupt practices, petitioned the Assembly on the subject, praying that the elections should be annulled. The petitions, however, owing to an excusable misapprehension, had not been accompanied by certain technical formalities, and could not be received by the House. When the omissions were discovered, the time for the observance of the formalities had passed, and there was thus no possibility of remedying the misapprehension into which the petitioners had fallen. It was felt by many disinterested persons that to give effect to the technicalities would be tantamount to a subversion of justice, and attempts were made to induce the House to waive the irregularities and receive the petitions. These attempts were opposed by the Government, and defeated. A Bill was then introduced by Sir Allan MacNab, whereby the time for receiving the petitions was

---

* See "The Political History of Canada," *ubi supra*, p. 27.

extended. This measure was supported, not only by the adherents of the mover, but by the French Canadian members, as well as by the advanced Reformers of British stock in both Provinces. The Ministry, acting under inspiration from the Governor, opposed the measure upon the ground that it was *ex post facto*, and that, irrespective of the truth or falsehood of the charges in the petitions, the sitting members had acquired a legal right to their seats. The Ministry put forth the whole weight of their influence; yet, so strong was the feeling of the Assembly on the subject that the measure was supported by many persons who ordinarily voted with the Government. In spite of all opposition, it was carried through its three readings by considerable majorities, and was sent up to the Legislative Council for the concurrence of that body. The Council, however, was much more subject to Government influence than the Assembly. They temporized by sending a message to the Assembly, asking for information as to the ground and evidence upon which that House had proceeded in passing the Bill. The evidence was soon forthcoming, but the Council refused to concur, and the Bill was therefore lost. The defeat was a sore point with the promoters of the measure, and it was felt that the Government had acted arbitrarily. They were accused of having beguiled the people of Canada with a counterfeit presentment of liberty. One Lower Canadian journal accused the Governor-General himself of having "suckled corruption and famished freedom." The Government were somewhat startled by the storm that arose all around them, and offered to consent to a committee of inquiry and an amended election law, but their opponents were not disposed to accept anything less than had been demanded by Sir Allan McNab's Bill, and so the matter was allowed to drop.* Upon the whole, the conduct of the Ministry in opposing the presentation of the petitions did not tend to strengthen their

---

* See Scrope's "Life of Sydenham," p. 242.

position before the country. A few days before the close of the session the Assembly unanimously passed a resolution to the effect that the House would proceed with the election inquiry early in the following session.

Among the useful legislation set on foot were various measures relating to public works and improvements, for which purposes sums exceeding a million and a half sterling were voted by the Assembly. An Act was passed to enable the Province to purchase the stock held by private persons in the Welland Canal, and the enlarging and deepening of that important enterprise was soon afterwards proceeded with as a public work. The improvement of the navigation of the St. Lawrence also formed a subject for Parliamentary deliberation, and more than a third of the entire sum voted for public works was assigned for that purpose. Provision was also made for the construction and improvement of roads and highways in various parts of the country. The money required for all these important public undertakings had to be borrowed, and an Act was passed to facilitate the negotiation of the requisite Imperial loan. A Provincial Board of Works Department was created with a view to the more efficient carrying out of the many public improvements which had been, or were to be, undertaken, and which it was justly deemed desirable to place under executive control, and thereby to lessen the opportunity for jobbery and corruption. Measures were also passed for securing the independence and uprightness of the judiciary, for the settlement of immigrants, for the readjustment of the currency and of the customs tariff, and for the reform of the criminal law.

An important Government measure which deserves a paragraph to itself was the Act to make provision for the establishment and maintenance of Common Schools throughout the Province. It was introduced by Solicitor-General Day on the 20th of July, and, after having been subjected to careful and repeated consideration in committee, passed its third reading on the 14th of September. It was passed by the Upper House without any amendment, and was assented to, with most of the other sessional measures, on the 18th of September. It embodied some of the most important of Mr. Arthur Buller's suggestions,* and provided an annual sum of $200,000 for the establishment of elementary schools in Upper and Lower Canada—$80,000 being apportioned to the upper, and $120,000 to the lower section of the Province.† A Chief Superintendent of Education was appointed for the entire Province, with assistants for the eastern and western sections. Under the provisions of this Act elementary schools were soon in operation all over the Province. The measure, though it was not free from objectionable features, proved a national blessing, and Lord Sydenham and his Ministry are entitled to full credit for it. As years passed by, more advanced legislation on the subject became necessary, but it served its purpose for the time, and paved the way for later enactments. It was superseded, so far as Upper Canada was concerned, in 1843; and in Lower Canada two years later.

The most important measure of the session was an Act to provide for the better internal government of the Upper Province by the establishment of local or municipal authorities therein. Prior to the coming into operation of this Act,‡ the inhabitants of the rural districts in Upper Canada had no power to form themselves into corporate bodies for the promotion of local improvements, or for the carrying on of public affairs. The measure of 1841, which was presented to the Assembly by Mr. Harrison on the 14th of July, provided that the inhabitants of each district should be a body

---

* See ante, p. 58.

† This apportionment was subsequently modified so as to accord with the respective populations of the two sections of the Province.

‡ The Act came into operation on the 1st of January, 1842. It was repealed by 12 Vic., cap. 80.

corporate within the limits prescribed by the Act. Provision was made for the formation of a municipal council in each district, to consist of a warden and councillors. Power was given to these councils to appropriate, assess and collect from the inhabitants such moneys as might be required for local purposes, and generally to adopt measures for the prosperity and good government of the respective districts. The Act was restricted in its application to Upper Canada alone, municipal institutions having previously been established in the Lower Province by ordinance of the Special Council. But the situation of the two sections of the Province was far from being analogous. In Upper Canada there existed a system of local taxation, imposed by the magistrates in Quarter Sessions. In the Lower Province there was no such thing as local taxation. The French Canadian members knew, however, that municipal institutions would render local taxation a necessity, and were consequently opposed to a municipal system altogether. The Upper Canadians wished to control their own expenditure, and though they wanted municipal institutions, they wanted the privilege of electing the principal municipal officers, such as the warden and treasurer. But Lord Sydenham could not concede to them a more liberal system than he had already conferred upon Lower Canada, and to make the officers in Lower Canada elective would be to make municipal institutions there a dead letter. The object, in a word, was to force municipal institutions upon a people unwilling to accept them ; and to effect this purpose it was necessary that the principal municipal functionaries should be appointed by the Crown.

The Municipal Bill was very warmly contested during its passage through the Assembly, and the clause enacting that Wardens should be nominated by the Crown was saved from defeat only by the casting vote of the Chairman of the Committee. The French Canadian members opposed the measure on principle, and because it would inevitably bring local taxation in its train. Sir Allan

MacNab and his Conservative following opposed it because it aimed at placing too much power in the hands of the people. Mr. Baldwin opposed it on the ground that it was not sufficiently liberal in its provisions, and he was supported in his opposition by all the more advanced of his coadjutors except Mr. Hincks. The Reform party as a whole were much divided on the measure, some voting for, and some against it. Mr. Baldwin himself proposed various amendments, and the Ministry, who had staked their offices on the Bill, announced their readiness to withdraw it in the event of any important amendment being carried. No such event took place, however, and the Bill passed its third reading, after an unusually prolonged debate, by a majority of twelve votes, on the 19th of August. It was unanimously accepted by the Legislative Council without amendment. On this important question Mr. Hincks—as may readily be believed most unwillingly—found himself opposed to all those gentlemen with whom he usually acted. He spoke and voted in favor of the Bill, and his support was greedily received by the Ministry, who gladly hailed the accession to their ranks of such a coadjutor. He was charged by some of the more outspoken of his party with having deserted from their ranks. He made a personal explanation on the floor of the House, and defended himself from the imputations which had been levelled at him. His defence, read at this distance of time, certainly seems to carry weight with it. He doubtless did not regard the Municipal Bill as being free from defects, but was disposed to accept it in default of a better; and in so doing he showed himself capable of rising above factious considerations. There was certainly no justification for accusing him of having deserted the Reform party. Although Mr. Baldwin and his more immediate followers opposed the measure, it was supported by many less advanced Reformers. Mr. Hincks's conduct was fully approved by his constituents. His services to his party had been such as could not be overlooked, and his fortunes were evidently rising. His voting on this and on several subsequent occasions with the Ministry was evidence of nothing except that he was capable of thinking and acting independently.* His action, however, produced a temporary rupture between Mr. Baldwin and himself which was not healed until the following year, when they were arrayed side by side as members of the Government.

Before the session was brought to a close another chapter was added to the history of Responsible Government in Canada. It may be premised that notwithstanding Mr. Draper's admissions on that subject early in the session, there was a widespread distrust of the Ministry among the French Canadian members and the advanced Reform members from the Upper Province. It was thought desirable that all doubts on the subject should be resolved before adjournment, and on the 3rd of September Mr. Baldwin moved a series of resolutions with a view to testing the sincerity of the Ministerial professions. The motion was seconded by Mr. Viger. The Government, however, had a safe working majority in the House, and were not disposed to allow the Opposition to gain credit with the public for these resolutions. Mr. Harrison moved amendments to very much the same effect as the original resolutions, but somewhat more circumscribed in their application. The amendments passed with little opposition. As finally carried, they were as follows:—(1) " That the head of the Executive Government of the Province being, within the limits of his Government, the Representative of the Sovereign, is responsible to the Imperial authority alone; but that, nevertheless, the management of our local affairs can only be conducted by him, by and with the assistance, counsel and information of sub-

---

* "The Government announced its determination on what I thought at the time, and still think, justifiable grounds, to withdraw the Bill, if any important amendment were carried, and in this, as on several other occasions as the session advanced, I considered it my duty to support the Government."—See "The Political History of Canada between 1840 and 1855," by the Hon. Sir Francis Hincks, P.C., K.C.M.G., C.B., pp. 23, 24.

ordinate officers in the Province." (2) "That, in order to preserve, between the different branches of the Provincial Parliament, that harmony which is essential to the peace, welfare and good government of the Province, the chief advisers of the Representative of the Sovereign, constituting a Provincial Administration under him, ought to be men possessed of the confidence of the representatives of the people, thus affording a guarantee that the well understood wishes and interests of the people, which our Gracious Sovereign has declared shall be the rule of the Provincial Government, will on all occasions be faithfully represented and advocated." (3) "That the people of this Province have, moreover, a right to expect from such Provincial Administration the exertion of their best endeavours that the Imperial authority, within its constitutional limits, shall be exercised in the manner most consistent with their well understood wishes and interests." These resolutions, in the language of a distinguished Canadian writer of the present day, " constitute, in fact, articles of agreement upon the momentous question of Responsible Government, between the executive authority of the Crown and the Canadian people." * Mr. Baldwin endeavoured to obtain a still stronger recognition of his views on the question of executive responsibility. He moved a resolution asserting the constitutional right of the popular branch of the Legislature to hold the Ministry responsible for using their best exertions to secure Imperial acquiescence in the wishes of the Canadian people, so far as the latter's particular interests were concerned. This motion, however, was negatived in the Assembly, being opposed to the spirit of Lord John Russell's despatch of the 14th of October, 1839, already quoted from, whereby the principle of non-interference by Colonial Ministers in matters of Imperial concern was recognized. The great principles underlying Responsible Government, however, had been most unmis-

---

* See "Parliamentary Government in the British Colonies," by Alpheus Todd, Librarian of the Canadian Parliament, p. 56.

takably asserted in the foregoing three resolutions, which, though
moved by Mr. Secretary Harrison, were as matter of fact dictated by
the Governor-General himself, whose biographer claims that "these
several declarations contain a formal and complete record of Lord
Sydenham's views on the subject of Responsible Government." It
is at any rate safe to say that they embodied his Excellency's
views as to what it was desirable to concede to public opinion in
Canada. Whether, if his life had been spared, he would have seen
his way to the adoption of a policy as liberal as was desired
by Mr. Baldwin and his colleagues, must ever remain an unsolved problem. His earthly race was nearly run. He had
overworked himself ever since his arrival in Canada. His labours
throughout the session had been simply tremendous for a man
in such an uncertain state of health. The obstructions in his path
had been many, and he had been compelled to encounter them
almost single-handed, for his Ministers were able to serve him to
only a limited extent. The most capable of them did not, as we
have seen, enjoy the confidence of the popular side, and could not
be expected to lend themselves with much enthusiasm to the carrying out of the most liberal of the Governor's measures.* Mr.
Baldwin's secession had doubtless tended to add to his many
embarrassments, for Mr. Baldwin, more than any other man in
Canada, had the ear of the public, and would have been invaluable
to His Excellency as an exponent of the popular will. A man of
less tact and Parliamentary experience than the Governor would
have been unable, in a single session, to carry through such a mass

---

* "My officers (Ministers?), though the best men, I believe, for their departments that
can be found, were unfortunately, many of them, unpopular from their previous conduct, and
none of them [was] sufficiently acquainted with the manner in which a Government through
Parliament should be conducted, to render me any assistance in this matter. I had,
therefore, to fight the whole battle myself; and it has been a considerable pull on both
one's adroitness and temper—particularly as I had 'a ministerial crisis' on the very day of
the meeting."—Letter of Lord Sydenham; see Scrope's "Life," p. 244.

of important legislation, beset, as it was, with multitudinous details, and in the face of a keen and watchful Opposition ever on the alert. Too much praise cannot be awarded for the indefatigable manner in which he literally spent himself in the public service. The Government's policy was sustained on every material point. The only measure on which they sustained defeat was one which contemplated the starting of a bank of issue. To Lord Sydenham more than to any one else this almost uniform success was due. But it was not obtained without the payment of a high price, so far as his Excellency was personally concerned. He worked at high pressure, and at tremendous expenditure of vital force. Much of the most important legislation was actually drafted by his own hand. He was ever at his post, and worked early and late. He was accessible to any member, no matter to what party he might belong, who could frame a plausible excuse for intruding upon him in the public interests. His nervous system was kept in a state of perpetual tension. His appetite was capricious, and he was frequently unable to sleep. "The worst of it is"—he wrote to his brother, on the 28th of August—"I am afraid I shall never be good for quiet purposes hereafter; for I actually breathe, eat, drink, and sleep on nothing but Government and politics, and my day is a lost one when I do not find that I have advanced some of these objects materially. That, in fact, is the secret of my success. The people know that I am ready at all hours and times to do business, and that what I have once undertaken I will carry through; so they follow my star."[*] He had been discounting his physical constitution ever since he had accepted the Governor-Generalship, and had taxed his energies ruinously. For more than a year before the opening of the session he had been subject to frequent attacks of his hereditary malady, the gout, and had sometimes been unable either to write or dictate. To gout, fever and utter prostration of mind

---

[*] Letter of Lord Sydenham; see Scrope's "Life," p. 255.

The Last Forty Years.

Canada since the Union of 1841.

By John Charles Dent

Geo. Virtue, Publisher, Toronto

LORD ELGIN.

LORD ELGIN

LAKE MEMPHREMAGOG.

THE HON. OLIVER MOWAT.

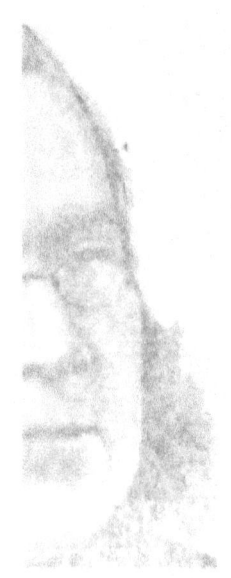

FALLS OF THE CHAUDIERE, NEAR QUEBEC.

and body were sometimes added. His removal from Montreal to Kingston, in May, caused some improvement in his health, but he complained that his strength did not come back to him, and that his work oppressed him as it had never done before. "I am ready to hang myself half a dozen times a day," he wrote, on the 5th of June. . . "I long for September, beyond which I will not stay if they were to make me Duke of Canada and Prince of Regiopolis, as this place is called." His ambition to tide over a Parliamentary session, however, and thus to see the new constitution in running order, was such that he would not resign until the wished-for goal had been attained, though it had all along been his intention to return home at the close of the session. The opening, the ministerial crisis, and the excitement of circumventing the Opposition seemed to stimulate him into abnormal activity for a time, and, as has been seen, he was able for many weeks to work even harder than before. On the 25th of July he forwarded his resignation to England, having already applied for and obtained leave of absence, which would obviate the necessity for his remaining at his post. Very grateful to his senses was the consciousness of his success. He knew that he had accomplished an arduous task, and felt a pardonable self-complacency.* He felt that he had won and deserved a place

---

* His Excellency believed that he had effectually solved all the difficult problems of the new constitution, and that all the wheels of administration would run smoothly for his successors. "I shall leave, I trust," he writes to his brother, towards the end of August, "a field which my successor, whoever he be, cannot mismanage. With a most difficult opening, almost a minority, passions at boiling heat, and prejudices such as I never saw to contend with, I have brought the Assembly by degrees into perfect order, ready to follow wherever I may lead; have carried all my measures, avoided or beaten off all discussed topics, and have got a Ministry with an avowed and recognized majority capable of doing what they think right, and not to be upset by my successor."—See "Life of Sydenham," pp. 253, 254. We now know that his Lordship's self-assurance carried him too far. Sir Charles Bagot staved off the impending conflict only by calling to his Cabinet some of those very French Canadians whom Lord Sydenham feared to trust with office and power; and Sir Charles Metcalfe proved by his unfortunate administration that the wheels of State would not run smoothly for him.

in history. On the 1st of September he wrote home in good spirits, saying that he had not thus far been compelled to act upon his leave of absence, and that he thought he could stand out the remaining few days of the session. He nursed himself more than he had ever before been in the habit of doing. He accustomed himself to take gentle exercise, and rode out on horseback almost daily. On the 4th of September he rode several miles out of town. He seemed to be much improved in health, and commented to his aide-de-camp on the beauty of the day. "We never," said his Lordship, "have such an atmosphere as this in England." He seemed to enjoy his ride, and the tone of his mind was apparently more hilarious than it had been for weeks. While returning homeward he put his horse to a canter, just as he began to ascend a little hill not far from Alwington House. When about half way up the ascent, the horse stumbled and fell, crushing his rider's right leg beneath his weight. The animal rose to its feet, and dragged Lord Sydenham—whose right foot was fast in the stirrup—for a short distance. His aide, who just then rode up, rescued the Governor from his perilous position and conveyed him home to Alwington House, which was close by. Upon examination, it was found that the principal bone of his right leg, above the knee, had sustained an oblique fracture, and that the limb had also received a severe wound from being bruised against a sharp stone, which had cut deeply, and lacerated the flesh and sinews.

It was evident that his Excellency had been subjected to a severe shock, and he was in a condition little suited to withstand any additional calls upon his nervous system. He himself took a despairing view of his case from the first, but his professional attendants did not for some time anticipate a fatal termination to the accident. He for some days continued free from fever, and his wounds seemed to be going on satisfactorily; but he was debilitated by an almost perpetual sleeplessness, and by inability to rest long in one position. His sufferings, too, were at times very severe. His mind, nevertheless, continued to busy itself with public affairs, and his interest in the sessional proceedings was apparently as active as ever. His Ministers and many of the other members of the Legislature were received by him with genial courtesy from day to day. On the 11th of the month the mail from England brought him the official notification that his resignation had been accepted, and that Her Majesty had been pleased to bestow upon him the Grand Cross of the Order of the Bath.

Such intelligence, read in the light of subsequent events, seems very much like a hollow mockery. Red ribbons and such like gauds are of little avail to one so near the hour of his utmost need as was Lord Sydenham at this time. He was about to pass the confines of a kingdom into which red ribbons, stars, garters and Windsor uniforms are no passport. It must surely have been more consoling to his Lordship, lying there so near his end, to reflect that, upon the whole, his conscience was clear; that he had, according to such light as had been given him, endeavoured to do his duty in his proper sphere; that he had had the manliness to stand up for the right, and to encounter harsh obloquy for his principles. Well for him if he could lay such flattering unctions as these to his soul, for his Lordship was about to appear before a Judge who is no respecter of persons; a Judge in whose eyes, it is to be presumed, the rectitude of a man's life weighs more than all the ribbons—red, blue, or otherwise—which it is the prerogative of Majesty to bestow.

His Lordship, however, notwithstanding his gloomy premonitions of the past week, rallied a little at receiving the intimation of the new dignity which had been bestowed upon him. He wrote to Lord John Russell the same day, expressing his thanks for the red ribbon, and giving an account of his accident. He hoped, he said, to be in a state to be moved by water to Quebec in time to sail for England during the autumn. The hope was not destined to be realized. Two days later, dangerous symptoms began to manifest themselves. Gout set in, and the fractured bone refused to knit. It had been settled that the prorogation should take place on the 15th, but it was now considered advisable to postpone the ceremony to the 17th. On Thursday, the 16th, he dictated the Speech with which he proposed to close the session. Next morning, though he was evidently very poorly, he insisted on revising and correcting the Speech, and he also transacted some public business. His personal attendance at the prorogation was out of the question for that day, and accordingly the ceremony was again postponed. His symptoms became still more alarming in the course of the afternoon, and his medical advisers were apprehensive of delirium. He accordingly issued a Commission appointing Major-General John Clitherow, the senior military officer who was then on the spot, to be Deputy-Governor, for the purpose of giving the royal sanction to the unreserved Bills which had been passed during the session, referring the reserved Bills for the signification of the Queen's pleasure, and proroguing the Parliament. It was too late to go through the ceremonial for that day. It was understood that if His Excellency's condition was not greatly improved on the following morning the commission to Major-General Clitherow should be acted upon. During the night it became evident that there was no hope of Lord Sydenham's recovery. His agonies increased, his little remaining strength gradually ebbed away, and his death was only a question of hours. There was, as is usual in such contingencies, an attempt to make the best of his condition to the world outside, but early on Saturday morning it was known all over Kingston that the end was rapidly approaching.*

---

* The *Montreal Gazette*, in an extra issued at Kingston early in the afternoon of Saturday, the 18th, announced the prorogation, and concluded as follows: "The state of His Excellency's health at the moment of our writing is most precarious. The latest bulletins from the Government House which we have seen are of the most gloomy character. The worst symptoms of his complaint have been aggravated during the night, and all hopes of

A few minutes after noon on Saturday, the 18th, the Deputy Governor, accompanied only by Captain Clitherow, his Aide-de-camp, and Mr. T. W. C. Murdoch, Chief Secretary to the Governor-General, repaired to the Legislative Council Chamber, where that body were then in session. The salutes and guards of honour usual on such an occasion were dispensed with, and the attendance of the heads of departments, officers, and other functionaries was not required. The Gentleman Usher of the Black Rod having been commanded to require the attendance of the Assembly, the Speaker and a large number of the members made their appearance at the bar. The unreserved bills were then presented by the Clerk of the Crown in Chancery, and the assent of the Deputy Governor, in Her Majesty's name, was given in the usual form by the Clerk of the Legislative Council. The first session of the First Parliament was then brought to a close by a Speech deploring the condition of the Governor-General, and congratulating the Legislature on the many important Acts which had been passed, and on the general harmony which had marked the Parliamentary proceedings.* The members then dispersed to their respective homes.

Notwithstanding the great bodily agony from which he suffered, Lord Sydenham bore up with wonderful fortitude. His mental faculties were unimpaired, and he knew that his end was very near. During the forenoon of Saturday he executed his will, in which was inserted a clause bestowing a legacy upon his friend and fellow-worker, Lord John Russell. "He was the noblest man it was ever

---

a recovery are now abandoned. The whole town appears to be deeply interested in the intelligence from hour to hour reported from Alwington House. But while life lasts there is still hope. God grant that those hopes may not prove fallacious!"

*The number of Bills to which the royal assent was given by the
    Deputy Governor was...................................... 67
Reserved for the signification of Her Majesty's pleasure............ 15
Previously sanctioned 20

Total passed during the session........................... 102

my good fortune to know," exclaimed the already dying Governor, as the clause was read over to him. In the course of the afternoon he gathered the members of his household about him, and united with them in partaking of the sacrament. He then took a personal farewell of each, after which he requested to be left alone with his chaplain. He spent the night in such preparation for the end as his sufferings permitted. He survived until seven o'clock on the following morning, which was Sunday, the 19th; when, after an agony of unusual sharpness, he breathed his last. The immediate cause of his death was inflammation, terminating in lock-jaw. He had completed his forty-second year only six days before.

Owing partly to an early disappointment in an affair of the heart, and partly to his feeble health—partly also, it may be presumed, to the absorbing nature of his pursuits—he had never married, and he left no successor to the title which he had so arduously won. In private life, notwithstanding the self-consciousness and pseudo-coxcombry alluded to by Greville,* he had many warmly-attached friends. His kindly disposition and ingratiating manners stood him in good stead, both in politics and in private life, and he left many sincere mourners behind him. Notwithstanding his absorbing occupations, he could always find time for works of kindness and charity. In a letter to an idle friend who had been remiss in correspondence, he once said, "Of course you have no time. No one ever has who has nothing to do."†

Considered merely as a member of society, however, Lord Sydenham was not so conspicuous that history is bound to take cognizance of him. Neither was his career in the House of Commons, notwithstanding his usefulness, of such a character as to bring him permanent fame. "His fame," says his biographer, "must rest, not so much on

---

* See note on pp. 38, 39, ante. Other biographies and one of the period amply corroborate Mr. Greville's estimate.

† See Scrope's "Life of Sydenham," p. 305, note.

what he did or said in Parliament as on what he did and proposed to do out of it."* The crowning work of his life, and that which renders his career specially interesting to Canadians, was his successful inauguration of the Union. For this he is entitled to whatever credit attaches to the measure itself. The conception was due to Lord Durham, the execution to Lord Sydenham. The latter enjoyed an advantage which was denied to Lord Durham—he was steadfastly upheld by the Home Government. He had not Lord Durham's fiery temper, and had no potent or bitter enemies to torture his life out of him by attacks in the House of Lords and in the public prints. He was moreover much more cool and calculating—more selfish, in a word—than Lord Durham, and knew how to make the most of his advantages. He seldom allowed personal pique to influence his public relations. He was no fanciful visionary, with a lofty ideal constantly before him. He had ever an eye to the practical side of life, and was much more frequently guided by experience than by theory. He was an able tactician and a shrewd man of business, skilled in finesse, and fond of exercising it. He had a largely-developed faculty for administration, and a perfect mastery over details. He lived long enough to see the new constitutional system fairly set going, but not long enough to encounter the inevitable strain to which sooner or later it was certain to be subjected. In this sense it may be said that he was as fortunate in his death as in his life. Had life and health been spared to him, and had he remained in Canada, some part of the struggle of which his successors were compelled to bear the brunt would doubtless have fallen upon his own shoulders.†

---

* See Scrope's "Life of Sydenham," p. 303.

† A very capable writer who acted as an occasional Canadian correspondent of the *New York Herald* during the summer of 1841 thus wrote of Lord Sydenham to that paper a few weeks before the close of the session :—" He owes his success in Canada as much to the absence of any leading men there as to anything else ; and I venture to predict he has

It is hardly probable, however, that Lord Sydenham would in any case have remained in Canada. At the end of August the Melbourne Ministry were compelled to resign. Sir Robert Peel succeeded to power, with Lord Stanley as Secretary of State for the Colonies. The question upon which the deposed Ministry had fallen was practically the oft-debated one of Free Trade *versus* Protection. Protection ideas were for the time in the ascendant. Lord Sydenham's Parliamentary reputation had been made—when he was plain Mr. Thomson—as the out-and-out advocate of Free Trade. The colonial policy also underwent various modifications upon the accession to power of the new Administration. Lord Stanley's views on the question of Responsible Government were by no means those entertained by Lord Sydenham, and it is not likely that the latter could have seen his way to continuing the administration of the affairs of Canada, even if there had been a disposition to retain him in his office. So that his death solved more problems than one.

Lord Sydenham has upon the whole been fairly judged, alike by his contemporaries and by those who have come after him. Miss Martineau, who, though she was not personally acquainted with him, had watched the later phases of his career with a good deal of interest, and whose knowledge of men and things in England entitled her to speak with some authority, passes the following judgment upon him: " He found his most favourable position when he went to Canada; but he neither entertained nor inspired political faith, nor drew towards himself any high respect or genial admiration. Though his last scene of action was his greatest and best, he was regarded, and is still, as one of the Whig failures—one of the Ministers of a critical period who, while possessed of consider-

---

tact enough to stay just sufficiently long for his reputation not to suffer. Time must consolidate and strengthen the elements of opposition to any Governor. Lord Sydenham, even if his health permitted him to stay, would leave these to be encountered by a successor at the proper period."

able talents and some good political qualities, have done more than many worse men to shake a nation's faith—if not in the principles of politics, at least in those who are the most forward in the profession of them. The professions of Whig Reformers while rehearsing the death-knell of abuses, have but too often reminded us of Dr. Johnson's knocking and summoning ghost;* the conclusion in both cases being that 'nothing ensued.' What is due to Mr. C. Poulett Thomson's memory is, that he should be regarded and remembered as Lord Sydenham, who governed Canada for two years on the introduction of Lord Durham; and that, if too much self-regard mingled—as his journal shows—with his inducements to the work, he still bore in mind Lord Spencer's more generous suggestion, that Canada offered 'the finest field of exertion for any one, as affording the greatest power of doing the greatest good to one's fellow-creatures.'"†

In compliance with Lord Sydenham's own expressed wish when he found the cold hand of death stealing over him, his body found a final resting-place in Canadian ground. He was interred in a vault beneath the floor of the middle aisle of St. George's Church, Kingston, on Friday, the 24th of the month. At the suggestion of the local authorities, the day was observed with all the solemnity due to "a time of mourning." All the shops and places of business were closed, and, notwithstanding the vast concourse, and the length of the procession, a funereal gloom reigned supreme. The flags of all the vessels in the harbour drooped at half-mast. Prominent citizens attended from various parts of the Province, as well as from some of the towns on the opposite side of Lake Ontario, to pay a last tribute of respect to the memory of the dead Governor. Eight

---

* The allusion is to the famous Cock Lane ghost. See Croker's edition of Boswell's "Life of Johnson," Vol. II., pp. 182, 183, note.

† "History of England during the Thirty Years' Peace," by Harriet Martineau; Book 5, Chapter XII.

clergymen attended at the obsequies, with the Venerable Archdeacon of Kingston at their head. The service was a peculiarly impressive one. "Never in this country"—says a contemporary account—"did the incomparably beautiful ritual of the Church of England for the dead appear with more striking effect, or produce a more heartfelt solemnity. The sacred edifice, with its galleries, pillars, pulpit, reading-desk and altar hung round with the sable drapery of death; the choir and organ chanting the requiem over the departed; and the church filled with people dressed in mourning, looking with anxious gaze on the last resting-place of their recent Ruler; these, with the dignified appearance of the venerable minister, as he stretched his hands over the grave, and solemnly pronounced those simple but eloquent words which go direct to the heart of every Christian—all these combined with the reflections upon the great loss of him, who, not many weeks ago, in the full enjoyment of intellect, had knelt in that building where now he lay a lifeless corpse, must have made an impression which, even in after years, will never be forgotten."*

And so Lord Sydenham slept his last sleep, three thousand miles distant from his native land and the tombs of his ancestors. Yet a few months, and Sir Charles Bagot reigned in his stead.

* Kingston correspondence of the *Montreal Gazette*; Friday, September 24th, 1841.

Chapter VIII.

THE CASE OF ALEXANDER McLEOD.

"On—wildly onward—sped the craft,
    As she swiftly neared the verge;
And the demon guards of the black gulf laughed,
    And chanted a hellish dirge;
And the booming waters roared anew
    A wail for the dead and dying crew.

"As over the shelving rocks she broke,
    And plunged in her turbulent grave,
The slumbering genius of Freedom woke,
    Baptised in Niagara's wave,
And sounded her warning tocsin far,
From Atlantic's shore to the polar star."

"THE DESTRUCTION OF THE CAROLINE;" a hysterical and very untruthful ballad published in the *Rochester Democrat*, a short time after the occurrence of the event described.

PON the death of Lord Sydenham the task of administering the Government devolved upon Lieutenant-General Sir Richard D. Jackson, Commander of the Forces in Canada, and an old warrior of the Peninsula. He was duly sworn in, and entered upon the discharge of his functions. He had had no opportunity of becoming acquainted with Lord Sydenham's views on questions of public policy, and wisely resolved not to assume any more of the attributes or powers of office than might be necessary for carrying on the political machinery. It was confidently expected by the members of the Government at Kingston that the recent change of Ministry at home would produce some corresponding change in the colonial policy and arrangements, and no little anxiety was felt as to who would be Lord Sydenham's successor.

That successor, as has been intimated, was Sir Charles Bagot; but before entering upon the events of his short Administration an episode must be noticed which, taken in connection with other serious causes of dispute, to be hereafter referred to, threatened, for a time, to embroil two great nations in a bitter and desolating war.

Most Canadian readers are familiar with the principal facts respecting the cutting-out and burning of the steamship *Caroline*. During the month of December, 1837, a number of the Canadian rebels, with William Lyon Mackenzie at their head, and a horde of American sympathizers under the command of an adventurer named Rensselaer Van Rensselaer, took up their quarters on Navy Island, situated in the Niagara River, nearly opposite Chippewa, several miles above the most tremendous waterfall on the globe, and within the boundary of Upper Canada. Here Mr. Mackenzie hoisted the "Patriot" flag, organized a Provisional Government, and, by way of burlesquing Sir Francis Bond Head, offered a reward of five hundred pounds for the Lieutenant-Governor's body. Entrenchments were thrown up, artillery and stores were obtained from the United States arsenals at several of the frontier towns, and fire was opened on the Canadian shore, where several houses were pierced with balls. A horse on which a Canadian citizen was riding was slain by one of the discharges, but the rider himself escaped injury. Enlistments went on from day to day on the American side of the river, and many of the citizens of the United States openly espoused the insurgent cause, and lent every assistance in their power to this miniature rebellion. There were undoubted violations of international law on the part of many Americans. Peaceable and unoffending Canadian farmers were fired upon by a "rout of American rascaldom" encamped on Grand Island, a little farther up the river. The local authorities of

New York State showed a very strong disposition to wink at these
proceedings; and there is no doubt that the sympathies of the
American people, almost to a man, were on the side of the rebels.
Volunteers were permitted upon the most flimsy pretexts to arm
themselves from the State military stores. One officer, whose duty it
was to prevent the State artillery from being removed, allowed
a cannon to be taken to Navy Island on being informed that
it was going to be used to shoot wild ducks.

Such a state of things was not to be quietly endured by the
Canadian authorities. Colonel (afterwards Sir Allan) MacNab,
Speaker of the Upper Canadian Assembly, after quenching the fires
of rebellion in the London District, hurried with his "Men of Gore"
to the Niagara frontier, where the militia, under the command of
Colonel Cameron, had already assembled in considerable force.
Colonel MacNab took the direction of affairs, and issued a remonstrance to the United States authorities, calling their attention
to the fact that succours and supplies were daily furnished to the
insurgents by American citizens, and that the movement, in fact, had
largely assumed the form of a petty invasion of Canadian territory
by marauding Americans. His representations, however, for some
time produced no practical effect. The "army" of the "Provisional
Government" on Navy Island continued to be reinforced by
American volunteers, and supplies continued to be furnished from
Buffalo, Black Rock and Batavia. "General" Van Rensselaer spent
his few sober moments in delivering ruffianly harangues to the baser
sort of his fellow-countrymen, and in solicitations to them to "rally
round the cause of freedom and liberty."* A small steamboat, called

---

* Poor Robert Gourlay, who was then at Cleveland, Ohio, wrote to Van Rensselaer,
under date of January 17th, 1838, pointing out the fatuity of the *soi-disant* General's course.
"Never," said Mr. Gourlay, "was hallucination more blinding than yours. At a moment
of profound peace, putting on armour, and, led on by the little editor of a blackguard newspaper, entering the lists of civil broil, and erecting your standard on Navy Island, to defy
the armies of Britain! David before Goliath seemed little; but God was with him. What
are you, in the limbo of vanity, with no stay but the devil!"

the *Caroline*, belonging to one William Wells, a citizen of Buffalo, was cut out of the ice at that place and taken down the river, where it was employed for the purpose of conveying men and stores between Navy Island and the eastern mainland. A number of Americans gave a bond to the owner, indemnifying him against loss in case of her capture. The collector of customs at the port, well knowing the purpose to which the steamer was to be put, made out and signed a license, and she was taken down the river to Navy Island. On the afternoon of the 28th of the month several Canadians saw the *Caroline* plying between the island and Schlosser—a village on the American side of the river—conveying munitions of war to the rebels, and acting as an easy and rapid medium of communication between them and the shore. They lost no time in repairing to Chippewa and apprising Colonel MacNab of the circumstance. The open employment of the little vessel in broad day for such purposes nettled the gallant Colonel, a gentleman who was not conspicuous for discretion at any time. After a brief council of war, it was determined that "the piratical craft," as she was called, must be arrested in her mischievous career. Sir Francis Head, the Lieutenant-Governor, having been applied to by Colonel MacNab, is said to have given his consent on the evening of the 28th to the capture or destruction of the *Caroline*;* and during the following night her capture and destruction were effected. The expedition, the charge of which was confided to Captain Drew, of the Royal Navy, consisted, at the outset, of seven boats,† containing an aggregate of about sixty men, armed with pistols, cutlasses and boarding-pikes. Few of the men were aware of the precise nature of the service required of them,

---

* He at any rate expressed his unequivocal approval of the act after it had been done. See his despatch of 30th December. See also "The Emigrant," Chapter X.

† See "The Life and Times of William Lyon Mackenzie," by Charles Lindsey, Vol. II., p. 146, *note*.

nor were they in a temper to search too curiously into its nature. They were in a superlatively loyal mood, ready and anxious to take part in any desperate deed of derring-do. It was only necessary for Captain Drew to signify that he required "a few fellows with cutlasses, who would follow him to the devil," and the full complement of men was obtained more rapidly than their names could be enrolled. The achievement proved to be nothing very desperate, after all, for they encountered no serious resistance. The expedition started from the mouth of the Chippewa River about an hour before midnight of the 29th. One of the seven boats grounded *en route* on a small island in the river. Another was inadequately supplied with oars, and the crew being unable to keep up with the others, were compelled to abandon the enterprise, and return to the Canadian shore. The number of boats was thus reduced to five, in each of which were nine men, so that the number of persons actually engaged in making the capture was forty-five. The rowers pulled with a will, and the boats, which kept pretty close together, were soon off Navy Island. It was then perceived that the *Caroline* was moored at the wharf at Schlosser, on the American side. The boats were accordingly pulled across the stream, and were not discovered by those on board the steamer until they were within fifteen or twenty yards of her. The crew of the steamer consisted of ten persons, but there were twenty-three others on board who had obtained permission to pass the night there, upon the ground that the taverns were full. The invading force reached the steamer about midnight. As the boats neared the vessel's side the sentinel on deck gave the alarm, and discharged a pistol or musket. There was however nothing worthy of being called a conflict. The crew and other occupants of the steamer were unarmed, or nearly so, and were moreover panic-stricken by being so summarily aroused from their slumbers at dead of night. Captain Drew and his little band were in possession in considerably less time than it takes to tell the story. There was a good deal of noise, which was made up in part of the clashing of swords and the discharge of firearms, and in part of hallooing and profanity. An American sailor who attempted to oppose the capture was cut down by Captain Drew, and a few others were disabled. The doughty Captain also drove three men before him from the steamer to the wharf, occasionally accelerating their motions by prods from the point of his sword.* Lieutenant John Elmsley then, by Captain Drew's orders, went ashore with several men, and cut the steamer from her moorings. The doomed *Caroline* was then towed out from the wharf by the five boats, set on fire, and abandoned to the strength of the current. The craft was old and dry, and the fire soon did its work, so that not much of it was left by the time it made the fearful leap over Niagara Falls. The rebels on Navy Island were treated to a magnificent spectacle of fireworks, of which Mr. Mackenzie himself has left a brief account. "We observed," he says, "about one o'clock A.M., a fire burning on the American side of the river, in the direction of the small tavern and old storehouse, commonly called Schlosser. Its volume gradually enlarged, and many were our conjectures concerning it. At length the mass of flame was distinctly perceived to move upon the waters, and approach the rapids and the middle of the river above the falls. Swiftly and beautifully it glided along, yet more rapid in its onward course as it neared the fathomless gulf, into which it vanished in a moment, amid the surrounding darkness. This was the ill-fated steamboat *Caroline*." †

After abandoning the steamer to her doom, the crews of the boats

---

* See the evidence of Mr. (afterwards Colonel) William Smart Light, of Woodstock, given on the trial of McLeod. Young Light himself was not the least active member of the expedition.

† See Lindsey's "Life of Mackenzie," Vol. II., pp. 144, 145. The captors intended to tow the steamer across the river to the Canadian shore, but found the current too strong, and were compelled to abandon her to its force.—*Ib.*, p. 150.

pulled back to camp on the Canadian shore, not a little proud of having so successfully accomplished the object of their expedition. They were warmly congratulated by Colonel MacNab and their brother officers, and were for a time the lions of the camp. Some of them doubtless went to their graves years afterwards with the conviction firmly rooted in their minds that their little adventure on the night of that 29th of December, 1837, had been a patriotic and chivalrous exploit. One of them—Lieutenant McCormick—was wounded somewhat severely during the assault, and several others received slight wounds which obtained for them honourable mention in the official despatches.

In the skirmish—it did not deserve a more dignified name—an American named Amos Durfee was slain. It was asserted by some of the crew that several other persons had met their death by fire or by drowning. No trustworthy evidence was ever offered to substantiate the assertion, although it is possible enough that other casualties may have occurred, as the occupants of the vessel at the time of her capture were mostly strangers to each other and to the neighbourhood, and belonged to a vagabond class of society, the representatives of which are not easily traced. One death, however, there undoubtedly was. When Wells, the owner of the *Caroline*, escaped from the steamer to the shore, he saw Durfee's body lying near the old storehouse mentioned in the above extract. He had been shot through the head, and his brains were scattered around near where he lay, so that it is not surprising to learn from a Buffalo newspaper of the period that "the vital spark was extinct."

It is easy enough to say that the destruction of the *Caroline* was an unwise and unnecessary act. That it was so is beyond dispute, but the facility with which people become wise after the fact is proverbial. The loyal inhabitants of Upper Canada were stirred to their inmost depths, not by the conduct of the rebels alone, but by the active sympathy of many American citizens in the outbreak, and by the apathy or supineness of the State authorities. It was a sore trial of patience to discover that American ruffians were permitted to appropriate public arms and stores to aid what was in reality an invasion of Canadian territory. The gorge of the loyal Canadian militia rose at this novel exhibition of international neutrality. Most of them were old enough to remember, and many of them were old enough to have taken part in, the troubles of 1812-'14. The Head of the Upper Canadian Government was a man greatly wanting in prudence and judgment, fond of producing startling and dramatic effects. Colonel MacNab was full of patriotism and military ardour. Add to all this that, according to the better opinion, the destruction of the *Caroline* was legally justifiable—although Great Britain eventually thought fit to apologize for the act*—and the whole transaction seems natural enough. Colonel MacNab was knighted and feasted, and was a conspicuous man for the rest of his life. He and Captain Drew received the thanks of the Upper Canadian House of Assembly for their gallantry, accompanied in each case by a costly sword; and it was not till the public excitement had to some degree cooled down, and till a demand for reparation had been made on behalf of the United States, that the Canadian public awoke to the fact that the destruction of the poor little steamer had upon the whole been rather a foolish deed.†

At the time of the occurrence of this episode, and for several years previously, a man named Alexander McLeod had been Deputy

---

* See post, Chapter X.

† Sir Francis Head, in "The Emigrant," Chapter X., says: "This act of calm justice and cool vengeance produced febrifugal results highly beneficial. It struck terror into those who, with bands and banners, were marching from all directions to invade us; and by thus inducing them to halt, the United States Government were not only obliged, but were enabled to exert themselves." No statement could be farther from the fact. Instead of striking terror into the hearts of American sympathizers with the rebels, the destruction of the *Caroline* roused a spirit of rage and aggression, and in many instances converted passive sympathizers into active participants in the invasion.

Sheriff of the Niagara District. He was of Scottish birth and descent, and at this time was nearly forty-two years of age, having been born on the 17th of January, 1796, at Carnoustie, in Forfarshire. He had been a soldier in his youth, and had attained the rank of a serjeant in the Twelfth Royal Lancers. His emigration from Scotland to Upper Canada took place in or about the year 1825. He for some time kept a small store at Kingston, and afterwards removed to Toronto, where he kept a grocery on what is now the corner of Church and Front Streets. He afterwards obtained the appointment of Deputy Sheriff already referred to, and in that capacity it was almost inevitable that he should make a good many enemies. He was known for a man of indomitable courage and iron will, who never hesitated to carry out an official duty merely because it was a disagreeable one. He was a fervidly loyal subject, and upon the breaking out of Mackenzie's rebellion he hurried over to Toronto, and took part in the affair at Montgomery's tavern. After the rout of the rebels he returned to his official duties, but upon receiving intelligence of the encampment of Mackenzie and his allies on Navy Island he repaired to the frontier, to give what assistance he could to Colonel MacNab. On the evening of the 24th of December he was at Buffalo, and received information as to the proposed employment of the *Caroline*. He repaired to Chippewa and informed Colonel MacNab of what he had heard. On the afternoon of the 28th he accompanied Captain Drew on a reconnoitring expedition in a small open boat, and, notwithstanding that they were repeatedly fired upon by the rebels, they contrived to approach near enough to Navy Island to observe the movements of Mackenzie's adherents. They also perceived the *Caroline* engaged in the act of landing stores on Navy Island from the mainland. Upon their return they of course communicated to Colonel MacNab all that they had observed; and it was this information which induced the Colonel to resolve to destroy "the pirate steamer."

McLeod, however, had no further connection with the event at that time. He did not join the expedition on the night of the 29th, which was passed by him at the neighbouring village of Stamford; nor was he present when the vessel was boarded and captured. He certainly had nothing whatever to do with the death of Durfee.

In due course a demand for reparation was made on the British Government by the United States, for violation of the latter's territory. A good deal of diplomatic correspondence ensued, which for a long time came to nothing. Nearly three years passed by, when, on the 12th of November, 1840, McLeod was arrested at Lewiston, in the State of New York, for murder and arson. The more serious offence charged against him was the murder of Durfee. The alleged arson consisted of the burning of the *Caroline*. Evidence was offered to show that McLeod had admitted, and indeed boasted of, having been engaged in the cutting-out expedition, and of having been especially bloodthirsty on the occasion.* Notwithstanding

---

* Deposition of Leonard Anson, taken November 12th, 1840.—Lived in Lockport. Went to Canada in 1836, and remained there until after the attack on the *Caroline*. Was at Chippewa the day after the affair, at the tavern. A number of persons were present, among whom was McLeod. They were disputing among themselves who had done most in the attack. McLeod said "I killed one d–d Yankee, and there is his blood;"—exhibiting a horse-pistol, on the stock of which there was blood. He had a sword at his side. Witness had known McLeod six or eight months. Did not know any other person present [at the time of McLeod's assertion] except the bar-keeper. Became acquainted with McLeod at Chippewa. Does not recollect what the others said, but they seemed to agree that McLeod had done most.

Deposition of Norman Barnum, taken before Alderman Hall, at Buffalo, December 31st, 1837.—On the 29th December was at the British encampment at Chippewa. In the afternoon the *Caroline* was seen going from Schlosser to Navy Island. There was much excitement among the officers and troops. Some of the officers determined to seize the *Caroline*. An expedition was arranged, under the command of Captain Mosher. Heard Colonel MacNab say, that if the cavalry would let their swords and pistols go, he would be answerable for their safe return. At night, twelve boats set off. Lights were seen on board the *Caroline*, and it was known that she was moored at Schlosser. Witness knows that Captain Mosher, Rolland McDonald, and Alexander McLeod were of the party. Beacons were lighted on the shore, to which the boats pulled on their return. McLeod

much that has been written to the contrary, it is tolerably certain that McLeod never made any such boast. The only evidence of his having done so proceeded from persons whose enmity he had incurred through the discharge of his official duties. McLeod was not one of the most moral or high-minded of men, but he was no swashbuckler, and was by no means given to boasting about his achievements. Neither was he addicted to vaunting his exploits at the expense of truth. It would, moreover, have been the height of absurdity for him to lay claim to having been engaged in such an expedition as that of the 29th of December, as the names of all who took part in it were enrolled under the personal direction of Colonel MacNab, and were all well known on the following day. The simple fact is that the prosecution of McLeod was instigated by a republican mob, and there was no difficulty in procuring any evidence which the exigencies of the case might require. After a long and vexatious preliminary examination, the Grand Jury of Niagara County found a true bill against the prisoner, who was committed to stand his trial, and was confined in Lockport gaol.

No sooner did these facts become known to Mr. H. S. Fox, British Minister at Washington, than he demanded the immediate release of the prisoner. The British Minister avowed the destruction of the *Caroline* as the public act of persons in Her Majesty's service, and represented that it could not therefore be made the ground of legal proceedings against the individuals concerned in it. After this avowal, it is clear that even if McLeod had been concerned in the destruction of the steamer, he could not be made personally responsible for the act of his Government, any more than a soldier could be tried and punished in a foreign country for obeying the orders

---

boasted that his sword had drunk the blood of two. Colonel MacNab knew and approved of the expedition.

Many of the details in the foregoing evidence are certainly untrue, and but little weight should be attached to any of them where they are unconfirmed by other testimony.

of his superior officer in time of war. The demand for McLeod's release, however, was not acceded to. It was claimed on behalf of the Government at Washington that the jurisdiction of the several States composing the Union was within its appropriate sphere perfectly independent of the Federal Government, and that the offence with which McLeod was charged was committed within the territory of the State of New York. There, it was said, he must take his trial. To this Mr. Fox at once replied, reiterating his former demand, and adding that he had forwarded the official correspondence between himself and Mr. Forsyth, the Secretary of State to the Republic, to Her Majesty's Government in England. "I cannot but foresee," said Mr. Fox, "the very grave and serious consequences that must ensue if, besides the injury already inflicted upon Mr. McLeod of a vexatious and unjust imprisonment, any further harm should be done to him in the progress of this extraordinary proceeding." Nothing came of this remonstrance, and McLeod was still confined in gaol at Lockport.

Early in March, 1841, Mr. Fox received explicit instructions to the effect that the Home Government entirely approved of his demand for McLeod's liberation, and directing him to renew it. It was renewed accordingly, and in the following unmistakable language: "Her Majesty's Government have had under consideration the subject of the arrest and imprisonment of Alexander McLeod, on a pretended charge of arson and murder, and I am directed to make known to the Government of the United States that the British Government entirely approved of the course pursued by him. I am instructed to demand formally, and in the name of the British Government, the immediate release of Alexander McLeod, for the reason that the transaction was one of a public character, planned and executed by persons duly authorized by the Colonial Government to take such measures as might be necessary for protecting the property and lives of Her Majesty's subjects, and being therefore an act of public duty, they cannot be held responsible to the laws and tribunals of any foreign country."

The Federal Government of the United States reiterated the former plea, to the effect that it had no power to interfere with the jurisdiction of the State of New York. With the State of New York, as such, it was manifestly impossible for the Imperial Government to have any international relations. When the very explicit terms of the demand are taken into consideration, and when it is further borne in mind that there were also international disputes between the two countries on the subject of the boundaries between British America and the United States, as well as on other subjects of importance, it will not be wondered at if war was regarded as a not improbable event on both sides of the Atlantic. There seemed to be no disposition to recede on the part of either the Governments or people of the two countries. In July Term McLeod's counsel had him taken under a writ of Habeas Corpus before the Supreme Court of the State of New York. It was contended on his behalf, first: That he was absent, and did not participate in the alleged offences; and second: That if present and acting, it was in the necessary defence or protection of his country against a treasonable insurrection, of which Durfee was acting in aid at the time. The Court declined to give effect to these contentions, and discharged the writ. Judge Cowen, who pronounced this judgment, did not thereby add to his judicial reputation, for, in the estimation of nearly all the eminent United States lawyers of the time, to say nothing of those of Great Britain, he was not only wrong in his law, but absurd and self-contradictory in his reasoning.[*] McLeod,

---

[*] One of Judge Cowen's dicta was, in effect, that without the actual concurrence of the Congress of the United States or the Queen of England, no hostile act can lawfully be done by a portion of the American or the British people. In a subsequent part of his judgment he clearly repudiated that doctrine. "If," says an able American jurist, "by the phrase *actual concurrence*, in this proposition, is not meant that which it seems to mean, the proposition is a very sound and unassailable truism; if otherwise it is a very

however, was remanded to gaol to take his trial, and a spirit was aroused in the public mind which boded serious consequences. Lord Sydenham, who supposed that McLeod had really got himself into all his trouble through boastfulness, was profoundly disgusted with the aspect of affairs. "If McLeod could be hanged," he wrote to Lord John Russell, on the 20th of January, 1841, "without its committing us, I must say that it would not much signify, for he richly deserves it for his folly, not to say wickedness. I believe there is no doubt that he was not at the burning of the *Caroline*, but he has been boasting everywhere that he was, and doing what he could to get himself taken up. However, that cannot be, and if the Yankees really hanged him, which a Lockport judge and jury are pretty sure to do, it would be a case of war."*

bold absurdity. It would be worth while to *assist* at General Gaines's reception at his first visit to the Presidential mansion, if a party of Indians should come to beat up his head-quarters at Memphis, and he should stack his arms, and take steamboat to report at Washington that he had no intimation of the *actual concurrence* of Congress in his adopting measures of defence. The concurrence of the sovereign is necessary, without doubt, to constitute a lawful war, but it is a concurrence which, in a variety of circumstances, must be presumed. It is to be presumed that the Queen of England and the Congress of the United States mean that their frontier shall be defended whenever it is threatened, and the officers and soldiers who defend it may very safely rely on their *actual concurrence* in the defence, and would be very imprudent to entertain any doubt about the matter. According as Judge Cowen's words here are construed, his doctrine is altogether immaterial to the purpose in hand, or else it is not only not true, but admits of, or rather is, a *reductio ad absurdum*. If the *actual concurrence* of the sovereign in necessary hostilities for the defence of his territory, (this doctrine, of course, is independent of the question *what* hostile measures of defence may in any case be necessary,) if this is not to be understood as expressed in a general commission, or presumable, from the object of self-protection, incident to the organization of civil communities, there is small safety for the subject except as he seeks it close by the capital;—there is nothing to prevent our company on the Aroostook from installing itself next week in Quebec; the garrison at Quebec will point a cannon against them at its peril."—*North American Review*, October, 1841.

* See Scrope's "Life of Sydenham," p. 235, *note*. His Excellency had a very low opinion of American life, whether social, political or judicial—a lower opinion, it is to be hoped, than was really deserved. On the 25th of July he wrote: "My neighbour Jonathan is getting too bad. McLeod's business is a disgrace to any civilized country, but a pretty specimen of this land of liberty, where the pride of the people seems to be that they are entitled to *break*, as well as make, laws for themselves." Eleven days later he wrote still

After repeated delays, motions, postponements and relegations, McLeod was finally put upon his trial on the 4th of October, 1841, before the Circuit Court of the State of New York, at Utica. He had then been in prison about eleven months. After a tedious trial which lasted eight days he was pronounced by the jury to be not guilty. Many persons who had taken part in the capture and destruction of the *Caroline*—among them Colonel MacNab himself, who had meanwhile become Sir Allan MacNab—went over from Canada, and testified that the prisoner had had no part in the expedition, and that he had not been present at the time when Durfee must have been killed. Several other witnesses proved an *alibi* on the part of the prisoner. The case for the prosecution was not particularly well managed, and a good deal of testimony was adduced on its behalf which bore perjury on the face of it. In short, the jury could not possibly arrive at any other conclusion than the one they did. Their verdict probably prevented war.

After his discharge from custody, McLeod proceeded to Montreal, where he was more or less lionized for a time. He subsequently kept a grocery at Drummondville, near Niagara Falls. Within a year after his enlargement he had occasion to visit Buffalo on business matters. He was recognized and maltreated by ruffians on the street, and narrowly escaped bodily injury. He made repeated applications to the Imperial Government for compensation for the losses and indignities to which he had been subjected. His applications were supported by the authorities here, and were finally suc-

---

more strongly. "McLeod will now take his trial, and his conviction or acquittal will depend altogether on the political opinions of the judge and jury. If they are Whigs he will be acquitted; if Loco-foco he will be found guilty. The merits of the case, or the acknowledged fact that he was no more at the burning of the *Caroline* than I was, will not weigh a feather in the scale, either way. Read Judge Cowan's [? Cowen's] judgment on the point of law! And the same thing exactly would happen if the case were carried either before the Senate of New York or the Supreme Court of the United States. What a people—what a country!" *Ib.*, p. 237.

cessful in obtaining for him a grant of £200 per annum, which he thenceforward continued to receive during the remainder of his life. For some years before his death he resided in the immediate neighbourhood of Niagara Falls. He died of paralysis on the 27th of September, 1871. A pension of £100 per annum has been continued to his widow, who still resides with the younger members of her family in the house in which he died.

At the time of McLeod's discharge, Lord Sydenham had been dead nearly a month, and many eyes were anxiously turned across the Atlantic to see what manner of personage was to be sent over as his successor.

Chapter IX.

SIR CHARLES BAGOT.

Bolingbroke. Call forth Bagot.
—King Richard II., Act IV., sc. 1.

Jaques. He hath been a courtier, he swears.
Touchstone. If any man doubt that, let him put me to my purgation.
—As You Like It, Act V., sc. 4.

HERE were no political events of much importance in Canada between the death of Lord Sydenham and the arrival of his successor. It was known before the close of the year that the new Governor-General was to be the Right Honourable Sir Charles Bagot, who had been appointed to that office on the 7th of October. Intelligence of the birth of the Prince of Wales on the 9th of November reached Canada soon afterwards, and the public seemed to take as lively an interest in the one item of news as in the other. For a week or two, indeed, the news of the Governor's appointment may almost be said to have been cast into the shade. The birth of an heir-apparent to the British throne was too important an event to be lightly passed over by the loyal population of Canada. Even the French in the Lower Province thought it incumbent upon them to mark the event by more or less enthusiastic demonstrations. Festivities were held in Montreal and Quebec, as well as in many of the towns and villages of the Upper Province. Then public attention began to be directed to the personality of the new viceroy, who, it was announced, had sailed from Falmouth for New York on the

23rd of November, in the line-of-battle ship *Illustrious*, of seventy-four guns.

Sir Charles Bagot was a member of an old aristocratic Staffordshire family, the head of which was in 1780 created first Baron Bagot, of Bagot's Bromley, Stafford, in the peerage of Great Britain.* Sir Charles was the second son of this staunch old Tory Baron. On his mother's side he was descended from Viscount St. John, brother and heir of the brilliant and dissolute Minister of Queen Anne, declared by Pope to be the first writer, as well as the greatest man of his age, but characterized by Dr. Johnson in much less flattering terms.† Sir Charles had left school in early youth, owing to the feebleness of his constitution, and had been bred to a diplomatic career. He had inherited the political proclivities of his ancestors, and had throughout his life been identified with the most pronounced high-Toryism. His physical constitution being weakly, and his intellect not above the average, his rise had not been rapid, though his industry and ambition had enabled him to make his way surely and steadily in the public service. In 1806 he became Under Secretary of State for Foreign affairs. On the 22nd of July in the same year he married Lady Mary Charlotte Anne Wellesley, eldest daughter of William Lord Maryborough, late Earl of Mornington. In 1814, when he was thirty-three years of age, he acquitted himself creditably of a special mission to Paris. He was subsequently a Minister Plenipotentiary to the United States, and

---

* A baronetcy had existed in the family for more than a century and a half, the chief representative having been created by King Charles the First, in 1627. An ancestor of Sir Charles probably went over to England with the Conqueror, as the name is undoubtedly Norman, and when Domesday Book was compiled a Bagot was in possession of the estate of Bagot's Bromley.

† "Sir, he was a scoundrel, and a coward: a scoundrel for charging a blunderbuss against religion and morality; a coward because he had not resolution to fire it off himself, but left half-a-crown to a beggarly Scotchman, to draw the trigger after his death."—See Croker's edition of Boswell's "Life of Johnson," Vol. II., p. 15. The "beggarly Scotchman" alluded to was David Mallet.

again acquitted himself entirely to the satisfaction of the Government of the day. An embassy to the Russian Court, and another to the Hague, were successively undertaken by him, and though his discharge of his official duties on both occasions was such as to gain for him additional respect, his health was completely broken down by his labours, and he was compelled to retire for a time from the diplomatic service. He was offered several lucrative and honourable appointments—one of them being the Governor-Generalship of India—but was compelled to decline them on the score of his continued feeble health. In 1834 he was sufficiently recovered to undertake an important mission to the Court of Austria, the objects of which he accomplished with credit to himself and to the Government which he represented. In recognition of his public services he was created Knight Grand Cross of the Bath. During the tenure of office of Lord Melbourne's Administration he does not seem to have been conspicuously before the public in any capacity; but upon Sir Robert Peel's accession to power in 1841 he again came to the front. The important post of Governor-General of Canada was offered to him by the Colonial Secretary, Lord Stanley. Being at that time in what, for him, was considered a remarkably good state of health, he accepted the offer, and, as has been seen, started for his destination in November. At the date of his appointment he had just passed his sixtieth birthday, and notwithstanding the fact that he had always been delicate, he looked considerably younger than his years.

The *Illustrious*, with Sir Charles and his suite on board, was delayed by heavy weather and contrary winds, and did not reach the quarantine ground off New York until the last day but one of the year. It was remarked at the time that she was the first line-of-battle ship that had reached that port since the close of the Revolutionary War. In consequence of the tempestuous weather that prevailed, Sir Charles did not disembark until the afternoon

of the day following his arrival. Mr. Jefferson Brick, or some
American journalist of his kidney, would seem to have been in full
force on the occasion, for a New York newspaper of the next day
contained minute accounts of the appearance and movements of the
"haughty aristocrat of an effete monarchy." The public were
informed that Sir Charles Bagot's retinue of servants was large
enough to colonize one of the western territories, and that the
luggage of himself and his suite weighed exactly forty-two tons.
Two cumbrous-looking, awkwardly-made English carriages, it was
said, formed part of this rather formidable array of personal
belongings, and it was suggested that the vehicles had doubtless
been imported under the belief that such things were unprocur-
able on this side the Atlantic. The searching criticism of this
"journalist of the period" did not prevent the suitable entertainment of the distinguished visitor by some of the leading personages
of New York. Sir Charles proceeded to Canada by way of Boston
and Albany. He left New York on the 4th of January, and reached
Boston on the morning of the 5th. In the course of that day he
attended the session of the Massachusetts Legislature, and also
visited the Navy Yard. From the *Boston Atlas* of Friday, the 7th,
we learn that "On Wednesday evening (the 5th) Mr. Grattan* gave
a party at his house in Franklin Street to the Governor-General and
his suite, at which were present his Excellency Governor Davis, his
Honour Lieutenant-Governor Hull, the President of the Senate, the
Mayor of the city, and other public functionaries and distinguished
citizens." He left Boston on the morning of the 6th, and proceeded
by way of Albany, Utica and Watertown, crossing the St. Lawrence
River at Cape Vincent. The citizens of the States of Massachusetts
and New York were very attentive to him all along the route, and
he did not reach Kingston until the afternoon of Monday, the 10th.

* The British Consul.

A very hospitable and flattering reception was accorded to him at the Canadian capital. In compliance with his own request there was no formal public reception, but the people of Kingston and the country thereabouts turned out in great numbers, in sleighs and on foot. The Kingston correspondent of the *Montreal Gazette* describes the arrival at some length. The Governor-General is referred to as a striking specimen of the fine old English gentleman, of about middle stature, with a pleasing and rather handsome countenance, and noble forehead. "His hair," said the writer, "is gray, and he is somewhat bald. He is, on the whole, a fine-looking man, and well calculated to grace, by his presence, the Colonial Court of his Sovereign." *

On the day before his arrival an express had been despatched to Toronto, to summon three of the judges of the Court of Queen's Bench to Kingston, for the purpose of administering the oath of office to the Governor. Immediately upon receipt of the summons Chief Justice Robinson and the two puisné judges—Jonas Jones and Archibald Maclean—set off on their journey. They reached their destination on the night of Tuesday, the 11th, and at one o'clock in the afternoon of the day following, his Excellency was duly sworn into office at Government House. The conclusion of the ceremony was announced by a salvo of artillery, and Sir Charles Bagot was, *de facto* as well as *de jure*, Governor-General of British North America. He forthwith proceeded to hold his first levee, when a great number of persons availed themselves of the opportunity to pay their respects. The road from the town to Alwington House was thronged with sleighs until the early winter nightfall, by which time his Excellency had become personally acquainted, not only

---

* "Of course," adds this correspondent, at the end of his letter, "all is in the dark, as yet, as to declaration, policy, instructions, etc. We have had plenty of rumours about town for the last few days to the effect that the Seat of Government will be removed from this place; but these rumours, many 'old heads' think, are got up by intending purchasers to influence intending sellers."

with all the principal officials, but with all the leading inhabitants
of Kingston and its neighbourhood.* At the close of the levee an
address was presented to the Governor on behalf of the people of
Kingston, congratulating him upon his appointment, and expressive
of their trust and confidence in him. His Excellency briefly responded, and the day, officially speaking, was at an end. A proclamation was issued, announcing the assumption of the Government
by his Excellency, and continuing "all and singular Her Majesty's
Officers and Ministers in the said Province of Canada" in their
several offices. Sir Richard Jackson, glad enough to be relieved of
the responsibility of office, surrendered his functions, and proceeded
to Montreal.

Sir Charles having all his life been an ultra Tory, many Canadian
politicians regarded it as probable that he would reverse much of
Lord Sydenham's policy, and adopt one of a much more Conservative
cast. The Reformers contemplated the proposed change with much
apprehension. The rump of the Family Compact, as was natural
enough, contemplated it with ill-concealed gratification. The members of both parties reckoned without their host. Sir Charles Bagot,
old-fashioned Tory as he was, had learned the trade of politics in a
constitutional school. The lessons of his past diplomatic career now
proved of incalculable service to him. Allusion has been made to his
mission to the Hague. That mission had involved intricate negotiations having reference to the consolidation of the union between
the two little states of Holland and Belgium. Sir Charles had then
been brought face-to-face with various questions closely analogous
to those involved in the union of Upper and Lower Canada. The
analogy, indeed, extended so far as to be nearly complete. In each
case there was a difference of race, of religion, and of language. In

---

* "His Excellency looked remarkably well, and was dressed in a splendid uniform,
richly decorated with silver. He was surrounded by an unusually brilliant staff."—
Kingston correspondent of the *Montreal Gazette*, January 12th, 1842.

each case there was an equality of representation, combined with a disproportionate population. In each case there was a large public debt on the part of the less populous division, which was imposed equally upon the solvent and more populous one. In each case a powerful policeman stood at the threshold, ready to take advantage of any complication which might justify his interference in the domestic affairs; ready, indeed, to take bodily possession upon any plausible pretext. Such a state of things required a cool and prudent judgment on the part of the head of the household. Sir Charles proved equal to the occasion. He was wise enough to learn from the signal example of King William of Holland, and to avoid falling into errors similar to those which had been committed by that monarch almost under his own eye.

His Belgic experiences had probably been the factor which had weighed with Lord Stanley in determining to send him over to Canada. At any rate, Sir Charles did credit to the Colonial Secretary's choice. He manifested a wise discretion, and carefully abstained from identifying himself with any party or clique. He felt that he had been sent over to Canada to administer a constitutional Government, and not to indulge his own political likings or predilections. Lord Stanley was no hard and fast friend to Responsible Government, but as Responsible Government had been expressly conceded to the Canadians he—at all events for the time—showed a proper respect for the acts of his predecessor, and issued his instructions to the new Governor-General accordingly. Upon those instructions Sir Charles Bagot uniformly acted throughout the term of his Administration. Strong efforts were vainly made by the rival parties to draw him this way or that. It was not possible to extract from him even an expression of his individual preference. Addresses were presented to him in which he was personally referred to as a staunch member of "that great Conservative party now entrusted with the Administration of the affairs of the British

Empire." His Excellency, as a matter of course, replied with his characteristic blandness and courtesy to such flattering effusions, but resolutely declined to commit himself. He even went the length of calling on all Her Majesty's loyal subjects to lay aside their political differences, and to coöperate with him in a common effort to promote the internal prosperity and happiness of the Province, and to strengthen the bonds which united it to the mother country.* He worked with praiseworthy assiduity, and devoted himself to studying the Canadian question in all its bearings. He had much to learn, for prior to his appointment his mind had been turned in other directions, and had been little better than a blank as to everything relating to British North America.

He dealt out even-handed justice to all parties. His appointments to office were marked by such perfect impartiality that he seemed to the Tories to be guided largely by caprice in his selections. But in reality there was nothing of caprice about the matter. On the contrary, there was much of prudent conscientiousness, and of desire to govern according to the well-understood wishes of the majority. By this discreet method of procedure he soon inspired a large measure of popular confidence. The conviction was forced upon the public mind that for the future the land was to be governed according to the principles of domestic, and not of trans-Atlantic, policy.† He was especially complaisant to the French Canadians, who, he felt, had had scant justice doled out to them by his predecessor, and whose cause was espoused by the advanced wing of the Reform party in both Provinces. The only members of the community who, as a class, openly resented this system of administration, were the

---

* See his Excellency's reply to an address from the inhabitants of Hamilton and its vicinity, presented at Kingston on the 27th of January, 1841, and published in the newspapers of the period.

† See "Some Remarks upon Sir Charles Bagot's Canadian Government," by the Rev. Dr. (Egerton) Ryerson ; Kingston, 1843.

Tories, by some of whom the Governor was accused of having abetted the rebellion *ex post facto*.

Sir Charles had made a very favourable impression upon the people of the United States during his embassy to Washington some years before; and his recent passage through their country on his way to Canada had revived his name in the public mind. The press of New York and Boston congratulated the Canadians upon having a gentleman at the head of affairs who knew something of the working of American institutions, and who, though he had been reared according to the straitest doctrines of high Toryism, had sufficient breadth of mind to appreciate some of the features of a republican form of government. The leading exponent of cultivated public opinion in New England congratulated the people of the United States upon the possession of a friendly neighbour.* Other prominent periodicals contrasted Sir Charles Bagot's demeanour towards the United States with that of Lord Sydenham, and the contrast was always made to appear very much to the latter's disfavour. Such things were indicative of the tone of public opinion across the border, and were not without importance, in view of the current disputes between the States and Great Britain. Those disputes were kept prominently before the public mind by certain injudicious acts on the part of American citizens. The McLeod episode having come to an end, it might have been hoped that the peace of two great nations would not again be endangered by any repetition of such an absurdity. In the early spring of 1842, however, Mr. John Sheridan Hogan, an Irish Canadian journalist, and a resident of Hamilton, was arrested at Rochester on a charge of

---

* "It is matter of satisfaction to every good citizen of the United States, that this critical trust [the Governor-Generalship of Canada] has fallen into the hands of one who is represented by those who know him best to be honourable, able and conciliatory; combining qualities of head and heart which fit him to be not only a good Governor, but, what is full as important in the present aspect of affairs, a good neighbour."—*North American Review* for January, 1842.

having been concerned in the destruction of the *Caroline* and the murder of Durfee. After an examination before a magistrate he was set at liberty, and he forthwith returned to Canada. He soon afterwards had occasion to pay another visit to Rochester, when he was again arrested on the same charge. His second arrest was due to the machinations of Doctor—or "General," as he styled himself—Edward Alexander Theller, a mendacious Irish American who had taken part with the insurgents in 1837 and '38, and had himself been a prisoner in Canada.* After being subjected to a vexatious delay, Mr. Hogan was again discharged from custody, and he once more returned to Canada, where a tragical fate awaited him.† He put in a claim for indemnity, but it was ignored, and the only compensation he ever received for the indignities to which he had been subjected was the notoriety which for a time attached to his name. A few months later, McLeod himself, as narrated in the last chapter, was subjected to contumely and ill-treatment on the streets of

---

*Theller was confined as a prisoner at Quebec for some time. He made his escape—probably through the connivance of one of his guards—and afterwards wrote a book called "Canada in 1837-38, showing the Causes of the attempted Revolution, and of its Failure, together with the personal adventures of the author." It was published at Philadelphia in two small 8vo volumes in 1841. As a narrative it is not deficient in interest, but as a contribution to history it is utterly untrustworthy, the writer's mendacity and want of judgment being constantly apparent. As he had a good many acquaintances in Canada, and as some curiosity may be felt as to his subsequent career, the following facts may be not uninteresting. Some years after the publication of his work on the Canadian rebellion Dr. Theller removed to California, where he engaged in journalism, and became Superintendent of Public Schools. He died at Hornitos, California, in 1859.

†Sixteen years after his imprisonment at Rochester, Mr. Hogan (who had meanwhile removed from Hamilton to Toronto, and become well known as a vigorous writer for the press) was returned in the Reform interest to the old Canadian Assembly, as member for the county of Grey. His ability was undoubted, and he made a more than average mark in Parliament. One dark night in the month of December, 1859, he was murdered by a gang of ruffians whom he encountered on the bridge crossing the River Don, in the eastern part of Toronto. His body was cast into the river, and no clue was obtained as to his mysterious disappearance until the discovery of his remains, more than a year afterwards. His Prize Essay on Canada was a well-known pamphlet in its day, and received high praise from the Canadian press.

Buffalo. Such occurrences as these did not tend to increase the goodwill of the Canadian people to their neighbours; but the cordial relations existing between the Governor-General and the authorities at Washington doubtless had a perceptible influence for good.

For some months, however, Sir Charles had quite enough to do to familiarize himself with internal affairs. The strain which had been inevitable ever since the Union now began to make itself felt. The task before Sir Charles Bagot was of a very different nature from that which his predecessor had assigned to himself, and was one scarcely less difficult. Lord Sydenham had to introduce a new constitution, but no sooner had he set it fairly in motion than the sceptre dropped from his hands by death. It was his successor's part to keep up the motion, and this, under the circumstances, could hardly be done without some friction.* Lord Sydenham's Administration had been calculated to serve his Lordship's own immediate purposes, and not to stand the whips and scorns of time.† It had

---

* "Lord Sydenham had a Constitution of Government to establish : Sir Charles Bagot had a system of Government to work. Lord Sydenham had two Provinces to unite : Sir Charles Bagot had two Provinces to cement. The former had an Administration to create : the latter had an Administration to establish. The one had to inspire the country with hope and confidence : the other had to inspire it with charity and enterprise."—"Some Remarks upon Sir Charles Bagot's Canadian Government," by the Rev. Dr. Ryerson ; Kingston, 1843.

† "It was a good Cabinet for Lord Sydenham, who was his own Prime Minister, and a capital manager of colleagues ; but for a Governor-General who wishes to play the easy part of Representative of the Crown, and therefore to govern through responsible Ministers, or for one who would govern in person, but who possesses neither the Canadian experience, nor the active, fagging, managing qualities of Lord Sydenham, the Executive Council which Lord Sydenham left is a most defective instrument. Everybody is satisfied that it cannot last six months in the state in which Lord Sydenham left it. Then why, you may ask, not form another, as we should do in such a case at home, of men able to command a majority in the Assembly ? Because, the answer is, there is not, in the first place, any preponderating party in the Assembly ; and, secondly, the new Governor-General has come here an utter stranger to the country, and could not by himself find out which was the preponderating party, if there were one. With some mending Lord Sydenham's Council may perhaps enjoy, more than any other set of men, the confidence

been his policy to break down—or at any rate to *keep* down—every
darty but his own, and the consequence was that before he had been
many weeks in his grave there was no strongly preponderating
party in the country. The Cabinet, as has been seen, was composed
of heterogeneous materials, and wanted coherence. A similar
characteristic prevailed in the Assembly itself. The only approximately coherent party there was the French Canadian party; and
their coherence was due to the simple fact that they *were* French
Canadians. By themselves, they were a hopeless minority. Their
dreams of a separate nationality had been dispelled. The Union
had been forced upon them by Lord Sydenham. How then could
it be expected that they would not unite in condemnation of Lord
Sydenham's policy, and in distrust of his Ministry which had
survived him. That Ministry had contrived to command a safe
working majority all through the first session, but it was already
doubtful if it could hold together through the first half of a second.
There was, moreover, no good reason for the existence of a Cabinet
so dubiously constituted. It was certain that when the House
should next be called together there would be clamour from the
French Canadian members, and a demand that some of their own
nationality should be admitted to take part in directing the Councils
of the State. In this demand they would most certainly be seconded
by their allies, the advanced Reformers of Upper Canada, who had
gradually attracted to themselves additional support. Their leader,
Mr. Baldwin, was steadily rising in the public esteem, and would
doubtless make his presence sensibly felt upon the meeting of
Parliament. The Governor-General accepted the situation without

---

of the Assembly; but.at this moment they would not have a majority; and if they were
dismissed in a body there is not another set of men who could get beyond a small minority
of followers among the representatives of the people. Sir C. Bagot will have trouble
enough in mending effectually, without troubling himself to destroy and reconstruct."—
EDWARD GIBBON WAKEFIELD, in a letter dated 26th January, 1842, published in the
Colonial Gazette, London.

a qualm. He resolved to govern the country according to the letter and tenor of his instructions. Whatever set of men should be proved to have the support of a majority in the Assembly, that set of men should be his Ministers; and he was not to be moved from this resolution by foolish diatribes against Radicals and ex-rebels. If the country preferred to be governed by Radicals and ex-rebels, so much the worse for the country (perhaps), but that was simply none of his business. His business was to see that the constitutional principle of governing by means of a Parliamentary majority was carried out. Where the Parliamentary majority would be could not, of course, be known to a certainty until the meeting of the Houses, which were summoned for the 8th of September.

Meanwhile his Excellency devoted his energies to practical subjects connected with the internal welfare of the country. He gave directions for the immediate construction of various public works, and spent much time in conference with Mr. Killaly, who had been appointed President of the Board of Works a few months before. He urged upon the President the immediate construction of good roads, and showed more insight into the economic necessities of the country than could have been expected from one whose life had been chiefly passed in courts, and in the mazes of diplomacy. He declared that in a country like Canada good roads should actually precede settlement in all the best agricultural districts. Well-built highways, he said, would pay for their construction in very few years, besides opening up to the farmers a readily-accessible market for their produce. During the spring he visited Toronto, where a warm and even ostentatious welcome awaited him, and where, on the 23rd of April, he laid the foundation-stone of King's College. The following month he paid a visit to Montreal, in time to hold an imposing levee on Her Majesty's birthday. His Excellency spent several weeks in Montreal, during which period he formed the acquaintance of many leading French Canadians, as well as of all the most prominent members of the old British party not previously known to him. He left for the east on the 22nd of June, and, after a brief stay at Sorel, or William Henry, at the mouth of the Richelieu, he proceeded by steamer down the St. Lawrence to Quebec. His reception by the inhabitants of the old metropolis of Canada was most enthusiastic. Addresses poured in upon him from numerous bodies of French Canadians, in many of which warm testimony was borne to the high sense entertained by the signatories and their fellow-countrymen of his perfect impartiality and justice in the distribution of official favours.

His Excellency remained at Quebec until early in August. Towards the end of July he was joined by Lady Mary Bagot* and his daughters, whom he had not seen for more than eight months, and who had just arrived from England by way of Halifax. Before proceeding westward her Ladyship held a Drawing-Room in the old Parliament buildings. It was attended without distinction of race or party, by representatives of nearly every prominent family in Quebec. Her Excellency and her daughters won golden opinions from all by their sweet and gracious affability, and by their evident desire to establish kindly relations with the Canadian people.† Equally pleasant was the impression made by her Ladyship at Montreal and Kingston; and at the present day there are venerable old dowagers—they were fair young maidens forty years ago—who

---

* She is called simply "Lady Bagot" in the Canadian newspapers of the day, but, as has been seen (ante, p.180) she was the daughter of an Earl, and as such she preserved her own rank, and was entitled to be called "Lady Mary Bagot."

† "One general expression of congratulation is heard, that the Province has now at the head of society the Lady of the Governor-General, accompanied by a family of daughters, who cannot fail in giving a tone to the manners of her circle, which will shed the most beneficial influence on the manners and morals of that numerous class who borrow their examples from the great, and are prone to fashion their conduct on the example set by their superiors in station, more especially of those who hold the first position in the land."—*Quebec Mercury.*

think and speak of Lady Mary Bagot as the most queenly and accomplished woman who has ever been seen in Canadian society in their time.

On the 18th of July a proclamation was issued by authority, summoning the Provincial Parliament to meet for the despatch of public business on the 8th of September. Certain changes, to be more particularly referred to in a future chapter, had meanwhile taken place in the composition of the Ministry, and still further modifications had become inevitable. There were rumours, too, that the seat of Government was to be changed, and that the ensuing session would be the last held at Kingston. It was hinted that the Governor intended to establish the Provincial capital at Montreal. Others suggested that there would probably be alternate sessions of Parliament at Toronto and Quebec. On this subject, however, no one was likely to have any definite information until the opening of the session. Before the day appointed for the meeting of the Legislature, the public mind was for a time engrossed by an event of considerable importance in Canadian history. On the 9th of August the Ashburton Treaty was concluded and signed at Washington.

Chapter X.

THE ASHBURTON TREATY.

"At this date, we look back with bewilderment at the extraordinary series of negotiations which ended in the establishment of the Maine boundary,—a result which converted undoubted British territory into foreign soil, which alienated the allegiance of thousands of British subjects, without their consent, and which made a direct connection on our own soil, between Central Canada and the Atlantic, an impossibility. . . . No Canadian can reflect, without pain and humiliation, on the sacrifice of British interests in the settlement that was made. . . The Imperial authorities recognize the lesson taught by the Ashburton Treaty, in adopting the policy of the federation of the British American Provinces, and in acting on the principle that no Canadian interest shall hereafter be discussed in Imperial negotiations without the presence of a Dominion representative." SANDFORD FLEMING, C.E. : *The Intercolonial ;* a Historical Sketch, pp. 234, 235.

"If not immediately, at least in the not distant future, the historian of the American Union, reviewing dispassionately its relations with this country, will do justice to the moderation displayed by English diplomatists, though it has hitherto had no other effect than to encourage pertinacity and to enlarge pretensions."—*Westminster Review*, January, 1862.

REFERENCE has more than once been made in these pages to the disputes between Great Britain and the United States. The *Caroline* imbroglio has already been discussed at sufficient length. The other causes of dispute were various, and involved, *inter alia*, the right of Great Britain to board and search American vessels which were believed to be engaged in the slave-trade. As matter of fact, no such *right* was claimed by Great Britain, nor would there have been any legal justification for the claim. The right could exist only by the rules of international law, or by the mutual agreement of the two nations. With respect to the former, international law recognizes no such right; and there was no compact between Great Britain and the United States whereby any such privilege was conceded to either party. By the Treaty of Ghent, however, which terminated the invasion known to our history as the War of 1812, and which was executed on the 24th of December, 1814, the traffic in slaves was declared to be irreconcilable with the principles of humanity and justice. It was mutually agreed between Great Britain and the United States that they would use their best endeavours to accomplish the abolition of the slave-trade. The Congress at Washington subsequently imposed the penalties of piracy on any citizen of the republic who might be caught engaging in it. But when Great Britain proposed to enter into an arrangement with the States whereby representatives of each of the contracting parties should have the right to board and search merchant vessels sailing on the coast of Africa, and flying the flag of the other, the Washington Government returned an elaborately-worded refusal. Great Britain had already made treaties with the chief maritime states of Europe whereby the right of search was mutually conceded, and her seamen were in the habit of exercising it. This, of course, was not done upon the assumption that "Britannia rules the waves," but in the interests of humanity, and under the provisions of specific treaty. In some instances, notwithstanding the absence of any such treaty with the United States, the vessels of that nation were boarded and searched in like manner, and sometimes with the happiest results to the cause of humanity, for the boldest and cruelest slavers were fitted out from New Orleans and Charleston. These vessels, be it understood, were not boarded as American vessels, but as slave-traders. American ships employed for legitimate purposes, and known or believed to be so employed, were never interfered with. But it was an all but universal practice for slavers to sail under United States colours, and when the captain of a British man-of-war, cruising along the African coast or the Mosquito shore, encountered a craft which he had good reason to believe to be engaged in the slave-trade, he was not always deterred from boarding her by the mere fact that she hoisted the stars and stripes. This the United States Government would not tolerate.* Congress remonstrated; Britain replied. It was in vain that British diplomatists pointed out the anomaly that the most notorious slaver might ply his infamous traffic with impunity by simply taking the precaution to keep a set of United States flags in his cabin. Nay, as a matter of strict legal right, if the captain of an English cruiser found a slaver *in flagrante delicto*, loading her cargo of human freight, he could not interfere, provided the trafficker in flesh and blood ran up what was currently known among sailors as "Jonathan's Gridiron" to his mast-head. As may readily be conceived, such a state of things was fruitful in grounds for quarrel. The diplomatic correspondence on the subject would fit out a small library, but in the beginning of the year 1842 no satisfactory adjustment of the question had been arrived at.

The refusal of Great Britain to surrender American slaves who had once gained a footing on English soil was also a cause of offence in the eyes of the Government at Washington. No matter by what means—stress of weather, accident, underground railway, or what not—the slave contrived to "touch one dust of England's ground," the shackles fell from his limbs, and he was a slave no longer, but a man. He was a man, clothed with certain rights and responsibilities as a member of society, and there was no power on earth that could infringe the majesty of his manhood with impunity. And for such a purpose any British colony, or the deck of any British ship, no

---

* "In the interests of humanity we, at great cost, keep up a cruising squadron on the coast of Africa. . . . A suspicious vessel heaves in sight; the captain of a British man-of-war believes that she is a slaver. She hoists the American colours; but any pirate may do this; and in order to ascertain her genuine character she is boarded; and when it is discovered that she really is an American ship, she is instantly allowed to proceed on her way. But the United States Government would not allow this. Their flag is sacred, and covers the ship and all that it contains. They would permit no visitation except at our own peril; and if we persisted they would go to war."—*Quarterly Review*, Vol. CXI., p. 262.

matter where situated, was English ground. Of course, if the slave had committed murder or felony—otherwise than in winning his way to freedom—there was a more or less righteous claim for his surrender; but if he was surrendered it was not as a slave but as a criminal—as an offender against the law of nature, and a fugitive from justice. There had been many remonstrances from Washington on this subject in past times, but they had almost ceased before the year 1842, for this was the one and only question on which the British mind had long been fully made up. England would not even condescend to discuss the question. On that rock she took her stand, and there was no power in diplomacy potent enough to shift her from her position. This fact had come to be pretty generally recognized by the American people. "It is idle," said an American writer, in 1841, "to imagine that England will ever be brought so much as to entertain a question upon that point. Her determination that whoever sets foot upon her soil shall be free, is without doubt irrevocable, and beyond the power of any coercion to shake it."* In this respect Massachusetts, Ohio, and other free States of the Union emulated, so far as they were able, England's noble example; but under the Federal Constitution they were bound to surrender *fugitive* slaves.

There was, moreover, no satisfactory arrangement between Great Britain and the United States as to the mutual extradition of criminals. By Jay's Treaty, signed in London on the 19th of November, 1794, provision had been made for the surrender of murderers and forgers, but it had been stipulated that the article containing the proviso should remain in force only twelve years—a term which had long since expired. With regard to all the other crimes in the calendar no provision for extradition had ever been made, a circumstance fraught with great inconvenience and injury to

---

* *North American Review*, October, 1841.

the cause of justice in the case of the States and Canada, lying side by side, and having an almost interminable frontier.

But the crowning apple of discord was the boundary question. There had for many years been a conflict of opinion between English and American diplomatists as to the true location of the boundary-line between New Brunswick and the State of Maine. By the Treaty of Peace, ratified at Paris on the 3rd of September, 1783, this line had not been defined with sufficient accuracy, and its precise whereabouts had thus been left an open question. It was provided that the frontier should begin "from the north-west angle of Nova Scotia, viz., that angle which is formed by a line drawn due north from the source of St. Croix River to the highlands; along the said highlands which divide those rivers that empty themselves into the St. Lawrence from those which fall into the Atlantic Ocean to the northwesternmost head of Connecticut River; thence down along the middle of that river to the forty-fifth degree of north latitude," etc., etc. This mysterious clause—mysterious to future generations of American politicians, who only wished to understand it in one way; though it was doubtless intelligible enough to its framers—this mysterious clause, we repeat, proved well-nigh as prolific of argumentative dispute as erstwhile did the famous Statute of Frauds. What was meant by the rivers "which fall into the Atlantic Ocean?" Was the application restricted to those streams which flowed directly into the ocean, or were the northern tributaries to be included? Especially, were the northern tributaries of the St. John included in the designation? Where was the northwest angle of Nova Scotia? Nay, where was the St. Croix River? For, strange as the assertion may seem, the geography of that region was so little known in 1783 that almost as soon as the ink was dry upon the Treaty, a dispute arose as to which of three rivers was intended to be designated by that name. It was not till Jay's Treaty was signed eleven years afterwards that the spot indicated by the words "the source of the St. Croix River" was definitely ascertained, whereupon a monument was erected to mark the place for the enlightenment of future generations.

But these were not the only anomalies. It was even doubtful what precise locality was meant by "the northwesternmost head of Connecticut River." Again, was the boundary-line to be drawn north of the upper bend of the St. John River, or south? New Brunswick, which became a separate Province in 1784, the year following that in which the Treaty of Peace was made, contended for the latter construction. Maine took the opposite view, and was backed in her contention by the entire diplomatic ability of the republic. By the Treaty of Ghent an attempt was made to adjust the dispute by the appointment of Commissioners to make a map and agree upon a boundary. The attempt ended in confusion worse confounded. The Commissioners were compelled to relinquish the task as hopeless, neither side being willing to give up its convictions to the other. And there, for a time, the matter rested. Meanwhile the absence of any clearly-defined boundary gave rise to periodical quarrels, and even to skirmishes, between the inhabitants along the frontier. In 1818, 1826, and 1827, there were further vain attempts at adjustment. There was also an attempt at arbitration, which signally failed. When the Commissioners under the Treaty of Ghent had found themselves unable to arrive at any decision they had, under the authority of a clause in the Treaty, referred the matter to the King of the Netherlands. His Majesty accepted the reference, and went into the question with praiseworthy industry, and an honest desire to do justice in the premises. Representatives of each of the contending parties repaired to the Hague, and presented their respective views, supported by a formidable array of maps and documents. All to no purpose. On the 10th of January, 1831, His Majesty of the Netherlands delivered what he was pleased to call his award. The document was a conclusive proof of his inability to grapple with the complicated questions involved. His

Majesty pronounced judgment on only two out of the three points submitted to him, and as to the third declared that there was no evidence to guide him to a decision. He however endeavoured to adjust the matter by proposing a new boundary-line which had not been suggested by either of the parties, and which was a mere conventional compromise. Great Britain professed her willingness to acquiesce, but the Legislature of the State of Maine, as well as the Senate of the United States, declined the proposal, and the question seemed to be no nearer to a settlement than before.

There the matter rested for more than two years. In 1833, while Lord Palmerston held the office of Secretary of State for Foreign Affairs in Earl Grey's Government, a proposition for a settlement was submitted on the part of General Jackson, President of the United States. The proposition seems to have been liberal enough—so liberal, indeed, that it was in after years denounced by an able American statesman—Albert Gallatin—on the ground that it conceded altogether too much to Great Britain. "Why the proposal was made, and why it was not accepted," wrote Mr. Gallatin, "cannot be otherwise accounted for, so far at least as regards the offer, than by a complete ignorance of the whole subject."* Lord Palmerston, however, thought proper to reject the proposal, and matters along the frontier went on from bad to worse. Innumerable diplomatic communications passed to and fro between the two Governments, but any satisfactory adjustment seemed as far off as ever. The people along the frontier on both sides began to lose patience, and to assume a warlike attitude. The situation grew more and more unpromising from month to month. In 1842 matters had arrived at such a pass that a settlement could no longer be delayed, if war was to be avoided.

---

* "That the proposal fell to the ground must be attributed entirely to the fact that the Imperial Government declined to concur in it, unless cumbered with conditions which a President of the United States had no power to accept."—*The Intercolonial*, by Sandford Fleming, p. 35.

The Last Forty Years.

Canada since the Union of 1841.

By John Charles Dent.

THE HON. SIR ALEXANDER T. GALT.

ALEXANDER T. GALT.

KAKABEKAH FALLS.

THE HON. ADAM CROOKS.

FALLS OF SHEWANEGAN

The northwestern boundary was another fruitful source of dispute. It attracted less attention than the question respecting the boundary to the northeast, because it had reference to a remote and sparsely-populated region; but the settlements were spreading overland with marvellous celerity, and it was apparent enough that the day of reckoning could not much longer be deferred. All the circumstances being considered, it was not without reason that Canadians, during the first year of the Union, regarded another war with the United States as a not improbable event. In these more modern days of Geneva Arbitrations and Fishery Awards, it seems astonishing that such sources of dispute should have for so many years imperilled the good understanding between the two great English-speaking nations of the world. But the simple fact was that War was at their very doors, and needed only a little hot-headed imprudence on the part of the statesmen of both countries to force her over the threshold.*

In the month of February, 1842, Lord Ashburton was sent out to the United States by Sir Robert Peel's Government as a Special Commissioner, to make one more attempt to settle the various questions in dispute. Lord Ashburton was in some respects well fitted to undertake such a negotiation. He was intimately associated with the United States by commercial and family relations. His connection with the great mercantile and banking house of the Barings, which had long had large dealings on this side of the Atlantic, had rendered it necessary that he should devote much attention to American affairs. In comparatively early life he had

---

* "What is to come of it all? Who can tell? But it does seem as if matters could hardly stand as they are, and that something must come soon. It will be strange undoubtedly, if, in this reasonable nineteenth century, two such nations as Great Britain and the United States shall not be able to see the right as to the questions between them, and be willing to render mutual justice, instead of going to work to harm themselves, while they distress each other, and break the peace of the world."—*North American Review*; October, 1841.

spent some time in the States, had married a lady of Philadelphia, and had written a pamphlet on the subject of international relations between the United States and Great Britain. He was personally acquainted with many of the leading persons of the republic, and had devoted much time to the study of American political and social questions. He had even a certain amount of theoretical sympathy with republican institutions—i.e., he considered them to be, on the whole, very well suited to the United States. He was personally a man of honour and fairmindedness. But there his fitness for his mission ceased. He had had little or no experience in conducting diplomatic negotiations. He was far too complaisant and yielding; too ready to make any man a present of his opinions; too ready to surrender those opinions for the sake of amity and good-fellowship, even when he knew that he was in the right. He lacked an element which is necessary to the success of nearly all complicated diplomacy, and which was peculiarly essential in carrying on an international negotiation with Daniel Webster— namely, downright physical force. Mr. Webster was then Secretary of State, and to him was officially entrusted the task of conducting the negotiation on behalf of the United States Government. His leonine face and figure were an index of his mental constitution. "Faculty" was a quality whereof "the Thunderer of the Senate" possessed a larger share than any American of his time, or probably of any other time. Whenever he bent his powerful mind to the elucidation of any knotty problem in law or politics, it was felt by all parties concerned that there was indeed a Daniel come to judgment. His sonorous, deep-mouthed voice, large presence, and earnest manner, were formidable adjuncts to such rare mental endowments, and Metternich or Talleyrand would have found full employment for all their subtlety if called upon to conduct a negotiation against him.

Lord Ashburton spent some time in the United States before

entering upon the active duties of his mission. The negotiations were not formally commenced until the 17th of June. They extended over nearly two months, and were productive of a definite result. The Ashburton Treaty, as it is generally called,* was concluded and signed on the 9th of August.

By the terms of the Treaty seven-twelfths of the territory in dispute between New Brunswick and Maine, including that portion of the French settlement of Madawaska lying south of the St. John, were ceded to the United States. The remaining five-twelfths, including certain heights commanding the St. Lawrence, fell to the share of Great Britain. The boundary, as then settled, was a purely arbitrary one. It was stipulated that, beginning at the monument already referred to as having been set up at the source of the St. Croix, the line should run thence north to the middle of the river St. John; thence up the middle of the main channel of the stream to the mouth of the St. Francis, and along the middle of the St. Francis and of the lakes through which it flows to the outlet of Lake Pohenagamook; thence southwesterly to the Metjarmette portage, between the head waters of the Penobscot and Chaudière rivers; and thence along the crest of the highlands to the Connecticut.† This arrangement was a compromise, whereby each of the contracting parties professedly yielded something to the other. It must be owned, however, that the compromise bore a striking resemblance to the immortal Irishman's reciprocity, which was all on one side. True, Mr. Webster accepted about five thousand square

---

* Lord Palmerston subsequently stigmatized it by the name of "the Ashburton Capitulation." The treaty was not a masterly stroke of diplomacy on the part of Lord Ashburton, but any reflections upon it come with a singularly bad grace from the statesman who had had such a chance as came to Lord Palmerston in 1833, and who had let it slip.

† The foregoing description of the boundary is not a literal transcript from the Ashburton Treaty, but it gives in few words as much information on the subject as the general reader requires.

miles less of territory than was claimed on behalf of the people of Maine, but the relinquished tract was largely composed of a sterile waste. Lord Ashburton, on his side, gave up a territory nearly equal to the combined areas of the two States of Massachusetts and Connecticut. The greater part of the territory so surrendered is fertile, well-timbered, and favourable, not only to settlement and cultivation, but likewise to the construction of railways.* It included the valley of the Aroostook, which the loggers of Maine have since turned to such profitable account. The navigation of the river St. John was declared to be free and open to both the contracting parties.

A long stretch of the northwestern boundary was also settled by the Ashburton Treaty. The line westward from the Lake of the Woods to the Rocky Mountains had previously been fixed upon, but that from the Lake of the Woods eastward to Lake Superior, and thence through the lakes and rivers to the Neebish Channel, was still more or less open to controversy. Here again the wide-awake

---

* Captain Yule had already made a survey through the ceded territory for a trunk line of railway, to connect Quebec with St. Andrews, on Passamaquoddy Bay, New Brunswick. By that route, as it might, and probably would, but for the cession of the territory by the Ashburton Treaty, have been deflected, Montreal would have been brought within 380 miles of St. Andrews, 415 miles of St. John, and 650 miles of Halifax. The distance from Quebec to St. Andrews "need not have exceeded 250 miles; 67 miles less than to Portland. Fredericton, the seat of local government, would have been on the main line to Halifax, and distant from Montreal about 370 miles; and these lines, moreover, would have been wholly within the limits of the Dominion, had the international boundary been traced according to the true spirit and intent of the Treaty of 1783. The distance between Montreal and Halifax might thus have been lessened nearly 200 miles. St. Andrews would have taken the place of Portland as the winter terminus of the Grand Trunk Railway, and would have commanded, together with St. John, a traffic now cut off from both places, and centred at a foreign port. The direct route would have brought the Springhill coal fields of Nova Scotia some 200 miles nearer to Montreal than by the present line of the Intercolonial, and would have rendered it possible to transport coal by rail at a comparatively moderate cost."—See *The Intercolonial*, by Sandford Fleming, pp. 39, 78. How much nearer the Atlantic would have been to the Pacific if our rights had been preserved in 1842, and, by consequence, how much shorter the route and how much less the cost of constructing the Canada Pacific Railway would have been, are matters not impossible to calculate with some approach to accuracy.

Daniel Webster proved too good a geographer for the British Commissioner. About four millions of acres to the west of Lake Superior, being a tract which had always been claimed by Great Britain, went to satisfy the thrifty appetite of the republic. So also did some large and valuable islands, including Isle Royale, in the northern reaches of Lake Superior, and George's or Sugar Island, in St. Mary's Strait.

The boundary to the west of the Rocky Mountains was not defined, but was left open to become a source of further wrangling and negotiation several years later. By the eighth and ninth articles of the Treaty provision was made for the suppression of the slave-trade. It was stipulated that each of the contracting parties should prepare, equip and maintain on the African coast a naval force of vessels carrying not fewer than eighty guns, "to enforce, separately and respectively, the laws, rights and obligations of each of the two countries for the suppression of the slave-trade." The question respecting right of search was presumed to be tacitly waived by Great Britain during the currency of the Treaty, and has not since been raised by her. The tenth article provided for the extradition of criminals, the offences for which extradition might legally be demanded, however, being much more circumscribed than the geographical situation of the two countries renders desirable. The crimes enumerated were murder, assault with intent to commit murder, piracy, arson, robbery, forgery, and the utterance of forged paper. The arrangement did not, of course, include either fugitive slaves or political offenders. It was agreed that the article referring to extradition should continue in force until one or the other of the parties should signify a wish to terminate it, and no longer.* The twelfth and last article stipu-

---

*The tenth article of the Treaty continued to be acted upon without interruption until the summer of the year 1876, when, owing to a difference of opinion between the two Governments, its operation was temporarily suspended. The facts with reference to this matter will be given in their proper place. Before the close of the year the British Government receded from the position they had taken, and the operation of the tenth

lated that the Treaty should be ratified in London within six months. With respect to the affair of the *Caroline*, which was not referred to in the Treaty, but which formed the subject of prolonged discussion and a voluminous correspondence, Lord Ashburton persisted in the declaration previously made on behalf of the British Government, that the invasion of United States territory on that occasion had been a necessity, owing to the inaction of the State authorities. An acknowledgment of the sacredness of the neutral rights of the people of the United States was however made by his Lordship on the part of Great Britain, and regret was at the same time expressed that any invasion of United States territory on the part of British subjects should have become necessary. This, in plain English, amounted to an apology, and as such it was regarded by all parties concerned. Thereupon the United States waived all claims for reparation, and the *Caroline* imbroglio was at an end.

Such, then, are the most important subjects determined by the Ashburton Treaty. Lord Ashburton himself won great and wide popularity during his sojourn in the republic. The press from one end of the land to the other lavished the most generous laudation upon him.* His Lordship, after his return home, received the thanks of the British Parliament, as well as the congratulations of several representatives of foreign States who were then resident in London.

---

article was restored. For an exposition of the present state of the law of extradition as between Canada and the United States, see *In re Williams*, 7 Ontario Prac. Reports, p. 273. See also, *Regina vs. Browne*, 31 U. C. C. P. Reports, p. 484.

* The following, from the *New York Commercial Advertiser*, is a fair sample of how he was treated by the press of the United States :—" He, too, the distinguished stranger, the Ambassador Extraordinary, who came among us on a mission of peace ; an Englishman, indeed, to the heart's core, yet one who cherished strong attachments to this Republic. A few months of diligent and unremitted attention to his duties have accomplished the object of that mission ; and Lord Ashburton has the highest satisfaction of uniting in cordial pressure the hands of the mother and the daughter. Distinguished stranger, thou art welcome here ; may the blessing promised to the peacemaker rest upon thee." The blessing would probably have been less devoutly invoked if his Lordship had known and firmly insisted upon the undoubted rights of the nation which he represented.

In England, and in British America, the Treaty was subjected to a good deal of hostile criticism from the time when its provisions became known to the public. That Lord Palmerston should find fault with it was not so much to be wondered at; though, considering the opportunity he had thrown away of making a more equitable settlement, prudence, to say nothing of good taste, ought to have dictated forbearance on his part. But the Liberal press generally condemned the Treaty, and declared that Great Britain, and above all Canada, had been shamefully abused in the transaction. Erelong certain facts came to light which did not tend to reconcile the nation to the one-sided bargain. It came out that there had been a *suppressio veri*, and even a *suggestio falsi*, on the part of the American negotiator. Not only had the British contention respecting the northeast boundary been perfectly just and right, but Mr. Webster and some of his compatriots had all along known, or at any rate had had strong reason for believing it to be so. In spite of this knowledge they had refused justice. They had suppressed the facts, and had put forward documents which it is scarcely an abuse of language to call spurious. They had persistently contended for the wrong, and when they had finally triumphed through their adversary's weakness, and from his want of the very information which they possessed, they slyly congratulated each other on the success of their "deal." The *Morning Chronicle* denounced this line of procedure in no studied terms, and characterized it as "a sharp Yankee trick." The present writer is not disposed to call the characterization in question. Moreover, there *is* a point at which a sharp Yankee trick, when played off on the part of a great and powerful nation, and by a statesman of Daniel Webster's intellectual calibre, begins to assume very much the appearance of petty larceny.

The facts may be briefly stated. In the month of February, 1842 —several months before the commencement of the negotiations for the Ashburton Treaty—Mr. Jared Sparks, the American historian and biographer, who was then on a visit to Paris, made an important discovery. While ransacking the *Archives des Affaires Étrangères* for historical materials, he came upon an original letter of Benjamin Franklin, written to the Count de Vergennes, on the 6th of December, 1782, six days after the preliminaries of peace had been signed by the representatives of Great Britain and the United States. Mr. Franklin, it must be borne in mind, was at that date Minister Plenipotentiary from the American Congress to the French Court. He had from the first represented the United States during the negotiation of the Treaty of Peace with Great Britain. No man, therefore, was more likely than he to know what were the precise terms of settlement. His letter to the Count de Vergennes was written in reply to a letter sent by the Count to himself on the previous day. The Count's letter had enclosed a map of North America with a request that Mr. Franklin would mark upon it the boundary-line of the United States, as just settled. This map was returned by Mr. Franklin with the observation that he had complied with the Count's request by marking the boundary with a strong red line.* The letter containing this observation was the one found by Mr. Sparks, who, being familiar with the precise character of the controversy which had long been in progress as to the boundary between Maine and New Brunswick, at once perceived the importance of discovering this map marked by Mr. Franklin's own hand. He proceeded to explore the American division in the geographical department of the archives, and, after a diligent search, found a map of North America by

---

* The following is the text of the letter:

"PASSY, *December 6th, 1782.*

"SIR:

"I have the honour of returning herewith the map your Excellency sent me yesterday. I have marked with a strong red line, according to your desire, the limits of the United States, as settled in the preliminaries between the British and American plenipotentiaries.

"With great respect, I am, etc.,

"B. FRANKLIN."

D'Anville, dated 1746, in size about eighteen inches square, and having *a strong red line* drawn along the boundary of the United States. It tallied exactly with the description in Mr. Franklin's letter. "The line," wrote Mr. Sparks,* "is bold and distinct in every part, made with red ink, and apparently drawn with a hair pencil, or a pen with a blunt point. There is no other colouring on any part of the map." There was thus a very strong probability that the map was the identical one enclosed in Benjamin Franklin's letter, and marked by him for the information of his correspondent. "Upon any other supposition," says Mr. Sparks, "it would be difficult to explain the circumstances of its agreeing so perfectly with his [Franklin's] description, and of its being preserved in the place where it would naturally be deposited by Count de Vergennes." This line of reasoning is plausible enough. Mr. Sparks doubtless felt proud of his discovery, though his complacency may well have been held in check by his perceiving that the red line ran wholly south of the St. John, and between the head waters of that river and those of the Penobscot and Kennebec. "In short," observes Mr. Sparks, "it is exactly the line now contended for by Great Britain, except that it concedes more than is claimed. The north line, after departing from the source of the St. Croix, instead of proceeding to Mars Hill, stops far short of that point, and turns off to the west, so as to leave on the British side all the streams which flow into the St. John, between the source of the St. Croix and Mars Hill. It is evident that the line from the St. Croix to the Canadian highlands is intended to exclude *all the waters* running into the St. John."

These important facts, together with a copy of so much of the map

---

* In a letter to Mr. Senator Rives, Chairman of the United States Committee of Foreign Relations, dated February 15th, 1842. Mr. Rives delivered the letter to the Senate assembled in Secret Session at Washington, on the 17th of August, 1842, only eight days after the signing of the Ashburton Treaty. The Senate subsequently dissolved the injunction of secrecy, and authorized the publication of Mr. Rives's speech on the occasion.

as was necessary to show the Maine boundary, were forthwith communicated to Mr. Webster, who consequently entered upon his negotiations with Lord Ashburton with a full knowledge of Mr. Sparks's discovery. He nevertheless carefully concealed it from his Lordship, and proceeded with the negotiations as though he believed the claims put forward by him to be just and righteous. After the British envoy had yielded nearly everything that grasping selfishness and dishonest greed, as personified in the Maine Commissioners, thought fit to demand, the Senate at Washington hesitated to confirm the arrangement, on the ground that the terms were not sufficiently favourable to Maine. There was no limit to their rapacity.* Some of the members did not even deem it necessary to make any pretence to fair dealing in the matter. Anything gained from Britain, by whatsoever means, was apparently regarded by them as a legitimate spoiling of the Egyptians. Then it was that Mr. Webster—for the sake of "whipping the Senate into line," as one of themselves tersely expressed it—authorized Senator Rives to produce Mr. Sparks's letter and the copy of the map. The argument made use of by the Senator may be thus briefly stated: "If you refuse to ratify this Treaty there will have to be another arbitration. You will then stand a good chance to lose the whole territory in dispute, for no arbitrator, with the present facts before him, will give you an acre of land to the south of the St. John." How little the Senate cared for mere questions of right and wrong was then made clear. They said, in effect: "Never mind what we are in justice entitled to. How much can Britain be coerced into giving us?"

* "The popular feeling in the United States was adverse to retrocession. It was desperately resisted in the American Senate. It involved the still greater family question of State rights. Maine raved like a maniac, and was ready for a free fight with all creation. She defied England, ran a muck at Canada, and shook her impious fist in the face of her own maternal Government. The two countries were brought to the verge of war."—*How Treaty-Making unmade Canada;* a paper read before the Literary and Scientific Society of Ottawa, by Lieut.-Col. Coffin, and reprinted in the *Canadian Monthly* for May, 1876.

Mr. Thomas H. Benton, the senator from Missouri, declared that he had long been aware of the existence of maps which showed the boundary-line as running wholly south of the St. John. He produced a map which, taken by itself, would have gone far to establish Britain's contention. Taken in connection with Mr. Sparks's discovery, it made the British position morally impregnable. It was printed and published at Paris in 1784, the year after the Treaty was signed, and was entitled on its face: "*Carte des Etats Unis de l'Amérique, suivant le traité de paix de 1783.*" It was engraved by Lattré, *graveur du Roi*, and was "dedicated and presented to His Excellency Benjamin Franklin, Minister Plenipotentiary of the United States of America, near the Court of France." Upon comparing it with the copy of the map found by Mr. Sparks, it was found that the two corresponded in every respect. The boundary-line was depicted precisely in accordance with what Great Britain had always claimed.*

Could there have been stronger secondary evidence that by the Treaty of 1783 the boundary-line had been fixed to run wholly south of the St. John River? Yet Mr. Webster, who had all along been in possession of these facts, did not scruple to suppress them. Not only did he suppress them, but he deliberately, and in writing, expressed to Lord Ashburton his confidence in the validity of the American claim. He put forward a map in the accuracy of which he could not have had any confidence, and insisted upon its forming the basis of the boundary. Yet his course was pronounced by one of the leading organs of public opinion to have been "dictated by scrupulous propriety, by usage in similar cases, and by the soundest wisdom and discretion."† The Senate, with a very bad grace, gave

---

* There were various other maps disclosing a similar boundary-line, one of which was produced by Lord Ashburton during the negotiations, but it was not clearly authenticated, and therefore could not be accepted as evidence.

† See *North American Review*, Vol. LVI., p. 479.

up the contest, and consented to accept the terms which Mr. Webster had made on their behalf.

Upon this subject some of our own writers, while admitting—as indeed, cannot be denied—that but scant justice was done to us by the Ashburton Treaty, have gone out of their way to find arguments in Mr. Webster's favour. "It is but fair to state," says Colonel Coffin, " in explanation of the course taken by Daniel Webster, that although, doubtless, the Franklin or 'red-line' map discovered by David *(sic)* Sparks . . was in his hands during these negotiations, this piece of evidence was not conclusive. It afforded strong presumption, but not absolute proof, of the correctness of our claims under the Treaty—claims, however, which we had abandoned when we abandoned the Treaty itself and accepted an arbitration."* The Treaty here referred to is that of 1783 ; and the answer to Colonel Coffin's argument is obvious enough to any one acquainted with the facts. We "abandoned the Treaty"—not because we were dissatisfied with its provisions, or because we had any doubts as to what we were entitled to under it; but because its language was not entirely free from ambiguity, and we were not in a position to prove that our contention was sound. We "accepted an arbitration," in 1818, because the other party to the contract contended for a construction which the language did not legitimately bear, but the correctness of which they professed to be able to prove. They claimed that we were wrong, and deliberately set to work to prove us so, although they had documents in their possession which proved that we were right. These documents were suppressed by them until they had gained an undue advantage, and until an erroneous basis of settlement had been arrived at. So far as to the merits of the controversy itself. To say that there was no "absolute proof of the correctness of our claims" is at best a lame plea. Whether the proof

---

* See Colonel Coffin's paper in the *Canadian Monthly, ubi supra.*

was absolute or partial, both sides should certainly have been placed on an equality as to its reception. But, it is said, an advocate cannot be expected to make out his adversary's case. To which it may be replied that, so far as a suit in a court of law is concerned, this doctrine is unassailable. But in a forum where the judges are the representatives of great nations—nations which claim, and justly claim, to lead the van of humanity and civilization—in such a forum the primary object should be, not to gain an undue advantage for anybody, but to get at the truth, and to do perfect justice. In such a forum, truth and justice demand that the judges should be placed in possession of all the material facts; and in the case under consideration material facts were deliberately concealed by one of the judges from the other.

It is too late, however, to serve any useful purpose by discussing the ethics of the transaction. Lord Ashburton had been authorized to treat with the United States on behalf of Great Britain. He had made a wofully bad bargain, but Britain never dreamed of discrediting her representative. The Treaty was accepted, the ratifications were formally exchanged at London on the 13th of October, and it became the law of the land. The amicable relations between Lord Ashburton and Daniel Webster continued without interruption, and the latter named one of his grandsons in honour of his Lordship. Whatever consolation was to be derived from such a compliment it is to be hoped Lord Ashburton enjoyed, for assuredly there was no other phase of the transaction upon which he had any reason to greatly felicitate himself.

Before proceeding to Ministerial and Parliamentary business, it is worth while to refer to another Imperial transaction of this period which was fraught with considerable importance to Canada; namely, the partial relaxation by Great Britain of her protective policy. In those days Sir Robert Peel halted between two opinions on the protection question, but it was evident to those who were admitted to mark the inner workings of his mind that he was gradually surrendering himself to the principles of Free Trade. There was a disposition on his part to relax the duties on various imported commodities, and upon this disposition he finally acted, in spite of the vehement remonstrances of many of his chief supporters. Up to this time the duty imposed upon Baltic timber was fifty-five shillings sterling per load, whereas on Canadian timber the impost was only ten shillings. These rates were relaxed to thirty shillings and one shilling respectively—the latter being regarded as nearly equivalent to no tax at all. This step was viewed by the merchants of Montreal and Quebec, as a class, with undisguised anxiety and alarm. It was regarded as the thin end of the wedge. But this was not all. The free importation of United States flour into Canada was put an end to, and the inhabitants of the West Indies were permitted to import their flour direct from the United States on payment of a duty of two shillings a barrel. Prior to this time, as has been seen,* Canada had enjoyed the exclusive privilege of furnishing the West Indies with lumber and provisions. These things, and others of a like character, tended seriously to reduce the trade of the St. Lawrence. The falling-off was very perceptible, and was very sensibly felt. In 1842 the number of vessels entering the St. Lawrence from the sea was 377 less than in 1841. This occurred, too, at a time when the mercantile community were ill-fitted to bear any falling-off of revenue. Commerce was much depressed, and there was a great scarcity of money. Several prominent firms were compelled to suspend payment—a matter of much greater significance to commercial credit in 1842 than it would be at the present day. The merchants in the chief centres of population, as has already been intimated, were alarmed. They feared—and as the event proved, with good reason—that this was only a

---

* See *ante*, p. 56.

foretaste of what was to come. If such inroads as this were to be made on the protective system, they sincerely believed that the commercial trade of the country would be shattered to pieces.

These ideas, however, though common among Canadian merchants in 1842, were not universal. Several of the most intelligent and far-sighted gentlemen belonging to the mercantile world of Montreal had already pronounced in favour of Free Trade. Specially conspicuous among these were two merchants who afterwards won wide recognition throughout Canada, not only in matters commercial and political, but likewise for their great intellectual and moral worth. Their names were Luther Hamilton Holton and John Young.

The latter though not unknown to Canadian Parliamentary history, is chiefly remembered for his active commercial life and his connection with various important public works. He was in the best sense a self-made man—the sole architect of his own fortunes. He was Scotch by birth, but came to Canada when he was only fifteen years of age, and had ever since been engaged in mercantile pursuits; first, as a clerk in a grocery-store at Kingston; next as a clerk in a wholesale house at Montreal; then as junior partner in a mercantile firm at Quebec; and finally as a partner in the great Montreal house of which the late Mr. Harrison Stephens was the senior partner, and which was then carried on under the name of Stephens, Young & Co. He had already risen to a moderate degree of wealth, and had begun to display much enterprise and public spirit. Only a year before this time he had given a signal illustration of the practical common-sense character of his mind. It has been seen that an effusive loyalty was evoked in Canada by the birth of the Prince of Wales.[*] Montreal was especially conspicuous for the fervour of its enthusiasm, and subscribed a large sum of money to commemorate the event by a costly banquet and ball.

---

[*] See *ante*, p. 179.

Mr. Young was a hard-headed Scot, to whom banquets and balls were merely so many interruptions to important business. At a public meeting held for the purpose of appointing a committee to make suitable arrangements for the impending entertainment, he made a motion eminently characteristic of the man. He moved that the money subscribed for the proposed feasting and revelry should be expended in purchasing a tract of land, and in building thereon an asylum for the poor. In the speech made by him in support of this motion he drew attention to the depressed condition of trade, and the great poverty and suffering that had been engendered thereby. He deprecated the expenditure of a large sum of money at such a time, and in such a manner as to leave no permanently beneficial traces behind it. Though not a practised orator, he made the most of his theme, and aroused the sympathies of his audience. His motion was carried by a large majority. The asylum project, however, was altogether too prosaic to satisfy the patriotism of a certain element of the population. Mr. Young's motion was subsequently rescinded, and the money was spent as had at first been proposed.

Mr. Young, during the summer and autumn of 1842, and during many subsequent seasons, did his utmost to inculcate Free Trade doctrines among the mercantile community of Montreal, and to convince them that the new Imperial customs regulations would eventually enure to the benefit of the colonies. For some years his advocacy was not attended with much visible success, but there can be no doubt that by his conversation and his contributions to the press on the subject he in some degree helped to prepare the minds of Canadian thinkers for the Imperial policy of 1846. He was subsequently largely instrumental in founding a Free Trade Association in Montreal. At present it is unnecessary to follow his fortunes any farther, though we shall meet him more than once in future pages.

Mr. Holton, owing to his long Parliamentary career, and to his prominent position in the ranks of the Liberal party, was even more widely known in his day and generation than Mr. Young. He was a Canadian, and had been connected with mercantile life in Montreal from his early boyhood. When he was about thirteen years of age he became a clerk in the office of the great Montreal forwarding-house of Hooker & Co. He displayed great aptitude for commercial life, and after the lapse of a few years became a partner in the firm, which was thereafter known as Hooker, Holton & Co. The business was very large and profitable, and the firm shared with the prominent house of Macpherson & Crane in carrying on the bulk of a trade which the advent of railways was destined to supersede. It chiefly consisted of the conveyance of merchandise from the ports of entry to the various inland cities and towns, the transportation being effected by means of wagons, batteaux, and Durham boats. In 1842 Mr. Holton was by no means so widely known as he subsequently became, but he had established a reputation for much commercial foresight and ability, and was known as a man of great integrity and uprightness of character. He from the first coöperated with Mr. Young in promulgating Free Trade doctrines, and even in 1842 endorsed the Imperial policy of relaxing the tariff, although it seemed to threaten such serious consequences to the trade of the St. Lawrence. In politics and other matters he avowed opinions which, in those days, were regarded as remarkably advanced and liberal. He will occupy no insignificant figure in future chapters of this work.

Chapter XI.

RECONSTRUCTION.

"Whilst it has been theoretically admitted upon all sides that our French fellow-subjects are fairly entitled to a representation in the Councils of the Sovereign, as well as of the people, Sir Charles Bagot has been assailed with unwonted bitterness for the selections which he has made—charge as inconsistent and as irrational as it would be to admit the right of the people of Great Britain to representation in the Executive Council of the nation, and then to denounce Her Majesty for selecting such men as a Peel and a Wellington; since the same British principles of State policy, and the same means of information which suggested to Her Majesty Sir Robert Peel and the Duke of Wellington as the most influential and appropriate advisers of the Crown on behalf of the people of Great Britain, suggested to Sir Charles Bagot certain individuals whom he has selected as the most influential and appropriate advisers of the Crown on behalf of the French people of Canada; a measure so just, so wise, so expedient, as to induce the Honourable Mr. Draper not only to advise it, but to regard his own retirement from the power and emoluments of office a not too great a sacrifice for its accomplishment."—EGERTON RYERSON. *Some Remarks upon Sir Charles Bagot's Canadian Government.*

URING the summer of 1842 certain significant changes took place in the composition of the Ministry. On the 9th of June Mr. Hincks accepted the post of Inspector-General of Public Accounts, an office corresponding to that of the present Minister of Finance. The appointment was of course made at the instigation of his Excellency's advisers. Mr. Hincks's talents, his taste for politics, his familiarity with the details of the political situation, and more especially his aptitude for dealing with the finances of the country, made him a decided accession to the Government;* but his appointment gave great umbrage

---

*That competent critic, Mr. Edward Gibbon Wakefield, thus wrote to the *Colonial Gazette*, under date of 28th May, 1842, respecting Mr. Hincks's contemplated acceptance

to the Conservatives, who considered that a member of their own party should have been preferred. Some of the newspapers poured out the vials of their wrath with no stinted hand. The Governor was accused of a glaring leaning towards Radicalism, and Mr. Hincks was openly denounced as one who had abetted Mackenzie's rebellion. As matter of fact the Governor had no choice. He was bound, under Responsible Government, to act upon the advice of his Ministers. His Ministers stood in need of Mr. Hincks's knowledge and services, and advised his admission to the Government. Mr. Hincks, however, was as acceptable to his Excellency as to the Ministry, and his energy was soon made apparent in the orderly state of the public accounts. His acceptance of office was not significant of any modification in the Government policy. It has been seen that during the latter part of the previous session he had been to a considerable extent a supporter of the Government. Lord Sydenham had been much impressed by his aptitude for dealing with questions of finance, and by the readiness with which he disposed of complicated matters of account. His Lordship had discussed with some of the Ministers the advisability of requesting him to accept office as Inspector-General, and overtures would doubtless have been made to that end had the Governor's life been spared.*

---

of the Inspector-Generalship: "This appointment has all the appearance of being wisely designed. The leading merchants and bankers of Montreal, who are very fit to judge of any man's financial capacity, consider Mr. Hincks highly qualified to bring the muddled finances of the Province into a state of order and security. He is popular with the commercial classes wherever the political-economy bent of his mind happens to be known as existing in conjunction with his practical disposition and talents. His energy and industry are acknowledged by all who know anything about him."

* Major Richardson says that had Lord Sydenham carried his favourite Bank of Issue project Mr. Hincks was to have been placed at the head of it, with a seat in the Council. See "Eight Years in Canada," p. 192. It is constantly necessary to have recourse to the saltcellar in reading the productions of the Major, and nowhere is his untrustworthiness more frequently displayed than in this so-called "Review of the Administrations of Lords Durham and Sydenham, Sir Charles Bagot, and Lord Metcalfe." That Lord Sydenham would have been willing to avail himself of Mr. Hincks's financial skill in the management of the Bank is probable enough; but his Lordship never had it in contemplation to directly

The death of his Lordship caused a temporary suspension of the Government policy, Sir Richard Jackson's official acts being almost entirely restricted to the merest formalities. Mr. Hincks's entry into the Cabinet had accordingly been postponed, but it had been well understood among the Ministers themselves that he should be admitted whenever a favourable opportunity should present itself. Direct overtures were made to him towards the end of May, and he returned a favourable reply within a day or two afterwards. His acceptance of office tended to widen, for a time, the breach between himself and his former leader, Mr. Baldwin. His constituents in Oxford, on the other hand, approved of his conduct, and reëlected him by a sweeping majority over the Opposition candidate. Upon accepting office he thought proper to sever his proprietary connection with the press, and disposed of his interest in the *Examiner*, which however was carried on by his immediate successor in the interests of the Administration, and for some time bore internal evidence that its policy continued to be largely shaped by Mr. Hincks. It subsequently passed into other hands, after which its policy underwent various modifications.

The animadversions upon Mr. Hincks's appointment to the Inspector-Generalship were not confined to members of the Conservative party. The advanced Reformers felt his alleged desertion keenly, and did not hesitate to accuse him of having sold himself for a price. Mr. Hincks was not disposed to sit down tamely under such accusations, and replied to all upbraidings with acrid raillery. In later times he was referred to by Lord Metcalfe's biographer as having "a tongue that cut like a sword, and no discretion to keep it in order."[*] Whatever opinion might be

---

identify the Bank with the Government by making its manager a Cabinet Minister. Such a proceeding would not have been tolerated by the country, and no one knew that such was the case better than did Lord Sydenham himself.

[*] See Kaye's "Life and Correspondence of Charles, Lord Metcalfe;" Revised Edition, Vol. II., p. 342.

formed as to his discretion, there could be no doubt whatever as to
the incisive sharpness of his tongue when he was roused by the
attacks of his opponents. It may be asserted of him that throughout the stormy discussions of those times he generally succeeded in
fully holding his own. So far as can now be judged, his conduct
in entering the Government and afterwards seems to have been
due to a modification of policy rather than of opinion, and in this
respect he by no means stood alone among Upper Canadian
Reformers. Upon the opening of the session of 1841 he had conscientiously enough ranged himself on the side of the advanced
wing of the Opposition. In common with his coadjutors, he had
anticipated a vote of non-confidence in the Ministry as a result of
Mr. Baldwin's resignation. That anticipation had proved to be not
well-grounded. The "united Reform Party of Upper Canada" had
proved to be less indissolubly united than had been supposed. As
the session advanced, Mr. Hincks, finding that the Government was
sustained by a large majority—a majority including many sincere
Reform members—saw no good purpose to be served by a fruitless,
and, as it appeared to him, a factious and hopeless opposition; more
especially as the principal grounds of his opposition had been removed
by the ministerial admissions on the subject of Responsible Government. Again, it seems not improbable that he was to some extent
surprised into admiration of Lord Sydenham by the comprehensive-
ness of that Governor's plans, and by the boldness and originality
of some of his measures.* There were doubtless other motives
personal to himself. He does not appear to have taken very kindly
to his French Canadian allies at that time, and they, in their turn,
were not favourably impressed by him. He was moreover ambitious,
and it must have been apparent enough to a man of his keenness of
perception that if he determined upon remaining in Opposition he

* See correspondence of "B.," on "Sir C. Bagot's Policy," in the Halifax *Nova Scotian*,
June 29th, 1842.

would be compelled to play a waiting game. His going over to the Ministerialists would not necessarily involve any sacrifice of Liberal principles, for the Government claimed to be, and to a large extent was, of a Liberal complexion. Lord Sydenham, who, at any rate during a great part of the session, had been his own Prime Minister, was a man whose Liberalism did not admit of doubt. On the Municipal Bill, and on other measures which did not appear to him to involve any essentially political principle, Mr. Hincks, in common with other Reformers, had voted with the Government. It is not to be wondered at, however, that his sincerity and consistency were impugned by his old allies, as well as by ultra-Conservatives, for no man had been more vehement in his antagonism to the Government during the early days of the session. He had even gone out of his way to proclaim the uncompromising character of his opposition at the time of Mr. Cuvillier's election as Speaker to the Assembly,* and had been the sharpest thorn in Mr. Draper's side during the debate on Responsible Government.† It is probable that both Mr. Hincks and Mr. Draper were constrained to modify some of their opinions of each other before the former's acceptance of office, and that the members of the Government agreed to meet upon something like common ground with respect to the principles of Colonial Government.

Ever since Mr. Baldwin's resignation of the office of Solicitor-General for Upper Canada—embracing a period of more than a year—that office had remained vacant. Shortly before Mr. Hincks's entry into the Government the post was offered to Mr. John S. Cartwright, member for Lennox and Addington, an ultra-Conservative, and a right-hand supporter of Sir Allan MacNab. That gentleman, however, would have nothing to say to the Solicitor-Generalship, and in a somewhat captious letter written at Kingston on the 16th of May, and addressed to the Governor-General in person, refused to accept any office whatever in a Government containing such heterogeneous

---

* *Ante*, p. 114.   † *Ante*, p. 134, *et seq.*

materials. He was disgusted at seeing men appointed to offices in both Provinces who, less than five years before, had announced themselves as being opposed to any longer maintaining the connection between Canada and the mother country. "I would not hide from your Excellency," wrote Mr. Cartwright, "that the Conservatives of Upper Canada view some of the late appointments as utterly indefensible, and as evidence that the Government was indifferent to the political principles of men, even although those principles were inimical to British supremacy in these colonies." How far Mr. Cartwright, an honourable and well-meaning man enough, was able to read the signs of the times, is apparent from his views, as enunciated in this letter, on the subject of Responsible Government. "On the question of Responsible Government I have already explained to your Excellency my views of its dangerous tendency; and the more I reflect upon it the more I feel convinced of its incompatibility with our position as a colony—particularly in a country where almost universal suffrage prevails; where the great mass of the people are uneducated, and where there is little of that salutary influence which hereditary rank and great wealth exercise in Great Britain. I view Responsible Government as a system based upon principles so dangerous that the most virtuous and sensible act of a man's public life may deprive him and his family of their bread, by placing him in a minority in an Assembly where faction, and not reason, is likely to prevail." Such language as this was not to be misunderstood. The Government could not hope to enrol Mr. Cartwright in its service. The post of Solicitor-General for Upper Canada was then offered to Mr. Henry Sherwood, an able Nisi Prius lawyer of Toronto, and a very pronounced Conservative, who had not then any seat in Parliament. Mr. Sherwood, greatly to the surprise of many of his friends and political allies, accepted the proposal, and was sworn into office on the 23rd of July.* There

*The *Kingston Herald* expressed the almost unanimous sentiment of the Conservative

were persons who did not scruple to allege that he had taken office with the deliberate intention of promoting the overthrow of the Government. The allegation emanated from Mr. Sherwood's personal and political friends, but does not seem to have had any foundation in fact. Such a course, indeed, unless distinctly avowed, would have been in the highest degree inconsistent with honour, and Mr. Sherwood was a very unlikely man to lend himself to any project of the kind.

A month before this date the Solicitor-Generalship for the Lower Province had become vacant, Mr. Day, the incumbent of that office, having been appointed, on the 20th of June, to a judgeship of the Court of Queen's Bench for Lower Canada. There was no successful attempt to fill the vacancy until after the meeting of the Houses.

The Government looked forward with a good deal of solicitude to the opening of the second session under the Union. Under Lord Sydenham they had been strong enough to feel safe, but their strength had been largely derived from Lord Sydenham himself, and by his death they had been deprived of that powerful support. By this time they well knew that upon the assembling of Parliament they would be compelled to encounter the determined opposition of two widely divergent schools of politicians. The French Canadian members, with one or two exceptions, might be depended

---

party on Mr. Sherwood's acceptance of office, which was the more surprising in consequence of Mr. Cartwright's recent refusal. "How it is," remarked the *Herald*, "that Mr. Sherwood has taken an office declined by Mr. Cartwright, it is, of course, impossible for us to say, for the former is, or was, quite as much a Tory as the latter.   It will probably be found that Mr. Sherwood expects, or perhaps has been promised, some concession to his principles.   At all events the Provincial Ministry is curiously constructed. Instead of being a coalition of moderate men, it is a coalition of fierce extremes. How they can meet at the Council Board and not laugh in each other's faces, if in merry mood, or come to fisticuffs, if in angry one, must be an eighth wonder of the world." The London *Herald*, Hamilton *Gazette*, Cobourg *Star*, Belleville *Intelligencer*, Cornwall *Observer*, Ottawa *Advocate*, and Kingston *Whig*, *News* and *Statesman*, all adopted the same attitude on Mr. Sherwood's acceptance of office—an acceptance not approved of by any members of the Conservative party outside of Toronto, where the new Solicitor-General resided.

upon to act in unison with the advanced Reformers of the Upper Province who acknowledged the leadership of Robert Baldwin. The ultra-Conservative members from Upper Canada, who followed the lead of Sir Allan MacNab and Mr. Cartwright, represented the other extreme of political ideas ; but they had one motive in common with Upper Canadian Radicalism and French Liberalism—dislike to the existing Administration.* The coalition of these two bodies† was ominous, for Mr. Baldwin's party had steadily gained ground all through the recess, and the French Canadian party had received a material accession of strength by the return of several of the ablest of their compatriots to Parliament. Mr. Baldwin and his following stood loyally by their French Canadian allies, and the united vote of French Canadians, Baldwinites, and Upper Canada Conservatives would be almost certainly fatal to the Ministry. The French Canadians were numerically the strongest of the three, and as they voted with absolute uniformity it was evident that they could not much longer be excluded from a share in the Government. It seemed not improbable that the balance of power would erelong be in their keeping.

The discontent of the Conservatives grew apace from day to day all through the summer. Sir Charles Bagot had greatly disappointed them. When the fact of his appointment to the Governor-Generalship had first been announced, they had looked forward with much confidence to something like a return of the (to them) golden age of Sir Peregrine Maitland and Sir John Colborne. Ever since his arrival in the country this confidence had been gradually diminishing. His treatment of them had been courteous and conciliatory in tone, but in this respect had not differed from his treatment of French Canadian ex-rebels and Upper Canadian Radicals. He

---

* History sometimes repeats itself with remarkable fidelity. We shall find the leading circumstances almost identical when we come to treat of the coalition of 1854.

† They had temporarily coalesced several times during the preceding session ; notably on the measure respecting the Lower Canada elections. See *ante*, pp. 143, 144.

rebuked the spirit of intolerance and persecution wherever he found it,* and displayed a good deal of quiet, statesmanlike firmness. He felt himself to be a constitutional ruler, and governed himself accordingly. A new Commission of the Peace was promulgated, which included the names of men of various origin, and of various political sympathies. His Excellency early recognized the importance of reconciling the French Canadians to the new order of things. In his appointments to office he knew no distinction between French Canadians and British Canadians. A French Canadian, in the person of M. Joseph Remi Vallières de St. Real, was appointed Chief Justice of the District of Montreal. Another was appointed Judge of the District of Three Rivers. Dr. Jean Baptiste Meilleur, whose nationality is sufficiently indicated by his name, was appointed Superintendent of Public Instruction for Lower Canada. In the Upper Province a similar disposition was manifested to appoint to office persons who enjoyed the confidence of the majority. "Some of the most notorious rebels of the Province," whines Major Richardson, himself a disappointed office-seeker, " having influence with certain members of the Legislature, whose support the Administration was solicitous to secure, were gazetted to situations of high trust and importance."† During the interregnum between Lord Sydenham's death and Sir Charles Bagot's arrival, Mr. Andrew Norton Buell, of Brockville, a very pronounced Radical, had been appointed to the Treasurership of the Johnstown District. This was one of the few appointments which Sir Richard Jackson had been prevailed upon to make, and it gave great offence to the Conservative party, for Mr. Buell was charged with having been an active sympathizer in the

---

* In a communication to Mr. Cartwright, written in reply to the letter of that gentleman already quoted from in the text, occurs the following sensible and dignified rebuke : "I trust that I am not doomed to have my earnest efforts for the well-being of this great colony defeated by the continuance of petty struggles or party animosities, for which, in its present state, and with its present prospects, there appears to me to be no longer room."

† See "Eight Years in Canada," p. 190.

rebellion. Some time after Sir Charles Bagot's arrival in Canada a petition, signed by many Conservatives of the county of Leeds, was presented to him, charging various matters of more or less gravity against Mr. Buell, and praying for that gentleman's removal from office. Here again Sir Charles proved that he understood his position. He courteously declined to inquire into the political sins of an official appointed by his predecessor, unless the petitioners could furnish proof of misconduct on the part of the official since his appointment.* In all these embarrassments he proved his determination to govern the country through its Parliament, and not through any faction whatever.

Such was the state of affairs when Parliament met on the 8th of September. A good many changes had taken place in the membership during the interval which had elapsed since the prorogation. There had been a considerable increase in the membership of the Legislative Council. Of the twenty-four members originally appointed by Lord Sydenham, three (Augustus Baldwin, Olivier Berthelet, and Etienne Maynard) had officially resigned their seats during the first fortnight of the session of 1841. His Lordship had added two members during the progress of the session, in the persons of Messieurs Gabriel Roy and P. H. Moore. One member, M. Jules Quesnel, had died. To the remaining twenty-two were now added seven members: Robert Dickson, of Niagara, George Jervis Goodhue, of London, Levius P. Sherwood, of Toronto, Simeon Washburn,

---

* "He, whose once high family would have shrunk dismayed from the idea of bestowing favour on a base-born traitor, even as they would have done from conferring honour on the perpetrator of a sacrilege, blushed not to reply (of course, in obedience to the dictates of his Council), that he was not responsible for, and would not interfere with, any appointments made previous to his arrival. The answer so pained and disgusted every honourable and loyal man in the country, that, whilst cherishing feelings of deepest indignation, they looked upon the Province as wholly lost to the Empire; nor were there wanting sagacious minds who came to the humiliating conclusion that the Ministry of England, Tory even as they were, were unscrupulously sacrificing not only the best interests of their Sovereign, but those of the colony, to a most unworthy principle of expediency."—*Eight Years in Canada*, p. 209. This author's views fairly reflect the opinions of Upper Canadian Conservatives at that period.

of Picton, William Walker, Amable Dionne and Joseph Dionne of the District of Quebec. In the Assembly the changes were many and important, and nearly all of them tended to strengthen the hands of the Opposition. Mr. Day's retirement from public life had left vacant the representation of the county of Ottawa. In his stead had been returned Denis Benjamin Papineau, a brother of the more celebrated Louis Joseph Papineau, who was still in exile, in consequence of his identification with the Lower Canadian rebellion. Mr. Morin had also retired, for the time, from public life, and had accepted a judgeship in his native Province, thereby leaving vacant the representation of the county of Nicolet. He had resigned the judgeship after retaining it a short time, but had not again offered himself to his old constituents, who had returned as their representative Louis Michel Viger, a cousin of the member for Richelieu. Various other changes had occurred, but the only one calling for special mention is the return of Mr. Lafontaine for the Fourth Riding of York. Mr. Lafontaine, who was one of the ablest men his Province has produced, and who was destined to take a conspicuous place in its political and judicial history, deserves a paragraph to himself.

At the time of his return to the First Parliament of United Canada, Louis Hypolite Lafontaine was only about thirty-four years of age. He was born near the village of Boucherville, in the county of Chambly, in 1807. From his earliest childhood he gave evidence of possessing a soaring ambition and a capacious mind.* He devoted himself to the law as his profession in life, and after his call to the bar he began practice at Montreal. He was successful, both in his profession and out of it, and rapidly accumulated considerable

---

* "Au collége de Montréal, où il fit cinq années d'études, Louis-Hippolyte se fit remarquer par la solidité de son jugement et l'opiniâtreté de son caractère. Il aimait à faire les choses à sa guise, travaillait sans se fatiguer et supportait difficilement le régime sévère des colléges du temps. On l'appelait 'la grosse tête.'"—*Biographies et Portraits*, Par L.-O. David; Montreal, 1876.

pecuniary means, which were augmented by an advantageous marriage. He held what in those days were considered very advanced opinions on matters political, and was a disciple—albeit not always a subordinate one—of Mr. Papineau. He served the popular cause in the District of Montreal by his writings in *La Minerve*, a paper founded in the national interests in 1826, and conducted with great ability for some years by Mr. A. N. Morin. Between Mr. Lafontaine and Mr. Morin a warm friendship sprang up; a friendship which was preserved unbroken throughout the whole subsequent course of their lives. It has been said that each of these two eminent men formed an appropriate complement to the other:* that each possessed what the other lacked, and that the union of their forces gave a formidable impetus to the cause which both had at heart. Mr. Morin was a man of rare ability, but he had the modesty which frequently accompanies true genius. He was not given to self-assertion, and passed with most of his acquaintances at much less than his true value. Mr. Lafontaine, on the contrary, was essentially a man of the world; a man of high ambitions; a man brilliant and showy, fully capable of asserting and maintaining all that of right belonged to him. He early took

---

*"M. Morin, timide et modeste, trouva dans M. Lafontaine la direction énergique dont il avait besoin. Racontons, en passant, un fait qui donnera une idée de l'amitié de ces deux grands hommes et de leur caractère. M. Morin avait l'habitude de donner aux pauvres jusqu'à son dernier sou, et même, souvent, de rembourser les clients dont il avait perdu les causes, de sorte que, sa pension payée, il ne lui restait jamais d'argent pour s'habiller. Un jour, M. Lafontaine lui dit qu'il ne voulait plus le voir paraître dans les rues avec l'accoutrement bizarre qu'il portait, que c'était un scandale. Il lui mit vingt-cinq louis dans les mains et lui enjoignit d'aller s'habiller. M. Morin s'en allait chez un tailleur, lorsqu'il rencontra un client malheureux dont il avait perdu le procès ; le client l'attendrit tellement sur son sort et sur le résultat de ce procès, que M. Morin lui mit les vingt-cinq louis entre les mains en lui recommandant bien de ne pas en parler à M. Lafontaine. Mais M. Lafontaine, le voyant toujours avec la même *toilette* les jours suivants, se décida à lui demander des explications. M. Morin hésita un moment, mais, ne pouvant mentir, il finit par raconter l'affaire. M. Lafontaine le gourmanda, malgré l'envie de rire qu'il avait, et lui dit qu'il était décidé, cette fois, à l'emporter. Il l'emmena chez un tailleur et lui fit faire un habillement complet."—*Biographies et Portraits*, pp. 97, 98.

rank among his compatriots as a leader of men. In 1830, when he was twenty-three years old, he was returned to the Lower Canadian Assembly, where he advocated the rights of his compatriots with much fervour and eloquence, until the breaking out of the rebellion. That Mr. Lafontaine would have been glad enough to see that movement succeed may safely enough be taken for granted, but he was too prudent to identify himself with it. After the engagements at St. Denis and St. Charles he found himself placed in an embarrassing position. The rebels looked to him for active support; but he knew the hopelessness of the insurrection, and had no idea of imperilling his liberty or his life in a lost cause. On the other hand, he found himself an object of suspicion to the Government. After an ineffectual appeal to Lord Gosford to convoke the Houses he quietly withdrew from the Province. He repaired to England, and thence to France, where he remained until after the amnesty proclamation was issued, whereupon he returned to Canada. His views had undergone some modification during his exile. He had previously held at naught the power of the priesthood, who in their turn had looked askance at him, and regarded him as heterodox in his religious beliefs. After his return he adopted a different policy. Mr. Papineau was out of the way, and there seemed to be no probability of his early return to Canada, as he had been expressly excluded by name from the amnesty that had been declared. Mr. Lafontaine accordingly found himself in the position of leader of his fellow-countrymen, and he was too wise to continue his opposition to so potent a power as was that of the Lower Canadian clergy. He set himself to conciliate them, and with success. "Whether from conviction or from policy," says the author of the *Washington Sketches*, "he went regularly to mass, and, his moral conduct being irreproachable, it is to be presumed that he was sincere, though the coincidence of interest and devotion is striking." However that fact may have been, Mr.

Lafontaine soon had the clergy on his side, and became all-powerful among his compatriots generally. He still held radical views in matters political, and would doubtless have been ready enough to head another insurrection if it could have been proved to him that such a movement would have been attended by any likelihood of success. He was for some time an object of suspicion to the authorities, and erelong the suspicion took an active form. An incautious letter written by him to a professional friend contained a sentence which seemed to indicate something more than a strong sympathy with the insurrection. The contents of the letter became known to the authorities, and a warrant was issued for the writer's apprehension. On the 7th of November, 1838, he, in common with the Vigers and other influential French Canadians, was arrested and committed to prison. The time was one of great excitement, as Robert Nelson was then making his foolish attempt to establish a Canadian republic. There was no evidence against Mr. Lafontaine, and he was soon released. His imprisonment, brief as it was, served rather to confirm than to weaken his position as leader of his compatriots, and he continued to retain their confidence to the end of his life. A short time before the Union Act came into operation the Governor-General—then Mr. Thomson—offered him the Solicitor-Generalship for Lower Canada, of course upon the understanding that he would support the Government policy. Mr. Lafontaine declined the proposal. He was one of the most vehement opponents of the Union, which, in common with nearly all of his fellow-countrymen, he rightly regarded as a scheme to destroy the French Canadian nationality. The imposition of the debt of the Upper Province upon them he regarded in the light of a legalized robbery. As already recorded in these pages,* a meeting was held at Montreal under his auspices, where, on his own special motion, a protest against the impending Union was adopted. When the project had become

---

* *Ante*, pp. 46, 47.

an accomplished fact, however, he bowed to the inevitable with
such grace as he could summon to his aid. As circumstances
would not accommodate themselves to his mind, he bent himself to
accommodate his mind to the circumstances. He offered himself to
his old constituents in Terrebonne as a candidate for a seat in the
First united Parliament. He was opposed by Dr. McCulloch, with
what result has already been narrated.* There can be no doubt that
Mr. Lafontaine would have been returned had the franchise been free
and unrestricted. As it was, he was defeated, and was compelled
to bide his time. Mr. Baldwin's double return gave him the opportunity for which he waited. Mr. Baldwin and he were of one mind
on all the principal questions before the public. They were also of one
mind as to the true policy required at the hands of the Government.
They had moreover conceived for each other a high personal esteem
and friendship, which were maintained without interruption during
the remaining years of their respective lives. After Mr. Baldwin,
on the 25th of August, 1841, had made his election to sit for the
county of Hastings, he presented his Lower Canadian ally to the
electors of the Fourth Riding of York. Mr. Baldwin's influence
was paramount there, and Mr. Lafontaine was returned on the 21st
of September, three days after the close of the first session under
the Union. The man who had long been the recognized leader of
his compatriots was now able to take his place as their leader in
Parliament. He was from the first a conspicuous figure there. He
had a massive, Napoleonic cast of countenance, and an argumentative style of oratory which impressed all who heard him. He was
an eloquent and large-minded man, with a statesmanlike intellect,
and his return had greatly strengthened the hands of the party
which he represented. With such a leader, it was impossible that
the French Canadian element could much longer be excluded from a

---

* *Ante*, pp. 48, 49.

share of power. That element looked up to him, not perhaps with the rapturous enthusiasm which Mr. Papineau had been wont to inspire, but still with a confidence and respect which were highly honourable to the recipient. His countrymen admired him for his abilities, for his intellectual power, for his undoubted devotion to their interests, for the imprisonment which he had undergone, and for the circumstances under which he had declined to accept office under Lord Sydenham. The fact that some French Canadians must be admitted to office was by this time fully recognized by the members of the Administration, and at the time when Parliament assembled the advisability of making overtures to Mr. Lafontaine to take a share in the cares and responsibilities of carrying on the Government had already been discussed. The result of the discussion will presently appear.

The second session was opened in the Legislative Council Chamber at two o'clock in the afternoon of Thursday, the 8th of September. The Speech from the Throne was read by his Excellency in a strong, clear and distinct voice, and spectators remarked upon the contrast between his appearance and that of Lord Sydenham. Sir Charles was in particularly good health, and, so far as could be judged, many years of work were yet in store for him. The Speech set out by deploring "the melancholy event which marked the close of the last session"—namely, the death of Lord Sydenham. It next referred to the birth of the Prince of Wales; to the failure of the recent attempt upon the life of Her Majesty;[*] and to the conclusion of the Ashburton Treaty. The Assembly were informed that the Imperial Government had fully redeemed the promise made by their predecessors to guarantee a Provincial loan. The extension of various public works throughout the country was

---

[*] Viz., the attempt of John Francis, on the 30th of May, to shoot Her Majesty on Constitution Hill, London, on the selfsame spot where Edward Oxford had made a similar attempt about two years before.

glanced at, as was also the question of immigration. The condition of the public revenue was declared to be highly satisfactory. The Speech then referred to contemplated amendments to the Act respecting the establishment of Municipal Councils, as well as to the School Act. A reorganization of the militia was also recommended. "It is my earnest hope," said his Excellency, in conclusion, "that a spirit of moderation and harmony may animate your councils and direct your proceedings. The Province has at length happily recovered from a state of severe trial and danger, and a bright dawn now opens upon its prospects. The promise of peace secured upon an honourable and advantageous basis, the re-establishment of tranquillity and security, the restoration of financial credit and commercial confidence, with the enjoyment of free and permanent institutions, are blessings for which Canada has reason to be grateful, and which, I feel assured, it will be your effort to preserve, and your pride to perpetuate."

In the Legislative Council an address echoing the Speech was moved and passed without delay. Upon the return of the members of the Lower House to their own chamber, Monday, the 12th, was appointed for the consideration of the Speech. During the intervening days it was apparent enough that something of importance was under discussion. The atmosphere was electric with rumours of impending changes in the Administration. Caucuses were held every night up to a late hour. The canvassing of members throughout the day was unremitting, except when the House was actually in session. On the appointed Monday a great crowd was in attendance, anxious to hear the debate which it was well known would take place when the subject of the reply to the Speech came up in order. The audience, however, was doomed to disappointment, for the consideration of the question was postponed, at the instance of Mr. Secretary Harrison, until the day following.

Meanwhile, the Ministry and the Governor-General were busily engaged in discussing the terms upon which a further reconstruction of the Administration might most advantageously be brought about. No definite conclusion was arrived at until about noon of the 13th, when his Excellency addressed a letter to Mr. Lafontaine, as the acknowledged leader of the French Canadian members, suggesting that he should accept office in the Administration as Attorney-General for Lower Canada. As an inducement to that gentleman to enter into the Governor-General's views, the Solicitor-Generalship of Lower Canada was placed subject to his nomination, with the proviso that the office should be filled by a gentleman of British origin. It was stipulated that Mr. Ogden, the then incumbent of that office (who was absent in England on leave), should be provided for by pension. The Commissionership of Crown Lands, with a seat in the Cabinet, was also placed at Mr. Lafontaine's disposal, as well as the Clerkship of the Executive Council, which was then vacant. It was well understood that Mr. Lafontaine would not accept office unless his friend Mr. Baldwin also consented to do so; and as a further inducement he was authorized to offer the Attorney-Generalship of Upper Canada to Mr. Baldwin. Mr. Sherwood, the new Solicitor-General for the Upper Province, being then absent from Kingston, it was suggested that his office should remain in abeyance until his arrival, when it should become the subject of consideration. The Commissionership of Crown Lands had not previously been a Cabinet office. Its incumbent was Mr. John Davidson, who had never been in Parliament, but who was an old and efficient public servant. It will be seen that the reconstruction, as contemplated, involved the retirement from office of Mr. Draper and Mr. Ogden, Attorneys-General respectively for Upper and Lower Canada.

The offer was flattering enough; but Mr. Lafontaine and Mr. Baldwin believed themselves to be masters of the situation, and refused to accept. They doubtless hoped to be able to compel the Ministry to resign, whereupon they would have had the forming of a new one.

This, however, the Ministry, as a body, refused to do. Mr. Draper knew that the time was up, so far as he was concerned, and tendered his resignation with apparent cheerfulness, but the other members of the Government clung to their offices with tenacity. Such was the condition of affairs on the afternoon of Tuesday, the 13th of September, the day to which the debate on the Address had been adjourned. The Governor's letter had been written and delivered to Mr. Lafontaine between one and two o'clock in the afternoon, and the recipient had only returned his hurried answer in the negative a few minutes before the meeting of the House.

On that day the crush was greater than ever, and the audience was regaled with a lively and prolonged debate. At half-past three o'clock in the afternoon the Address was moved by Mr. C. J. Forbes, member for Two Mountains, and seconded by Mr. John Sandfield Macdonald, of Glengarry. The discussion was then set going by Mr. Draper, who throughout fully maintained his well-earned reputation for eloquent plausibility. He said that ever since the promulgation of Lord John Russell's celebrated despatch he had felt that no Government should be continued which could not command the confidence of the House and of the country. That, he declared, had been his fixed principle, and he should have been false to his own professions, to his own feelings, and to the despatch itself, had he tendered any other advice to the Head of the Executive Government. Acting under such a system of administration, and feeling the full force of its propriety and necessity, not only in theory but in practice, he had always been of opinion that the Government never could be carried on in unison with the principles contained in that despatch so long as the great body of the French Canadian members took no part in the administration of affairs. This had at all times been his opinion, but under the Administration of the late Governor-General he had had no power to carry out his views. During the last session he had twice tendered his resignation of the office of Attorney-General. He added that he had within the last forty-eight hours tendered his resignation for the third time, to the end that his continuance in office might be no obstruction to the reconstruction of the Government upon that firm and satisfactory basis upon which he felt it ought alone to stand. He admitted that at the outset of the previous session he had entertained prejudices against the French Canadians, but added that his prejudices had been removed by the more intimate knowledge which he had since acquired of them by personal intercourse. Feeling that there was in fact no difference in sentiment between the honourable gentlemen opposite and himself and his colleagues, he had used his best endeavours to carry a union between them into full effect. He had endeavoured to bring about that political and national harmony upon which he hoped to see the Government stand. Although his feelings had at all times been such as he now stated them to be, he had had no opportunity of carrying them out to any practical result, till the arrival of the present Head of the Government. In negotiating an arrangement such as that to which he had been alluding, he felt that no proposal should be made to the gentlemen opposite but such as honourable men could accept. With that view, and knowing that the honourable member for Hastings (Mr. Baldwin) had forfeited office for them, and that, as honourable men, they could not take office without him, he made no proposal to the gentlemen opposite which did not include the honourable and learned gentleman from Hastings. In making a proposition to include the member for Hastings he knew, he said, that he was making one to exclude himself, and it would be derogatory to him and also to the member for Hastings for both to act together in the same Cabinet. He had therefore at once given in his own resignation. He and his colleagues had submitted those views to the honourable and learned gentleman opposite (Mr. Lafontaine), the leader of the French Canadian people. It was not for him (the

Attorney-General) to say why their proposals had been rejected; but whatever might be the motives which had dictated the refusal, he yet hoped to see the day when such a union would be formed, and when the principle of administering the Government in harmony with the wishes of the people would be fairly carried out. Mr. Draper then read a copy of the letter addressed by the Head of the Government to Mr. Lafontaine. He concluded his remarks by saying that whatever might be the result, he felt consoled that he had tendered what he conceived to be the best advice he was capable of giving; and having so performed his duty, he would leave the whole matter to the impartial consideration of the House.

Mr. Lafontaine then briefly addressed the House in the French language, stating that he would afterwards explain his motives for declining the offers made to him. He added that his motives were more of a personal than of a public nature.

Mr. Baldwin made a speech of nearly an hour's duration, in the course of which he remarked that it was some consolation to him to find that the very advice which eighteen months before he had tendered to Lord Sydenham—the very advice for persisting in which he had retired from office—was now confirmed by the unanimous voice of the whole Cabinet. He had not expected that such ample testimony would be so soon borne to the correctness of his views. He expressed his desire to see a strong Government established; not one like those in a neighbouring country, blown about by every wind, and bending before every storm, but one that, being anchored in the affections of the people, would be enabled to ride triumphantly over every adverse wave. "The learned Attorney-General," pursued Mr. Baldwin, "now comes forward with proposals to the Reform party. If he is sincere in making such proposals, the period of the Union was the proper time for making them. He acknowledges that he was at all times impressed with the sentiments of liberality to which he has this day given utterance, but if such were his feelings during the last session, why did he not express them? Why did he allow twelve or eighteen months to elapse, and still keep his feelings to himself? Why did he not tell Lord Sydenham what he has told Sir Charles Bagot?" After a searching review of the Speech from the Throne, Mr. Baldwin concluded by moving an amendment to the Address, expressive of a want of confidence in the Government. The motion was seconded by Mr. J. G. Barthe, member for Yamaska, and supported by a speech from the Hon. D. B. Viger; after which Mr. Lafontaine again addressed the House in the French language, stating the offers that had been made to him by the late Lord Sydenham, and also by Sir Charles Bagot. He added that he looked upon the whole as hollow and insincere, and that he could not think of taking office by pensioning off the old incumbents. Other speeches followed, and a fiery war of words was kept up until half-past eleven at night, when Mr. Parent moved the adjournment of the debate to the day following. The motion was seconded by Mr. Hamilton, and unanimously concurred in.

Next day the galleries were again closely packed by a great crowd, eager to hear the conclusion of the debate. Even before the Speaker had taken his chair it became evident that some mysterious influences had been brought to bear since the noisy debate of the previous afternoon and evening. All excitement and anger appeared to have completely subsided. Those who had so recently been pitted against each other in fierce antagonism were now seen side by side in friendly converse. Voices which a few hours since had made themselves heard in loudest objurgation were now hushed and subdued. For a few minutes the Assembly Chamber might almost have been taken for a Castle of Indolence.

"A pleasant land of drowsy-head it was."

The Independent and the Conservative members were at no loss to understand what this portended, and were hardly taken by surprise when Mr. Hincks, soon after the House had been called to order, rose in his place, and after a few observations, moved that the debate on Mr. Baldwin's amendment be postponed until Friday, the 16th. He added that after what had taken place on the previous day the subject had necessarily engrossed the serious attention of the Administration. Mr. Baldwin expressed his assent to the postponement; and if there had previously been any doubt as to what was in contemplation, doubt could exist no longer. The Opposition members preserved a stolid silence. Several gentlemen who were classed as "Independents" expressed their disapproval of the proposed delay. Dr. Dunlop,* Huron's representative, declared his

---

* Dr. William Dunlop was perhaps the most eccentric man who has figured in our Parliamentary history. He was a Scotchman of undoubted but irregular ability, and had had a somewhat chequered career. In his youth he was a surgeon in the famous regiment (the 88th) known as the Connaught Rangers. He was in Canada during the War of 1812-'14, and fought against the American invaders with the indomitable courage which has always been the special attribute of his regiment. He subsequently saw some service in India, where he edited a newspaper, and where he killed so many tigers that he acquired the name of "Tiger" Dunlop. His intellect was keen, and he was an omnivorous reader, so that notwithstanding his unsettled and irregular life he contrived to pick up a good deal of desultory scholarship. Upon returning to his native land he became a contributor to *Blackwood's Magazine*, and the collaborateur of Professor Wilson and the Ettrick Shepherd. Later on he was one of the band of literary rowdies that Dr. Maginn collected about him during his editorship of *Fraser's Magazine*. His portrait, as he appeared in those days, may be found in the seventh volume of *Fraser*. It also appears in the well known group by Maclise, which at present does duty as a frontispiece to the "Reliques of Father Prout." He published several works of the most diverse character, and at one time delivered an extraordinary course of lectures in Edinburgh on medical jurisprudence. He came out to Canada in 1826 with Mr. John Galt, the Canadian Superintendent of the Canada Company, father of the present Sir Alexander T. Galt. The Doctor spent the rest of his life in this country, and for some time after his arrival held a sort of "roving commission" in the service of the Canada Company. On the 23rd of April—St. George's Day—1827, he assisted Mr. Galt in performing the "inaugural ceremonies" attendant upon the founding of the town of Guelph. He was also largely instrumental in settling the Huron tract in Upper Canada, and in founding the town of Goderich. In 1833 he published "Statistical Sketches of Upper Canada, by a Backwoodsman," which was a useful and readable book in its day. He was returned to Parliament for the first time in 1841. For some further interesting particulars respecting the Doctor's career, and for a certified copy of his extraordinary last will and testament, the reader is referred to "The Scot in British North America," by William J. Rattray; Vol. II., pp. 445-456.

conviction that some underhand scheme was afoot which he, in common with other Independent members, could not support. Mr. Johnston, of Carleton, followed in a still more vehement strain; but all to no purpose. The motion was carried, and the House soon afterwards adjourned.

Before the appointed Friday the negotiations with Mr. Lafontaine had been successful, though all the details had not been definitely settled. Mr. Draper's resignation had been accepted, and Messieurs Lafontaine and Baldwin had agreed to accept the offices which had been tendered to them. There is no need for going over the negotiations and conferences from day to day. On the 16th Mr. Baldwin voluntarily withdrew his amendment. On the 25th Mr. Aylwin accepted office as Solicitor-General for Lower Canada. The Government was not entirely reconstructed until the end of the short session, which was brought to a close on the 12th of October. As then reconstructed the membership was as follows:

The Hon. L. H. Lafontaine, Attorney-General for Lower Canada.
" " Robert Baldwin, Attorney-General for Upper Canada.
" " R. B. Sullivan, President of the Council.
" " J. H. Dunn, Receiver-General.
" " Dominick Daly, Provincial Secretary for Lower Canada.
" " S. B. Harrison, Provincial Secretary for Upper Canada.
" " H. H. Killaly, President of the Department of Public Works.
" " F. Hincks, Inspector-General of Public Accounts.
" " T. C. Aylwin, Solicitor-General for Lower Canada.
" " J. E. Small, Solicitor-General for Upper Canada.
" " A. N. Morin, Commissioner of Crown Lands.

Such important changes as those indicated by the foregoing list necessarily evoked much criticism from Sir Allan MacNab and his followers, as well as from those members who called themselves Independents. It was not to be wondered at if the in-coming members were charged with inconsistency, and if gloomy vaticinations were indulged in by the disappointed and disgusted Opposition. The party press of course reflected the party sentiment. "The composition of the present Cabinet," remarked one of the leading organs of Conservative opinion in the Lower Province, "is the commencement of division and ill-feeling in his Excellency's Government in Canada; the re-creation of subdued national feelings and irritations, and, we much fear, the germ of the colonial separation from the mother country. We are convinced that these results must follow from a Cabinet composed, on the one hand, of those who have openly and undisguisedly exhibited their opposition to British connection, and on the other, of men of republican feelings, or who want honesty sufficient to retire unreservedly from place, when opposed to principle." Yet it was admitted by the adherents of all shades of party that the French Canadians were fairly entitled to be represented in the Government. If so, they were surely entitled to a voice in the selection of their representatives, and Mr. Lafontaine had succeeded to the place once held by Mr. Papineau in the estimation of his compatriots. In Upper Canada there could be no doubt whatever that Mr. Baldwin was the popular tribune of the people. These facts had been admitted by Mr. Draper himself, not only in words, but by the mere fact of his retirement from office. It may as well be admitted, without disguise, that the formation of the new Ministry was to some extent a measure of political expediency. There was probably not a single member of it who felt unbounded confidence in all his colleagues. If any one of them had been allowed to pick and choose, he would without doubt have ordered things differently. Mr. Lafontaine and Mr. Baldwin would doubtless have preferred not to sit on the same benches with Mr. Sullivan and Mr. Hincks. Mr. Hincks and Mr. Aylwin had recently, in the course of public debate, used language towards each other which neither of them could have entirely forgotten or forgiven. But the members doubtless felt that they had not been sent there merely to give effect to their personal likes and dislikes. Something was due to public opinion, and something was due to expediency. The old members of the Government enjoyed the power which proverbially springs from possession. Had Mr. Lafontaine continued to reject the Governor's overtures, it was not quite certain that he could have carried the Assembly with him. The members of the old Ministry who retained their places were moreover familiar with the duties of their respective departments. Some of them were exceptionally efficient. Mr. Hincks was probably the best man in the country for the post of Inspector-General. Under such circumstances a compromise was indicated, and finally carried out, with the results already recorded. At first, as has been seen, there was a fixed resolve to compel the Ministry to resign, and to this end Mr. Lafontaine declined the Governor's proposals, in the belief that the resignation would take place, and that he and Mr. Baldwin would then be asked to form a new Administration. When the Ministry, however, firmly refused to resign, Mr. Lafontaine did not deem it prudent to push the combat à l'outrance. On one point, however, he was firm. He would not consent to accept office on the condition that the Minister whom he thereby deposed should be pensioned by the in-coming Government. The old Ministers yielded something in their turn, and agreed to leave the pension question an open one, with power to all parties to vote as they thought fit. They also, as will already have been inferred, yielded so far as to advise his Excellency to declare Mr. Sherwood's office vacant, and thus to render feasible its acceptance by Mr. Small. And thus matters were accommodated.

The Ministry then formed is popularly known as the first Lafontaine-Baldwin Ministry, to distinguish it from that of 1848, called the *second* Lafontaine-Baldwin Ministry. As matter of fact, however, the former was not a new Government, but merely a reconstructed one. The statement made by a deceased Lower Canadian historian* to the effect that the old Ministers retained their places on condition of conforming to the policy of their new chiefs is an error. So, at all events, asserts Sir Francis Hincks, the sole surviving member of that Ministry, and the only person now living who is entitled to speak upon the subject with full authority.† In a reconstructed Ministry, in the absence of any stipulation to the contrary, the precedence of members is determined by the dates of their commissions. Newly-admitted members, therefore, are junior to the older ones; and in strictness, Mr. Lafontaine and Mr. Baldwin were junior to all the six gentlemen who retained office in the reconstructed Administration. The new Attorneys-General, however, were the recognized leaders of their respective parties in the two Provinces, and were the most important members of the Government; so that the use of their joint names to designate the Administration which they directed can hardly be termed a misnomer.

The reconstruction involved consequences the reverse of welcome to Messrs. Ogden, Sherwood and Davidson, whose offices had been declared vacated. Mr. Ogden had accepted the Attorney-Generalship of the Lower Province at a time when that office had been technically a non-political one. He had done loyal service to more than one Governor. At the time when his office was declared vacant he was absent from the Province on leave. His long and uninterrupted public services had somewhat impaired his health, and within a few days after the close of the session of 1841 a minute in Council had been passed granting him leave of absence for six months. This term was subsequently extended by Lord Stanley,

---

* "Les ministres qui restaient dans le Cabinet . . conservaient leur siége à la condition de se conformer à la politique de leurs nouveaux chefs."—LOUIS P. TURCOTTE: Le Canada Sous l'Union; Premiere Partie, Chapitre II.

† "No such stipulation, nor any other, except on the subject of the pension vote, was proposed."—See "The Political History of Canada," etc., ubi supra, p. 25.

the Colonial Secretary, but upon condition that he should be entitled to only half his usual salary during his absence. When his office of Attorney-General was declared vacant he was still absent, and he was not consulted as to the matter. Within the period covered by the extended leave of absence he returned to Canada by way of New York. It was not until he reached Albany that he learned that his office had been vacated, and that he had been sacrificed to the exigencies of the Government.* From all which it is apparent that if the principle of granting pensions was to be admitted at all, it was not difficult to make out a case for him. Mr. Sherwood, of course, had no claim to a pension, nor did any one dream of demanding one on his behalf, as he had accepted office only a few weeks before, and had not even been returned to Parliament. Mr. Davidson, however, had long been in the public service as Commissioner of Crown Lands. He had never been in Parliament, and had declined to enter public life at the Union, when it was suggested to him that his commissionership might probably erelong be made a Cabinet office. The time had now come when his office was needed, and it was considered unfair that such an old and respected public servant should be dismissed without any provision for his future. His case was accordingly considered by many persons to be a fair one for a pension. On the 3rd of October the Governor-General issued a message to the Assembly on the subject, recommending that a superannuation allowance of a sum not exceeding £625 per annum should be granted to Mr. Ogden, and a sum not exceeding £500 per annum to Mr. Davidson, " to be enjoyed during life, unless hereafter they shall hold under Government any office or equivalent of greater value within the Province." On the day before the close of the session Mr. Hincks moved that the message be taken into consideration by the Assembly, but the House was not in a pensioning

---

* See "The Humble Petition of Charles Richard Ogden, late Attorney-General of Canada," presented to Her Majesty in 1848.

mood. An amendment, proposed by Mr. Neilson, to the effect that
the Governor's message should be taken into consideration next
session, was carried by a vote of thirty-five to fifteen. Messieurs
Lafontaine and Baldwin both disapproved of the motion, but were
not present when the vote was taken, both of them being absent
in their respective constituencies;* it being necessary under Responsible Government, that they should be reëlected after taking
office in the Government. The difficulty regarding the pension
matter was finally got over by the appointment of Mr. Davidson
to the office of Collector of Customs at Hamilton, and by the
appointment of Mr. Ogden by the Imperial Government to the
Attorney-Generalship of the Isle of Man. The latter appointment,
however, was not made until considerably more than a year had
elapsed.

As for Mr. Sherwood, although there was no question of pensioning in his case, he naturally felt that he had been treated with but
scant consideration. At the time when he had agreed to accept
office he had presented to the Governor-General a memorandum
containing a statement of his political opinions. In that memorandum he had represented himself as being actuated by Conservative
principles. He had declared his views to be opposed to those of some
members of the Executive Council, but professed that he felt it to
be his duty to assent to the proposal of Her Majesty's representative in Canada to take part in the Administration; reserving to
himself, nevertheless, the option of voting as his judgment might
dictate upon the question of the Lower Canadian elections alleged
to have been carried by unjustifiable means. With regard to all
other questions he had declared that in the event of his acceptance

---

* Sir Francis Hincks is of opinion that "under different circumstances neither Mr.
Lafontaine nor Mr. Baldwin would have disputed the propriety of awarding pensions to
two old public servants deprived of their offices owing to the introduction of a new
principle of Government."—See the "Lecture" already frequently quoted from, p. 26.

of office he should feel himself bound to support any measure determined upon by a majority of the Council in accordance with the views of his Excellency, or else to resign office. This conduct on the part of Mr. Sherwood was frank, open, and straightforward. The Governor fully concurred in the terms of the memorandum, and Mr. Sherwood was sworn in as Solicitor-General accordingly. He was soon afterwards directed by his Excellency to proceed, in his capacity of Crown Officer, to St. Catharines, to investigate and report upon certain disturbances which had arisen there. He departed on his mission, and it was while he was acting in the discharge of this public duty that the reconstruction took place. Having completed his investigations, he started from St. Catharines for the seat of Government, being still unaware of the changes in the Administration. Upon reaching Toronto he received from a personal friend at Kingston, on the night of Wednesday, the 14th of September, a copy of the letter of the Governor-General to Mr. Lafontaine dated the previous day. In that letter, as has been seen, the Governor made an attempt to keep Mr. Sherwood's office open until that gentleman's arrival at Kingston, doubtless with a view to affording him an opportunity to resign. Mr. Sherwood, however, did not wait to reach Kingston, but at once wrote out his resignation, being well assured that that would be the most effectual means of preserving his dignity. The letter of resignation was not forwarded, as the Solicitor-General was about to leave for Kingston without delay, and preferred to place it in his Excellency's hands in person. Upon reaching Kingston he found that he was too late, and that his office had not only already been declared vacant, but had also been filled up. He felt indignant that he should thus have been superseded without notice, and wrote a long letter to his Excellency expressive of his feelings. The Governor doubtless felt that "impatience hath his privilege," and replied in a conciliatory manner. And thus ended Mr. Sherwood's connection with an Administration in which he ought never to have accepted a place. His political career, however, was not at an end. As will hereafter be seen, he was destined to be successively Solicitor-General and Attorney-General for Upper Canada.

Mr. Lafontaine, upon returning for reëlection to his constituents in North York, was returned by a flattering majority of more than two hundred votes over his opponent, Mr. William Roe, of Newmarket. Mr. Baldwin did not fare so well. He was opposed in Hastings by Mr. Edmund Murney. At this election the total number of votes polled was 915. Of these, 482 were recorded for Mr. Murney, and only 433 for Mr. Baldwin, who was therefore defeated by a majority of forty-nine. The most glaring bribery and corruption were practised during this contest. Ruffianism was rampant, and mob-law prevailed to such an extent that many electors, after being beaten and otherwise maltreated, were forcibly prevented from recording their votes.* It happened just after this

---

*The outrageous proceedings at this election rendered it a memorable event in the history of the county of Hastings. It seems incredible that such scenes should have taken place in a well-settled, and presumably well-civilized community in Upper Canada less than forty years since. The ruffianism which prevailed during two days is thus described in the Prince Edward *Gazette*, the proprietor of which visited Belleville for the purpose of obtaining accurate information on the spot: "On Wednesday [the 5th of October] it appears that bodies of voters, armed with bludgeons, swords, and fire arms, generally consisting of men who had no votes, but attached to opposite parties, alternately succeeded in driving the voters of Mr. Baldwin and Mr. Murney from the poll. In the melée which took place several persons were severely wounded. One man, named Cuverly, had his arm nearly cut off by the stroke of a sword, and two others, named Curtis and Madden, are not expected to live, from the blows which they received. Two brothers, of the name of O'Brien, one of whom keeps a tavern, were seriously injured. The tavern-keeper had the windows of his house knocked in by those to whom he was opposed. All the persons injured, whom we have mentioned, were the supporters of Mr. Baldwin, but we understand that the riotous proceedings were about as great on the one side as on the other. On Wednesday the poll was closed about three o'clock p.m. In the course of the afternoon it was deemed expedient by the magistrate of Belleville and Mr. Baldwin to send down to Kingston for a detachment of troops, for the preservation of the public peace. In the course of Thursday [the 6th] two attempts were made to open the poll, but, from the violent conduct of the people it was closed immediately, before even a single vote could be taken. On the arrival of the troops, on Thursday afternoon,

THE HON. THOMAS MOSS.

THE HON. THOMAS MOORE.

BROCK'S MONUMENT, QUEENSTON HEIGHTS.

THE HON. EDWARD BLAKE.

THE HON. SIR CHARLES TUPPER.

time that a new election became necessary in the Second Riding of York, in consequence of the return of the sitting member, Mr. George Duggan, having been pronounced void. Some of Mr. Baldwin's friends rashly put him forward as a candidate without his knowledge or consent, he having meanwhile decided on running for a Lower Canadian constituency. He did not visit the constituency pending the canvass, and his interests were not even judiciously attended to in his absence. That he should be beaten under such circumstances was almost a foregone conclusion. Mr. Duggan again offered himself to his constituents, and on the 22nd of November was returned by a majority over Mr. Baldwin of forty-three votes. Mr. Baldwin may thus be said to have sustained two successive defeats, although as matter of fact he never sanctioned the action of his friends in putting him forward for the second constituency. His consistent championship of his Lower Canadian allies was then acknowledged by the latter in a very practical shape, several Lower Province constituencies being at once placed at his disposal. He would have had no difficulty about securing a return in an Upper Canadian constituency, but he showed his appreciation of the good offices of his eastern friends by selecting the county of Rimouski, where the sitting member, Mr. Borne, made way for him. On the 30th of January, 1843, he was declared elected. The anomaly was thus presented of the Upper Canadian leader sitting for a Lower Province constituency, and the leader of Lower Canada sitting for a constituency in the Upper Province. Mr. Aylwin had it all his own way in Portneuf, where he was reëlected without opposition. Mr. Small, the new Solicitor-General for Upper Canada, was opposed in the Third Riding of York by Captain John Simcoe Macaulay, whom he defeated by a considerable

---

consisting of a body of one hundred and fourteen men of the 23rd, under the command of Captain Crutchley, the town was restored to comparative good order."

majority. Last, but by no means least among the new Ministers, came Mr. Morin. His portfolio of Commissioner of Crown Lands had previously been offered to his fellow-countryman, Mr. J. J. Girouard. That gentleman had been charged with active participation in the Lower Canadian Rebellion, and a reward of five hundred pounds had been paid for his apprehension. He was a popular man among his compatriots, and his appointment to office would have been gratifying enough to their feelings, but he himself saw fit, for personal reasons, to decline the overture.* The portfolio was then tendered to, and accepted by, Mr. Morin, who was returned for the county of Saguenay, which constituency was rendered vacant by the appointment of the sitting member, Mr. Etienne Parent, to the post of Clerk of the Executive Council.

Such were the changes brought about by the reconstruction of 1842. The newly-formed Government was a strong one; so strong that anyone unfamiliar with the chances and changes of political life might naturally have predicted that it would be able to make light of any opposition that could be brought to bear against it for years. In a House of Assembly containing eighty-four members the Opposition could not muster more than twenty-eight, consisting exclusively of the Conservatives of the two Provinces—arrayed under the banners of Sir Allan MacNab and the Hon. George Moffatt—and of the two or three members calling themselves Independent. When Parliament next met the twenty-eight had shrunk to twenty-four, and Mr. Sullivan, the President of the Council, who for some years previously had been more of a Conservative than anything else, was able to boast that the Government had its foot firmly planted upon the neck of the Conservative party. The Conservatives of both Provinces were naturally depressed, and the

---

* Mr. Girouard was the gentleman to whom Mr. Lafontaine's incautious letter had been addressed, as narrated ante, p. 231. The text of the letter, in English and French, may be read in the columns of the *Montreal Gazette* for February 9th, 1843.

Reformers were proportionately elated. The French Canadians were especially jubilant at the turn of affairs. Heretofore, since the Union, they had been excluded from all share whatever in the conduct of public business. They now saw their leader the actual leader of the Government, and another highly-esteemed compatriot holding the important office of Commissioner of Crown Lands. For the first time for years they began to contemplate the situation with some degree of complacency, and to ask each other whether it might not be possible, after all, to regard the Union of the Provinces as a yoke possible to be borne with composure.*

---

* The French Canadian view of the situation is very clearly depicted by Mr. Turcotte : "L'Union était toujours un mal, mais un mal d'où pouvait resulter le bien : car le gouvernement responsable donnait au peuple un élément suffisant de réparation pour le passé et pour le présent et de garantie pour l'avenir. D'ailleurs, avec les concessions faites par Sir Charles Bagot, l'Union pouvait être tolérée par les Canadiens-Français, tout en travaillant à l'amender autant qui possible."—*Le Canada Sous l'Union*, Premiere Partie, p. 141.

Chapter XII.

THE SHADOW OF DOWNING STREET.

"Sir Charles Bagot succeeded in reconciling and attaching to the British Government . . people whose affections had been in a great degree alienated by former misgovernment. The test of his capacity for the high office which he held was his complete success. The evidence of that success is to be found recorded in the journals of the House of Assembly, where opposition was absolutely silenced; it is to be found in the addresses that poured into him, not from a party or faction, but from a united people; it was manifested in the heartfelt prayers put up for his recovery when he was languishing on that bed of sickness which he never left."—Letter of "A Canadian," dated August 13th, 1844, and published in the *Morning Chronicle* (London).

HE legislation of the second session under the Union was not of permanent historical importance, and may be passed over with very brief mention. The Acts passed were thirty in number, in addition to two which were reserved for the further signification of Her Majesty's pleasure thereon.* Among the most important measures which became law was an Act to provide for the freedom of elections, and to prevent such unseemly passages of arms as had just taken place in the county of Hastings, as mentioned in the last chapter. Some of its clauses were marked by what seemed to many of the old-fashioned voters of those days to be unnecessary severity. It was enacted that any person convicted of a battery committed during any part of any day on which an election was held, and within two miles of the hustings, might be fined twenty-

---

* One of these reserved Acts was to impose a duty on foreign wheat imported into Canada. It in due course received the royal sanction, and became the law of the land.

five pounds, and imprisoned for three calendar months, or either, in the discretion of the Court.* The penalties in case of bribery were heavy, and candidates were prohibited from paying even the common expenses incidental to an election, such as the hiring of wagons to convey voters to the polls. The exhibiting of any ensign, standard, colour, flag, ribbon, label or favour whatsoever, or for any reason whatsoever, or for any election, on any election day, or within a fortnight before or after such day, was prohibited under a penalty of fifty pounds and imprisonment for six months, or either.† The Act had the desired effect of making an orderly and decorous election contest possible, and of enabling an honest voter to exercise his franchise without running the risk of losing his life or of being deprived of the use of his limbs.

Another measure of importance was an Act to make uniform the law for vacating the seats of members of the Legislative Assembly accepting office. The ancient boundaries and limits

---

* It may be interesting, and even instructive, for readers of the present day to see a specimen of the worst and most unfair species of criticism to which public men and measures were subjected in those times. The following were the *Toronto Patriot's* editorial remarks on the clause referred to in the text :—" Oh rare and inimitable legislation! Oh, most profound and wisest of all long-eared law-givers! A scoundrel may insult or strike an honest man, or try to force his way into his house, on the morning of some election held two miles off, and if the latter very properly knocks him down, he is fined twenty-five pounds and sent to gaol for three months under Mr. Attorney-General Baldwin's most merciful and sapient Act of Parliament."

† "So that any body of honest electors who for a fortnight after any election (being a period of one month,) shall dare to hoist the Union Jack of Old England, or wear a green or blue ribbon in the button-hole, shall be fined fifty pounds, or imprisoned six months, or both, under Mr. Baldwin's Election Bill! We defy the whole world to match this Bill for ridiculous enactments and for grinding and insupportable tyranny. In British annals it has no parallel since the days of the Curfew—when our French invaders, assisted by domestic traitors, bound down the old Saxon race in the most degrading servitude—when after the tolling of the evening bell the hearthfires and lights throughout the broad bounds of Merry England were extinguished at the whim of a foreign tyrant."—*Ib.* Strange to say, such rhodomontade as this passed current with many people for sound, sensible argument.

of the cities of Quebec and Montreal were restored, and certain Ordinances of the late Governor and Special Council of Lower Canada were repealed. Much of the legislation simply repealed or amended measures which had come into operation under Lord Sydenham,* and there was a manifest desire to legislate in such a manner as to conciliate the French Canadians. There was a good deal of agitation during the session on the Seat of Government question, and resolutions were passed by a majority of forty to twenty to the effect that Kingston was not a desirable place for the capital of the Province. The changes in the Administration had been of such importance that it was deemed wise to make the session a very short one, as it was hopeless for the reconstructed Government to attempt to formulate a wise or carefully-considered policy while the Legislature was actually in session.

Parliament was prorogued at one o'clock in the afternoon of Wednesday, the 12th of October, after a session of less than five weeks. His Excellency's Speech was very short, and indicated an early reassembling. It concluded by the expression of a hope that the members, upon their return to their homes, would use their influence in promoting unanimity and good feeling in their respective districts. The Governor-General seemed to be in the enjoyment of excellent health, and it was remarked of him that he was more at home with his duties than he had appeared to be at the opening of the session. "He was accompanied to the House," says a flippant newspaper writer of the period, "by a guard of the Lancers, and received by a company of the Third Fusiliers, amid the roar of cannon and a general uncovering of upper works. He acquitted himself of his duties creditably, and returned to his

---

* "Ainsi, presque toutes les *grandes mesures* de Lord Sydenham et du conseil spécial furent ou rappelées ou amendées, de manière à satisfaire le peuple." *Le Canada Sous l'Union, Premiere Partie*, p. 131. "Presque toutes," however, is a somewhat stronger statement of the case than the facts warranted.

domicile instantly after the ceremony."* It was remarked of his Excellency that he seemed to have grown younger since his arrival in Canada, and that he was evidently destined for a green old age.

The indications were illusory. Scarcely had the session been brought to a close when the Governor's health began rapidly to decline. Early in November he was prostrated by a severe and dangerous illness. One physician pronounced his disease to be dropsy. Another declared it to be hypertrophy of the heart. Both proved to be correct. There was a general breaking-up of the constitution, and though the patient rallied once or twice it soon became apparent that his earthly career was nearly run. Parliament had been prorogued until the 18th of November. The Governor's ill-health rendered a further prorogation necessary. His medical advisers recommended, as the most effectual means of prolonging his life, that he should at once return to England, or that he should at least repair to some land where he might be subjected to a less trying climate than that of Canada in winter. The first recommendation harmonized with his own inclinations and those of his family, and he lost no time in requesting his recall. Long before any reply could be received from the Imperial authorities, however, lake and river navigation had closed, and winter had set in with unusual severity. The inclement season did its work upon his debilitated frame, and he was soon too weak to undertake the journey. He bore up with such fortitude as he could command, and transacted business with his Council whenever he felt able to do so, but in the actual work of carrying on the Government he was able to take but a very slight share.

Before the close of the year it began to be rumoured in political circles that the exciting cause of Sir Charles Bagot's illness was worry and anxiety of mind, induced by animadversions on his

---

* "H.," in the Montreal Gazette of October 15th.

conduct from the Home Office. How far these animadversions were really responsible for his condition it is difficult to say. As has already been intimated, he had never enjoyed a vigorous constitution, and he was at this time sixty years of age. Still, he had always lived regularly, and, unlike his predecessor, whose habits were not in all respects conducive to longevity, he had husbanded his physical resources by a careful observance of the laws of health. Up to a few days before his first attack he had seemed to be so vigorous and buoyant that he was complimented by members of his family upon having renewed his youth. It is certain that on the very day before his prostration he had received an official communication from Lord Stanley, the Colonial Secretary, and that he had been greatly annoyed and worried thereby. The contents of this missive, and of subsequent missives from the same quarter, have never been given to the world, but there can be little doubt that they contained severe censure of his action with reference to the change of Ministry. The particular ground of censure can only be guessed at, but Lord Stanley at this time looked with no favourable eyes upon Responsible Government as applied to Canada, and it is at least probable that he was averse to seeing persons placed in power in this country whose loyalty had so recently been, to put the matter very mildly, open to grave suspicion. Downing Street was less indifferent to Canadian affairs than it had been prior to the publication of Lord Durham's Report, but it could not be expected to understand the position of matters here as well as Sir Charles Bagot, who had spent ten months in acquiring a knowledge of the political needs of the country. The London *Times*, which then, as now, was culpably ignorant on everything relating to Canada, lectured the Governor with patronizing sternness for having taken Mr. Lafontaine, "a man who had had a price set upon his head," into his Council. The Imperial assent to the Governor's request for his recall, however, was not understood as implying any censure upon his conduct, but merely as a compliance with his will, imposed by the declining state of his health.

The Opposition press of Canada, which had assailed Sir Charles with merciless rancour ever since the reconstruction of the Administration, did its utmost during the closing months of his life to disseminate erroneous views as to his character. It is possible enough that in many instances these views were honestly entertained, but that they had no solid foundation must be apparent to all who will take the trouble of careful investigation. It was represented that the Governor was a man of feeble will and capacity, and that he was a mere puppet in the hands of the members of his Council. Even the most rabid of his assailants admitted that he was "a good and excellent man, with so much station and character as should prevent public indignation from rejecting him;" but it was charged that he was so slenderly endowed intellectually as to be "incapable of detecting any intrigue, or resisting any pretension." No evidence of these assertions has ever been offered to the public, and the known facts all point to a different conclusion. It is true that he had no pretensions to commanding talents or brilliant statesmanship, but his abilities were at least of a respectable order, and his long career in the public service had given him a knowledge of the world and a familiarity with departmental details which afforded him great advantages in his capacity of a constitutional Governor. He proved that he was at least great enough to rise above the trammels of party. He was a Conservative by descent, by training, and by predilection. He found the tone of Conservative society in Canada much more to his taste than that of the Reformers. He was jealous for the prerogatives of the Crown. Yet he did not hesitate to call to his Council, and to work cordially with, persons of the opposite extreme of political opinion, when he found that such persons enjoyed the popular confidence. He acted up to the spirit of the resolutions passed by the Assembly in September, 1841.*

---

* See *ante*, p. 150.

He refused to render Responsible Government in Canada a nullity, merely because his own sympathies would never, perhaps, have led him to originate such resolutions. As has been said of him by a Canadian historian, he "went on the broad principle that the constitutional majority had the right to rule under the constitution."* The constitutional majority included persons whose political opinions were widely different from his own, but that fact did not seem to him to afford any reason why he should run counter to the declared principles of the constitution itself. Had the Conservative party been in the ascendant, his task would doubtless have been far more congenial to him than it was under the state of things which actually existed. It would also have been far more easy, for the reconstruction of the Ministry could have been accomplished without either trouble or delay. As it was, the reconstruction rendered much deliberation necessary, as well as much apparent waste of time. The delay which occurred was in a measure due to his desire to conciliate the Conservatives.† After postponing the meeting of Parliament until further postponement was not to be thought of, he called the Houses together. No sooner were the members in their places than it was made apparent that under no conjunction of circumstances whatever could the Conservatives be

---

* See MacMullen's "History of Canada," p. 497.

† "To place the leaders of that [the Conservative] party in power, he would have resorted to any constitutional steps. He consulted with them; he obtained their opinion as to the result of a dissolution of Parliament; and, finally, he offered office to the only one of them [Mr. Sherwood] who would accept it on such terms as it was in his power to offer. He postponed the meeting of Parliament almost to the last moment, in the vain hope of making some arrangement by which he could at the same time secure the necessary Parliamentary support for his Government, and obtain the assistance of the leaders of that party to which he was personally attached. To effect this object he would have sacrificed those members of his Ministry who could not have acted with the Tories. One thing he would not do, and that was to quarrel irrevocably with those who were possessed of public confidence, and either suspend the constitution or dissolve Parliament, when the leaders of the Conservative party themselves admitted to him that they had no hope of success by an appeal to the people." Letter of "A Canadian," in the (London) *Morning Chronicle*.

induced to support the Government as it stood. The Conservative leaders from both Provinces—Sir Allan MacNab, Mr. Cartwright, and the Hon. George Moffatt—at the same time admitted their inability to form an Administration which could hope to command the support of Parliament. The ablest Conservative in the country —Mr. Draper—already held office in the Government. He was wise enough to comprehend the situation, and though he was very reluctant to resign his portfolio, he gave to the Governor the best advice in his power—well knowing, at the same time, that if his advice were followed he could not hope to retain office in the same Government with Mr. Baldwin. His counsels prevailed, and the result was the formation of a Government so strong that, as has already been intimated, it seemed impregnable. It is now admitted on all hands that Sir Charles acted wisely, and that if he had acted otherwise he would soon have found himself in a position somewhat analogous to that in which we shall hereafter find his successor, Sir Charles Metcalfe. Such a result, however, though clear enough to us at this day, was by no means perfectly obvious at the time; and the fact that the Governor-General had the sagacity to take in the main points of the situation, and to forecast the probabilities of the future, affords evidence that he was not, as has been alleged, a mere weak puppet, liable to be driven hither and thither at the will of his advisers. A weak, a vacillating, or even a stubborn man, would have been almost certain to blunder at such a crisis. He would not have seen the wisdom which lurked in the counsel of the Attorney-General. He would have been very likely to enact the rôle of Charles I., and to set himself up in opposition to public opinion, as we shall find his successor doing a year later.

That he exhibited weakness after the hand of disease had been laid heavily upon him is undeniable; but the weakness, even then, was physical rather than mental, and there is no evidence that it was ever abused by his Councillors. So far as can now be ascertained, the relations between him and them seem to have been of a frank and cordial nature.* Whenever the state of his health admitted of his taking a share in the active duties of Government, he seems to have done so. That his Ministers did not press work upon him when he was physically unfit for work, is very probable. It is also probable that they took more upon themselves than they would have presumed to do if the Governor had been in good health; but that they should do so was a necessary incident of the position in which they found themselves, and forms no ground for censure, or even for criticism. After Sir Charles became so much prostrated as to be unable to transact even the most formal functions of Government, all matters of great importance which required Executive action were held over until the arrival of his successor.

In the middle of February, 1843, it became known in Canada that Sir Charles Bagot's request for his recall had been granted, and that Sir Charles Metcalfe, late Governor of Jamaica, had been appointed in his stead. Before entering into particulars respecting Sir Charles Metcalfe's appointment, and his subsequent Administration of affairs in Canada, the little that remains to tell about Sir Charles Bagot may as well be chronicled. The Governor had not yet relinquished the hope of living through the winter, and of proceeding to England in the spring. His successor reached Canada towards the end of March, and on the 30th of the month the reins of Government were surrendered into his hands by the retiring Administrator. Just before relinquishing his authority Sir Charles Bagot held his last Cabinet Council. He was compelled to receive the Ministers in his bedroom at Alwington House, for he had become too weak to leave his bed. He bade them a cordial and tender farewell, accompanied by an earnest injunction to *defend his*

---

* "His uniform frankness and cordiality had so won upon his Ministers that there was not one of them that would not have gone the utmost length in his power to meet and forward his views."—Letter of "A Canadian," in the (London) *Morning Chronicle*.

memory. He doubtless anticipated trouble between the new Governor and the Ministry, in which case his own conduct would not improbably come in for serious animadversion. The tone of his communications from the Colonial Secretary for some months past had been such as to satisfy him that he need expect no defence from that quarter. He doubtless felt that his conduct was capable of being defended, and that the proper persons to undertake that task were his sworn advisers. The interview is described as being a very affecting one, and it is said there was not a dry eye in the room. Such a scene would not have been likely to take place if the Governor had, as alleged by the Opposition press, been smarting under a sense of tyranny and injustice on the part of his Ministers.

Sir Charles Metcalfe did not disturb Sir Charles Bagot and his family in their occupation of Alwington House. The invalid was soon compelled to relinquish the hope of dying in his native land. He grew weaker and weaker from day to day. He lingered until three o'clock in the morning of Saturday, the 19th of May, when his earthly sufferings were terminated by death. His remains were conveyed from Kingston to England by way of Oswego and New York. They were honoured with marked tokens of respect while passing through the United States. His memory was long cherished with warm affection by French Canadians of every degree, and he is not yet wholly forgotten by them. He was the first Governor-General to mete out to them even-handed justice, and they were not insensible to the wise and impartial policy by which his Administration was characterized. The British press on both sides of the Atlantic, without distinction of party, bore testimony to his personal good qualities, and mourned his death.*

---

* To this there were several exceptions. The *Toronto Patriot*, which, as will have been inferred from previous quotations, was the deadly and uncompromising enemy of the Administration, referred to the dead Governor as an imbecile and a slave. Major

Lady Mary, with her family, returned to England immediately after her husband's death. She survived him less than two years, and died on the 2nd of February, 1845.

Richardson states that "other journals, even less guarded in their language, boldly pronounced a wish that his death might free the country from the state of thraldom to which it had been reduced."—See "Eight Years in Canada," p. 213.

Chapter XIII.

SIR CHARLES METCALFE.

"A tallow dip is an excellent thing in the kitchen candlestick. It is only when you stick it in silver and introduce it into the drawing-room that it seems dim and ineffectual. Alas for the worthy man who, like that candle, gets himself into the wrong place."— GEORGE ELIOT: *Scenes of Clerical Life.*

SIR CHARLES THEOPHILUS METCALFE, the statesman who had been appointed to succeed Sir Charles Bagot as Governor-General of Canada, had passed many years of an industrious life in the Civil Service of India, and had more recently administered the Government of Jamaica. In both hemispheres he had won a high and honourable reputation, not only in various official capacities, but also as a man. The testimonials to his efficiency as a public servant, as well as to his intellectual and moral worth, were strongest and loudest where he was best known. "The ablest civil servant I ever knew in India," said Macaulay,* " was Sir Charles Metcalfe." " In his public career," said Lord William Bentinck,† "I think no man has shown greater rectitude of conduct, or more independence of mind. . We served together for nearly seven years; his behaviour to me was of the

---

* In a speech delivered in the House of Commons on the second reading of the India Bill. In consequence of his being compelled to bring this masterly effort to an abrupt and premature conclusion, Macaulay did not judge it worthy of a place in the collected edition of his speeches. The reader will find some of the most salient passages of it, including the above tribute to Sir Charles Metcalfe, in Trevelyan's "Life of Macaulay," Harpers' Library Edition, Vol. II., p. 287, *et seq.*

† In a letter to Lord Melbourne. See Kaye's "Life of Metcalfe," revised edition, Vol. II., p. 233.

noblest kind. He never cavilled upon a trifle, and never yielded to me upon a point of importance." In Jamaica the encomiums lavished upon him were all pitched in the same key. When he embarked for England, after resigning the Governorship of that island, crowds of people of all classes attended him to the place of embarkation to bid him "God-speed." The old island militia-men volunteered to form his escort. The coloured population knelt to bless him. "All classes of society and all sects of Christians sorrowed for his departure; and the Jews set an example of Christian love by praying for him in their synagogues."* "The universal voice of the colony seemed to be lifted up in a chorus of benediction."† After his departure the people erected a statue to his memory in the public square of Spanish Town. Upon his return to England the Colonial Society presented him with an address in which it was declared that Colonial Governments could never thereafter be conducted on any other principles than those of his administration.‡ His kindly nature, his open-handed benevolence, and his noble generosity of heart left their impress behind them whithersoever he went, and love for the man was as profound as was respect for the just and right-minded administrator. His reputation had steadily grown with his increasing years, and his praise was in the mouths of all men. His name was well and favourably known in every land where the supremacy of Great Britain was acknowledged, and when it was announced in this country that he was to be Sir Charles Bagot's successor in the Governor-Generalship the intelligence was received with a feeling akin to pride.§ England, it was said, had at last given us of her best.

---

* See Kaye's "Life," p. 303.   † Ib., p. 300.   ‡ Ib., p. 304.

§ "Perhaps there had never been a previous instance of a Governor—a personal stranger to those whom he was about to govern, and yet separated from them by an entire ocean—obtaining such a hold upon the affections and good will of a people, as Sir Charles Metcalfe did, from the very moment that his name was confidently mentioned as the future Governor-General of Canada."—*Eight Years in Canada*, by Major Richardson, p. 214.

The facts of his early life may for the purposes of this work be briefly stated. He was born at Calcutta on the 30th of January, 1785, and was the second son of an English gentleman of much wealth, named Theophilus Metcalfe, a Major in the Bengal army, and a Director in the East India Company. He was from infancy destined by his parents for the Company's service, and, as was usual in the case of youths of his rank, he was sent home to England to be educated. He stood well in his classes at Eton College, and was known for a jovial-hearted, generous boy, although somewhat self-willed, and fond of having his own way. He returned to India in his sixteenth year, and was soon afterwards appointed to a writership in the service of the great Company. This position he filled for about seven years, when he was appointed to the charge of a mission to the court of Lahore, where he succeeded so well that other high offices of trust were conferred upon him. He rose steadily and surely, and in 1827 took his seat as a member of the Supreme Council of India. By the death of his father and elder brother he had meanwhile succeeded to the family estates and title, and had become Sir Charles Metcalfe. Additional wealth and honour awaited him at every step in his career. Upon Lord William Bentinck's resignation of the Governor-Generalship of India in 1834, Sir Charles was provisionally appointed to that position, which he filled until the arrival of his old schoolfellow, Lord Auckland, as Governor-General, in 1836. During this interval he brought about many liberal and much-needed reforms, one of the most important of which was the emancipation of the Indian press from certain embarrassing restrictions to which it was liable to be subjected by any Governor who might be despotic enough to enforce them. By this one act he won the lasting gratitude, not only of the press itself, but of the countless thousands of whose sentiments the press was the exponent. Upon Lord Auckland's arrival Sir Charles sailed for England, where he took up his abode at Fern Hill, an estate which he had inherited from his father, and which is situated near the historic old town of Windsor. He had never married, but he had near relatives to whom he was fondly attached, and who fully reciprocated his affection. In their society he passed most of his time, and he looked forward to spending the evening of his life among them. But he was not destined to enjoy a long retirement. In the summer of 1839, just as he had begun seriously to contemplate the step of entering the House of Commons, he was prevailed upon by the Ministry of the day to accept the post of Governor of Jamaica. The Government in that island was in a very disorganized condition, and presented little inducement to any man who had the option of living a life of dignified leisure, as had Sir Charles Metcalfe. A war of races prevailed there, and the coloured population were declared to be unmanageable except as slaves. Sir Charles accepted, however; partly with the hope of adding fresh laurels to his crown, and partly, no doubt, from a high sense of duty, and a desire to render service to the State. The result was such as fully to satisfy any ambition which he could reasonably have entertained. He converted strife and disaffection into peace and loyalty, and this not by rule of thumb, but by the exercise of a systematic justice. He made himself beloved by all classes of society. After administering the Government between two and three years he had the proud satisfaction of leaving the island in a state of tranquillity. How he was honoured upon his departure has already been told.

His resignation was due to the ill effects of the climate upon his constitution, and to the progress of a painful and serious disorder by which he had long been afflicted—cancer of the left cheek. This malady had begun to manifest itself some years before his departure from India, but its real nature had not been suspected until it had made considerable progress. After his arrival in England from Jamaica he submitted to a painful operation at the hands of Sir

Benjamin Brodie and other surgeons of experience. The anguish he endured was great, but he bore it with the fortitude of a man who, in governing others, had learned the art of governing himself. The result of the operation seemed to be very satisfactory, and for a while it was hoped that all danger to life was over. The terrible disease, however, had merely been checked in its progress, and it remorselessly bided its time.

Early in January, 1843, it began to be whispered in English political circles that Sir Charles Metcalfe was to succeed Sir Charles Bagot in the Governorship of Canada.* The rumour proved to be true. And in order that some plausible solution of subsequent complications may be arrived at, it is necessary to inquire somewhat narrowly into the circumstances attendant upon his appointment.

And first, a word as to Lord Stanley, the Colonial Secretary. This distinguished member of a noble and historic English family held office by virtue of his talents, not less than by his high social position, and the amount of Parliamentary support which he could command. Though an aristocrat by descent and by natural leanings, he had opinions, of his own, to which he was not afraid to give expression. He had at one time been (theoretically) one of the most radical of Whigs, and had taken no undistinguished part in the debates in favour of the Reform Bill. As Chief Secretary for Ireland in Earl Grey's Administration he was responsible for two bold measures—one relating to national education; the other to the Irish Church temporalities, which resulted in the abolition of ten Irish bishoprics. The natural tone of his mind, however, was

---

* "The report had been mentioned at a dinner party at which Mr. [Edward] Gibbon Wakefield was present, and that gentleman, who was as well versed in colonial politics as any man in the country, had asked Mr. Mangles, who was another of the party, if he were a friend of Sir Charles Metcalfe, to inform him that neither he nor any other statesman would act wisely in accepting the Governor-Generalship of Canada without making certain stipulations with, and receiving certain powers to act from, the Home Ministry."—Kaye's *Life of Metcalfe*, Vol. II., p. 312.

eminently Conservative, and his secession from the ranks of the
Reform party sooner or later was inevitable. His mind was not
receptive of new ideas. He was an elegant and accomplished
scholar, proficient in the classics, and somewhat inordinately fond
of airing his classical attainments in the House of Commons. His
knowledge of political economy, of the science of governing, and
of scientific matters generally, was inconsiderable, and he on one
occasion boasted of having been born in the pre-scientific age.* In
1834 he became alarmed by a measure for appropriating the surplus
of the Irish Church temporalities to secular purposes, and withdrew
from the Administration. He then joined the Conservative party,
with whom his own interests continued to be bound up for the rest
of his long and active life. He was an ardent protectionist, and upon
the formation of Sir Robert Peel's Ministry in 1841, as has been seen,†
he accepted office in it as Colonial Secretary. With such instincts
as he possessed, it was to be expected that there would be more or
less change in Britain's colonial policy. The expectation was
realized. For some time past Governors of Liberal tendencies had
been sent out to Canada. Lords Durham and Sydenham had been
identified with the most advanced Liberalism. Lord Stanley re-
versed this by sending out a staunch Conservative in the person of
Sir Charles Bagot. The events of Sir Charles's Administration
greatly disappointed the Colonial Secretary, and the effect of the
latter's censures upon the Governor to whom they were addressed
has already been hinted at.‡ The disappointment seems to have been
shared by Sir Robert Peel and the other members of the Administra-

---

* "He had very little, indeed, of that class of information which the modern world
requires of its statesmen and leaders. Of political economy, of finance, of the development and the discoveries of modern science, he knew almost as little as it is possible for
an able and energetic man to know who lives in the throng of active life, and hears what
people are talking of around him." *A History of Our Own Times*, by Justin McCarthy,
Chapter II.

† *Ante*, p. 160. ‡ *Ante*, p. 256.

tion in only a limited degree. Evidently Lord Stanley did not feel his position to be strong in the matter of his censures, for, as has been intimated, the despatches containing them were not published, and he afterwards mildly defended Sir Charles Bagot in the House of Commons. Sir Charles having resigned, it now became necessary to supply his place. The question is: Why did the Secretary conceive the idea of appointing Sir Charles Metcalfe?

To this pertinent query, it may be replied that Sir Charles Metcalfe was a very likely man to be selected for such an appointment, inasmuch as he had already approved himself to possess many high qualifications. He was personally incorruptible and high-minded. He had had a long and varied experience in the Civil Service. He had been entrusted with more than one important mission, and had always acquitted himself in such a manner as to deserve and obtain high commendation. In the performance of his last important service to the State he had displayed statesmanlike qualities which even those who knew him best had scarcely credited him with possessing. In a land "still convulsed by a social revolution," he had "calmed the evil passions which long suffering had engendered in one class, and long domination in another."* Was it not reasonable to suppose that the man whose life had hitherto been a series of successes would continue to justify his reputation? There was certainly much to be said in favour of such an appointment. But—there was another side to the question.

Sir Charles's thirty-and-odd years of public service had nearly all been passed in India, and in connection with a Government which was largely despotic in its character. In the constitution of that great empire the representative element was wholly wanting. The right of the people to have a voice in public affairs was not recognized. So far as they were concerned, an imperious Governor could,

---

* See the well-known epitaph on Lord Metcalfe, by Macaulay.

if so disposed, lay claim to practical irresponsibility.* Sir Charles's despotism had always been exercised in a beneficent manner, but his Indian experiences had certainly not been of a nature to fit him for the direction of Canadian affairs. It may be doubted whether they had not rather a tendency to disqualify him.† In Jamaica he had, as already recorded, effected a pacification of hostile races, but he had previously obtained a complete ascendency over the so-called representative Assembly, and had had everything his own way.‡ His will had been so manifestly good, and his measures had so manifestly conduced to the public welfare, that there had been no serious opposition to anything he had thought fit to propose. So that his administration there could not be taken as a test of his ability to administer the affairs of a country provided with a constitution, and where both ministers and people were strenuous in asserting their constitutional rights. He had gone out to the West Indies armed with authority to virtually suspend the constitution. His chief task after his arrival had been to prove to the employer and the

---

* "Sir Charles Metcalfe, with a nature courageous and honourable, generous in expenditure, boundless in liberality, with great experience, great skill and fine taste in composition, had been trained in a country where suspicion [of] and contempt for the natives, formed the general rule of administration. It is the first lesson that a cadet learns in India, and he has not forgotten it when, after forty years of service, he is elevated to the rank of Governor-General."— See "The Speeches and Public Letters of the Hon. Joseph Howe," edited by William Annand, M.P.P., Vol. I., p. 324.

† The Hon. R. B. Sullivan, in replying to the Rev. Dr. Egerton Ryerson's defence of Sir Charles Metcalfe, in 1844, put forward this view of the matter very speciously. He remarked that if Dr. Ryerson had said that *notwithstanding* Sir Charles's residence in India he might yet be a good man and a benevolent man, he would not deny his proposition; "but," added Mr. Sullivan, "to say that governing slaves for forty years gives a man experience in the government of free British subjects is to tell the latter they are, or should be, slaves." See "Letters on Responsible Government," by *Legion*, p. 15.

‡ "Metcalfe, by his popularity, talents and private wealth, was enabled to pacify parties, and to control the *soi-disant* representative Assembly."— See "Review of *The Colonial Policy of Lord J. Russell's Administration*, by Earl Grey, and of Subsequent Colonial History;" by the Right Hon. Sir C. B. Adderley, K.C.M.G., M.P. [now Baron Norton], p. 231.

employed that their interests were identical. This he had effectually succeeded in doing, but he had not to deal, as in Canada, with the conflicting and more or less matured views of opposite schools of politicians. There had been no important fiscal projects to mature; no great commercial problems to solve. A representative constitution had been introduced into the island nearly two hundred years before,* but in so very simple a form that complicated disputes on obscure constitutional questions could not well arise. The Legislative Council was likewise the Executive Council, and the members of it held their offices during good conduct. Generally speaking, the Governor was wont to exercise the executive authority without reference to the Council.† Such a school as this could hardly be expected to furnish a suitable training for a ruler who was to administer the affairs of a colony possessed of Responsible Government. Of Parliamentary Government, as understood and practised in this country, he had had no experience, and he undoubtedly entertained exalted ideas as to the nature of the royal prerogative. It was alleged that he was a man of Liberal ideas. His emancipation of the Indian press, and the general course of his official policy, had been of a character to lend colour to the allegation. His biographer states that he was "saturated through and through with Liberal opinions." Such, indeed, was the estimate currently formed of him in England; and justly, for, though he had had no opportunity of formally identifying himself with either of the rival political parties there, he favoured the abolition of the Corn Laws, vote by ballot, the extension of the suffrage, amelioration of the Poor Laws, equal rights to all sects of Christians

---

*See "Parliamentary Government in the British Colonies," by Alpheus Todd; p. 74.

†See Sir Charles Metcalfe's despatch to Lord John Russell, dated February 12th, 1841, on the Constitution of the Local Government of Jamaica, quoted in "Selections from the Papers of Lord Metcalfe," edited by John William Kaye, p. 373, et seq.

in matters of religion, and equal rights to all men in civil matters.*
It is plain enough, however, that though his generous mind led him
instinctively to favour such projects as these, his doing so was rather
matter of instinct than of deliberate conviction. He saw only their
philanthropic side, and had not carefully weighed the political consequences of their adoption. It is not improbable that one or two
sessions in the House of Commons would have brought about a
considerable modification of his views on these and other leading
questions of the times. In the East he had put many of his Liberal
ideas into practice, and had acquired the reputation of being an
advanced Reformer, but any enlightened Tory would have found
himself in the same position. The code of political ethics at Calcutta
was by no means identical with that which prevailed at Westminster.
A line of policy which would constitute advanced Liberalism in an
Indian Viceroy might require a very different classification if the
venue were removed to England, where the Reform Bill was in
operation, and where Chartism was by no means at its nadir.
Popularly, however, Sir Charles Metcalfe was rightly regarded as a
Liberal, and always honestly professed himself to be such. Why,
then, did a hard-and-fast Conservative Government have recourse
to him in such a contingency? He had not sought for employment, and was even averse to accepting any. He was unmarried,
and had not the usual incentives to a life of exertion. He felt that
he had done his share of life's work, and hoped to spend the
remainder of his days in retirement and ease.

"The choice of an Indian statesman of reputed ability, but without
any experience whatever of Parliamentary Government, was at least
singular," says Sir Francis Hincks, who is of opinion that Lord
Stanley had formed a determination to overthrow Responsible Government, and that he selected Sir Charles Metcalfe as the most

---

* See his letter to his friend Mr. R. D. Mangles, dated January 13th, 1843, quoted in Kaye's "Life," pp. 312, 313.

fitting agent for the purpose.* This, be it understood, is merely the expression of Sir Francis Hincks's individual opinion, and not a statement of ascertained historical fact. It must be owned, however, that the propounder of the theory argues it out with a good deal of plausibility, and the circumstances attendant upon Sir Charles Metcalfe's appointment prove clearly enough at any rate that there were motives at work which were not then, and have never since been, made known to the world.

On the 14th of January, 1843, the Colonial Secretary wrote to Sir Charles from Downing Street, asking if the state of his health was such as to enable him to take upon himself "most honourable, but at the same time very arduous duties in the public service." Such are the precise words of the first official communication from the Government to Sir Charles on the subject of the Governor-Generalship of British North America. Personally, be it understood, Sir Charles was not known either to Lord Stanley or to any other member of the Government. "Should your answer to this preliminary inquiry be unfortunately in the negative," continued the missive, "I need not, of course, trouble you further; but in the event of your entertaining no insuperable objection to again giving this department the advantage of your valuable services, I would beg you to favour me by calling here any day next week which may be most convenient to yourself, when I should be happy to enter upon an unreserved communication with you upon the subject."† Sir Charles was unable to withstand such an appeal. He went up to London and accepted the appointment, but, as his correspondence shows, with many and serious misgivings. He seemed harassed by the consciousness that he was being sent on a "forlorn-hope" expedition.‡

---

* See the Lecture on "The Political History of Canada," p. 29.
† Kaye, Vol. II., p. 314.
‡ See Sir F. Hincks's Lecture, p. 30.

On the 19th of the month he wrote thus from Mivart's Hotel to Captain Higginson, who afterwards became his private secretary: "I have accepted the Government of Canada without being sure that I have done right. For I do not see my way so clearly as I could wish. Neither do I expect to do so before I reach my destination."* Three days later he wrote to another correspondent, Mr. R. D. Mangles: "I never undertook anything with so much reluctance, or so little hope of doing good, but I could not bring myself to say No, when the proposal was made. . . I fear that the little reputation that I have acquired is more likely to be damaged than improved in the troubled waters of Canada. I know, from experience, that the chief embarrassment of a colonial Governor is the interference of the Home Government. At the same time it is impossible to stipulate that they shall not control the Government of a colony. I must urge what is right and resist what is wrong, and come away as soon as I see that I can do no good. If I do any, I shall be agreeably surprised."† To Lord Monson he wrote on the 10th of February: "Never did a man go so unwillingly to anything by his own consent. Going, however, I am; and grumbling is useless. If I succeed in reconciling local dissensions, and promoting attachment between the colony and the mother country, I shall rejoice in having undertaken the charge. If I fail, which, from the state of things, is more probable, I must console myself with the assurance that for the rest of my days I shall be left undisturbed in the retirement that I love."‡

The question arises: What was the occasion of these wailing jeremiads? And why did the Colonial Secretary refer to the duties to be undertaken as "very arduous?" Unless the new Governor was to be hampered by secret instructions—unless he was to be sent out to Canada to inaugurate a new and an unpopular line of

* Kaye, Vol. II., p. 315.   † Ib., pp. 316, 317.   ‡ Ib., p. 317.

policy—the administration of affairs in this country did not seem to involve any insuperable difficulties. If Sir Charles Bagot's policy was to be maintained, and if Responsible Government was to be continued as a reality, why should Sir Charles Metcalfe look forward with something approaching to dread to the duties before him? Why should he be almost hopeless of being able to accomplish what was required of him? Why should he have doubts as to whether he had done right in undertaking such a task? Why should he fear damage to his reputation? There was no apparent reason for any particular solicitude. The Union was fairly under way. Responsible Government had been conceded, and was established. The newly-formed Administration was so strong that it could almost afford to despise the feebleness of the Opposition.* It seemed as though Sir Charles's duties, instead of being "arduous," would be much less so than had been those of his two predecessors. Sir Francis Hincks is of opinion that Sir Charles's language is inexplicable on any other assumption than that the arduous duty required of him was to overthrow Responsible Government.† It seems tolerably certain, at any rate, that Sir Charles came over to Canada charged with some task which bade fair to involve him in controversy, and the nature of which does not appear from the public despatches. It is always presumptuous to dogmatize where all the facts are not certainly known; but it seems not improbable that Lord Stanley had conceived the idea of reversing, or at any rate modifying, Sir Charles Bagot's policy, and that he had chosen Sir Charles Metcalfe as his agent because the latter's devotion to the Crown was undoubted, and because his reputation was such as to inspire respect for the Government of which he was the

---

* "Lord Grey's Administration in 1833 was hardly so strong as respects the constituencies."—See "A Letter on the Ministerial Crisis," by the Old Montreal Correspondent of the *Colonial Gazette*, of London (Edward Gibbon Wakefield). Kingston, 1843.—In a House containing 684 members Earl Grey had a clear working majority of 182.

† See the "Lecture," p. 30.

emissary. More than this, in the absence of additional facts, cannot wisely be averred.

Sir Charles Metcalfe, then, accepted Lord Stanley's proposal. On the 27th of February he was entertained at a splendid banquet given in his honour by the Colonial Society at the Colonial Club, St. James's Square.* Several days afterwards he dined at Buckingham Palace with Her Majesty and the Prince Consort. On the 4th of March, accompanied by his suite, he sailed from Liverpool for Boston in the Cunard steamship *Columbia*. The vessel touched at Halifax on the 18th, and Sir Charles spent several hours on shore there as the guest of Lord Falkland, the Lieutenant-Governor.† He reached Boston on the 20th, and during his two days' stay there received many civilities from persons in authority. On the 22nd he set out on his overland journey to Kingston, by way of Albany, Schenectady and Utica. From Utica to Kingston the journey was made in sleighs, in which conveyances the party crossed over the St. Lawrence and Lake Ontario on the ice, "both being frozen over, and covered with snow, like the rest of the country."‡ He reached his destination on the afternoon of the 29th, when he found the troops and a large crowd of people

---

* Among the guests was Sir Francis Bond Head, who, in the course of a racy after-dinner speech, proved that he had not gained wisdom since the close of his disastrous administration of affairs in Upper Canada. Not satisfied with declaring that the new Governor-General was about to leave for Canada taking with him the confidence of the whole empire, which was the simple truth, he prophesied that Sir Charles's accession to office would prove a blessing to the colony over the destinies of which he had been selected to rule. He also volunteered some advice which Sir Charles was far too prudent to act upon.

† The "Lord of the Bedchamber" of Mr. Joseph Howe's well-known effusion, and the husband of a natural daughter of King William IV. by Mrs. Jordan. Lord Falkland's quarrels with his own ministers about Responsible Government and other important public questions occasioned his recall several years afterwards. See "The Speeches and Public Letters of the Hon. Joseph Howe," edited by William Annand, M.P.P., Vol. I., p. 530.

‡ See letter of Sir C. Metcalfe to his sister, Mrs. Smythe, quoted in "Kaye," Vol. II., p. 323, *et seq.*

waiting to receive him with the honours due to his position. A long procession, chiefly made up of the members of the national societies, various fire companies, and other local institutions, met him at the entrance to the town. He was escorted to his residence by a detachment of the Incorporated Lancers and a guard of honour of the 23rd regiment. He took up his quarters in a new and previously untenanted private house hired for the occasion,* begging Sir Charles and Lady Mary Bagot to continue their occupation of Government House until their departure for England—the possibility of the invalid's being able to cross the Atlantic not yet having been wholly abandoned. On the 30th he was sworn into office, and issued a proclamation announcing that he had entered upon his duties as Governor-General.

---

*The following announcement appears in the local papers: "His Excellency's temporary residence is in Mr. Palmer's new house, in King Street, where he will receive visits daily (Sundays excepted) between the hours of 11 and 1 o'clock." The *Whig* expresses great solicitude for the Governor's health, and deprecates his being housed in such quarters. "From the lamentable and untimely death of one Governor-General," says that paper, "and the dangerous illness of another, Kingston has unfortunately attained an ill-fame for healthfulness; and now, it appears that another Governor, an aged man, and one used to tropical climates, is to be put into a newly-built house, never inhabited, the walls of which are filled with moisture, that would take two hot summers to dry up; and a house, too, in which no single stove has been lighted during this long and tedious winter. They had better put him in a coffin at once. We look upon the taking of this house as a deliberate attempt made upon the life of the new Governor; and should he fall ill, not only ought Kingston to be exonerated from causing his sickness, but the parties who hired the house should be brought to condign punishment." The Kingston correspondent of the Montreal *Gazette* made the following reference to the Governor's personal appearance: "Sir Charles Metcalfe is a thorough looking Englishman, with a jolly visage. He looks older than he really is, but this may proceed from the fatigues of his very rough journey."

Chapter XIV.

WHAT IS TO BECOME OF THE GOVERNOR-GENERAL?

"He was called upon to govern, or to submit to the Government of Canada, by a party; and the party by which he was to govern was one with which he had no sympathy. It was rather a combination of parties than a single faction—a combination of two parties, the principles of neither of which Metcalfe could bring himself to approve."—KAYE'S *Life and Correspondence of Charles, Lord Metcalfe*. Revised edition. Vol. II., p. 336.

"We do assert, and on this ground we take our stand, that the Governor is bound by that power which granted a Representative System to Canada, to submit to the opinions of the Parliament, and to the advice of a Council who are nominated by the Governor because they are known to possess the confidence of such Parliament."—*Hamilton Journal*, 19th July, 1839.

IN entering upon the momentous struggle between Sir Charles Metcalfe and the Lafontaine-Baldwin Ministry, it is to be premised that no fair and impartial account of that struggle has ever been given to the world. The literature of the subject is very extensive—so extensive that even the most industrious student must make up his mind to devote many months to the theme ere he can boast of having made himself a thorough master of it. The official despatches between Sir Charles Metcalfe and the Home Office are among the most important documents requiring attention. The Provincial newspapers of the time are almost entirely engrossed by the struggle. Ever since, whenever a constitutional question having the slightest conceivable bearing on Responsible Government has arisen in Canada, the precedent of Sir Charles Metcalfe and his Ministry has been put forward with more or less appositeness, and with more or less knowledge of the essential nature of the dispute.

Some of these discussions may be consulted with advantage. The pamphlets on the subject may be counted by the score, and of course all the histories of the period devote more or less space to it. The newspapers of Great Britain and the official journals of the House of Commons furnish their quota to the discussion. The periodical literature of the neighbouring republic did not deem it unworthy of attention, though the opinions expressed therein do not appear to have been formed with much care, or to have been founded upon an accurate knowledge of the principles involved. And after passing the whole of this undigested mass of special pleading through his mind—for every page and every column of it is to some extent tinged by partisanship—the student's interpretation will have to be evolved from constitutional principles which were by no means well understood, even among statesmen, in the year of Grace 1843. Still, it is not impossible to arrive at a just apprehension of the merits of this memorable quarrel, the narrative of which involves one of the most salient passages in our constitutional history.

That Responsible Government—however much or however little was involved in that principle—had been conceded, was a matter no longer open to dispute. Whether Governor Simcoe had any such thing in his mind when he remarked[*] that the Province of Upper Canada was blest, "not with a mutilated constitution, but with a constitution which has stood the test of experience, and is the very image and transcript of that of Great Britain," may perhaps be doubted. Mr. MacMullen, in a note to his history,[†] ventures the remark that the Governor evidently forgot the irresponsible Executive of Canada when he indulged in such a flourish of trumpets. But Lord John Russell's instructions to Mr. Thomson, afterwards Lord

---

[*] In his Speech from the Throne, at the close of the first session of the First Provincial Parliament of Upper Canada, on the 15th of October, 1792.

[†] See MacMullen's "History of Canada," p. 235.

Sydenham (embraced in various despatches),* Lord Sydenham's own admissions, and those of his Attorney-General, Mr. Draper,† and more especially the resolutions adopted by the Assembly on the 3rd of September, 1841—quoted in a former chapter of this work‡ —had at least established beyond question that Responsible Government was to be regarded as the law of the land. This fact was repeatedly admitted by Sir Charles Metcalfe himself, both before and after his arrival in Canada. The precise meaning to be attached to the term "Responsible Government," however —how much it embodied, and how much was excluded—was not so clear as to render misapprehension impossible. The responsibility involved was the responsibility of the Executive Council to the will of the people, as expressed by a majority in the Legislative Assembly. Where did the responsibility end? It could scarcely be contended that it was illimitable? The highest Canadian authority admits that "the system itself was imperfectly understood, and mistakes were made on all sides, in the application of this hitherto untried experiment in colonial government to the practical administration of local affairs."§ A calm and dispassionate review of all the circumstances must lead an inquirer of the present day to the conclusion that Sir Charles Metcalfe was wrong in his interpretation of the principle. But it is at least equally evident that he was not *culpably* wrong; that he was not, as was charged upon him, a wilful and stubborn tyrant; that he honestly endeavoured to carry out the instructions which had been imposed upon him; that his failure to satisfy popular opinion in this country arose from his inability to understand the refinements

---

* See more especially the despatches of September 7th, October 14th, and October 16th, 1830.

† *Ante*, pp. 125-136.

‡ *Ante*, pp. 149, 150.

§ See "Parliamentary Government in the British Colonies," by Alpheus Todd, p. 58, and authorities there quoted.

of what to him was a new and untried system; and that whatever blame attaches to his conduct should rest upon the shoulders of the Imperial Government that sent him to fulfil a task for which he was intellectually and by previous training unfitted. Sir Charles Metcalfe, during his Canadian Administration, was merely a glaring instance of the round peg in the square hole. He was like David with the armour placed upon him by Saul—an armour which he had not used, and in the management of which he was unskilled. It is devoutly to be wished, for his own fame and peace of mind, that the analogy had been carried still further, and that he had said to Lord Stanley as David said to the first king of Israel— "I cannot go with these, for I have not proved them." In his own sphere, as Administrator of an Oriental Government, he had approved himself not only a man of just mind, but a man of very great diplomatic ability. As such he stands out in the history of British India in conspicuous relief. As Administrator of a colony which boasted the possession of Responsible Government he was Samson shorn of his hair, and become as any other man—any other man who had not enjoyed a constitutional training, and who, at fifty-eight years of age, was too old to be inoculated with new ideas. It was very much more his misfortune than his crime.

The shadow of the future began to fall across his pathway ere he had been many weeks in the Province. It has been seen that during his residence in England he had not formally allied himself with either of the two political parties in the country. He professed himself, and with perfect truthfulness and good faith, to be opposed to partisanship. During his tenure of office in Jamaica he had successfully applied himself to obliterating or softening the party-lines in vogue there. Upon his arrival in Canada he for the first time saw the fire of partisanship actively aflame. Both parties were bent on conciliating the new Governor, and both deluged him with addresses conceived in the most opposite spirit. Many of these addresses were mere expositions of an ultra party platform. "The curse of faction," says his biographer, "appeared before him so swollen and exaggerated that he wondered the evils with which he had contended during his former Government had ever disquieted him at all."* He found the Conservative party, which had stood loyally by the Crown during the troubles of 1837-'38, and which embraced a large majority of the wealthy and educated people of the country, in Opposition. The Reform party he found strongly entrenched in power. In an official despatch penned within a month after he assumed the Government he truthfully referred to this party as including in its ranks "some who actually went into rebellion, some who stood aloof on that occasion without taking any active part in defence of the Government, and some who, although acting with the Reform party before the rebellion, performed their duty as loyal subjects when that occasion arose."† He found representatives of the two classes last named holding high office in the Ministry. As for the French Canadians, he found them much mollified by the concessions made to them by his predecessor, but with political views purely French Canadian, directed to the maintenance and extension of their own power, and resenting all attempts at Anglification.‡ By coalition with the Reformers of Upper Canada, the French Canadians enjoyed a share of power. The only party which exercised no power was the party upon whom, as he remarked, "the mother country might confidently rely in the hour of need"—namely, the Conservatives. He naturally felt his own sympathies go out to the members of that party, and deprecated their exclusion from power. He seems at this time, however, to have fully realized his position with respect to them. Referring to the existing state of things, he informed the Colonial Secretary that he saw no remedy, "without

---

* Kaye, Vol. II., p. 330.
† See his despatch of 25th April, 1843, in "Selections from the Papers of Lord Metcalfe," edited by J. W. Kaye, p. 406.
‡ Ib., p. 405.

setting at defiance the operation of Responsible Administration which has been introduced into this colony, to an extent unknown, I believe, in any other. . . Fettered as I am," he continued, " by the necessity of acting with a Council brought into place by a coalition of parties, and at present in possession of a decided majority in the Representative Assembly, I must in some degree forego my own inclinations."[*] He feared lest the excluded party might identify him with the Council, and thereby become incensed against him personally, but congratulated himself upon the fact that, so far, opposition to the Council was not identical with opposition to the Governor or to the Home Government.[†] Meanwhile he adopted a policy of great conciliation towards the Opposition, and seems to have been almost imprudently frank in his public expressions of good-will in certain individual cases.

It is thus plain enough that the statement made by his biographer, and placed at the head of this chapter, was literally true. He was compelled to govern Canada by a party, and by a party with which he had no sympathy. Now, it is true that a man of warm heart and strong opinions cannot avoid having sympathies, but a man placed in the position of Governor of a colony where representative institutions prevail, should bear in mind that the people also have their sympathies, as manifested in their choice of their representatives in Parliament. He should remember that he occupies a public position, and that it is his duty to subordinate his personal likings and predilections to those of the majority. To contend for any other view would be to advocate the most pronounced absolutism; and it is here that Sir Charles's Indian training first asserts itself.[‡] The

---

[*] See his despatch of 25th of April, 1843, in "Selections from the Papers of Lord Metcalfe," edited by J. W. Kaye, pp. 408, 409.

[†] Ib., p. 410.

[‡] "As a Constitutional ruler he had no business to have sympathies, and if he had them he had no right to act upon them. How had he seen the Queen, his Sovereign, act, within the period of his return to England and his departure for Canada? Had he not seen her transfer her confidence from Lord Melbourne, for whom she had a filial attach-

sympathies of a large majority of Canadians had been manifested by their return of members who had sanctioned the advent to power of those very persons with whom the Governor had no sympathy, and with whom it was therefore inevitable that he should sooner or later come into collision. They had once been excluded from power themselves, and had never till lately tasted the sweets of office. They had once been legitimate objects of the sympathy of all good men who had any sympathy to spare, and were surely entitled to all the good things which the Union had brought them.

Differences between the Governor and some of his Councillors—differences so slight at first as scarcely to be perceptible, but still differences—began to manifest themselves before the former had been many weeks in the country. He conceived that his Ministers were unnecessarily brusque and unceremonious in their intercourse with him. This he could have borne, so far as he was personally concerned, but he could not endure that his high office should lose any of its dignity while it was in his keeping. On the other hand, his Ministers were no children. They were men, and, for the most part, men of strong individuality. Some of them were probably not easy to manage. They had fought a long and hard battle for the right, against tremendous odds. They had won, and they fully appreciated the importance of their victory. Under such circumstances it was only natural that they should not be in the least disposed to yield anything that of right belonged to them. The system of irresponsibility against which they had so long contended in vain had been a rude training-school. It is easy to conceive that they may have been less diplomatic in their relations with the Governor than men of less sincerity and earnestness, men who had been less sorely tried, would have proved. When the Governor suggested something

---

ment, to Sir Robert Peel, whom she never really liked? And why? Because she knew, as a Constitutional Sovereign, that her business was to give her confidence to, and call to her councils, those men who had the support of the representatives of the people."—*The Irishman in Canada*, pp. 488, 489.

which was opposed to the policy they had outlined for themselves, it is quite probable that they signified their disapproval without unnecessary circumlocution. They very keenly felt any, even the slightest, attempt at infringement upon what they considered their privileges. They claimed an absolute right to be consulted as to all appointments to office. They did not relish Sir Charles's apparent desire to conciliate the Opposition, and listened with impatience to any suggestions, whether emanating from the Governor himself or from any of his satellites, pointing to the filling of any vacant offices from the Conservative ranks. That this feeling should be entertained by them was a necessary consequence of their position; almost, indeed, a necessary consequence of Government by party. But Government by party had been established in Canada, and, much as the Governor was opposed to party government, he was wise enough to perceive that no other system was practicable under the then-existing order of things. He again and again declared his full and free acceptance of the doctrine of Responsible Government. While admitting so much, however, he was jealous for his prerogative as the representative of the Crown, and was disposed to claim at least a share of the Government patronage.

During the first week in May an episode occurred which, unknown to the Ministry, tended not a little to stimulate this jealousy on the part of the Governor. Mr. Lafontaine dined with his Excellency at the latter's lodgings in King Street, where he still remained, owing to Sir Charles Bagot's continued occupancy of Alwington House. At table Mr. Lafontaine sat next to Captain Higginson, the Governor's private secretary. During dinner the conversation turned upon the office of Provincial Aide-de-camp for Lower Canada, which had been for some time vacant. Among the candidates mentioned either by Captain Higginson or by Sir Charles Metcalfe himself was a gentleman of whom Mr. Lafontaine, for political reasons, did not approve. This gentleman was Mr. DeSalaberry, son of the hero of Chateauguay. Mr. Lafontaine remarked to Captain Higginson that such an appointment would not be regarded with favour in Lower Canada. In the course of conversation Captain Higginson expressed a desire to talk over the political state of the country at some length with one so competent to afford information on the subject as Mr. Lafontaine, and an appointment was made for the next day at noon, at Mr. Lafontaine's office. Captain Higginson called at the time and place fixed upon, and the two gentlemen, who had the office all to themselves, conversed together for nearly three hours. The respective accounts subsequently given by them of the conversation do not agree in all particulars. It is only reasonable to infer that some part at least of the discrepancy arose from misapprehension of Mr. Lafontaine's meaning on the part of the secretary. The purport of the discussion seems to have been substantially as contained in the following paragraph. Captain Higginson, it is to be presumed, may fairly be taken to have been the Governor's mouthpiece on the occasion,* and as the conversation embodies the clearest account to be found anywhere of the various points upon which the Governor and his Ministers soon afterwards found themselves at variance, it is considered desirable to detail it at some length.

The Attorney-General was asked by Captain Higginson to explain to him what was meant by the phrase "Responsible Government." In compliance with the request Mr. Lafontaine delivered his views on that important subject, explaining that the Councillors were responsible for all the acts of Government with regard to local

---

* It will be seen that in the course of the conversation, Captain Higginson stated that he was not charged by the Governor-General to discuss the matter with Mr. Lafontaine. "Charged" is a strong word. The secretary would certainly not have entered upon such a discussion under such circumstances, unless he had been carrying out the express or implied instructions of the Governor. There is not even the shadow of doubt that the views expressed by him were those of Sir Charles Metcalfe, from whom he doubtless derived all his inspiration on the subject.

matters; that they were so held by the members of the Legislature; that they could only retain office so long as they possessed the confidence of the representatives of the people; and that whenever this confidence should be withdrawn from them, they must retire from the Administration. "These principles," added Mr. Lafontaine, "were recognized by the resolutions of the 3rd of September, 1841, and it was on the faith of these principles being carried out that I accepted office." He further informed Captain Higginson that inasmuch as the responsibility of the members of the Administration extended to all the acts of the Government in local matters, including appointments to office, consultation of the Ministers by the Governor in all those cases was necessary. The Governor, it was admitted, was not obliged to adopt the advice tendered to him, but, on the contrary, had a right to reject it; but in this latter case if the Members of Council did not choose to assume the responsibility of the act that the Governor wished to perform contrary to their advice, they had the means of relieving themselves from it by exercising their power of resignation. The secretary combated this view, observing that it did not appear to him that this was the sense of the resolutions of 1841. He urged that the Governor, being responsible to the Imperial authorities for the acts of his Government, ought himself to bear the responsibility of those acts in local matters, and that he could not relieve himself from it by throwing it upon his Councillors; that this responsibility could not be understood as Mr. Lafontaine understood it—"for," said Captain Higginson, "it must then be considered that the act is not the act of the Governor, and in that case it would not be just that the Imperial Government should hold him responsible for it; but as the act is the act of the Governor, and as the Imperial Government hold him responsible for it, it would be equally unjust that he should throw the responsibility on his Councillors." Captain Higginson added that for this reason it appeared to him that the Governor must be free to act with or without the advice of his Councillors; admitting, nevertheless, that it was desirable that he should take their advice in the generality of cases; that for his (Captain Higginson's) own part, he did not see the possibility of putting the resolutions of 1841 in practice as explained by Mr. Lafontaine, unless the Imperial Government should expressly relieve the Governor from all responsibility as to local matters. Even in that case, it was urged, there would still be the objection that the Governor would be reduced to a cipher, and that such a system would make the colony an independent state. The Captain added that even supposing the resolutions of 1841 could be interpreted in the sense given to them by Mr. Lafontaine, he did not think that this would include the exercise of patronage, and that he did not see why the representatives of the people should hold the Councillors responsible for it; that he looked on the distribution of offices as a prerogative of the Crown that the Governor must exercise on his own responsibility, not having to render any account of it except to the Imperial Government. In answer to a question put by Mr. Lafontaine, Captain Higginson stated that, in his opinion, the sense of the resolutions of 1841 was that the Governor should choose his Councillors from among those supposed to have the confidence of the people; that it was desirable that those persons, or the majority of them, should have seats in the Legislature, to explain there the views and the measures of the Government; that if it happened that one of them should cease to possess the confidence of the representatives of the people, it would be the duty of the Governor to replace him by another more likely to gain that confidence, in order to maintain harmony, as far as possible, between the different branches of the Legislature; that each member of the Administration ought to be responsible only for the acts of his own department, and consequently that he ought to have the liberty of voting with or against his colleagues whenever he judged fit; that by this means an Administration composed of the principal members of each political party might exist advantageously for all parties, and would furnish the Governor the means of better understanding the views and the opinions of each party, and would not fail, under the auspices of the Governor, to lead to the reconciliation of all. Mr. Lafontaine then informed the secretary that if the opinions which he had just expressed were those of the Governor-General, and if his Excellency was determined to make them the rule for conducting his Government, the sooner he made those facts known to the members of his Council the better, in order to avoid all misunderstanding between them; and he added that in such case he, for one, would feel it his duty to tender his resignation, convinced as he was that such a system was in opposition to the principles recognized by the resolutions of 1841, and that the difference between it and the old system that had formerly prevailed in Upper and Lower Canada was so trifling as to be scarcely perceptible. The secretary replied that in speaking thus, he must not be considered as expressing the opinions of the Governor-General, but merely his own individual views, and that he was not charged by his Excellency to hold any conversation on the subject with Mr. Lafontaine.

As to the next part of the conversation there is a conflict between the parties. Captain Higginson's account, as published in the Toronto *Colonist*, charges Mr. Lafontaine with language to the following effect: "The attempt to carry on the Government on principles of conciliation must fail. Responsible Government has been conceded, and when we lose our majority we are prepared to retire. To strengthen us, we must have the entire confidence of the Governor exhibited most unequivocally, and also his patronage, to be bestowed exclusively on our political adherents. We feel that his Excellency has kept aloof from us. The Opposition pronounce that his sentiments are with them. There must be some act of his, some public declaration in favour of Responsible Government, and of confidence in his Cabinet, to convince them of their error. A declaration of the Governor to that effect would put a stop to political agitation, which the Opposition keep up as long as they have the slightest hopes of office. Let them know that the game is up, and all will go right, and many come round. The differences in religion in Upper Canada will always prevent amalgamation. You must first make them all of the same religion, like ourselves in Lower Canada."

Mr. Lafontaine, on the other hand, denied having used such language, and claims to have said, in reply to Captain Higginson's suggestion of conciliatory measures towards the Conservatives, that such measures would not succeed; that the best means of conciliation was frankly to give effect to the resolutions of 1841, and to conduct the Government with the assistance of a Council whose members should have views in common both with regard to legislation and administration, and who should possess the confidence of the representatives of the people and of the Governor. Thereupon, as Mr. Lafontaine alleges, allusion was made to the rumour then very currently reported that the members of the Administration did not enjoy the confidence of his Excellency; and Mr. Lafontaine remarked to Captain Higginson that if any fact came to their knowledge of such a nature as to convince them that they had not such confidence they would not allow a day to pass without tendering their resignation. Captain Higginson assured him that there was no foundation for the rumour. "The Councillor," says Mr. Lafontaine, writing of himself in the third person, "never said at any time, or in any place, much less to Captain Higginson, that the patronage of the Governor ought to be *exclusively* exercised in favour of the partisans of the Ministry. The Councillor has never professed such a doctrine; but the Councillor answered a question thus put by Captain Higginson, that, as a general rule, when two candidates offered with equal qualifications, the one not opposed to the Administration should have the preference; that were a contrary rule to prevail—if, in the distribution of offices, the Governor were to let it be seen that opposition to the members of his Administration was a title to his favour—he would be wanting in what was due to himself, as well as to his Councillors; that so long as he retained them in his Council he was supposed to give them his confidence, and that he ought to do nothing which would have the effect of destroying the influence of his Administration, but, on the contrary, should strengthen that influence by every legitimate means in his power." Mr. Lafontaine added that he and his colleagues had a right to expect that his Excellency would thus act towards them; that otherwise it would be infinitely better for his Excellency to relieve them from their duties and appoint their successors; that as for appointments to office he could appeal to the past to prove that there had been nothing exclusive about them; that as the love of place appeared to be the influencing motive with a considerable number in their opposition to the Government, he was convinced that the political agitation which was the consequence of it would diminish much in its force so soon as these individuals should see that such opposition had ceased to be a title to employment; that the opposition would then become more honourable and constitutional, for it would bear on the principles of legislation and administration according to English practice. Captain Higginson called the attention of Mr. Lafontaine to the fact that there existed more divisions among the population of Upper Canada than among that of Lower Canada, and begged of him to explain the cause of it. Mr. Lafontaine said that it appeared to him that in Upper Canada there existed a profound hatred between the party called Tory and that called Reform; that the Government prior to the Union having always been in the hands of the first of these two parties, this hatred appeared to have been created by its bad administration, which after all had been the effect of the then bad system of Colonial Government; that in Upper Canada there existed a great number of religious denominations more or less numerous, and that, moreover, the population was in a great part composed of people, natives of different countries—viz.: *native* Canadians, English, Scotch, Irish, Americans, Dutch—that all this might serve to account for the divisions which prevailed in Upper Canada; while in Lower Canada the population was more homogeneous, consisting principally of French Canadians, and a very great majority professing the same religion. Religious differences, Mr. Lafontaine alleged, were scarcely known in the Lower Province, and as for past political divisions they arose from the circumstance that a small number of individuals and of families, principally of the cities of Quebec and Montreal, had been rendered masters of the Government and the Governors, and altogether engrossed it, and conducted it according to their own whims, to the prejudice of the mass of the population, English as well as French. The Union, Mr. Lafontaine added, had caused the leaders of the Tory party of Lower Canada to disappear from the House, and all this would help to explain the reason why the divisions which prevailed in Upper Canada did not exist in Lower Canada.

Such, as reported by the two gentlemen who took part in it, is the substance of the principal points of the conversation which took place, at the request of Captain Higginson, between him and Mr. Lafontaine. As a matter of course the former lost no time in reporting the whole to Sir Charles Metcalfe, who took the matter very seriously to heart, for he knew that Mr. Lafontaine's defection would involve the defection at least of Mr. Baldwin and Mr. Morin, and that the inevitable result would be a general break up of the Administration. To yield all that was demanded of him, however, seemed utterly out of the question. What then would become of the Governor-General? The idea that if he yielded to pressure he would become "a mere cipher" was gall and wormwood to him. Yet the Governor did full justice to Mr. Lafontaine's motives, and did not attempt, as Sir Francis Head would have done under similar circumstances, to impugn his personal character.* After pondering the matter for a week he wrote to Lord Stanley as follows: "I learn that my attempts to conciliate all parties are criminal in the eyes of the Council, or at least of the most formidable member of it. I am required to give myself up entirely to the Council; to submit absolutely to their dictation; to have no judgment of my own; to bestow the patronage of the Government exclusively on their partisans; to proscribe their opponents; and to make some public and unequivocal declaration of my adhesion to those conditions—including the complete nullification of Her Majesty's Government. . . Failing of submission to those stipulations, I am threatened with the resignation of Mr. Lafontaine for one, and both he and I are fully aware of the serious consequences likely to follow the execution of that menace, from the blindness with which the French Canadian party follow their leader. . . I have no intention of tearing up her Majesty's commission by submitting to the prescribed conditions. . . The sole question is, to

---

* The following is the deliberate estimate of Mr. Lafontaine formed by Sir Charles Metcalfe, as reported by the latter's biographer: "All his better qualities were natural to him; his worse were the growth of circumstances. Cradled, as he and his people had been, in wrong, smarting for long years under the oppressive exclusiveness of the dominant race, he had become mistrustful and suspicious; and the doubts which were continually floating in his mind had naturally engendered indecision and infirmity of purpose. But he had many fine characteristics which no evil circumstances could impair. He was a just and an honourable man. His motives were above all suspicion. Warmly attached to his country, earnestly seeking the happiness of his people, he occupied a high position by the force rather of his moral than of his intellectual qualities. He was trusted and respected rather than admired." - Kaye, Vol. II., p. 342. The estimate is by no means accurate in all points. For instance, no one who knew Mr. Lafontaine well could have been made to believe that he was infirm or undecided of purpose. Sir Francis Hincks, in the lecture which has so often been quoted from in these pages, declares that he never met a man less open to such an imputation. In point of fact Mr. Lafontaine was imperious, if not tyrannical; one of the last men to accept the judgment of others in preference to his own. The mistake, however, is a mere error of judgment on Sir Charles Metcalfe's part. The characterization, as a whole, proves that the Governor was upon the whole a fair and just-minded man, capable of rising above little personal considerations in his intercourse with mankind.

describe it without disguise, whether the Governor shall be solely and completely a tool in the hands of the Council, or whether he shall have any exercise of his own judgment in the administration of the Government? Such a question has not come forward as a matter of discussion; but there is no doubt that the leader of the French party speaks the sentiments of others of his Council besides himself. . . As I cannot possibly adopt them, I must be prepared for the consequences of a rupture with the Council, or at least the most influential portion of it."

There was, however, no present outbreak between the Governor and his Councillors, though there were frequent indications that perfect harmony did not exist between them. There were several vexed questions which demanded attention, and the business of the country was not neglected. Perhaps the most embarrassing matter to be dealt with was the location of the Seat of Government. The idea of continuing Kingston as the permanent capital of the Province was acceptable to no one except the inhabitants of that town and its neighbourhood. The merits and demerits of various localities had been considered. Montreal had a great many advocates, and was favoured by a majority of the members of the Government, but no settled conclusion had been arrived at. The claims of the present capital of the Dominion—then known as Bytown—had been put forward by Mr. James Johnston, the member for Carleton, but had been rejected by an all but unanimous vote of the Assembly during the last session. The only certainty about the matter was that whatever locality should be selected there would be great dissatisfaction from all other localities.*

---

* "Place the capital in Upper Canada, and the Lower Canadians will be dissatisfied. Place it in Lower Canada, and the Upper Canadians will be so. In proposing Montreal, therefore, I do not mean to promise that such a decision will not produce great dissatisfaction in Upper Canada, for I am inclined to believe that it will, and I have been told that it will lead to a motion for the repeal of the Union."—Despatch from Sir C. Metcalfe to the Colonial Secretary, quoted in Kaye's "Life," p. 352.

This, however, was merely one of many subjects which distracted the mind of the Governor-General. The evils of excessive partisanship appeared more glaring in his eyes day by day. The Irish element in the population, as is their wont, entered into the party struggles of the time with keen zest. On the Conservative side were arrayed the Orange lodges; while the Hibernian societies, composed chiefly of Roman Catholics, ranged themselves on the side of the Administration. Occasionally, small aggregations of these opposite factions encountered each other on the public streets and highways, and whenever such encounters took place the peace of the community was disturbed. During the year 1843 the agitation in Ireland on the subject of the Repeal of the Union was at its height, and it seemed, as the Governor's biographer remarks, that all the evils of Irish party-strife had crossed the Atlantic only to appear in Canada in an aggravated shape. During the summer several hostile meetings between the rival factions occurred. On the 12th of July the Orange lodges of Kingston, chiefly, it is believed, in deference to the Governor's request, abstained from the usual procession through the streets, and contented themselves with celebrating the day of pious and immortal memory within doors. At night the lodge rooms were besieged by mobs of Irish repealers. The troops were called out to preserve order, and succeeded in dispersing the crowd, but not until several persons had been wounded, and Robert Morrison, a young man of sixteen—a non-partisan, and a mere casual spectator—shot through the head, and slain. On another occasion the streets of the Provincial capital were placarded with bills announcing a meeting for the avowed object of promoting a repeal of the Union between Great Britain and Ireland. Counter placards were at once issued under the auspices of the Orange societies, announcing that the meeting would not be permitted, and that they would obstruct it, peaceably or forcibly, according to the necessities of the case. The Governor was invoked to put forth his authority to prevent the repeal meeting from being held. He showed his good sense by first suggesting persuasion, which was successful, and what would doubtless have resulted in a riotous and bloody demonstration was peacefully suppressed.

There seems to be tolerably good reason for believing that the Governor, even at this early period of his Administration, did not on all occasions act with perfect openness and good faith towards his Councillors. He felt satisfied that the Attorney-General East, in the conversation with Captain Higginson, had not been talking at random, but had given utterance to the deliberate convictions of himself and his colleagues. That those convictions would be acted upon, should occasion arise, the Governor could not doubt, and he was haunted by the consciousness of coming strife. He believed the position taken by his Ministers to be wholly untenable, so far at any rate, as the question of patronage was concerned, and he was thus led to entertain a secret antagonism towards them. He regarded them in the light of persons who were disposed to demand, more than their due, and the inherent firmness, not to say stubbornness, of his nature, was aroused. There was an evident reserve in his manner towards them at the Council Board. The simple truth of the matter seems to be that he was incapable of studied, persistent dissimulation, and could not personate a confidence and good-fellowship which he did not feel. But the disingenuousness did not begin and end here. He established intimate relations with several prominent members of the Opposition, and if their own accounts are to be credited he even went so far as to hint very strongly at the want of cordiality existing between himself and his Councillors. He made no secret of his kindly feelings towards several leading members of the Conservative party, and repeatedly invited them to private conferences. About two months after the conversation between Mr. Lafontaine and Captain Higginson, the

THE LAST FORTY YEARS.

CANADA since THE UNION OF 1841.

BY JOHN CHARLES DENT.

GEO VIRTUE
PUBLISHER
TORONTO

THE HON. SIR JOHN A. MACDONALD, K.C.B., D.C.L.
(*From a recent Photograph by Topley, of Ottawa.*)

SCENE IN MUSKOKA.

THE HON. D. L. MACPHERSON.

THE UNIVERSITY OF NEW BRUNSWICK, FREDERICTON.

Governor had a long interview with Mr. Ogle R. Gowan, one of the most pronounced Conservatives in the country. This gentleman was not at that time a member of Parliament, but he was the editor and proprietor of one of the most ably conducted Opposition newspapers in Canada, and was unsparing in his criticism of the existing Administration. He was also Grand Master of the Orange body, and as such wielded a tremendous political influence. The Governor sent for this gentleman a few days prior to the anniversary of the battle of the Boyne, for the ostensible purpose of inducing him to put forth his power as Grand Master to prevent the Orangemen from engaging in any public demonstrations on the 12th of the month. The success of this appeal has been chronicled in the preceding paragraph. But it appears that the conversation was not confined to such topics. Mr. Gowan's account of the interview, as given in a letter to his partner, and subsequently published in the newspapers, was to the effect that he and the Governor had had a long and confidential discussion on the political situation. Mr. Gowan seems to have suggested certain changes in the Ministry. That one in Sir Charles Metcalfe's position should have tolerated such a suggestion from such a source, much less that he should have listened to it with favour, seems almost incredible. Mr. Gowan's letter, however, is very specific. It says: "Don't be surprised if Baldwin, Hincks and Harrison *walk*, or that Cartwright succeeds the latter. This may be all done without offending the Radicals, and without losing the interest of either of the three who retire. This, to you, must appear a paradox, but it is so, nevertheless. I have received in writing, marked 'Private' his Excellency's thanks for my memorandum of plan." That Mr. Gowan in thus writing to his partner made the most of the conversation, for the purpose of exalting himself in that partner's eyes, is exceedingly probable; but that some such topics were discussed between him and the Governor there seems to be no good ground for doubting. Of course, nothing of all this was known to the Ministers until the publication of the letter, which did not take place until the following year. It is hard to believe that the Governor could have been so ignorant of the fitness of things as not to know that he was acting with most culpable impropriety in thus intriguing against his sworn advisers with one of their bitterest enemies. It is charitable to hope that the intrigue was not deliberately planned on the part of his Excellency, and that in an unfortunate moment he was betrayed by Mr. Gowan's confident and insinuating manner into using incautious expressions. Still, after all allowances and deductions have been made, it must be admitted that the Representative of Majesty was culpably oblivious of what was due to his Sovereign, to his Ministers, and to himself, in permitting even the most distant allusion on Mr. Gowan's part to such matters as those indicated in the letter.

The Governor's incautious expressions to several persons unconnected with the Government, and his private conferences with prominent Conservatives, erelong gave rise to a widespread belief that his Excellency was disgusted with his Councillors, and would be glad to be rid of them; that their arrogant pretensions alternately aroused his anger and contempt.* It was said that all his sympathies were with the Opposition. These rumours almost daily found their way to the ears of the members of the Cabinet, to whom they were very

---

* That the Governor did really entertain such feelings as those attributed to him seems, to say the least, probable. His despatches and private letters abound with what may be characterized as suppressed sneers. "The Council," wrote he to Lord Stanley on the 24th of April, "are now spoken of by themselves and others generally as 'the Ministers,' 'the Administration,' 'the Cabinet,' 'the Government,' and so forth. Their pretensions are according to this new nomenclature. They regard themselves as a responsible Ministry, and expect that the policy and conduct of the Governor shall be subservient to their views and party purposes."—Kaye, Vol. II., p. 332. Again: "He was wont," says his biographer, "writing to his Indian friends, to compare his position to that of an Indian Governor, who might have to rule through the agency of a Mahomedan Ministry and a Mahomedan Parliament. I find the same form of expression used in more than one letter, but I am not sure of the correctness of the analogy."—Ib., p. 371.

unpalatable, as they naturally tended to weaken the popular respect for them, and raised difficulties in their path which otherwise would have had no existence. The rumours, however, were not sufficiently direct or specific to justify any conference with the Governor on the subject, and the Ministers carried their coals with such patience as they could command. They had abundance of hard work on their hands. As the summer glided by, they were busily occupied in preparing measures for the ensuing session of Parliament, which, after repeated prorogations, had been summoned to meet on the 28th of September. Much hostile comment, on the part of the Conservative press, was evoked by the return from exile of a number of persons who had been compromised in the troubles of 1837-'38. Conspicuous among these were Dr. John Rolph, Dr. Charles Duncombe, Dr. Thomas D. Morrison, David Gibson, Nelson Gorham and John Montgomery, to each of whom a pardon had been granted under the Great Seal. Dr. Wolfred Nelson had returned some months previously, and had resumed the practice of his profession at Montreal. On the 28th of August a *nolle prosequi* was entered in the Court of Queen's Bench at Montreal, with respect to Dr. Nelson and two of his former coadjutors, Dr. E. B. O'Callaghan and Thomas Storrow Brown. This was done at the instigation of Mr. Lafontaine, who pressed upon his Excellency the expediency of granting a general amnesty for all political offences. His Excellency was disposed to yield his assent, with an express reservation in the case of the ringleaders, Papineau and Mackenzie. Mr. Lafontaine declined to acquiesce in the proposed reservation, and the Governor finally gave way so far as to authorize the entry of a *nolle prosequi* against Mr. Papineau also. The authority was at once acted upon, but Mr. Papineau, who was then living at Paris, France, did not avail himself of his privilege until long afterwards.

The Governor seems to have tried hard to understand, and make the best of, his singularly uncongenial position. He devoted much of his leisure time to the study of the Canadian constitution. The fact that much time was needed was of itself tolerably good evidence that he was not in his proper element, for he enjoyed peculiar advantages in being able to prosecute his studies on the spot, and with the aid of competent advisers, who would willingly have afforded him the benefit of their judgment on all questions of difficulty. But he distrusted all his official advisers except Mr. Daly, and had no mind to consult them. As for Mr. Daly, he was intellectually the weakest man in the Council, and, as subsequently appeared, was himself hopelessly at sea on matters relating to the constitution. He was an old bureaucrat, fond of his office and his salary, who believed his mission in life to be to support the existing Imperial Government, no matter who might be at the head of it, and no matter what might be its policy. The Governor was wise enough to perceive that not much weight could be attached to Mr. Daly's judgment, and does not appear to have sought that gentleman's advice at this time. He read over Lord Durham's report and the various despatches between the Home and Colonial Governments for several years past. These he pondered in his own mind, and seems to have been lost in a maze of contradictory evidence. He could perceive easily enough that Lord Sydenham's views on the question of Responsible Government had from time to time undergone various modifications. He was thus led to conclude that Lord Sydenham, in his most liberal concessions, had either made a great mistake, or had been acting under a sort of political duress. In neither case did he consider himself bound to sacrifice at Lord Sydenham's shrine. This appears very clearly from his despatch to Lord Stanley dated the 5th of August.* "I find," says the missive, "that in the early portion of his [Lord Syden-

---

* For the full text of this remarkable despatch, see "Selections from the Papers of Lord Metcalfe," pp. 412, 413.

ham's] despatches, whenever Responsible Government is alluded to, in the sense in which it is here understood, he scouts it. . In composing his Council of the principal executive officers under his authority, in requiring that they should all be members of the Legislature, and chiefly of the popular branch, and in making their tenure of office dependent on their commanding a majority in the body representing the people, he seems to me to have ensured, with the certainty of cause and effect, that the Council of the Governor should regard themselves as responsible; not so much to the Governor as to the House of Assembly. In adopting the very form and practice of the Home Government, by which the principal Ministers of the Crown form a Cabinet, acknowledged by the nation as the Executive Administration, and themselves acknowledging responsibility to Parliament, he rendered it inevitable that the Council here should obtain and ascribe to themselves, in at least some degree, the character of a Cabinet of Ministers. If Lord Sydenham did not intend this, he was more mistaken than from his known ability one would suppose to be possible; and if he did intend it, he, with his eyes open, carried into practice that very theory of Responsible Colonial Government which he had pronounced his opinion decidedly against. I cannot presume to account for this apparent inconsistency otherwise than by supposing either that he had altered his opinion when he formed his Council after the union of the two provinces, or that he yielded against his own conviction to some necessity which he felt himself unable to resist." Sir Charles then draws consolation from the supposed fact that Lord Sydenham " was little accustomed to consult his Council, and that he conducted his Administration according to his own judgment"—an assertion which will by no means bear investigation. Lord Sydenham was a man of an extraordinarily active mind, who was sent out to this country to accomplish extraordinary work. He acted, to a large extent, as his own Prime Minister, and obtained great ascendancy over his Executive Councillors. He could generally persuade the latter to adopt his views of public questions, but he did not venture either to act without their consent or to run counter to their advice. "The term 'Responsible Government,'" continues the despatch, "was derived, I am told, from the marginal notes of Lord Durham's report. Previously to the publication of that document, the democratic party in Upper Canada had been struggling for a greater share than they possessed in the administration of the government of the country; but they had no precise name for the object of their desires, and could not exactly define their views. Lord Durham's report gave them the definition, and the words Irresponsible Government, Responsibility of the Government, Responsibility of the Officers of the Government, occurring repeatedly in the marginal notes, it is said furnished the name." Such erroneous statements as these prove beyond doubt that the Governor was chiefly indebted to his own researches, rather than to competent Canadian authorities, for his opinions on Canadian political affairs. It also proves that his researches were restricted within very narrow bounds. There was not one of his official advisers—nay, there was hardly a public man in the country—but could have set him right on this point. The term "Responsible Government" was at least as old as 1828. For more than ten years before Lord Durham's report was published the expression was a household word in Upper Canada, as well as in Nova Scotia. Though not so widely known in Lower Canada, it was not uncommon there. It would be easy to fill a volume with extracts from the newspapers of that period, proving that the phrase was nearly as common in men's mouths in the Upper Province as that of "Representation by Population" subsequently became. Robert Baldwin, his father, Dr. Baldwin, Peter Perry, and indeed all the leading members of the Reform party in Upper Canada, constantly employed the term in their public speeches. As early as 1830, nine years before the publication of Lord Durham's report,

Mr. Ogle R. Gowan published at Toronto a pamphlet entitled
"Responsible or Parliamentary Government," in which the theme
was discussed with much clearness and vigour. In 1836 there was
a battle between Sir Francis Head and his Councillors on the subject, the echo of which rang from one end of the Province to the
other. When Mr. Hincks started *The Examiner* at Toronto, in the
summer of 1838, months before Lord Durham's report was written,
he adopted as the motto of his journalistic venture, "Responsible
Government and the Voluntary Principle." Joseph Howe, the
present Sir William Young, and others had made the phrase well
known in Nova Scotia. In fact, it was a familiar term throughout
the British North American Colonies for years before Lord Durham
was connected with Canadian affairs. Lord Durham simply adopted
the phrase which he found in vogue throughout the country, and
no more invented the name than he invented the thing itself. Sir
Charles Metcalfe's despatch from first to last is a bundle of errors
and misconceptions. Its tone is one of anxiety, almost of despondency. Lord Stanley, after perusing it, could not have been in doubt
as to the inevitable future, and if he had wished to preserve
Responsible Government in Canada it would seem that he ought
to have lost no time in recalling Sir Charles Metcalfe and appointing his successor.

The time was approaching when the opposing forces of the
country were to encounter each other. During the late summer
and early autumn his Excellency sought relief from the manifold worries and cares of office by a hurried tour through the
more settled districts of the Province. He successively visited
Bytown, Montreal, Quebec, Three Rivers and the Eastern Townships, returning to Kingston by way of Cornwall during the first
week in September. After resting a day or two he set out on
a western tour extending as far as London, and including all the
more important towns on the route. That he should be well

received wherever he went, and that he should be made the recipient of numerous congratulatory addresses, was a necessity of his position. "Colonial communities," says his biographer, with a patronizing air, "are an essentially address-presenting people."[*] In the addresses which now poured in upon the Governor the most diverse sentiments were expressed as to the true policy required for the country's good. In nothing did the virulence of party strife appear to less advantage. In an address from the inhabitants of the township of Pelham, in the Niagara District, "unfeigned sorrow" was expressed that efforts had been made to weaken his Excellency's opinion of Messieurs Baldwin and Lafontaine and the other members of his Cabinet; and it was hoped that his confidence in those Ministers would not be diminished by any representations made by the enemies of Responsible Government. In another address, from the people of Orillia, his Excellency was recommended to dismiss Messieurs Harrison, Lafontaine, Baldwin, Hincks and Small from his Councils—a proceeding, which, it was suggested, would tend to the "real good, happiness and prosperity of the country."[†] In at least one instance there was so little local unanimity of sentiment that the inhabitants could not agree upon the terms of an address for presentation, and it became necessary for the Governor to receive and reply to two different addresses from the same community.[‡] From all which it is apparent that his Excellency's position was one calling for the exercise of great tact, prudence and discrimination. He mildly rebuked the unbecoming rancour of party spirit wherever he found it, and exhorted the people to lay aside the animosities engendered by a condition of things which no

---

[*] Kaye, Vol. II., p. 355. [†] Ib., pp. 357, 358.

[‡] "The Talbot District was a very hotbed of faction. On Metcalfe's arrival he had received two addresses from it, one calling upon him to support the liberal institutions of the country; and the other denouncing Responsible Government as a dangerous innovation that must lead to the disruption of the colony from the mother country."—Ib., p. 359, note.

longer existed. On the subject of Responsible Government the remarks in some of the addresses were so pointed that he could not avoid numerous references to it. He frequently admitted that he had found the system in vogue upon his arrival in Canada, and he uniformly professed himself as its friend and upholder. That his Council and himself were not agreed as to what was included in the term "Responsible Government," however, and that a collision between them would take place sooner or later, was rendered clear enough. In his reply to an address from the people of the Talbot District he made use of the following ominous language: "It"— *i.e.*, Responsible Government—"may be pushed to an extreme which would render it impracticable; and that is the case when it is attempted to render the Governor merely a tool in the hands of a Council, demanding that the prerogative of the Crown should be surrendered to them for party purposes."*

The Governor-General returned to Kingston on the 24th of the month, in time to open Parliament at the date appointed.

---

* Kaye, Vol. II., p. 359.

Chapter XV.

ON THE EDGE OF THE STORM.

King John. So foul a sky clears not without a storm.—KING JOHN, Act IV., sc. 2.

"To appoint to office is an undoubted prerogative of the Crown, but a Cabinet Councillor's whole duty, as such, is to advise upon the exercise of undoubted prerogatives of the Crown. No one denies the legal right of the Crown to exercise any of its prerogatives, without the advice of Councillors; but Councillors who would remain responsible for appointments to office, when their claim to be advised with upon them was denied, would be worse than anomalies—they would be fools and deceivers."—LEGION'S *Letters on Responsible Government,* pp. 58, 59.

HE approaching session had for some time been looked forward to with anxious expectation, and even with solicitude, by all classes of politicians. It was known that several questions of vital importance must engage the attention of Parliament, upon each of which there would be wide divergence of opinion. Rumours of impending complications between the Governor and his Ministers had got abroad, and had given rise to the most absurd conjectures on the part of the enemies of the Administration. For several days before the opening, considerable numbers of people, in addition to members of Parliament, continued to arrive at Kingston from all parts of the Province. The hotels and places of public entertainment were filled to repletion, and the little town had never presented so stirring an aspect.

Several new members of the Assembly call for a few special words of mention. Conspicuous among them was Henry Sherwood, ex-Solicitor-General for Upper Canada. Since his demission of office, a

year before this time, he had been returned to the Assembly for the
city of Toronto, in the place of Mr. Isaac Buchanan.* He now
came down to Kingston in a frame of mind which impelled him to
make the most of any grounds of opposition to the Administration
which might present themselves. Jean Chabot, a French Canadian
advocate of some ability, also now took his seat in the Assembly for
the first time, having just been returned for the city of Quebec, upon
the resignation of the previous member, Mr. David Burnet.† M.
Chabot's limited knowledge of the English language prevented him
from taking as conspicuous a part in the debates of the time as he
was otherwise well qualified to do, but he exercised much influence
over his compatriots, and was recognized as one of the political
forces of Lower Canada.

A more remarkable man than either of the preceding was Edward
Gibbon Wakefield, who had been returned for the constituency of
Beauharnois, upon the resignation of Mr. J. W. Dunscomb. Mr.
Wakefield was an Englishman by birth; a man of great talents and
much learning, more especially in the department of political economy. He was born in 1796, and had passed through some rather
strange mutations of fortune. From his youth he had devoted
much attention to colonial affairs, his knowledge whereof may
almost be said to have been to some extent inherited, for his father
was an enthusiast in matters relating to colonization, and had written
one or two pamphlets on the subject. The son was one of the practical school of politicians that grew up in England during the second
and third decades of the present century. He wrote much for the
newspaper press, and before he was thirty years of age he was
known to some of the leading Whigs as a remarkably well-informed

---

* Mr. Buchanan resigned his membership in the Assembly on the 2nd of January, 1843.
Mr. Sherwood was elected in the following March.

† Mr. Burnet resigned on the 26th of August. M. Chabot was elected on the 18th
of September.

man on colonial and economical questions. His opinions inspired
general respect among such students of the national polity as were
familiar with his writings, and it seemed as though a future of
great brightness was before him, for he was ambitious, and in
some directions barely stopped short of genius. But, unfortunately,
his moral qualities were not upon a plane with his intellect and
his learning. His pecuniary means were small, and in 1824 an
unfortunate investment deprived him of nearly all he had. Then
commenced the *descensus Averni*. Adversity tries the temper of
men's souls, and the soul of Edward Gibbon Wakefield was not
found equal to the ordeal through which he was compelled to
pass. In endeavouring to retrieve his fortunes he connected himself with more than one transaction of questionable repute, and
finally with a transaction as to the character of which there
could be no question at all. In plain English, he entered into
a conspiracy for the abduction from a boarding-school of a wealthy
young lady of fifteen years of age. The motive of the abduction
seems to have been wholly mercenary, and it is to be feared
that the transaction had few exculpatory features about it. The
story is not an agreeable one to tell, and shall not be told at
length in these pages. Those who wish to go into the matter may
consult the authorities quoted below.* Suffice it to say that there
was a family conspiracy between Mr. Wakefield, his brother, and
his stepmother; that by means of forged letters and the grossest
falsehoods the young lady was induced to put herself in Mr. Wakefield's charge, and afterwards to accompany him to Scotland, where
there was a Scotch marriage by the Gretna Green blacksmith, David

---

* "Trial of Edward Gibbon Wakefield, William Wakefield, and Frances Wakefield, indicted with one Edward Thevenot, a Servant, for a Conspiracy, and for the Abduction of Miss Ellen Turner, the only Child and Heiress of William Turner, Esq., of Shrigley Park, in the County of Chester." London, 1827. See also, "The Member for Beauharnois: a True Narrative," published at Montreal in 1842; Blackwood's Magazine, Vol. XXI., p. 522; also Vol. XXII., p. 63; Edinburgh Review, Vol. XLVII., p. 100; Annual Register, Vol. LXIX. (1827), pp. 316-326; Canadian Portrait Gallery, Vol. II., p. 32.

Laing. This marriage was subsequently annulled by Act of Parliament. Mr. Wakefield, who at the time of the exploit was thirty years of age, and a widower, was arrested, tried, convicted, and sentenced to a term of two years' imprisonment in Newgate. After serving his term he came out of prison, amended his ways, and employed his great talents in maturing a scheme of colonization. He for some time gave himself wholly up to a literary and journalistic life. He edited and published an edition of the great work of Adam Smith. He also published several other suggestive and valuable works, the most widely known of which was issued anonymously in London in 1833, under the title of "England and America: a Comparison of the Social and Political State of the Two Nations," which was highly eulogized by competent critics. His past misdeeds, however, and the imprisonment he had undergone, had left a stain upon him which could never be wholly obliterated, and which rendered it impossible for him to attain high and honourable distinction in his native land. His plan of colonization recommended him to the notice of some of the leading statesmen of Great Britain, among whom were numbered Earl Grey, his son-in-law, Lord Durham, and Lord Stanley. Lord Durham found him a man of very remarkable intellectual power and originality, and when that nobleman came out to Canada in 1838 as Governor-General and Lord High Commissioner, Mr. Wakefield accompanied him as one of his *attachés*. That Mr. Wakefield's knowledge and services were of inestimable value to Lord Durham is unquestionable, and it is at least probable that some able practical suggestions embodied in the famous report may have originated with him. He remained in Canada after Lord Durham's departure, but eventually followed his Lordship to England, where, in conjunction with his friend Mr. Charles Buller, he concerted a scheme for raising money in Great Britain to be expended in local improvements in Canada. In furtherance of this project he again came out to this country. He for some time acted as the Canadian correspondent of the *Colonial Gazette*, and many of his letters to that periodical display an unusual degree of economical knowledge and political prescience. In July, 1842, Mr. Dunscomb, the sitting member for Beauharnois, resigned his seat, in consequence of his prospective appointment as Warden of Trinity House, Montreal. Mr. Wakefield offered himself to the electors of that constituency as their representative, and was elected in the following November. During the canvass all the unsavoury details connected with his past life were raked up and published for the edification of the people of Canada. He now took his seat as an avowed and earnest supporter of the Administration. In personal appearance he was stout and portly, with a full face and a florid complexion. As a public speaker he appealed to the reason rather than the imagination, and there was little of the *ad captandum* orator about him. He was better calculated to impress educated men than the public at large, and by consequence was not well fitted for the labours of an election campaign, although he possessed many rare qualifications for a legislator.

The Legislative Council had also received several additions, the most important of which was Mr. Draper, late Attorney-General for Upper Canada, who had been appointed to a seat in that body on the 10th of April. Dr. William Warren Baldwin, father of Robert Baldwin, was gazetted a member of the Council, but did not take his seat during the ensuing session, owing to ill health. Before another meeting of Parliament had been summoned he was no more, so that he never sat in the Legislative Council.*

A measure providing for the removal of the Seat of Government from Kingston to Montreal having been resolved upon by the Ministry, Mr. Harrison, Provincial Secretary for Upper Canada, was constrained to hand in his resignation. He sat in the Assembly as member for Kingston, and felt bound to his constituents to ad-

---

* Dr. Baldwin's death took place on the 8th of January, 1844.

vocate the retention of the capital there.* The Ministry having determined upon the removal, as a Government measure, he had no alternative but resignation, and this alternative he adopted at the opening of the session.† The abolition of the office which he held had been determined upon by the Ministry some time before, and there was no attempt or intention to appoint a successor. Mr. Harrison, after his resignation, continued to yield a general support to the Government so long as the session lasted.

His Excellency's Speech at the opening, which took place at two in the afternoon of the 28th, was quiet, dignified, and comprehensive as to details. The fashion and beauty of the Provincial capital were fully represented in the Council Chamber. After alluding to the birth of a princess,‡ the Governor spoke in sympathetic terms of the death of his predecessor. He next referred to the Imperial Act which had been passed, whereby the importation of Canadian wheat and flour into the United Kingdom was facilitated. Referring to the Provincial tour which he had just completed, he expressed his gratification at the evidences of progress and loyalty which he had encountered. The character of some of the more important measures which were to be submitted to Parliament was briefly hinted at; and the insufficiency of the prison and asylum accommodation commented upon. It was noticed that his Excellency carefully abstained from any reference to subjects likely to lead to prolonged debate. His delivery was marked by a firm manliness of tone, but some of those nearest to him observed that his usually placid countenance bore traces of anxiety. He doubtless felt much solicitude as to what

---

* At a public meeting of the inhabitants of Kingston held soon after the opening of the session, Mr. Harrison stated that he had been elected without any express pledge, but that as the Government had been brought there, and was actually there at the time of his election, he felt that there was an implied pledge on his part to maintain the Seat of Government within Upper Canada, so far as he might be able to do so.

† His formal resignation is dated the 30th of September.

‡ Alice Maud Mary, who was born on the 25th of April, 1843.

the session would bring forth. He was moreover not free from anxiety on the subject of his bodily health. The cancerous formation had of late begun to assume a malignant appearance, and had given rise to serious forebodings. Its nature was of course unknown to the public, but his face was somewhat disfigured by the fleshy tumour, as it seemed, of about the size of an acorn, in the middle of the left cheek. In every other respect he seemed to be, as to his outer man, the very model of a colonial Governor. He was about the middle height, with just sufficient corpulency to impart an appearance of prosperous dignity. His countenance was full, and rather massive, and his capacious brow was indicative of much intellectual power. His silvery locks betokened mature, but not advanced age, and he carried his nearly three-score years with a quiet and becoming dignity.

Although the Speech from the Throne had been prepared with a view to avoiding debate, it did not pass unchallenged. The Address in reply gave rise to considerable discussion in both Houses. In the Legislative Council the debate was closed on the last day of September by an able speech from Mr. Sullivan. In the Assembly it was protracted for some days longer. The Opposition felt their numerical weakness, and displayed much factiousness. The most memorable episode of the debate was an encounter which took place on the 3rd of October between Sir Allan MacNab and Robert Baldwin. Sir Allan, in the course of a speech delivered in opposition to the Address, singled out different members of the Government for personal attack. During his onslaught upon Mr. Baldwin he referred to the fact that that gentleman had gone out with a flag of truce to the rebels at Gallows Hill, near Toronto, in the month of December, 1837. "Is it not notorious," said the Knight of Dundurn, "that the traitor Rolph was the bosom friend of the Attorney-General? Is it not notorious that the Attorney-General was the person who, in company with him (Rolph), carried the flag of truce to the rebels who had assembled in the vicinity of Toronto with the intention of attacking it?" The implication was that Mr. Baldwin had himself been a disloyal and deceitful man. For such an innuendo there was of course not the shadow of justification. The facts, briefly stated, were these.* In December, 1837, Mackenzie and his adherents were encamped to the north of Toronto, and contemplated an attack upon the city. Sir Francis Bond Head, the Lieutenant-Governor, in order to gain time, determined upon parleying with the insurgents. He despatched an emissary to Mr. Baldwin, with a request that the latter would be the bearer of a flag of truce. Mr. Baldwin complied with the request, stipulating only that some one else should join him in his embassy. The other person selected was Dr. John Rolph,† who, unknown to Mr. Baldwin, was as deeply implicated in the rebellion as was Mackenzie himself. The pair proceeded on horseback to Gallows Hill, and had an interview with Mackenzie, who demanded their credentials. They were not provided with any, and the insurgent leader refused to hold any discussion with them until they could show him written authority from the Lieutenant-Governor to enter into negotiations. They then rode back from the rebel headquarters to Toronto, to obtain the credentials demanded by Mackenzie. Sir Francis Head, however, was by this time reinforced, and felt safe. He declined to ratify his embassy. Dr. Rolph's share in the transaction requires no further allusion in this place. He soon afterwards fled from the Province to escape the consequences of his treason, and did not return until a special pardon had been issued to him in the summer of 1843, as already recorded.‡ By Sir Francis Head's refusal to furnish

---

* For a much fuller account of this episode, see the sketch of the life of the Hon. Robert Baldwin, in "The Canadian Portrait Gallery," Vol. I., pp. 32–35.

† Marshall Spring Bidwell had previously been proposed by Mr. Baldwin as his companion on the expedition, but that gentleman had declined to go. It was after his refusal that Dr. Rolph was applied to.

‡ *Ante*, p. 299.

the credentials demanded, Mr. Baldwin was placed in an equivocal light, and without the satisfaction of having accomplished any good. This was the part played by Mr. Baldwin, for which he was now taunted by Sir Allan MacNab. He had been subjected to similar taunts before, and had deemed it beneath his dignity to reply to them, but on this occasion he adopted a contrary plan. He rose to his feet, and addressed the Assembly with calm and impressive earnestness, detailing the particulars with such minuteness as to render it impossible for any one to misunderstand the story. He sat down amid resounding cheers from all parts of the House, and it was felt that he had only done simple justice to himself in making his explanation. It is fair to Sir Allan MacNab to say that he had never before clearly understood the precise nature of Mr. Baldwin's mission to the insurgents, and that he subsequently made a public apology for his remarks.

The debate on the Address having been disposed of, and the Address itself having been passed without amendment, the Government were at liberty to devote their attention to other measures. It was not necessary to take much account of the Opposition, who were totally without anything deserving the name of a policy, and who were too feeble in point of number to be dangerous. The rank and file of the Opposition had comparatively little to say in Parliament. The leaders chiefly confined their assaults to raking up old tales about disaffection and disloyalty. On only one important measure did the Administration encounter serious obstruction; namely, on the Seat of Government question. On the 9th of October the Hon. Mr. Daly, in response to a motion made some days previously by Sir Allan MacNab, presented a message from his Excellency relative to the contemplated removal of the capital. The correspondence between the Home and Colonial Governments on the subject did not accompany the message, which, however, contained the substance of a despatch from the Colonial Secretary, conveying an intimation to the effect that Her Majesty's Government declined coming to any determination upon the subject of the permanent location of the Seat of Government in Canada without consulting the Legislature of the Colony.* It was intimated that any addresses either from the Assembly or the Legislative Council upon that question, in favour of Montreal or Kingston, would be favourably recommended to Her Majesty, provided that such addresses were accompanied by an appropriation to cover the necessary expenses of removal and permanent location. Toronto and Quebec were both mentioned in the despatch, and the unsuitableness of both was admitted, as also was the project of holding alternate Parliaments in each. The choice was entirely restricted to Montreal and Kingston. The matter was thus brought squarely before the Legislature, and the debate upon it in both Houses was long and loud. In the Legislative Council the Government policy was upheld by Mr. Sullivan with even more than his customary brilliancy and vigour. In the Assembly the debate was not brought to a close until early in November. The Opposition, though they were in a hopeless minority, fought every inch of the ground. They urged the implied undertaking of Lord Sydenham that the capital of the Province should be in Upper Canada. That undertaking, it was claimed, had been one of their chief inducements to consent to the Union.† It was to be expected that Upper Canadians would look with disfavour upon the project of removal to Montreal, and the lines of party discipline could not be drawn with sufficient tightness to compel obedience to the dictates of the Government on the part of all their supporters. William Hamilton Merritt and Malcolm Cameron,

---

* Sir Charles Metcalfe, at the instance of his Councillors, had consulted the Secretary of State as to the expediency of removing the capital from Kingston.

† By some of the members it was represented as having been an implied undertaking on the part of Mr. Thomson, afterwards Lord Sydenham. Others—Sir Allan MacNab and Mr. Cartwright among the number—claimed that the undertaking had been express, but private.

who generally gave in their adhesion to the Ministerial measures, were
against the Government on this question, and supported the alleged
claims of Upper Canada with much vehemence. Nearly all the Upper
Canadian members, other than the members of the Government,
either voted against the Ministry or abstained from voting altogether.
The strength of the Administration was such, however, that they
could well afford to wink at the defective party allegiance of a
few of their supporters on this vexed and vexing question. On
the 2nd and 3rd of November the debate was brought to a close, and
the Cabinet resolutions, moved by Mr. Baldwin and seconded by
Mr. Lafontaine, were carried by a vote of fifty-one to twenty-seven.
It was resolved that "in the opinion of this House it is expedient
that the Seat of Her Majesty's Provincial Government for this
Province should be at the City of Montreal." The hotly contested
matter was therefore disposed of, and before the next meeting of
Parliament the Seat of Government, together with all the para-
phernalia of office, had been removed from Kingston. Local predilections apart, there can be no doubt that the step was a wise
one. Montreal was nearly as central as Kingston, and had long
been a focus of commercial and social life. It was the port at
which the greater part of the Provincial revenue was collected, and
where the chief fiscal arrangements of the country were managed.
Kingston, on the other hand, had nothing to recommend it but its
central position.[*] Its unsuitableness was patent to all, and an
agitation for removal had been on foot ever since Lord Sydenham
had fixed upon it as the site of the Provincial capital. This agitation
would doubtless have been maintained, to the great loss of the public

---

[*] Charles Dickens, at the time of his visit to Kingston, in 1842, pronounced it to be "a
very poor town, rendered still poorer in the appearance of its market-place by the ravages
of a recent fire." "Indeed," he added, "it may be said of Kingston that one half of it
appears to be burnt down and the other half not to be built up. The Government House
is neither elegant nor commodious, yet it is almost the only house of any importance in
the neighbourhood."—*American Notes*, Chap. XV.

time, and to the detriment of legislative business. The Montreal experiment eventually proved a failure, but the failure was due to causes which no human wisdom could have foreseen or provided against in the year 1843.

The session, during the first few weeks of its progress, was a very busy one. Some important measures were passed, and others of equal importance were inaugurated, but not carried through, owing to the complications to be detailed in the following chapter. Ever since the meeting of Parliament the antagonism between the Governor and his Councillors—Mr. Daly always excepted—had been slowly but surely gaining ground. There had been no unpleasant words at the Council Board, but a chilling coldness of atmosphere pervaded the deliberations there. The chilliness was rendered all the more apparent by the warm cordiality which marked the Governor's demeanour towards Mr. Daly, who was not in good odour with his brother Councillors, some of whom suspected him of intriguing with the Governor and the Opposition against them. As for the Governor, he showed an increasing disposition to make light of the responsibilities of his Ministers, and at the same time to magnify his own. After giving his consent to the introduction of a Bill for the suppression of secret societies, and after the measure had run the gauntlet of opposition in both Houses, he had, without a word of explanation, announced his determination to reserve it for the signification of Her Majesty's pleasure. The first intimation of this fact came to the Ministry in a roundabout fashion from a gentleman who was not even a member of Parliament, and who was a staunch opponent of the Administration. That the Governor had the right to reserve the Bill was undeniable, but the Ministers considered that they had been treated cavalierly in not being vouchsafed a full and cordial explanation, and they were, rightly or wrongly, under the impression that he had determined to reserve it for no other reason than to display his power over them. They considered that in any case they ought to have been the first to hear of his intention. Their position, moreover, was rendered increasingly intolerable by the rumours afloat to the effect that his Excellency governed the country as he thought proper, and neither sought nor desired advice from his Ministers. Notwithstanding Mr. Lafontaine's strongly expressed opinion* as to the necessity for the Governor's consulting his Ministers on all appointments to office, it was found that appointments were offered, and in some cases actually made, without a word on the subject having been communicated by the Governor to his Councillors. It came to the knowledge of the Ministers that the Speakership of the Legislative Council—which had been vacated by Mr. Jameson with strong expressions of contumely in consequence of the vote on the Seat of Government resolutions—had been offered successively to Mr. Levius Peters Sherwood, a leading Conservative, and to Mr. Neilson, of Quebec, by both of whom it had been refused. The vacancy was at last filled on the 8th of November, by the appointment of Mr. Caron to the post. Other appointments, it was said, had been expressly promised by his Excellency to friends of the Opposition, and with respect to none of them had he thought it worth while even to deliver a hint of his intentions to his Ministers. The influence of the latter with his Excellency was currently reported to be far less than that of Sir Allan MacNab, Mr. Cartwright, Mr. Draper, or Mr. Sherwood. The Ministers were covertly taunted on the very floor of the House with the Governor's disrespect for them. Finally, at the beginning of the fourth week in November, it was ascertained that a Mr. Francis Powell, son of Colonel Powell, an old-time Conservative, had been appointed by his Excellency to the vacant post of Clerk of the Peace for the Dalhousie District. The information came to them from a prominent member of the Opposition, who had boasted some days before in the presence of Mr. Baldwin that he would induce the Governor to make the appoint-

---

* Ante, pp. 286-291.

ment in the teeth of his Ministers. The Ministers were disposed to discredit the news, but next day they received a brief and formal notification from the Governor of the fact of the appointment. How disagreeable such a piece of intelligence must have been may be understood when it is known that Mr. Baldwin had himself promised the position to a firm supporter of the Administration. The Ministers, of course, would be regarded by the country as being responsible for this appointment; an appointment as to which they had not been consulted, and as to which they would never have given their consent. It was the last straw on the back of the camel. The pitcher had gone to the well once too often. The Ministry, with the largest Parliamentary support at their back that any Canadian Administration had ever been able to command, found themselves practically ignored by their official head, and treated as though they were of no account. His Excellency was soon to learn, to his cost, that the meridian of Canada was not coincident with that of Bengal, and that Louis Lafontaine and Robert Baldwin were the last men in the world to enact the *rôle* of Ulric the Unimpeachable.

Chapter XVI.

RESPONSIBLE GOVERNMENT.

"Lord Metcalfe became involved in difficulties with his Council on a question relating to the distribution of patronage. His ministers retired, supported by a majority of the Assembly. Could the continued absence of English constitutional principles from Canadian government be more strikingly described?"—ADDERLEY'S "Review of *The Colonial Policy of Lord John Russell's Administration*, by Earl Grey, and of Subsequent Colonial History;" p. 27.

"Generally speaking, patronage in a country like England, is always exercised with a view to the acquiring or preserving Parliamentary support. Napoleon, the King of Prussia, and the Emperors of Austria and Russia might select individuals to fill offices on the sole ground of their superior fitness to discharge their duties. But in a free country suitableness for office is not the only thing to be attended to in deciding as to the comparative claims of candidates for official preferment: if they possess it, so much the better; but the primary consideration is, how is the Government to be carried on? Now that, it is plain, will be best effected by securing the active support of the friends of Government, and by weakening the party of their opponents; and the distribution of patronage is one of the principal means by which these objects are to be realized. A Government that should neglect to avail itself of this power could not long exist."—McCULLOCH'S GEOGRAPHICAL DICTIONARY. Article on *England and Wales—Constitutional Government*.

THE Ministers received their first notification of Mr. Powell's appointment on the afternoon of Thursday, the 23rd of the month. They felt that the time for self-assertion had arrived. The delicate task of conferring with the Governor was deputed to Mr. Baldwin and Mr. Lafontaine, who waited upon his Excellency at Government House on Friday, the 24th. There is no material conflict in the accounts given of the conversation by those who participated in it, though they differed widely as to the deductions to be drawn from it. The two Councillors began by deprecating the humiliating position in which they and their colleagues found themselves, owing to the Governor's reticence in his intercourse with them, more especially in the matter of public appointments. They called his attention to the fact that appointments had been offered, and in some cases actually conferred, upon persons who were no friends to the Administration. They complained that their influence was thereby brought to naught ; that they were sneered at by the Opposition ; that by the country at large they were held responsible for acts they had not sanctioned, and as to which they had not even been consulted. They also deprecated the reservation by his Excellency of the Secret Societies Bill, after he had sanctioned its introduction to Parliament. All through the interview his Excellency remained perfect master of himself, but he could not conceal his consciousness that a crisis had arrived in public affairs. He would not, however, recede by so much as a hair's-breadth from the position he had assumed. He admitted that he had made and offered appointments without consulting his Ministers, and claimed that he had simply exercised his prerogative in so doing. His interlocutors, without denying his rights in the matter, submitted that they also had rights of their own, one of which they would be called upon to exercise unless a satisfactory understanding could be arrived at. The right here referred to was of course that of resignation. On the subject of the reserved Bill, the Governor averred that he had given his consent to its being introduced into Parliament because he had promised, soon after his assumption of the Government, that he would sanction legislation on the subject as a substitute for executive measures, which he refused to adopt on account of their proscriptive character, although he deprecated the existence of societies which tend to foment religious and civil discord.* He then stated that ever since his arrival in the country he had observed an antagonism between his own views and those of his Ministers on

---

* See the Governor's reply to Mr. Lafontaine's "Note to Sir Charles Metcalfe," etc., dated from Government House, November 28th.

the subject of the prerogative. The Ministers expressed their astonishment and regret that his Excellency should have had this consciousness so many months without hinting at anything of the sort to his Councillors. The conversation lasted several hours. The upshot of it was that the Councillors demanded from the Governor that he would no longer ignore their existence in the matter of public appointments; that he would act upon their advice or not, as he thought fit; but that he would at any rate consult them beforehand.* His Excellency was not disposed to bind himself by any such stipulation, or indeed by any stipulation whatever. To do so, he declared, would be at once to degrade his office and to surrender the prerogative of the Crown.† After discussing the question with much earnestness, and apparently with entire good faith on both sides, they mutually agreed to leave it open until the following day, when the Council were to meet. Next afternoon the discussion was resumed at the Council Board, and the whole matter was gone over again and again, with no result except that both

---

* "When the members of the late Executive Council offered their humble remonstrance to his Excellency on this condition of public affairs, his Excellency not only frankly explained the difference of opinion existing between him and the Council, but stated that from the time of his arrival in the country he had observed an antagonism between him and them on the subject, and notwithstanding that the members of the Council repeatedly and distinctly explained to his Excellency that they considered him free to act contrary to their advice, and only claimed an opportunity of giving such advice, and of knowing before others his Excellency's intentions; his Excellency did not in any manner remove the impression left upon their minds by his avowal that there was an antagonism between him and them, and a want of that cordiality and confidence which would enable them in their respective stations to carry on public business to the satisfaction of his Excellency or of the country. The want of this cordiality and confidence had already become a matter of public rumour, and public opinion not only extended it to acts upon which there were apparent grounds for difference of opinion, but to all measures of Government involving political principles. His Excellency, on the one hand, was supposed to be coerced by his Council into a course of policy which he did not approve of, and the Council were made liable to the accusation of assuming the tone and position of responsible advisers of the Government, without, in fact, asserting the right of being consulted thereupon." See Mr. Lafontaine's "Note to Sir Charles Metcalfe, relative to the resignation of the late Cabinet," dated from Daly's Hotel, November 27th.

† See the Governor's reply to Mr. Lafontaine, *ubi supra*.

sides were, if possible, more firmly set in their respective opinions than before.* They parted for the day, however, without any actual rupture, the Governor repeatedly declaring that he subscribed entirely to the resolutions of the Legislative Assembly of the 3rd of September, 1841, and that he considered any other system of Government than that which recognizes responsibility to the people and to the representative Assembly as impracticable in Canada.† In vain did his Councillors point out to him his inconsistency. It was a simple waste of time. It was like describing the glories of sunrise to one who had been blind from his birth. He seemed to suffer from a congenital incapacity to perceive what he had made up his mind did not exist.

That night all the Councillors met and consulted together—all of them, that is to say, except Mr. Daly, who had had no part in any of the ministerial proceedings above described, and who had already announced his intention of standing by the Governor, come what come might. Throughout the whole of this episode, and indeed throughout the whole of his public career, Mr. Daly's conduct was of a piece with that of the valiant Frenchman of whom most of us have heard, who passed his life in coming to the rescue of the strongest. In his eyes the Governor was the Governor, the nominee of the Fountain of Honour, and his authority was paramount. Sooth to say, Mr. Daly was in about as false a position as the Governor himself. He was altogether out of his element. He could see no reason whatever for resigning the sweets and emoluments of office, and setting himself up in opposition to authority, merely to gratify a foolish, Quixotic notion about so trivial a matter as

---

* "Three or more distinct propositions were made to him [the Governor] over and over again, sometimes in different terms, but always aiming at the same purpose, which in his opinion, if accomplished, would have been a virtual surrender into the hands of the Council of the prerogative of the Crown, and on his uniformly replying to their propositions in the negative, his refusal was each time followed by 'then we must resign,' or words to that purport, from one or more of the Council." See the Governor's reply to Mr. Lafontaine, *ubi supra*. † *Ib*.

Responsible Government in one of Her Majesty's colonies. He was there to obey the behests of royalty, and royalty in Canada was represented by the Governor-General.

The result of the ministerial conference was that on Sunday, the 26th, nine out of the ten gentlemen comprising the Ministry (i.e., all except Mr. Daly) tendered their resignations to his Excellency, who signified his acceptance of them. In accordance with Parliamentary usage in England in cases of ministerial resignations, Mr. Lafontaine applied to the Governor for permission to explain to the Legislature the reasons which had led to the existing state of affairs. The permission, which was verbal only, was accompanied by a request that the ex-Ministers would put on paper the substance of the proposed explanation. This was done by Mr. Lafontaine, and the document was delivered to his Excellency early on Monday morning.* The fact of the resignation soon became known all over Kingston, and the anxiety and excitement on the subject were intense. The political world of the capital was taken completely by surprise. No sooner had the doors of the Assembly chamber opened at ten o'clock on Monday morning than every foot of space available for spectators was occupied. Before the commencement of the regular business of the day Mr. Lafontaine rose and addressed the House both in English and French. He announced that he and his colleagues, with the exception of the Honourable Member for Megantic, had deemed it their duty to tender their resignations. He added that the Governor-General had accepted the resignations, and that the ex-Ministry would at an early day explain to the House the reasons for their conduct. Immediately after this announcement the nine ex-Ministers vacated the Treasury Benches, leaving Mr. Daly there alone in his glory. Only formal business was tran-

---

* On this subject, see "*La Crise Ministerielle et M. Denis Benjamin Viger, etc., en deux parties;*" Kingston, 1844. Also "The Ministerial Crisis: Mr. D. B. Viger and his Position," being a review of the abovenamed pamphlet, by a Reformer of 1836 (? the Hon. F. Hincks). Kingston, 1844.

sacted, the Government measures which were the order of the day being necessarily postponed. The Assembly adjourned soon after noon, and during the rest of the day the resignation, and the presumed grounds of it, formed the staple of eager discussion throughout the city. On Tuesday the Governor prepared a counter statement to that of Mr. Lafontaine. As has already been stated, the two accounts did not materially conflict as to facts, but only as to the deductions to be derived therefrom. These deductions, however, struck at the root of the whole question at issue. It was claimed by the Governor that in Mr. Lafontaine's statement there was a total omission of the circumstances which he (the Governor) regarded as forming the real grounds of resignation. He stated that a demand had been made upon him by the ex-Ministers that he should agree to make no appointment, or offer of appointment, without previously consulting his Council; that the lists of candidates should in every instance be submitted to the Council, and that he (the Governor), in deciding after consultation with them, should make no appointment prejudicial to their influence : " in other words," remarked his Excellency, "that the patronage of the Crown should be surrendered to the Council for the purchase of Parliamentary support; for if the demand did not mean that it meant nothing, as it cannot be imagined that the mere form of taking advice without regarding it was the process contemplated." He stated that he had declined to "degrade the character of his office" by assenting to the demands made upon him. He further stated that he had objected to the exclusive distribution of patronage with party views, and maintained the principle that office ought, in every instance, to be given to the man best qualified to render efficient service to the State; and where there was no such preëminence, he asserted his right to exercise his discretion. On the subject of the Secret Societies Bill, the Governor's explanation was that he had received special instructions from Her Majesty to reserve every Act of an unusual or extraordinary character. "Undoubtedly," continued his Excellency, "the Secret Societies Bill answers that description, being unexampled in British legislation." With respect to his having given his consent to its being introduced into Parliament, he remarked that "permission to introduce a Bill cannot be properly assumed as fettering the judgment of the Governor with regard to the royal assent, for much may happen during the passage of the Bill through the Legislature to influence his decision. He then commented upon the opposition to which the Bill had been subjected, and added, "it was much better that it (the Bill) should not go into operation until confirmed by Her Majesty's Government than that it should be discontinued after its operation had commenced."

From time to time his Excellency sent for, and was closeted with, various leading members of Parliament, including Messieurs Daly, Draper, Viger, MacNab and Wakefield. The last-named gentleman had some time before this ceased to be a supporter of the Lafontaine-Baldwin Government. He had various special purposes of his own to serve in connection with the colonization scheme already mentioned, and had been unable to obtain ministerial concurrence therein. He was moreover specially intimate with Mr. Daly, whose cause he now espoused against the ex-Ministers. It was suspected by some shrewd persons that Mr. Wakefield, as soon as he found that he could not win over the Ministry to his views, had begun to intrigue with Mr. Daly against the other members of the Government. He at all events was one of his Excellency's most trusted advisers from that time forward. As Canadian correspondent of the *Colonial Gazette* he thenceforth did a good deal to mislead public opinion in England as to the real grounds of conflict between Sir Charles Metcalfe and his Ministers.[*]

---

[*] See especially his letter dated 11th December, 1843, republished at Kingston in pamphlet form.

On Wednesday, the 29th, Mr. Baldwin explained to the Assembly the grounds upon which he and his eight colleagues had resigned office. After reading the resolutions of the 3rd of September, 1841, whereby the principles of Responsible Government had in their fullest sense been conceded, he declared that he and his colleagues had taken office under those principles, and that when they found that the illustrious person at the head of the Government entertained views widely different from theirs on this subject, their duty bound them to take the course they had adopted. "Had those differences been merely theoretical," said Mr. Baldwin, "the Ministers would have been sorry to interrupt the harmony existing. But when they found that those differences existed with respect to appointments to office: when they found the Head of the Government making appointments without their advice (not that they pretend for a moment to say that he has not the right of doing this)—when they found also that proposals for appointments were made without their knowledge: when these took place, the difference of opinion ceased to be merely theoretical." But this, he added, was not all. It was ascertained that a Bill of a most important nature was not to receive the royal assent in this country, notwithstanding its having been introduced under the sanction of the Head of the Government. Some signification of the intention to withhold the royal assent to this Bill should, in his (Mr. Baldwin's) opinion, have been made to the Ministers on its passage, in order that the public might have been made acquainted with it. As it was, the Ministers were open to the imputation of having advised the Head of the Government in favour of a measure to which he could not consent; or else of having introduced it, knowing that it would be sent home to lie on the dusty shelves of the Colonial Office, where so many of their measures were already deposited. Had they remained in office they would have been responsible for acts which they had not advised. They had received a frank avowal from his Excellency that since his arrival in the country, and assumption of the Government, he had discovered an antagonism in their principles, and a difference in their views, although this communication had only lately been made known to them. Cordiality should exist between the Governor and his Council, and he (Mr. Baldwin) for one would never serve under any man who, after a lapse of months, told him there was an antagonism in their opinions. They (the Ministry) had conceded to his Excellency in its fullest extent the right of making appointments, but they claimed the right of advising the acts of the Governor. They claimed a right not to be left to know from third parties of decisions come to by the Head of the Government, which they should have known from the very first. An offer had been made of the chair in the Legislative Council, and this they were only aware of from the person to whom the offer was made, or from persons in the streets. Was that what the Assembly understood by Responsible Government, or what was expected from the responsible advisers of the Crown? Their interview with the Head of the Government had led to no hopes of a different course of conduct, but on the contrary had led to an assurance of a want of cordiality and assistance. Could the Ministers be expected to hold office under such terms—terms so pregnant with mischief to the Province, and so contrary to the avowed wishes of the country and its representatives in the House.

Mr. Baldwin was here interrupted by Mr. D. B. Viger, who inquired whether he (Mr. Baldwin) had the sanction of the Head of the Government to make these explanations. Mr. Baldwin replied that he had received permission to produce any facts necessary for the justification of himself and his colleagues. Had this been refused, the Ministers must have come down and claimed the support of the House in their justification. These explanations were necessary to obtain from the House its verdict, as to whether by their course of proceeding they had guarded the interests of the country or not.

Rumours had spread abroad as to this difference of opinion, by which it appeared either that the Governor acted under coercion, or else that he acted without their advice. Mr. Baldwin repeated his asseveration that had the difference been merely theoretical, the Ministers might have acceded, but that when they found a want of cordiality and confidence existing since the first moment of his Excellency's assumption of the Government, although only announced to them a few days since, they were bound as men of honour to resign, and were ready to be judged by the House and by the people. Such were the grounds for their resignation, and it was for the House to say whether they had done right or wrong in doing so.

Mr. Daly, who undertook to present the Governor's view of the matter to the Assembly, read Mr. Lafontaine's letter to the Governor, dated the 27th instant, and also his Excellency's reply of the 28th. His argument was a mere repetition of the points urged by the Governor, who, he alleged, had acted upon his own views with respect to Responsible Government, and would continue so to do. Mr. Daly concluded by a strong protest from his Excellency against the explanation of the late Ministry. That explanation, he alleged, was calculated to mislead the House as to the true causes of difference. After an ineffective attempt at further explanation on the part of Mr. Hincks, who was interrupted by various members on the grounds that the subject was not debatable, Sir Allan MacNab moved for an humble address to his Excellency for copies of all correspondence between the Head of the Government and the late Executive Council on the subject of the late resignations. The order of the day was then proceeded with, and the debate on the subject of the resignation was for the time at an end in the Assembly.

The explanation in the Legislative Council was made on Thursday, the 30th, by Mr. Sullivan, who delivered a long and powerful speech on the great question in dispute. This remarkable speech contains an exhaustive and admirable presentation of the argument from the ex-Ministers' point of view, and the most salient passages of it may be read with profit by anyone who wishes to understand the precise nature of the issue. He began by remarking that the course pursued in the Assembly had removed many of the difficulties that might have lain in his way, while showing the impossibility of himself and his colleagues remaining in office after understanding his Excellency's views. With respect to the degree of their responsibility to the country, he, Mr. Sullivan, had formerly stood on the floor of that House to defend every act of the Government, and in the other House his colleagues had been in the same position. They had been held accountable for every act of the Government, and often blamed, unjustly blamed, even by those on their own side, without having it in their power to excuse themselves; and it was not only by the two Houses of Parliament that they had thus been held accountable, but by every man in the country, no matter what his political sect. They had been held accountable for every official appointment, and for every act relative to local affairs. It had not been in their power consistently to reject that position. On it they had taken office. They had admitted it when they had met his Excellency for the first time, and when they had met Parliament; they had been allowed to pledge themselves to sustain that position, and not one voice or one word had been raised against it either in public or in private. And this had led to results highly disagreeable to the Ministers. Every act of theirs that was good, every act that was patriotic, was ascribed to the kind and beneficent individual who represented the Sovereign, but the blame of anything that gave offence, or that was unjust, was put upon them, and having assumed that position they were bound to stand or fall by it. If honourable gentlemen believed that it was for any slight difference in political opinion, or from any private or interested motives, that they would

have risked their present position, little was understood of their
heavy responsibility. It was unparliamentary to speak of the
Head of the Government, but he, the Speaker, could have wished to
see before him, on the floor, those who, by their secret advice, had
brought about the existing state of things. By that secret Administration a system of irresponsible Government had been begun.
The first step was already made, and he feared, from such a state of
political tranquillity as was never before known in Canada, a state so
contented as to cause no wish for a change, that new system would
cause a retrogade movement, ending in a contest between the people and the Representative of the Crown. God forbid that such a
contest should ever arise; and he declared that whether he was a
member of the Government or in Opposition he would be the very
last to shake the loyalty even of the greatest waverer, by any act of
his. The differences between the Governor-General and his Executive Council had first grown out of appointments to office without
their advice, and without their knowledge, until at last it had gone
so far that the first intimation they got of those numerous appointments was when it was told to them in the streets. He was not
going to reveal Government secrets, but affairs had been so carried
on until, on a late occasion, the honourable Speaker of that House
had declared that he would not sit in the chair any longer, and in a
few days after informed them that after repeated solicitations
his Excellency had refused to accept his resignation. Was it not
natural to think that, in that case, his Excellency would say, "Mr.
Sullivan, you have a seat in the Legislative Council, and therefore
ought to be acquainted with the feelings of that body. As one of
my advisers, can you tell me if it is the wish of the Legislative
Council that I should refuse to accept the resignation of your
Speaker?" But no! After the honourable Speaker had insulted
that House by telling them that he would consider it an indignity
to sit there any longer, his Excellency had continued him in that

situation without taking the advice of his Council. He (Mr. Sullivan), on a still later occasion, had been thanked by an honourable member of that House for having recommended him to fill the chair. In reply, he had expressed his regret to him that he had not accepted the proffered honour, for in reality he would have been happy to see that honourable gentleman as Speaker, but in spite of that he did not feel the less that his Excellency had humiliated his Council by not asking if they wished that appointment to be made. He would ask honourable gentlemen to suppose, with him, that at a period when he stood on the floor of that House in defence of a principle by which he had determined to stand or fall, some person who vigorously opposed that principle was appointed to an exalted office, would it not be a clear demonstration to the country that he (Mr. Sullivan) did not possess the confidence of his Excellency; in fact that his opponent was rewarded for his opposition? Such, nevertheless, was the case. He had heard in the streets that a gentleman* who had distinguished himself by his opposition to the Government had been sent for to take the situation of Speaker, but the gentleman having embarked for Toronto, the appointment had not taken place. If it had, the Council would have resigned then, instead of awaiting further insult. The same system had been carried on from day to day, until at last they had received a direct note informing them of some appointments, trifling in their nature, but in direct opposition to their views. Did they seize their advantage then, to embarrass his Excellency by tendering their resignation? No! and he had no doubt that if it were put to the votes of the House they would have been censured for not doing their duty by resigning. The appointments certainly were trifling, but he could not tell honourable gentlemen how humiliating it was for them to be taken by the hand, by persons of whom they knew nothing, or to receive half a dozen letters by post from persons whose very

---

* The Hon. Levius Peters Sherwood. *Ante*, p. 318.

names were unknown to them, thanking them for appointment to office. He could not tell, he could not give an idea to honourable gentlemen of their humiliation, when they saw in an opposition print that such an one was appointed to an office, but that the appointee did not mean to thank a rebel Executive for his appointment, but a higher and a better power! It was in consequence of the abovementioned note that the Executive had had a long discussion with his Excellency on Saturday, the 25th instant, when the question of appointments was put into every possible shape, at the same time to meet his views and to gain the degree of consideration for themselves which they felt to be their due. So long did they persist that at last they felt—and he was not sure that another person did not participate in the feeling—that any further efforts would only make it appear that they were holding on to office cringingly. At that discussion, as well as at the short one on the previous day, they had in vain endeavoured to impress on the mind of his Excellency that it was not their wish to direct or control his measures, but merely that he should say: "Gentlemen, you are my advisers, and I will not make any appointments without consulting you beforehand,"—so as to give them an opportunity to express their opinions upon those measures for which they were held accountable. The result of the discussion with his Excellency having made it necessary for them to resign, they had done so by letter, which together with his Excellency's answer, he would read to the House, and would afterwards comment on them both. In doing so he remarked that they followed the course usually pursued in England, where, when a Ministry resigns, they ask leave to explain on what grounds that resignation is made. The liberty, he added, was seldom or never refused, because it would place the ex-Ministry in a very advantageous position, as they could immediately turn round and say, "Leave is denied us to lay before you our reasons for resignation. You may form your own opinions

on such conduct, and we claim from you the same confidence as we
enjoyed on first taking office." (Here the honourable gentleman
read Mr. Lafontaine's note, and the reply of his Excellency.) With
respect to what his Excellency stated, as to an attempt made by the
ex-Ministers to show that the difference rested on the theory of
Responsible Government, he (Mr. Sullivan) distinctly stated that
that formed the ground of difference and no other. His Excellency
might be quite right in asserting that he would exercise his own
discretion in the Executive Government of the country, but he
(Mr. Sullivan) would merely say that as the Council had gone
before the last Governor-General with a distinct assertion of the
footing on which they would act, they could not recede from that
position unless with disgrace; and that not being to their mind,
they withdrew from the Government in time to save their honour.
If his Excellency chose to make use of his own discretion alone,
then the Executive Council was a useless body. The resolutions
embodying the principles of their Government were introduced
by a gentleman who, at the period of their introduction, was himself in opposition, perfectly understanding the delicacy of the
Home Government in admitting that there was a colonial Cabinet;
and what was still more, knowing that it would be as wise to
think of the Executive Council of Canada carrying on the Government of the British Empire, as to think of supporting any administration in opposition to the views of the Assembly. The first
principle established by the resolutions was that the Governor-
General is not accountable to the people of Canada, and can not
be called to account for any act of his. One part of the resolution
named those who were to be held responsible—"subordinate officers
by whose counsel and advice the Governor conferred appointments."
He, Mr. Sullivan, would ask if there was any one point on which there
was aroused a greater degree of wrath, which caused more vituperation or more envy, than the conferring of appointments. On that

point every one's local feelings were excited, and if his Excellency took that which most indisputably was the duty of the Council into his own hands, who was responsible ? Did the Councillors part from his Excellency on slight considerations, or did any man imagine that they threw themselves out of office on account of a few paltry appointments ? No! they withdrew from the Government, because they found their political existence was endangered, and because they could not sit any longer as members of a government whose principles were destructive of their very constitution. Another resolution laid down that the responsible officers should be persons enjoying the confidence of the people; and it was in that view that they informed his Excellency, when about to take a step offensive to them, that if he appointed those persons to office who were opposed to them in politics, a door would be opened to the people to charge them with a treachery and backsliding from their avowed creed; and if the right of advising him were taken away, and they staid in office, they would be justly charged with undermining the constitution under which they had consented to act; and perhaps, after months of crimination, would go back to the people without the confidence or the sympathy of any. Among other charges in his Excellency's letter, it was imputed to the late Executive Council that they wanted to purchase Parliamentary support by the conferring of offices. That he, Mr. Sullivan, denied. Was there a single case in which Parliamentary support was made a condition on taking office ? Beyond doubt it was true that Lord John Russell's despatch stated that no officer under Responsible Government should oppose the measures of that Government; that was a fundamental principle of the constitution; but it was notorious that five-sixths of the whole officials of the country were appointed by former Governors, and yet they were not interfered with by the Government for the sake of Parliamentary support. As to that part of his Excellency's letter which mentioned the injustice of giving office only to persons of the same political opinions with the existing Government, he said he had watched the course of different administrations in Canada for the last twenty years. He had been a member of administration for eight years, and yet during the whole length of that time, he did not remember ever to have seen any of the many different parties in power patronizing their enemies. In fact, if the proposition had been made he had no doubt it would have been laughed at as a piece of childish folly. There was another part of the letter from his Excellency to which he wished to draw the attention of honourable gentlemen. It was the reference to the Secret Societies Bill.* His Excellency remarked that the Bill was pressed on him with great pertinacity. He (Mr. Sullivan) admitted it, and could have wished that, at that time, the Ministers had been informed that as an extraordinary measure it would be reserved for the royal assent. If that course had been pursued not one voice would have been raised against it. But permission was given to introduce the Bill; it was passed by a large majority in the Lower House; by acclamation, he might say, in the Legislative Council; and not having the slightest knowledge of his Excellency's intention regarding it, honourable gentlemen might judge of his utter astonishment when he was told out of doors that his Excellency had reserved the Secret Societies Bill for the approval of Her Majesty. Some time afterwards an official notification was received, letting them know that what was already common rumour was in reality to be the case. Could anything more humiliating be conceived than that they, Her Majesty's advisers, did not receive any information from his Excellency that he intended to do so and so, until after it was publicly spoken of in the streets? Mr. Sullivan concluded by expressing the utmost admiration of the Governor-General's character, but stated that his ideas of governing were brought from other countries,

---

* See the antepenultimate paragraph of his Excellency's statement.

and that if the experiment were made in Canada of carrying on a Government without paying respect to the different parties, it would be unsuccessful; and although so much could not be gathered from his Excellency's letter, he (Mr. Sullivan) hoped that a coalition could be formed having the entire confidence of the people, and standing before the Assembly as responsible for their acts.

This speech, which, like other important Parliamentary speeches, was reported in the newspapers of the time, produced a marked effect upon the country, and tended to increase the very high reputation which Mr. Sullivan already enjoyed. Meanwhile his Excellency continued to send for and confer with leading members of Parliament with a view to the formation of a new Ministry. Such assistance as the chiefs of the Opposition, assisted by Messieurs Draper, Wakefield and D. B. Viger could give him, was entirely at his disposal, but the state of public feeling was such that the prospect of forming an Administration which would command Parliamentary support was not hopeful.

On the 1st of December the Governor, in reply to an address of the Assembly adopted on the previous day, transmitted to that House, through the medium of Mr. Daly, in his official capacity, a message, accompanied by a copy of the note of Mr. Lafontaine, and also of his own reply. Upon motion of Sir Allan MacNab two thousand copies of the message, as well as of the accompanying documents, were ordered to be printed in English, and as many in French, for the use of members. The documents then for the first time became public property. After the transaction of some formal business, Mr. James Hervey Price, member for the First Riding of York, rose and stated that he had a paramount duty to perform, from which he trusted he should not flinch, notwithstanding the embarrassing situation in which he was placed. He remarked that it was unprecedented for a Minister of the Crown to come down, as the Provincial Secretary for Canada East had done, with a message in reply to explanations from Ministers who had resigned. He, Mr. Price, did not know how to treat this message. He trusted he would treat it with all the respect due to the high character of the person from whom it emanated. If Responsible Government had not been conceded to them, he, Mr. Price, did not know what concession was. He had supposed the colony to be under the government of a head, advised in all its acts by a Council responsible to, and holding the confidence of the people through their representatives. He, the speaker, had always pursued one undeviating course in politics since his first arrival in the colony. He asked no favour from any Government; and they had nothing in their gift which they could bestow on him. But he wished to see the Government so conducted in this country that when a separation took place between parent and child (an event which he trusted would not occur in his lifetime) that separation should be made a mutual and friendly one between the two countries. He had always supported those Governors who had governed constitutionally and for the good of the country. He hoped that the present discussion they were about entering into would settle the question of Responsible Government at once and definitely—a question of such vast and vital importance to the Province. No man was more popular, or enjoyed more the confidence of the people of Upper Canada, than the late Attorney-General West—a popularity which he owed to the uniform consistency of his political life, and the honesty and integrity of his principles. He was afraid, at the opening of this session, when he saw appointments to office of persons politically opposed to the late Ministry, that there was an underhand back-stairs influence at work which was going to injure them in the opinions of their supporters. He had written to the late Attorney-General West, as far back as February, 1843, on the subject of these appointments, pointing out to him that if such a course was pursued in the exercise of the prerogative of the Crown (a right which he did not pretend to deny), it would be his (the Attorney-General's) duty to resign. He (Mr. Price) admitted, to its fullest extent, the right of appointments resting with the Governor-General, but he would maintain that these ought to take place only by and with the advice of his Council, who were responsible to the country, and best qualified to judge of the merits of the candidates for office. If this was not to be the case: if the Governor was to appoint to offices of importance in the Province without the advice of his sworn Council: then they were under a despotism, and not under a Responsible Government. There was a power behind the Throne which directed the Government of the country, and until that power was got rid of he would rather see the House of Representatives swept away, and the Province ruled by a Governor and Council, from whose decisions they could appeal to their Sovereign. He (Mr. Price) approached the subject of the message with much embarrassment, and would only touch upon two passages in that document. With respect to the passage referring to the patronage of the Crown being bestowed only for political purposes, he would refer to Sir Robert Peel, who was no mean authority, and who had refused to take office while the ear of the Crown was in possession of the ladies of the bedchamber, and of wives and relations of the Ministry he had supplanted, and who might exercise an influence hostile to his policy and Government. He highly approved of the conduct of the late Provincial Administration in a somewhat similar line of conduct, when they were permitted no voice in the appointments to office of persons who weakened their Government and political influence. He felt confident that if a dissolution took place the people of Upper Canada would mark their approval of the conduct of the late Ministry by returning them almost unanimously to their seats in the House. He trusted the Assembly would never again be placed under the yoke of that oligarchy under which Upper Canada had so long groaned, and to which she had been indebted for so many of her miseries. With respect to the Secret Societies Bill, he, Mr. Price, felt certain that had not the late Ministry resigned on being informed that the royal assent would not be given to it, they would have been scouted by all their honest supporters. His honourable friend, the Attorney-General West, had retired three times from office, rather than sacrifice his principles. In bestowing the patronage of the Crown on their supporters the late Ministry had only followed the course invariably pursued by their predecessors, who had at least monopolised nine-tenths of it. He thought the documents transmitted to the House were of a most extraordinary nature, in which the theory of Responsible Government was acknowledged, while its practical working was denied. He was certain that no Ministry could thereafter hold office in this Province for four and twenty hours who did not accept office under the principles of Responsible Government. He concluded by moving "That an humble address be presented to his Excellency, humbly representing to his Excellency the deep regret felt by this House at the retirement of certain members of the Provincial Administration on the question of their right to be consulted on what this House unhesitatingly avow to be the prerogative of the Crown—appointments to office; and further to assure his Excellency that the advocacy of this principle entitles them to the confidence of this House, being in strict accordance with the principles embraced in the resolutions adopted by the House on the 3rd of September, 1841."

The motion was seconded by Mr. Benjamin Holmes, member for Montreal, who declared that while he acknowledged in its fullest extent the prerogative of the Crown, he felt assured that the representative of the Crown in this country was not only bound to consult with his sworn advisers, but also to take their advice. Had the late Ministry retained office after being told that their advice would not be taken—that they had not the confidence of the Governor-General—they would have been looked upon by the whole country as degraded. Mr. Holmes spoke highly of his Excellency, but said he was certain that he was acting under some underhand influence which he trusted the country would be able to arrive at. He (Mr. Holmes) was confident that his Excellency could not rally round him a sufficient number of persons to carry on the Government of the country on adverse principles to those of the late Administration; and this the country would show if a general election should ensue from the resignation of the late Ministry, by returning them triumphantly to their seats in the House.

Mr. D. B. Viger trusted that this question would be settled without an appeal to the people. For the vote he would give on the present occasion he might be traduced as a traitor to his country. Let it be so. He had been accustomed all his life to the injustice of man. He was favourable to Responsible Government on constitutional principles. He condemned the documents which had been submitted to the House, and the course which had been pursued with respect to them he pronounced to be without precedent. His Excellency should never have been brought into personal collision with the House. It was as if they were now putting his Excellency on his trial.

Mr. Baldwin thought his honourable friend from Richelieu was labouring under a delusion. He repudiated the idea of their trying the Governor-General—that was out of the question. But the late Ministry were now on *their* trial, and the verdict of the House would decide whether they had acted up to the principles under which they had taken office, and he had no fears for the result. He concurred with the member for Richelieu as to the unparliamentary nature of the documents before the House. It was not until within an hour of the meeting of the House on Wednesday that they had been placed in the hands of himself and his colleagues. He thought the prerogative of the Crown had been more endangered by the production of those papers than by the concessions which the ex-Ministry had demanded. The Governor's reasons were not necessary. His simple announcement of the fact would have been quite sufficient. It was difficult and most embarrassing to know how to treat that anomalous document which had been laid before the House. It was neither a message nor a correspondence, yet it contained, written in indelible characters, facts which after they (the late Ministry) had ascertained, they could no longer retain office. Had they not resigned immediately on becoming acquainted with these facts they would have been looked upon as traitors to their country, and scouted by every honest man. There was but one unanimous opinion from one end of the country to the other as to the principles under which the Government had been lately conducted. The principle of Responsible Government had been fully conceded to the people of the Province, and formed part of the constitution. He firmly believed they would still continue to enjoy this blessing in defiance of all opposition. What had the late Ministry claimed but the right of advice on the subject of appointments to office? This had been denied them because they might advise appointments which would increase their political influence. Even so, could any Government be carried on which did not support its own party? Let those who thought otherwise go and fill the empty Treasury Benches, and see how long they would occupy them if they did not support their own party. He wished to know if a Governor, a stranger in a country, was qualified to judge of the respective qualifications of the various candidates for office. Were they, the sworn advisers of the Crown, to be mere puppets, subject to the back-stairs influence which lavished the patronage of the Crown on their political opponents and enemies, and they to be the last persons to hear of appointments made without their advice and knowledge. He alluded to Sir Francis Head, who dealt very largely in general declarations. Sir Francis had had the good of the country so much at heart that he would allow no one to be responsible to it but himself; and yet he had brought that country to the brink of revolution, and had entailed on it much misery and bloodshed. Neither he (Mr. Baldwin) nor his colleagues had ever thought of the Council being supreme, and the Governor a mere nullity; nor had they any intention of interfering with the independence of his Excellency's judgment. All they had claimed was the right of tendering their advice to the Governor, and resigning when that advice was not attended to. With respect to the Secret Societies Bill, they had not been anxious to legislate on the subject. They had not thought that that was the proper way of dealing with the evil. They had thought that executive measures, such as had been used in Ireland, would have met the case much better. But after legislation had been forced upon them they had been informed that the royal assent would not be given to the Bill in this country. Would not the upper section of the Province brand them with the imputation of not having been in earnest in its introduction? He thought the Province was now placed in nearly a similar situation to what it had been in under Sir Francis Head. He concluded by trusting that the late Ministry would receive the favourable verdict of the House for the course which they had felt it their duty to pursue.

Mr. Christie, of Gaspé, said that a very serious charge was contained in the documents before the House, amounting to impeachment against the late Ministry. By it they were accused of wishing to bestow the patronage of the Crown for the increase of their political influence, and thus of corrupting the House of Assembly. They were also accused by it of attempting to degrade the character of the Governor, by imposing conditions on him derogatory to his high station. He never for a moment could have imagined that they had attempted such a thing. He therefore could never believe that the document now before the House had emanated from his Excellency. Had not this document been produced a reconciliation might have taken place. This he regretted the more, as he felt confident that no Ministry could now be formed which would obtain the confidence of the House or the country. He felt confident that the stand taken by the late Ministry would be approved of from one end of the Province to the other.

Mr. Boulton (Niagara) did not see why the principles of Responsible Government could not be applied to them as well as to the parent State. He would support the late Ministry in the stand they had taken.

Mr. Cartwright could not understand how the member for Niagara could support the late Ministry after what had fallen from the member for the First Riding of York with respect to the oligarchy which had ruled Upper Canada to its destruction, when he (Mr. Boulton) had formed part of that oligarchy for sixteen years—that oligarchy among whom existed more truth, honour, loyalty, and attachment to the parent State than had ever existed under the humbug of Responsible Government. He thought the late Ministry might have chosen some more fit time for upsetting the State coach, and stopping so many measures *in transitu*, after a session of two months, and after an expense of thousands of pounds had been incurred. Their resignation was mere clap-trap, and resulted from their having discovered that they could not succeed in carrying through some of their obnoxious measures. By the motion now before the Chair they were actually impeaching and trying the Governor-General. Supposing the Governor to be supported by the Imperial authority, were they prepared to carry out the member for Rimouski's threat, to have Responsible Government in defiance of all opposition here or elsewhere? Were they prepared to resort to physical force to obtain this? He, Mr. Cartwright, thought that as candidates for office the natives of this Province had a prior claim. But he did not think they had much right to complain if some of their fellow-subjects from the parent State were sometimes

THE LAST FORTY YEARS.

CANADA since THE UNION OF 1841

By JOHN CHARLES DENT

GEO. VIRTUE

THE HON. LUTHER HAMILTON HOLTON.

THE HON. JOHN YOUNG.

WILLIAM LYON MACKENZIE.

THE HON. LUCIUS SETH HUNTINGTON.

appointed to office in the colony, when they reflected on the great
expense the mother country was put to in affording them her protection.
Could they expect that any independent man would ever
become their Governor to be a mere puppet in the hands of an
Executive Council—to move as they pulled the strings?

Sir Allan MacNab stated that the reasons why the late Ministry
had objected to the appointment of the present Speaker of the
Legislative Council (Mr. Caron) was because they had wished to
have their late colleague, the Honourable Mr. Sullivan, appointed
to that high station—he who had been confidential adviser to so
many different Governors, and held office under so many different
principles. He dared them (the late Ministry) to deny this statement,
and asked them at the same time if his Excellency had not
exercised a sounder judgment than they would have done. Had
they not also made Legislative Councillors whom they had ascertained
beforehand would support them in their votes on the Seat of
Government question? He regretted that Responsible Government
had ever been conceded to them, as he was certain it would hasten
the moment of separation from the mother country, which he
dreaded would occur in a very few years. He had heard a great
deal about the advantages they had derived from Responsible Government.
If those advantages consisted in depriving old and
faithful servants of the Crown of their situations, and replacing
them by political partisans at larger salaries, then they had certainly
enjoyed the blessings of Responsible Government. He perfectly
agreed with his Excellency in his views with respect to the Secret
Societies Bill, and those who had introduced that measure would
find out the error they had committed in introducing it when they
next appeared at the hustings in Upper Canada.

Colonel Prince, whose Liberal fit was, for the nonce, upon him,
remarked that he could not see how the Ministry could have acted
otherwise than as they had, holding office as they did under Respon-

sible Government, which had been conceded to them, and acknowledged by the authority of the Governor-General himself. He was happy that the question was debated without any influence being exercised on them by an Executive Council, as the popularity of the late Ministry would be more plainly evinced by the large majority which would be afforded them on the present motion by the independent members of the House. However unfortunate the time might be when the late Ministry had resigned, they had no option as men of honour on the Governor's opinion being intimated to them. He thought the country was highly indebted to the late Cabinet for their patriotism and integrity, and for the liberal measures which they had introduced to the House, and which he trusted would be passed ere that House dissolved. Responsible Government having been conceded, it now formed part and parcel of the constitution. He (Colonel Prince) did not wish to hold out any threats, but being a stiff old Englishman, he, for one, like the Barons at Runnymede, was prepared to maintain his rights at all risks. He had supported Lord Sydenham's Government, and felt proud that he had done so. The motion now before the Chair was not condemnatory of the Governor-General. He was certain that the late Ministry would be supported by the whole country in the stand they had taken, and this would be shown at the general elections which would ensue from the dissolution of the present House of Assembly; an event which he regarded as inevitable.

The debate was kept up with undiminished vigour until two hours past midnight,[*] when, on motion of Mr. Sherwood, it was adjourned to ten o'clock in the morning. The House promptly reassembled at the hour appointed, when Mr. Wakefield moved the following amendment to Mr. Price's motion: "That according to the principles of the British constitution as declared to exist in this Province by the resolutions of the House of Assembly of the 3rd of September,

---

[*] The number of speakers was forty-three.

1841, the members of the Executive Council are responsible to the people, and to this House as the representatives of the people, for the exercise of every royal prerogative within this Province; and that consequently, inasmuch as it would be most unjust to subject any man to responsibility for acts in which he had not participated, it is indispensable that the royal prerogative be exercised by his Excellency the Governor-General with the advice of the members of his Executive Council. That according to the aforesaid principles of the British constitution, the Provincial representative of the Sovereign cannot be responsible or in any way accountable for the exercise of any branch of the royal prerogative to any Provincial authority whatever; and therefore that he cannot constitutionally enter into any pledge, engagement or assurance with the members of the Executive Council, or with any other person or persons in the Province, respecting the future exercise of the prerogative. That the well-known practice of the British constitution recognizes one effectual means, and no other, of securing the observance of the aforesaid principles; namely, the resignation of the members of the Executive Council, whenever, on an occasion of sufficient importance to warrant the application of that legitimate check upon the exercise of the prerogative, the Governor-General shall have failed to ask or refused to follow their advice in some particular case or cases; but that if the Head of the Government were to enter into any general engagement with the members of his Executive Council, or even with this House, binding himself in any wise, whether directly or by implication, as to the future exercise of any of his functions as the representative of the Sovereign, he would openly divest the Crown of its acknowledged prerogative, degrade the royal office into obvious and proclaimed subordination to the Executive Council, and most seriously impair the constitution which it is the glory of this Province to possess."

In support of this amendment Mr. Wakefield delivered an argumentative and able speech. He said that unless the principles of Responsible Government, as laid down in the resolutions of September, 1841, were carried out, no good government could exist in any colony. Those resolutions scarcely laid down anything more than that the responsible advisers of the Crown should resign when they could no longer command a majority in the House. The obvious question which had now been raised between the representative of the Crown in this colony and his advisers was whether the former would not pledge himself to give up to them the royal prerogative. Had the Governor submitted to this he would have been recalled, as having endangered the rights of the Crown. If the Ministers found it necessary to differ in opinion from his Excellency, they should have resigned at once, without entering into any specific agreement with him on the subject. Such he (Mr. Wakefield) was certain would be the opinion of the people of England. Not that England would wish to coerce the people of this colony in their opinions, for if they wished to have, instead of a Governor divested of all royal prerogatives, a President with such powers as the late Attorney-General West would choose to give him, she would say to them, "Take what you wish, and let us part in peace;" for England was weary of the dissensions and civil war which had lately distracted the colony. But England would never submit to have the representative of the royal authority divested of all power, and a mere nullity in the colony. With respect to the time the late Ministry had chosen for their resignations, it was most inopportune, for they must have well known that his Excellency would never surrender what was demanded of him. This they knew full well, and therefore might have taken some other time for their demand, and not, by making it now, have put a stop to the whole business of the country. The member for Rimouski had acknowledged himself a party man. He (Mr. Wakefield) agreed with him in this. Mr. Baldwin was a party man—an ambitious party man—and had taken this step to

the prejudice of the Governor, and to increase his own influence in
the Province. With respect to the motion before the Chair, his
Excellency could not reply to it without the implication of pledging
himself as regarded the future patronage of the Crown. If it passed,
it would bring the House into direct collision with the Governor,
and cause a dissolution of Parliament and a general election, which
would throw the whole country into a state of excitement and
ferment, productive of much harm, particularly in Lower Canada.
Sir Charles Bagot had elevated the much-abused French Canadians,
and had afforded them a fair share in the general government of the
country. And this unanimity and peace was now likely to be
endangered, because Her Majesty's late Attorney-General West in
the Province had not succeeded in making his Excellency the
Governor-General agree with him in his theories about Responsible
Government; there was no other reason on earth. He (the late
Attorney-General West) owed his late position to the French Canadians, who had felt themselves bound by political honour to give
him a share in the Administration, in which he only occupied a
second-rate position, for at the time it was formed he could only
command five, or at the most six votes. In Lower Canada, beyond
the great cities little was known about Responsible Government,
but its people had confidence in that Government in which they
saw one of their own people occupying the high station of Her
Majesty's Attorney-General East. Could any one suppose that Sir
Charles Metcalfe's policy differed from the just and humane policy
adopted by Sir Charles Bagot? The Governor-General would have
deserved impeachment had he surrendered the rights of the Crown
into the hands of his late advisers. Suppose that the Imperial
authority supported him in the stand he had taken in defence of the
royal prerogative, in what situation would they be placed? Were
they (the people of this colony) prepared to appeal to the *ultima
ratio*? Let them ponder well on this. Did they imagine for a

moment that Sir Charles Metcalfe, who had passed forty years of political life without blame or reproach, would recede from the position he had taken ? Because his Excellency would not subscribe to the member for Rimouski's theories, they (the Assembly) were likely not only to be brought into collision with the Governor-General, but also with the Imperial authorities, and the whole country was likely to be convulsed with the turmoils of a general election.

Many able speeches followed, and several other amendments were moved. Mr. Lafontaine thought it necessary to offer some further explanations. He had not, he said, been anxious to take office, and when the appointment he had lately held was offered to him his opinions with respect to Responsible Government had been well known. To carry on any Government satisfactorily it was necessary for its Ministers not only to have the confidence of the House, and through it of the people, but also of the Head of the Government. If they were to have Responsible Government, let them have it; if not, let it be repealed; but he, Mr. Lafontaine, would never allow himself to be placed in a position in which he might be liable to the accusation of deceiving the House, the country, and his friends. He looked upon the present state of affairs as resulting from secret advisers about his Excellency's person.

The debate was prolonged far into the night. One of the most eloquent speeches of the session was made by the ex-Solicitor-General East, Mr. Aylwin; but as it did not throw any additional light upon the constitutional question, its insertion in these pages is deemed unnecessary. The several amendments having been voted down, the vote was finally taken on the original motion, which was carried by forty-six to twenty-three.* Mr. Boulton then moved

---

* The following is the division list :—

YEAS.—Messrs. Armstrong, Aylwin, Baldwin, Barthe, Berthelot, Boswell, Boulton, Boutillier, Beaubien, Cameron, Chabot, Child, Christie, Crane, Derbishire, DeWitt, Dunn, Durand, Gilchrist, Harrison, Hincks, Hopkins, Jobin, Lacoste, Lafontaine, Leslie

that the following additional clause be added to the resolution adopted:

"That this House, in dutiful submission to their Gracious Sovereign, and with the utmost respect for the exalted station and high character of his Excellency, is most anxious to guard against any misconstruction which possibly might be placed upon the affirmative declaration of their opinion upon this delicate and most vitally important constitutional question; and therefore most humbly beg leave to disclaim, in a negative form, any desire that the Head of the Government should be called upon to enter into any stipulation as to the terms upon which a Provincial Administration may deem it prudent either to accept of or continue in office : that mutual confidence, which is essential to the well being of any government, necessarily presumes that they are understood, while a due respect for the prerogative of the Crown, and a proper constitutional delicacy towards Her Majesty's Representative, forbid their being expressed."

The motion was seconded by Mr. Lafontaine, and, after considerable discussion, was carried by a vote of sixty to seven. An address to his Excellency, embodying the resolution and addition, was agreed to by the House, and ordered to be engrossed. Then, after one of the most momentous debates known to our Parliamentary history, the House adjourned.

Donald McDonald, John S. Macdonald, Merritt, Moore, Morin, Morris, Papineau, Parke, Powell, Price, Prince, Quesnel, Small, Harmanus Smith, Steele, Taché, Thompson, Thorburn, Turcotte, and Louis M. Viger—46.

NAYS.—Messrs. Black, Cartwright, Chesley, Dunlop, Forbes, Foster, Hale, Hamilton, Johnston, Sir A. N. MacNab, McLean, Murney, Neilson, Noel, Roblin, Simpson, Henry Smith, George Sherwood, Stewart, Denis B. Viger, Wakefield, Williams, and Woods—23.

Fourteen members were absent, namely, Messrs. Cook, Daly, Doggan, Franchère, Holmes, Jones, Judah, Kilhaly (resigned), McCulloch, Ogden, H. Sherwood, Taschereau, Turgeon, and Watts. The other member required to make up the full membership of eighty-four was Mr. Cuvillier, the Speaker.

CHAPTER XVII.

CHAOS.

"For nine months Sir C. Metcalfe has kept the chief offices of the Government vacant—it being actually more dangerous to fill them with men holding his opinions than to keep them vacant—and he has substituted his own inefficient, though certainly mild dictatorship, for that system of Responsible Government which the people of Canada had hoped, upon the restoration of a Constitution, to see established among them. He has engaged the people in a discussion upon the principles of Government, in which the experience of the neighbouring States cannot be disregarded; he has violated all settled opinions; and, perhaps unintentionally, has most seriously checked the improvement of the Province."—*A Brief Statement of the Dispute between Sir C. Metcalfe and the House of Assembly of the Province of Canada.* London, 1844.

THE country was left without a Ministry. Mr. Daly, the sole remaining ministerial official, was not seen in his place, ill health being the reason assigned for his absence.* From day to day, and almost from hour to hour, the Governor continued his conferences with various members of Parliament. The contest was no longer confined to himself and his Ministers merely, but was between himself and the Assembly. The final outcome of such a struggle could not be doubtful, but meanwhile the business of the country was impeded. A few days after the vote on Mr. Price's motion, Mr. D. B. Viger announced to the Assembly that the Governor had authorized him to say that his Excellency was engaged

---

* "The honourable member for Megantic has not shown up lately in his place on the Treasury Benches, having wisely fallen sick to avoid the badgering he would otherwise have been subject to, as the only representative of the Government in the House of Assembly."—Montreal *Herald's* report of the Parliamentary proceedings for Saturday, December 9th.

in forming an Administration. In reply to a question put to him by a member as to when the Governor expected to complete his undertaking, Mr. Viger replied that the Administration would be formed "as soon as possible." On the 9th of the month Parliament was prorogued, no Ministry having then been formed. Dominick Daly was the Ministry, and the Ministry was Dominick Daly.

This state of things could not last, but the Governor's difficulties were most serious, and the ingenuity of his unofficial advisers was taxed to the utmost to provide a remedy. Portfolios were offered right and left, and, in the parlance of that day, office went a-begging. Aspirants to office were numerous enough, but it would have been folly to appoint persons who could not command popular support, and the only persons who could command such support were the ex-Ministers. The latter doubtless expected to be recalled, as there seemed to be no other means whereby public affairs could be carried on with due respect to the constitution. But the Governor was resolutely set against adopting such a course, and declared that rather than do so he would resign.* Resignation, indeed, would have been his wisest policy, but there was a *via media*. He might have preserved himself from even the appearance of submission to his ex-Ministers by giving *carte blanche*, say to Mr. Viger, who might have approached Mr. Lafontaine and Mr. Baldwin with a reasonable certainty of being able to bring about an accommodation. But the Governor's foible about degrading the prerogative stood as an insuperable barrier in the way, and the outlook was far from hopeful.

On the 12th, three days after the prorogation, Mr. Daly was reinforced and kept in countenance by the swearing-in of two new Executive Councillors, in the persons of Mr. Viger and Mr. Draper.†

---

*See Sir Allan MacNab's address to the Hamilton electors during the campaign of 1844.

† "Mr. Viger representing the French party, and both Mr. Daly and Mr. Draper representing in some degree as to each both the British and moderate Reform parties."—Sir C.

Those gentlemen did not then accept offices of emolument, but merely formed a sort of Provisional Government, and it was understood that the offices would all be filled up without loss of time. Mr. Viger's action in coming to the Governor's assistance at this juncture encouraged his Excellency in the course he was pursuing. It was hoped and believed at Alwington House that Mr. Viger would be able to induce his fellow-countrymen to come round to the Governor's views. His undertaking such a task was a serious disappointment to a great majority of his, Mr. Viger's, fellow-countrymen. It was felt that his acts were inconsistent with his professions, and that he had falsified the record of a long life; a life which had in great part been spent in battling for popular rights. His support of the Governor of course placed him in antagonism to Mr. Lafontaine, and could not fail to produce more or less division among the French Canadian population, whose influence must thereby be weakened. It was said by many that he had covered himself with ignominy in his old age. Some of his friends were so indiscreet as to make excuses for him on the ground of senility, excuses for which there does not seem to have been any foundation, as his intellect, for all practical purposes, was still as vigorous as it had been in the days of the famous ninety-two resolutions. His motives cannot be pronounced upon with certainty. It is probable that he thought Mr. Lafontaine's popularity greater than that gentleman's services to his countrymen called for, and that a certain amount of mental hostility was, consciously or unconsciously, aroused in him in consequence. Mr. Lafontaine, when a youth, had been a student in his office. The student had won a higher place than the principal in popular regard. Mr. Viger must have felt that his own sufferings in the national cause had been immeasurably greater than Mr. Lafontaine's, and may have considered that those sufferings merited

---

Metcalfe's despatch of December 26th. How far Mr. Viger represented the French party appears from the text.

higher recognition than they had received. This, however, is nothing more than plausible conjecture. What is certain is that Mr. Viger did not clearly understand all that was implied in the contest; that he succumbed to the magnetic influence of Sir Charles Metcalfe; that, from whatever cause, he was sincere in his loyalty to the Governor, and that he did his utmost to win over French Canadian opinion to his way of thinking. The Governor, for some reason or other, was very sanguine as to Mr. Viger's prospects. That gentleman achieved, however, but a very slight measure of success. The French Canadian journals were loud in their condemnation of his conduct, the only exception being a journal which was largely subject to his own direction. On the other hand, the Conservative papers in both Provinces lauded him to the skies. A Montreal paper which, only six years before, when Mr. Viger was lying in gaol, had objected to his being "fattened for the gallows," now came forward as his staunchest champion, and invited its readers of whatever nationality, to rally round him. Addresses to the Governor-General poured in from all parts of the Province. The question between the Governor and his late Councillors came to be regarded (as in fact it was) as a direct issue between Conservative and Reform principles.* Sir Charles Metcalfe, the man said to be "saturated through and through with Liberal opinions," was thus made to figure in the rôle of an obstructionist and an opponent of the popular will.

The promise that the ministerial offices would speedily be filled was not kept, for the all-sufficient reason that persons who might hope to command Parliamentary support could not be induced to accept them. Constitutional Government in Canada was practically suspended. Days, weeks, months rolled by, and the functions of

---

* "The effect was to direct Parliamentary Government against the Governor personally, and the British Government of which he was the organ."—See "The Colonial Policy of Lord John Russell's Administration," by Earl Grey, Vol. I., p. 205.

nine Executive Councillors continued to be monopolized by the triumvirate, composed of Messieurs Daly, Viger and Draper. These gentlemen received much assistance from the Governor's private secretary, Captain Higginson, who was very improperly permitted to deal with affairs which ought only to have been deputed to a responsible Minister of the Crown. Mr. Viger found public opinion in his own section of the Province so strongly against him that he issued a pamphlet* during the early weeks of the new year, in which the argument from his point of view was supposed to be set forth, and in which he reproached the ex-Ministers for having, in the course of their explanations in and out of Parliament, violated their oaths of office, by revealing matters which they were bound to keep secret. The pamphlet afforded irrefragable evidence that the author did not understand the nature of the dispute. He professed his devotion to Responsible Government, and the principal charge brought by him against the ex-Ministers was that the latter had been guilty of breaches of official etiquette. The pamphlet called forth numerous rejoinders, and the member for Richelieu cannot be said to have improved his position among his fellow-countrymen by his effort.

The Governor's real tower of strength was Mr. Draper. That excellent lawyer's great tact, his subtlety of intellect, his power of lucid exposition, and his faculty for administration, were beyond all price at such a contingency. It was said of him by Sir Charles Metcalfe himself that his eminent capacity enabled him to take the place of half a dozen men.† That he made the best of the singularly infelicitous position in which the Governor was placed is undoubted; though the best was bad enough. The Governor could not have adopted any more effectual means of alienating the members of the Reform party from himself than by calling Mr. Draper to his assistance. Mr. Draper, though he had never been a member of the

---

* See *La Crise Ministerielle*, etc., quoted *ante*, p. 324.   † Kaye, Vol. II., p. 378.

Family Compact, was of as ultra-Conservative a cast of mind as it was possible for a man of his high intelligence to be. Some of the leading Reformers had in times past been made to feel the weight of his abilities, and this fact did not tend to make them more charitable towards his opinions. It has been seen that he yielded his assent to the principle of Executive responsibility in the Assembly,* but the concession had been wrung from him, and it was an open secret that his enthusiasm for Responsible Government was very moderate. He had been the great obstacle to liberal measures and smooth government prior to his resignation in September, 1842, and it was felt that his return to power at this time portended no good to liberal principles. There can be no doubt that the Reform party as a whole were unjust to Mr. Draper. They did not even give him credit for sincerity or good intentions. The historian of to-day, no matter what his political opinions may be, who contemplates Mr. Draper's career as an Executive Councillor, must doubtless arrive at the conclusion that he was wrong; that he was an obstructionist—a drag on the wheel of progress. But this fact was by no means so easy of recognition in 1844 as it is in 1881, and there is no good reason for impugning his motives, which, so far as can now be ascertained, were honourable and patriotic. No impartial mind can review the acts and characters of the leading members of the Conservative party of those times, and come to the conclusion that they were all selfish and insincere. Nay, it is evident enough that they were at least as sincere and as zealous for the public good as were their opponents. They lived in a time of transition, and their minds had not yet learned to accept new ideas. Their opinions are now held by no one on this side of the Atlantic, and can only be found flourishing in out-of-the-way corners of Great Britain and continental Europe. But in 1844 such opinions were com-

---

* *Ante*, p. 126, et seq.

mon enough in all parts of the civilized world, except, perhaps, in the United States. In Canada they were honestly entertained, and, generally speaking, as honestly acted upon. Nor are those opinions in the least to be wondered at. The persons who held them had been trained in the school of old-fashioned loyalty. Less than a decade had elapsed since a large section of their political antagonists had been in open rebellion. They themselves had proved their devotion to their principles and their Sovereign by arraying themselves on the side of authority. Scarcely had law and order been restored when they found that the "rebels" had won sympathy, and even respect, by their rebellion. A Reform Government succeeded to power soon afterwards, and it really seemed to the Conservatives as though the fact of a man's having been guilty of treason was the highest recommendation to ministerial favour. Persons who openly boasted of the parts they had played during the troublous times of 1837-'38 were appointed to honourable and lucrative offices, whereas the loyalists who had manned themselves in defence of the Government of the day were passed by. Was it any wonder if they smarted under a sense of injustice? Their intellectual vision, be it remembered, was limited. They did not recognize the fact that the rebellion had been the legitimate result of foul wrong. From their point of view, indeed, rebellion, for whatever cause, was a thing altogether hateful and foul. During the latter half of Sir Charles Bagot's term of office some of them had slightly modified their views on this subject, and two or three of their prominent members had even indulged in a little wild talk; but in the main their opinions were not only unchanged, but unchangeable. Independently of their political opinions, they were for the most part honourable but non-progressive men. Responsible Government seemed to them a delusion and a snare, and a long stride in the direction of severance from the mother country. Let Sir Charles Metcalfe indulge in as much sophistry as he might, they saw clearly enough that the real question at issue between him and his ex-Councillors was as to Responsible Government, and for this reason they espoused his side in the quarrel with hearty good-will.

As for the Governor himself, he, a professed Liberal, found himself deserted by nine-tenths of the Liberals of the Province, while the old high Tory party were, to a man, on his side. But he was thoroughly impracticable. He would not work in full accord with any party. He professed his firm belief that party government was the only thing for Canada, and in the next breath declared his antagonism to party government, and refused to be bound by the principles applicable to such a system. He never wearied of repeating that the patronage of the Crown must not be prostituted to party purposes. Now, whether party government is or is not a good thing may perhaps be open to question, but it is certainly anomalous that the necessity for party government should be conceded, while the details whereby its springs are kept in motion are scouted and repudiated.

Sir Charles, then, did not even make the most of his alliance with the Tories. The months rolled by, and still there was no Ministry. Meetings were held all over the Province, and the people were in a fever of antagonism and excitement. The speakers at the Tory meetings denounced the ex-Ministers. At the Reform meetings the Governor and his supporters were assailed with equal or greater opprobrium. A monster Reform Association was established at Toronto, with branches all over the Province. From one end of the country to the other nothing was heard but denunciations of Sir Charles Metcalfe and counter denunciations of the ex-Ministers. Never had party ferocity reached such a pitch in Canada. Meetings were broken up by sheer physical force, and in not a few instances stones and bludgeons were the most effective arguments employed. The political ethics of Galway seemed to have been imported into the country. The timid were afraid to espouse either side of the quarrel, and yet were estopped from remaining neutral. In public speeches delivered from Tory platforms, Lafontaine, Baldwin, and Hincks were declared to be intriguing to bring about the annexation of Canada to the United States. On the other hand, it is impossible to avoid the observation that the extreme wing of the Reformers were altogether too rancorous in their denunciations of the Governor and his allies. Their constitutional argument was sound enough. It was in the highest degree reprehensible that the ministerial offices should be left unfilled month after month. No more positive evidence could have been adduced that there was no intention to govern the country in accordance with the principles of Responsible Government.* But the ultra-Reformers, not satisfied with impeaching the Governor's unconstitutional conduct, reviled him as a deliberately false-hearted and despotic man who cared nothing for the rights of others, and who was eager to stamp out the liberties of the people. Others tried to hold him up to public contempt as an imbecile old dotard who had survived his faculties. They nicknamed him "Charles the Simple," and "Old Squaretoes,"†

---

* "If there had merely been a difference of opinion between the Governor and his Council, and if the principle of Responsible Government was intended to be observed, another administration would have been immediately formed. He [the Governor] had no other constitutional course. Any reason which pleased himself, however trifling, such as that he did not like the cast of an eye of one Councillor, or the colour of the hair of another, was a sufficient warrant for changing his advisers, but he was bound to replace them forthwith." Toronto *Globe*, March 5th, 1844.

† This cognomen is said to have been bestowed upon his Excellency by the Hon. Mr. Daly. Though originally applied in derision, it was taken up by the Governor's friends and converted into a term of affection; witness the following lines, being additional verses to "The Fine Old English Gentleman," as sung at a public dinner in Toronto, while the contest with Sir Charles Metcalfe was in progress :

> One verse the songster has forgot—he has another claim ;
> The brave Old Square-toed gentleman, he of the stainless name ;
> For Indian laurels grace his brow, Jamaica loves him too,
> And Canada will fight for him 'gainst all the Baldwin crew—
> The fine Old Square-toed gentleman, all of the present time.

and thereby degraded themselves much more than the representative of Sovereignty whom they assailed. That representative was at least entitled to their outward respect, even if he had been a much worse man than they pronounced Sir Charles Metcalfe to be. Mr. Draper and Mr. Viger were of course legitimate objects of attack, but they were assailed with a malignity which, in the light of the present day, seems very much like ferocity. The assaults were not confined to speeches at public meetings. Pamphlets innumerable were put forth on both sides, and in all parts of the Province. As for the newspapers, they were filled to overflowing with gall and wormwood. Charges the most outrageous and unfounded were made, on the one hand against the Governor and his chief supporters, and on the other against the ex-Ministers. In many instances it would seem that there was not the faintest attempt to keep within the bounds of truth in these criminations. The country had not been lashed into such a state of fury since the year of the rebellion.

Fortunately, all the contributions to the literature of the struggle were not of the malignant character above described. Dr. Egerton Ryerson's well-known pamphlet,* and the equally well-known collection of letters contributed to *The Examiner* by Mr. Sullivan under the *nom de plume* of "Legion," and subsequently republished in pamphlet form,† were such as might have been expected from the

---

So let our loyal shouts go forth, let traitors hear and quail,
And British hearts will leap for joy on every hill and vale;
And though the Baldwin clan may howl, though loud th' hyæna roar,
We'll rally round Old Squaretoes, and give him one cheer more;
The fine Old Square-toed gentleman, all of the present time.

The verses are not remarkably brilliant, but are said to have been furnished almost impromptu; and in any case they have an interest for the present generation, as being the production of a clever young lawyer named John Hawkins Hagarty, known to us in these later times as Chief Justice Hagarty.

*"Sir Charles Metcalfe Defended against the Attacks of his late Councillors." Toronto, 1844. The contents of this pamphlet were originally published in *The British Colonist* newspaper, in Toronto.

† *Legion's* "Letters on Responsible Government." Toronto, 1844.

24

character and abilities of their respective authors. The writers were wide as the poles asunder in the conclusions at which they arrived from the same set of facts, but they both went over the ground very fully from their opposite points of view, and these two pamphlets form valuable adjuncts to a proper understanding of the dispute. Dr. Ryerson was not a politician, and did not argue the matter from a politician's point of view. His plea for the Governor, however, was not without its effect upon public opinion, and Sir Charles proved his appreciation of the Doctor's services by appointing him Superintendent of Public Schools for Upper Canada, a position which he filled with credit to himself and benefit to the public for many years. Mr. Sullivan's letters were ostensibly written from a purely constitutional point of view, and, though unbecomingly flippant in many passages, they were eloquent and argumentative. They displayed the Governor's inconsistency in a very strong light, and provided his opponents with some unanswerable arguments. Mr. Isaac Buchanan also furnished his quota to the discussion.* Notwithstanding his zeal for Responsible Government, he took strong ground against the ex-Ministers, and in favour of Sir Charles Metcalfe. The other pamphleteers of less note were too numerous to need particular reference.

An important factor in the discussion, however, still remains to be mentioned. On Tuesday, the 5th of March, 1844, appeared the first number of the Toronto *Globe*. Its founder, Mr. George Brown, was then a young man of twenty-five. He was destined to play a very important part in public affairs, and as no man has more distinctly stamped his individuality upon the Canadian history of his time, some particulars of his previous career are in order in this place.

George Brown was born at Edinburgh, on the 29th of November,

---

* "First Series of Five Letters against the Baldwin Faction, by an Advocate of Responsible Government, and of the New College Bill." Toronto, 1844.

1818. He was the eldest son of Peter Brown, a gentleman of high intelligence and great force of character, who was engaged at different times in various mercantile and building operations in the Scottish capital. The son was educated, first at the High School, and afterwards at the Southern Academy of Edinburgh. He left school at an early age, and for some time assisted his father in his business pursuits. As he grew to manhood he developed a large vitality and force, accompanied by a high temper and strength of will which gave promise of a successful career. The promise of the boy was royally fulfilled in the performance of the man. At various conjunctures in his after life, George Brown was placed in positions which would have meant utter defeat and failure to any one less liberally endowed with vigour and determination of will; but he seldom failed, by the sheer force of his powerful individuality, to convert what seemed inevitable failure into a greater or less degree of success.

His early experiences were of a nature to fit him for a hand-to-hand struggle with the world. His precocity is sufficiently attested by the fact that before he had completed his eighteenth year he was sent to London to purchase goods and supplies.* In course of time reverses of fortune came, and in 1838 father and son emigrated from Scotland to New York, where they engaged in journalistic and other pursuits, and where they were soon afterwards joined by the other members of the family. Mr. Brown the elder was not only a man of great native intelligence, but was possessed of a large fund of political knowledge. Though he had been regarded in Edinburgh as an advanced Liberal—and justly so, taking the prevailing tone of Scottish Liberalism in those times into consideration—he was a zealous upholder of the monarchical

---

* This circumstance probably gave rise to the belief, asserted as undoubted fact in nearly all the published accounts of Mr. Brown's career, that he left home in his boyhood and sought to push his fortunes in London—an assertion for which there is no other foundation whatever.

principle, and of the connection between Church and State. He was regarded by the republicans of the New World as something nearly approaching to a Tory, but his knowledge and sagacity won recognition. He became a leading contributor to *The Albion*, a weekly newspaper published in New York in the interest of the British population. It was during his connection with this periodical that he wrote " The Fame and Glory of England Vindicated," in answer to a foolish book by an American, entitled "The Glory and Shame of England." In December, 1842, in conjunction with his son, he established *The British Chronicle*, as the organ of Scotchmen resident in America. During the same month the son for the first time came over to Canada with a view to obtaining subscribers and patronage for the new venture. The decision of the House of Lords in the famous Auchterarder case had been pronounced a few months previously, and the Disruption in the Scottish National Church was imminent. The Browns were vehement supporters of the Free Church party, a party which had a large following in Canada, and which had begun to feel the need of an organ. During a brief sojourn in Toronto, young George Brown formed the acquaintance of some of the leading citizens who espoused that side of the question. His force of character, and the apparent depth and earnestness of his convictions, made an impression upon all who conversed with him. It was felt that he might be a potent ally of the cause, and overtures were made to him to convert the paper which he represented into an exponent of Free Church views. These overtures he communicated to his father by letter, and meanwhile he proceeded on his tour through the Province in the interests of his paper. At Kingston he formed the acquaintance of Mr. Provincial Secretary Harrison, by whom he was introduced to other leading members of the Administration. He had a natural taste for politics. The training he had received under the paternal roof had of course been largely influential in forming his opinions, but he was by several degrees more advanced than his father, and was soon on good terms with the members of the Canadian Ministry. News of Sir Charles Metcalfe's appointment had just reached this country. Sir Charles Bagot was incapacitated from taking any share in the Government, and public business was for the time almost at a standstill. The prospective policy of the new Governor was a principal theme of discussion among politicians throughout the Province, and the Ministers themselves, as was to be expected, felt a vital interest in the theme. They were surprised at the ready and firm grasp of the situation which Mr. Brown displayed. Here was a young man, an entire stranger in Canada, without any political experience, who had nevertheless contrived in the course of a short time to master various important local details, and to gauge the merits of questions not easy of solution, even to persons to the manner born. The Ministers were much impressed by his native shrewdness and acumen, as well as by his large vitality. They little thought, however, that the tall, raw-boned, and somewhat awkward-looking youth before them would in a few years become one of the foremost men in Canada, and the founder of what may almost be characterized as a distinct school of politics.

After completing his tour of the Province, he returned to his home in New York with a glowing account of Canada. The overtures from Toronto were discussed, and the result of the final deliberations between father and son was that they removed to Toronto, where, on the 18th of August, 1843, *The Banner* was started under their auspices as the Canadian organ of the Free Church party. Though not professedly a secular paper, *The Banner* entered actively into the political questions of the time, and gave a vigorous support to the Administration. It had been in existence but little more than three months when the resignation of the Ministers occurred, and the struggle with the Governor began. *The Banner* espoused the cause of the ex-Ministers, and argued the constitutional side of the question with great ability, but its theological character interfered to some extent with its freedom of action, and its circulation was almost entirely restricted to adherents of the sect in the interests whereof it had been founded. The dispute with the Governor grew hotter and hotter as the winter passed by, and the defects of *The Banner* as a political power were felt more and more. *The Examiner* was still published in Toronto, but it was not conducted with the vigour which had characterized it during Mr. Hincks's proprietorship, and its popularity with the Reform party as a whole had diminished. That party felt the need of a paper which should be their recognized organ, and which should be carried on with spirit and vigour. Who so fit to conduct such an enterprise as the Browns? The masculine force and energy of the son would be admirably supplemented by the knowledge and power of expression of the father. The sincerity of the political professions of both was beyond question, and the "large discourse" of the younger could be turned to account on the hustings. Negotiations were entered upon, and the result was the establishment of a publication which, after a career of more than thirty-seven years, still stands preëminent as the leading newspaper of British America.

Mr. Brown was thus fairly launched upon his career in Canada. The *Globe* made a distinct impression upon the country from the issue of its first number, which, as has been stated, appeared on the 5th of March. For long subsequent to that date it was published merely as a weekly, and it was a very insignificant looking sheet as compared with the journals of the present day; but it was written with a vigour and robustness of expression which made it a powerful moulder of public opinion.* It battled valiantly for Responsible

---

*The above facts are not set down by way either of approval or disapproval of the political course pursued by the *Globe*, but merely to show the origin and causes of the widespread influence which that journal obtained. It will hardly be denied by any Canadian, whatever his political opinions may be, that the establishment of the *Globe* was an event in the political history of our country, and that as such it is entitled to be chronicled in a work like the present.

Government, according to the legitimate acceptation of the term, and against the restricted construction which Sir Charles Metcalfe and his advisers sought to put upon it. It was an undoubted factor in the contest, and its power, combined with that of *The Examiner*, was perceptibly felt by the Governor's adherents. It steadily gained ground in public favour, and eventually made its founder well known all over the Province. It is not necessary to pursue Mr. Brown's career any farther at this time. In future pages he will claim the share of attention due to a man whose widely-extended influence made itself felt to the remotest confines of the Province, and who stamped his name indelibly upon our political life.

The Address of the Gore Councillors, as it is called, and his Excellency's Reply thereto, deserve to be specially enumerated among the important contributions to the literature of the struggle. Among the flood of addresses by which the Governor was deluged during the winter of 1843-4 was one from the Warden and Councillors of the Gore District. It was couched in the most respectful tone, but declared the belief of the signatories that public opinion would fully sustain the late Executive in the stand taken by them "on the plainly defined and easily understood principles of the British constitution."* The reply of his Excellency is important, as showing his entire faith in his professions, and his utter inability to perceive the true merits of the question at issue. He represented himself as being responsible, not only to the Crown, Parliament and people of the mother country, but also to the people of Canada. He expressed his acceptance of the doctrine that it should be competent to the Council to offer advice on all occasions, whether as to patronage or otherwise; that the Governor should receive it with the attention due to his constitutional advisers, and consult with them in all cases of adequate importance; that there should be a cordial coöperation and sympathy between him and them; that the Council should

---

* The full text of the Address and Reply will be found in Kaye, Vol. II., pp. 477-480.

be responsible to the Provincial Parliament and the people; and that when the acts of the Governor were such as they did not choose to be responsible for, they should be at liberty to resign. Any student of our constitution at the present day will readily perceive that these statements, the sincerity of which is indisputable, involve more than one fallacy. To acknowledge responsibility to the people of Canada was, to say the least, misleading on the part of the Governor. Responsibility implies a certain measure of control on the part of the power to which the responsibility is due, and the people of Canada had no constitutional control whatever over the acts of the Governor. The only means of obtaining redress against him for any violation of his functions was through the Imperial authorities. The remarks of his Excellency on the subject of the responsibility of his Councillors have been humorously, and not ineffectively, paraphrased by a Canadian writer of the present day, in the following language: "How could the Council be held responsible for acts over which they had no control? . . Suppose a mistress were to say to her cook, 'Mary, I will cook the dinner, but if the veal is roasted to a cinder you will be good enough to take the responsibility. If the fish is sent up half cooked, if the soup is a mass of fat, if the turkey is raw, the whole brunt of the master's storming must fall on you.'"[*] The whole text of the Governor's reply was based upon false premises, and the conclusions, which were equally wide of the constitutional mark, were not even legitimate deductions from his assumptions.

The Government offices were removed from Kingston to Montreal soon after the opening of navigation, and in the course of the summer his Excellency also removed his headquarters from Alwington House to Monklands, a pleasant abode situated several miles westward of the last-named city.

Meanwhile, a struggle almost identical in principle with that between Sir Charles Metcalfe and his nine Councillors was in

---

[*] See "The Irishman in Canada," by Nicholas Flood Davin; p. 499.

progress in Nova Scotia, between the Lieutenant-Governor, Lord
Falkland, and the Reform members of his Cabinet.* Lord Falkland had seen fit to appoint an unknown and untried man to an
important office, and this without consultation with the Reform
Ministers, who accordingly resigned their seats, giving, in writing,
their reasons for doing so. The Lieutenant-Governor wrote a long
reply, which, like that of Sir Charles Metcalfe to Mr. Lafontaine's
note, was published in the local newspapers.† The two replies were
both set to the same tune. Both professed willingness to pay due
deference to the views of the Councillors, and to the popular wishes,
and both declined to give way on questions involving the royal
prerogative. The Tory party, however, were somewhat more powerful in the Nova Scotian Assembly than in that of Canada, and
after the matter had been under discussion for fourteen days, the
Lieutenant-Governor's action was sustained by a small majority.
But this was merely the beginning of the end, so far as Lord Falkland was concerned. Responsible Government, backed by Mr. Howe
and Mr. Young, eventually proved too much for his Lordship, and in
the summer of 1846 he was compelled to make way for his successor.

The contest with Sir Charles Metcalfe was maintained with
increased virulence. The country was in an uproar from end to end.
The great expectations which the Governor had been led to entertain respecting Mr. Viger proved to be unfounded. That gentleman
had betaken himself to Montreal and other parts of Lower Canada,
where he had addressed public meetings, had conferred with various
members of Parliament, and generally had done his utmost to bring
his compatriots round to his own and the Governor's views. In
vain. The French Canadians, as a body, held fast by Mr. Lafontaine and his colleagues, and would have none of Mr. Viger. This

---

*Messrs. Howe, Uniacke, and McNab.

†See "Nova Scotia, in its Historical, Mercantile and Industrial Relations," by Duncan Campbell (Montreal, 1873), pp. 352, 353.

was a sad disappointment to the Governor and Mr. Draper, who had been awaiting the result of Mr. Viger's exertions, and postponing arrangements in Upper Canada. Summer set in, and the ministerial offices still remained unfilled. Towards the end of June it was resolved that Mr. Draper should himself proceed to the Lower Province, with a view to definitely ascertaining the state of public feeling there. That gentleman accordingly repaired to Montreal, where he spent three weeks, a period quite long enough to enable him to gauge the situation. He wrote to the Governor that "after diligently prosecuting his inquiries, and extending his observations in all possible quarters, he could come to no other conclusion than that the aid of the French Canadian party was not to be obtained upon any other than the impossible terms of the restoration of Baldwin and Lafontaine."*

"Impossible terms," indeed; but the impossibility was of the Governor's own creation, and was simply attributable to his determination not to give way. It was, however, impossible that matters should remain as they were without utter ruin to the Province. The absence of any duly-constituted Executive would erelong bring commercial disaster to the country by destroying its credit. The public mind was in an unsettled and anxious state. There were grave nervous forebodings about the future. Extremists hinted at impending revolution and anarchy. Trade and industry began to be seriously affected. Merchants and manufacturers were afraid to launch out into new enterprises. The want of a responsible Attorney-General was already seriously felt in Upper Canada, and was daily becoming more imperative. Reform papers rang the changes upon Othello's phrase, "Chaos is come again." Where was the remedy? How was a Ministry to be formed? "After the lapse of seven months, during which the country had been without an Executive Government, Metcalfe was told by one of the ablest, the most clear-headed,

---

* Kaye, Vol. II., p. 380.

and the most experienced men in the country, that it was impossible to form a Ministry, according to the recognized principles of Responsible Government, without the aid of the French Canadian party, and that that aid it was impossible to obtain."* And why impossible to obtain? Because, forsooth, "to recall Baldwin and Lafontaine would be publicly to acknowledge a defeat, to lower the dignity of the Crown, and to pave the way for new embarrassments which might be more insuperable than the old."† Yet no Ministry which did not include them could gain the French Canadian vote, and without that vote no Ministry could hope to command a majority in the Assembly. Under Responsible Government, which the Governor admitted to be in full force in the Province, a Ministry without a majority of supporters in the Assembly was no Ministry at all. How then was the Government to be carried on consistently with the principles of the Canadian constitution?

August arrived, and this problem still remained unsolved.

---

* Kaye, Vol. II., pp. 380, 381. † Ib., p. 381.

Chapter XVIII.

AN APPEAL TO THE COUNTRY.

Theseus. How shall we find the concord of this discord?
—A Midsummer Night's Dream, Act V., sc. 1.

THE unpromising state of affairs in Canada naturally excited a certain amount of speculation in the mother country. In the House of Commons, so early as the 2nd of February (1844), Lord Stanley, in reply to a question from a member of the Opposition, declared that the course pursued by Sir Charles Metcalfe met with the entire and hearty approbation of Her Majesty's Government. On the 30th of May a discussion on the subject took place in the House, when Mr. Roebuck drew attention to the fact that the Province had remained for more than six months without an Administration. The speaker censured Sir Charles Metcalfe's procedure strongly, and asked for an official expression of opinion on the subject. Lord Stanley, in reply, speaking on behalf of the Government, again expressed approval of Sir Charles's conduct, but his remarks showed that he had been misled, at least as to details. He represented to the House that the Governor-General's Councillors had demanded of him that he should bind himself by writing, under his hand and seal, not to make, or offer to make, any appointments whatever, save with their concurrence. The same thing had frequently been declared in Canada, though not by authority of the Governor, so far as the "hand and seal" clause was concerned, and the ex-Ministers uniformly denied having made so arbitrary a demand. Lord

Stanley, however, of course made the statement in good faith, having been deceived, no doubt, by one of those sources of mischief which have so often misled men in his position.* He commended the Governor for having refused to surrender the patronage of the Crown, and defended his action in reserving the Secret Societies Bill. Lord John Russell and Sir Robert Peel followed, and pronounced eulogies on the conduct and character of Sir Charles Metcalfe, but both of them showed, in the course of their remarks, that they were not well-informed as to the precise nature of the dispute.

In Canada matters went on from bad to worse. Mr. Draper, upon whom the Governor almost exclusively relied for advice on important questions, rendered loyal service to his Excellency, but he was too patriotic to stand quietly by and see the Province drift into revolution or anarchy. As the summer passed by he became urgent in his counsels. Early in August he protested to the Governor that affairs could not much longer be carried on without an Administration. Sir Charles Metcalfe, who had been so chary of his dignity when dealing with Messrs. Lafontaine and Baldwin, took in good part the sharpest counsel that Mr. Draper saw fit to administer, and now began to bestir himself in good earnest. A systematic canvass of members of Parliament was set on foot. The post of Attorney-General for Lower Canada was successively offered to four leading French Canadians, and declined by them all. The latter were staunch in their allegiance to Mr. Lafontaine and Mr. Baldwin, and were not to be tempted.† After some further fruitless negotiations the Governor was driven to the conclusion that he must get along without French Canadian assistance, and must rely upon the British

---

*See "A Brief Statement of the Dispute between Sir C. Metcalfe and the House of Assembly of the Province of Canada." London, 1844.

†It is fair to give them credit for loyalty to their chiefs, although as matter of fact it would have needed no little temerity on their parts to brave public opinion in Lower Canada by deserting the popular side. This, however, as will presently be seen, was done by Mr. D. B. Papineau with a certain measure of success.

alone. He next offered the Attorney-Generalship for Lower Canada to two British residents of that part of the Province, by both of whom the post was declined. The portfolio had thus been successively offered to, and declined by, six persons. But perseverance met its reward. A seventh offer, made during the fourth week in August, to Mr. James Smith, was successful. Mr. Smith was entirely devoid of legislative experience, having never had a seat in Parliament, nor was he of any special note in his profession. He was merely a respectable member of the Montreal bar, of moderate opinions, and of fairly industrious habits. About the same time, in consequence of delicate approaches at second hand, Denis Benjamin Papineau was induced to accept the office of Commissioner of Crown Lands. He already had a seat in the Assembly, having, as has been seen,* succeeded the Hon. Charles Dewey Day in the representation of the county of Ottawa. The Governor considered it no slight triumph that he had been able to induce a brother of the arch-insurgent to accept office at his hands, as it could no longer be alleged that he had been entirely unsuccessful with the French Canadian element in the population. Mr. Papineau was a man of high character, and of more than average ability, but he suffered from partial deafness, an infirmity which to some extent interfered with his usefulness at the Council Board as well as in the House. A more important addition to the Ministry was William Morris, as to whom some particulars have been given on a former page.† He is correctly referred to by Lord Metcalfe's biographer as one of the most respected and respectable men in the Province. "He had been conspicuous in his opposition to the old exclusiveness of the dominant faction, but having subsequently arrayed himself against the late Council, he had been scouted by them as a Tory, and some persons had hesitated to join an Administration of which he was a member, lest the same imputation should

---

* *Ante*, p. 226. † *Ante*, p. 108.

be made against them. But in reality, though a loyalist, he was a man of liberal sentiments; and whilst the greatest possible assistance was likely to be derived from him by the Executive Council from his excellent habits of business, no collision of opinion was anticipated."[*] The office assigned to him was that of Receiver-General. The three new Ministers were sworn into office in the beginning of September. Mr. Draper at the same time became Attorney-General for Upper Canada, and Mr. Viger President of the Council. Mr. Daly retained the Provincial Secretaryship for Lower Canada. So that, after a ministerial interregnum of more than nine months, the six most important offices in the Cabinet were filled, and the Governor was disposed to summon Parliament for the despatch of business. To do so, however, would have been to encounter certain defeat in the Assembly, where the ex-Ministers could command an easy majority. A dissolution was accordingly resolved upon, and on the 23rd of September was carried into effect. On the following day writs, made returnable on the 12th of November, were issued for a new election. It was determined not to fill any more of the ministerial offices until the result should be known.

Such an election had never been witnessed in Canada. The first contest under the Union had been stormy enough, but that of 1844 stands out as a unique episode in our history. The well-wishers of Responsible Government felt that it was on its trial, and put forth their mightiest energies. The supporters of the Governor were fully awake to the importance of the crisis, and left no stone unturned to procure the return of candidates favourable to their policy. The Governor himself felt that his posthumous reputation was at stake, and he did not scruple to turn his personal influence to account, as well as to resort to stratagems which he despised, in order to win votes. From end to end of the Province the excitement was unprecedented. In many places there were rioting and bloodshed.

---

[*] Kaye, Vol. II., p. 387.

Wherever such a course was practicable the troops and militia were warned to hold themselves in readiness, and in several places they were actually called out. Nowhere was the bitterness of party strife more pronounced than in Montreal, and the local authorities dreaded the worst consequences from collisions between opposing factions. Mr. John Young, whose previous career has already been glanced at,* was appointed returning officer for the city. In that capacity he was specially deputed to preserve the peace, and to secure a fair and free exercise of the franchise throughout the city. To accomplish both those desirable ends was perhaps beyond his power. It was much that, with the aid of the troops, he was able to prevent serious loss of life. For a day or two prior to the commencement of the elections, hordes of ill-looking fellows poured into the city. Many of them were known to be armed. Mr. Young went systematically to work. Backed by the soldiery, and with the aid of an army of special constables, he instituted a rigorous search for secreted weapons. Whenever any such weapons were found they were impounded, and the persons carrying them were in many instances placed under arrest and kept in durance until after the close of the contest. So far, all was well. But, owing to the unjust system imposed, nothing approaching to a full vote was polled in the city. The simple fact of the matter is that the plan of alternate voting adopted by Mr. Young enabled a minority to elect their candidate. In the three centre wards, where the Conservatives had a majority, all the votes were recorded, whereas in the six suburban wards, where the Liberals had a decided majority, nothing like a full vote was polled. The alternate voting was neither more nor less than an election scheme concocted in the Governor's interest, and by its means many Reform electors of Montreal were, for the time, practically disfranchised.

---

*Ante, pp. 215, 216.

The result of the elections as a whole was a small majority for the Government.* Of course, both parties were accused of the most unblushing bribery and corruption, and there seems to be good reason for believing that many of the accusations on both sides were true. It was a contest wherein much was involved, and as to which both parties felt strongly. We may be sure that no petty scruples were permitted to stand in the way of obtaining votes. The influence of mob law was great in those days, and was in more than one instance turned to the fullest account. There seems to be no possibility of doubting that several returning officers were guilty of the most corrupt and criminal abuse of their opportunities. The excuses afterwards made by the Tories for flagrant corrupt practices was that they had helped the Governor to maintain his Sovereign's cause against a rebellious people; and doubtless this was a not uncommon feeling throughout the Province wherever Tory influence was predominant. Not a few moderate Reform votes were recorded in favour of his Excellency's policy from dread of the consequences of a prolonged interregnum. It was felt that the confirmed mild paternal rule, even of a Governor who did not believe in Responsible Government, was better than such a state of things as the country had seemed to be insensibly drifting into since the resignation of the Ministers nearly a year before.

In Lower Canada, all the influence which the Government could bring to bear succeeded in obtaining but a slight measure of success, so far as success is to be estimated by actual power in the Assembly.

---

* On the 23rd of November Sir Charles Metcalfe forwarded to Lord Stanley the following analysis of the election returns:

Upper Canada—Avowed supporters of the Government, 30; avowed adversaries, 7; undeclared and uncertain, 5.

Lower Canada—Avowed supporters of the Government, 16; avowed adversaries, 21; undeclared and uncertain, 4.

Total of both sections of the Provinces:—Avowed supporters of the Government, 46; avowed adversaries, 28; undeclared or uncertain, 9.—See "Selections from the Papers of Lord Metcalfe," p. 437.

Mr. Viger, the new President of the Council, was worsted in his constituency of Richelieu. And by whom ? By Dr. Wolfred Nelson, whose return from exile has been recorded on a former page,* and whose identification with the Lower Canadian rebellion had been as complete as that of Louis Joseph Papineau himself. Notwithstanding his defeat, Mr. Viger retained the Presidency of the Council, but did not find a seat in the Assembly until the middle of the following summer, when he was returned for the town of Three Rivers, which constituency had meanwhile become vacant through the death of the sitting member, Mr. Edward Grieve. Jean Baptiste Isaie Noel, who had represented Lotbinière in the First Parliament, and who had from the first supported Mr. Viger in his espousal of the Governor's side in the dispute with his ex-Ministers, presented himself to his constituents for reëlection, and was defeated by Joseph Laurin. Joseph Guilliaume Barthe, the only other French Canadian member who had openly supported Mr. Viger and the Governor, was defeated in Yamaska by Dr. Léon Rousseau, a supporter of the Lafontaine-Baldwin policy.† Austin Cuvillier, who had been Speaker to the late Assembly, and who was now suspected of a leaning towards the Government party, was defeated in Huntingdon by Benjamin Henry Lemoine. The veteran John Neilson, who had been on the Government side throughout the dispute, was left far behind in the race upon presenting himself to his old constituents in the county of Quebec. On the other hand, the Government policy received unexpected support in some important constituencies. Not only were Messrs. Daly and Papineau reëlected in Megantic

---

* *Ante,* p. 299.

† "With respect to Mr. Barthe, it is right to state that the loss of his election is attributed to there having been another candidate in the same county also avowing support to the Government, by which the votes of the Government supporters, forming an aggregate majority, were divided between two candidates, while those of the adverse party were given to one, who thereby obtained a majority over each of the others."—See Sir Charles Metcalfe's despatch to Lord Stanley, November 23rd, 1844.

and Ottawa—the latter without opposition—but Mr. Smith, the new Attorney-General for Lower Canada, was returned for Missisquoi, and the Hon. George Moffatt and Charles Clement Sabrevois DeBleury were successful against Mr. Drummond and Dr. Beaubien in the city of Montreal, where, as was well known, the Opposition ought to have been able to command a majority of votes. On the side of the Opposition, some prominent members were defeated, and others narrowly escaped defeat. The Lower Canadian members of the ex-Ministry were all returned. Mr. Morin was returned for two constituencies (Saguenay and Bellechasse *); Mr. Lafontaine, having resigned his seat for the Fourth Riding of York, in Upper Canada, was elected without a contest in his old constituency of Terrebonne; and Mr. Aylwin was returned for the city of Quebec.

In Upper Canada the loyalty cry was found most effective, and the Government had a very distinct triumph; a triumph which was signalized not only by the return of a large majority in favour of their policy, but by the defeat of some of the most conspicuous of their opponents. Messrs. Baldwin, Small and Price had too strong a hold to be dislodged in their respective constituencies (the Fourth,† Third and First Ridings of the county of York), but they were opposed by Government candidates with such pertinacity that their supporters were compelled to work with unflagging energy in order to secure their election. Mr. Hincks, much to the surprise of his late colleagues, was defeated in Oxford by Robert Riddell, a local candidate who had been set up by the Government party. The ex-Inspector-General had meanwhile become a resident of Montreal, where he had established a newspaper of a character similar to that of *The Examiner*. At the time of the

---

* He elected to sit for Bellechasse.

† Mr. Baldwin had issued a farewell address to his Lower Province constituents in Rimouski, and had returned to his old constituency, the Fourth Riding of York, for which Mr. Lafontaine had sat since the formation of the Lafontaine-Baldwin Administration. Mr. Lafontaine, as indicated above, returned to his old constituency of Terrebonne.

resignation of the Ministers the want of a Reform paper printed in the English language was much felt by the British residents of Montreal, where all the English journals espoused the Governor's side. There was another cause which made Montreal a likely spot for the establishment of an English Reform newspaper—it was soon to be the Seat of Government. Mr. Hincks accordingly established *The Pilot* there early in 1844. The paper was conspicuous for precisely the same qualities which had made *The Examiner* a power in the land so long as it remained in Mr. Hincks's hands. It did good service to the cause which its founder had espoused, but when Mr. Hincks went up to Oxford for reëlection he found that hostile influences had been at work, and that the Government party had obtained a large following. The contest was keenly fought out, and resulted in the return of Mr. Riddell by a majority of twenty votes. Mr. Hincks did not offer himself elsewhere, and did not sit in the Second Parliament. He for the time confined his energies to his paper, and we shall not meet him again until the next general election. His defeat was a decided triumph for the Government party, and an equally decided blow to the Opposition. John Henry Dunn, late Executive Councillor and Receiver-General, was badly beaten in Toronto, which returned two ministerialists, Henry Sherwood and William H. Boulton. James Durand, too, a firm adherent of the ex-Ministers, sustained defeat in his constituency of West Halton. The Hon. Henry John Boulton, formerly a member of the Family Compact, but now an adherent of the Lafontaine-Baldwin party, was beaten in the town of Niagara by Walter Hamilton Dickson, an out-and-out supporter of the Governor. These are merely a few of the most conspicuous defeats sustained by the Opposition in Upper Canada. The Government elected all their staunchest supporters. As already stated, all the Lower Canadian Ministers except Mr. Viger were returned. The only Ministers belonging to Upper Canada were Mr. Draper and Mr. Morris, both of whom had seats in the Legislative Council, and needed no election. While the elections were in progress Mr. Henry Sherwood accepted the office of Solicitor-General for Upper Canada, but without a seat in the Executive Council. He was reëlected to the Assembly by the citizens of Toronto.

Parliament met at Montreal on Thursday, the 28th of November. The state of parties in the Assembly was clearly defined by the vote on the Speakership. His Excellency desired the presence of the members of the Assembly in the Legislative Council Chamber, and announced, through the Speaker of that body, that he did not see fit to declare the cause of summoning Parliament until a Speaker of the Assembly should have been chosen according to law. The members of Assembly accordingly returned to their own Chamber, whereupon Mr. Attorney-General Smith proposed Sir Allan Napier MacNab as Speaker. The motion was seconded by William Henry Scott, member for Two Mountains. Colonel Prince, who had been reëlected for Essex, then proposed the ex-Minister, Mr. Morin, and his motion was seconded by Mr. Christie, who had also been returned for his old constituency—Gaspé. After much discussion the vote was taken, and Sir Allan was elected by a majority of three; thirty-nine votes being recorded for him as against thirty-six in his favour.* All the French Canadian members voted for Mr. Morin, except the new Commissioner of Crown Lands and Mr. De Bleury, one of the abovenamed new members-elect for the city of Montreal. Sir Allan laboured under the disadvantage of being unacquainted with the French language, but was in other respects well suited for the Speakership.

On the following day the session was formally opened by his Excellency. The Speech from the Throne was of considerable length,

---

* Seventy-seven members were present in the Assembly, seventy-five of whom recorded their votes as above stated. The two candidates did not vote, and the remaining constituencies were for the time unrepresented in the House.

and touched upon various topics of public interest, but it had not been very cunningly drawn. Its first clause tacitly acknowledged that there had been great delay in assembling Parliament, and an altogether insufficient reason was assigned for the delay. "I have assembled you at the earliest period that the completion of the general election would allow," said his Excellency. The obvious criticism suggested by such a remark is that the general election ought to have been held sooner, and that the business of the country had been prejudiced by the unnecessary delay. Towards the close of the Speech there was a quasi admission of impropriety on the part of the Governor in not sooner filling the various ministerial offices.

Just before the opening of the session John Neilson and James Morris had been appointed members of the Legislative Council. It now became apparent that the complexion of the Assembly had undergone important changes. Some prominent members of the last Parliament were conspicuous by their absence, and several personages whose names were destined to become well known throughout the Province now took their seats for the first time. Among the most conspicuous absentees were Francis Hincks, John S. Cartwright, Henry John Boulton, Edward Gibbon Wakefield, James Durand, and Austin Cuvillier. Among those who now for the first time sat in the Assembly were at least six personages deserving of special introduction to the reader.

Ogle Robert Gowan, the new member for Leeds, has already been more than once referred to in these pages. He was an Irishman by birth, and a native of the county of Wexford, where he had been prominently connected with the Orange body from his early youth, and had written several pamphlets on politico-religious subjects. He had also connected himself with two weekly newspapers, to both of which he had been a voluminous contributor. In 1829 he emigrated from Ireland to Upper Canada, and settled at Escott

Park, in the county of Leeds. He had not been much more than a year in the country when he wrote a pamphlet on Responsible Government,* which was the means of making him well known to Upper Canadian politicians. In due time he found his way into the old Parliament of Upper Canada, and to a connection with several newspaper enterprises. He became, as has been seen,† Grand Master of the Orange body in British North America, a position which he occupied for about twenty years, and which enabled him to exercise a vast influence. In politics he was a distinctly pronounced Conservative, so far as his fast and firm alliance with that body was concerned, but he entertained modern and enlightened views on some important public questions. During the rebellion he took a prominent part on the loyal side, and was present at the capture of Hickory Island, as well as at the engagement near Prescott, known as the battle of the Windmill. At the latter engagement he was thrice wounded. He had previously received from Sir Francis Head the command of a regiment of militia, and was afterwards promoted by Sir John Colborne to a company in the Queen's Own Rifles. Later still he attained the rank of Lieutenant-Colonel. He did not sit in the first Parliament under the Union, but did good work for the Conservative side by means of a vigorously conducted weekly newspaper established by him at Brockville some years before, and known as *The Statesman*. During the sojourn of the Government at Kingston this newspaper was removed thither. It opposed Lord Sydenham and Sir Charles Bagot with combined volubility and vigour. With Sir Charles Metcalfe its editor early established friendly relations.‡ When the rupture with the Ministry took place, Mr. Gowan became one of the staunchest allies of the Governor, and one of the fiercest assailants

---

* "Responsible or Parliamentary Government;" Toronto, 1839. Republished with modifications and additions, 1859. Referred to *ante*, p. 300.

† *Ante*, p. 297.   ‡ *Ante*, p. 297.

of the ex-Councillors. At the general election of 1844 he was returned for the county of Leeds, and upon the opening of Parliament took his seat in the Assembly as the uncompromising advocate of the Governor's policy.

Mr. Gowan's writings everywhere exhibit a considerable degree of rugged but uncultivated strength. It is impossible to read his articles without perceiving that he was not, in the modern, or indeed in any proper acceptation of the term, an educated man, or one who knew how to make the most of himself when his pen was in his hand. Still, there was a homely, coarse robustness in his writings which probably found its way to the understandings of his readers more quickly and effectually than articles written in the style of Mr. Gladstone's state papers would have done. As a speaker he was long known as one of the most effective in the Assembly. His training in Orange lodges had given him a readiness of expression which enabled him to do full justice to the vein of eloquence which is proverbially an attribute of his race, and which he inherited in no common degree. He was an able, active-minded man, destined to attain to higher distinction than had yet come in his way, and to leave distinct traces of his life's work behind him.

Dr. Wolfred Nelson has also received mention in former pages. He had obtained an unenviable notoriety by reason of his connection with the rebellion, but it is a circumstance worthy of being reported in his favour that he never lost the personal respect of even the most loyal of his former friends, in consequence of his action in aiding and heading an armed insurrection against duly constituted authority. Neither did he ever lose his respect for himself. No one ever ventured to doubt his perfect sincerity, disinterestedness, and good faith. It is a trenchant commentary upon the state of affairs which prevailed in the Lower Province in 1837-'38, that a man of respectable English descent, and possessing a high sense of moral rectitude; a man of irreproachable private character, of high standing in one of the learned professions, in good pecuniary circumstances, and of undoubted loyalty and good sense, should have been driven into hoisting the standard of rebellion.

He was born at the City of Montreal in 1792. After receiving his education he studied medicine, and even during his student days won a high reputation for surgical skill. Upon obtaining his license to practice, in 1811, he settled at St. Denis, a pleasant little village in the county of St. Hyacinthe. He was a large-hearted man, and, notwithstanding his English descent and training, was able to enter into the sympathies and feelings of the *habitans* who formed the bulk of the rural population. He spoke their dialect as glibly as his own, and soon found his way to the hearts of the entire French Canadian population in and about St. Denis. Patients flocked to him, and he was frequently not only their physician, but their adviser on temporal matters. During the war of 1812-'15 he served as surgeon of a battalion raised in the district, and acquired an unusual degree of familiarity with military tactics. At the close of hostilities he returned to his quiet home at St. Denis. He took a warm interest in public affairs, his sympathies being strongly on the popular side, insomuch that he was nicknamed "the Frenchified Englishman." He resisted all importunities to enter political life until he had reached his thirty-fifth year, by which time he had amassed a competent fortune, and was in a position to take liberties with his future. He certainly availed himself of his privilege in this particular to the fullest extent. In 1827 he was returned to the Lower Canadian Assembly. He made his mark in Parliament, not only as a fluent and earnest speaker, but as a man who entertained strong opinions which were worth listening to. He devoted himself to finding a remedy for the many grievances under which the people suffered, and after a time became a fellow-worker with Papineau. For years, however, he tried to stem the current which he foresaw would, if unchecked in its course, eventually lead to rebellion. Apart from the consideration that he had the sympathies of an Englishman, and was loyal to his Sovereign, he well knew that any attempt at rebellion in Canada must prove ineffective. His object was not disintegration, but merely to gain for British subjects in Canada the same rights which British subjects enjoyed elsewhere. Continued oppression and misgovernment, however, at last did their work. Hundreds of suffering and illiterate peasants looked to him for advice and support. Papineau hounded them on, and the Doctor was drawn into the vortex. The die having been cast, he threw himself into the struggle with characteristic energy. He was the most active organizer and director of the revolutionary measures. The Government were apprized of the drillings and manœuvres in progress in various parts of the Province. On the 23rd of November, Colonel (afterwards Sir Charles) Gore, a veteran of Waterloo, who was at this time on service in Canada, bore down upon St. Denis with a body of infantry and volunteer cavalry at his back. Dr. Nelson, with a little force of *habitans*, was entrenched there, and defended the place like a veteran. It is agreed on all hands that he conducted operations like one who had been a man of war from his youth. Colonel Gore and his forces were compelled to retreat, leaving behind them wounded soldiers who were ministered to in the kindest and gentlest manner by Dr. Nelson himself. There is no need to prolong details, nor to tell the tragical story of Lieutenant Weir. The repulse of Colonel Gore merely postponed the inevitable result. The rebellion was soon crushed, and the leaders fled. A reward of two thousand dollars was offered for Dr. Nelson's capture. After a few days, during which he suffered untold miseries from hunger, cold, and exposure, he was captured in the wilderness near the United States frontier, and conveyed to Montreal, where he was lodged in gaol with a number of his fellow-conspirators. The sufferings which he had undergone produced a prostration of the system from which he was long in recovering, but he conducted himself with a manly composure and self-possession which effectually proved the quality of his mind, and which won respect from all. He indulged in no useless repinings. He had played a desperate game, and had lost. He resigned himself to pay the penalty of death. But better things were in store for him. How he was banished to Bermuda by Lord Durham; how the ordinance was disallowed; how he was subsequently permitted to return to his native land, and to engage in medical practice in Montreal, has already been narrated. In his futile struggle he had lost nearly all his property, and was compelled to begin the world anew. He buckled on his armour for the struggle with true Saxon courage, and no one ever heard him complain of his lot. The inhabitants of Richelieu now testified their esteem for him by electing him to Parliament over the head of no less a man than Sir Charles Metcalfe's President of the Council. The rest of his life was passed in honour, without spot or stain. He was twice elected Mayor of Montreal, and subsequently rendered good service to his country as Inspector of Prisons. He contributed largely on professional subjects to the medical press of Canada and the United States.

Joseph Edouard Cauchon, who took his seat in the Assembly for the county of Montmorency, was—and is—one of the most remarkable French Canadians of his day. At the time of this present writing he is Lieutenant-Governor of the Province of Manitoba, and is known—not altogether favourably—from one end of the Dominion to the other. In 1844 he was known only to the people of Lower Canada, and even to them was notorious chiefly as a brilliant young journalist who had suffered persecution in the popular cause, and who was therefore deserving of their support. He was at this time in his twenty-eighth year, having been born at Quebec in 1816.

He came of a good French family, and had enjoyed an excellent scholastic training. As a young man he developed rare qualities of mind. He studied law, and was called to the bar, but devoted himself chiefly to journalism—a calling for which he was in some respects well fitted. He was a collaborateur of Etienne Parent* in the conduct of *Le Canadien*. When that gentleman was elected to Parliament, in 1841, Mr. Cauchon became editor-in-chief. His editorial career at this time was marked by unbounded energy and temerity, but by much indiscretion. He had entertained strong political sympathies almost from his childhood, and long before he could be expected to furnish any good reason for the political faith that was in him. The opinions of one who is guided by his sympathies and prejudices rather than by his reason cannot be of much value, and this was precisely the case of young Cauchon when he succeeded to the editorial chair of *Le Canadien*. He wrote wildly denunciatory articles, and erelong brought down upon himself the indignation of Government. His paper was suppressed, but soon after arose phœnix-like, as the *Journal de Québec*, which was conducted with equal ability and greater prudence, and soon won a prominent place among French Canadian newspapers. Mr. Cauchon's fame grew apace, and at the general election which forms the chief topic of the present chapter he responded to advances made to him to enter Parliament. The result of his response has already been chronicled, and he thenceforward continued to be "the member for Montmorency" for a continuous period of twenty-eight years. It is not necessary in this place to discount the evil repute which has attended Mr. Cauchon during the last decade or thereabouts. That repute, and the causes which led to it, will necessarily be noticed in future pages. In 1844 he took his seat as the ally of the ex-Ministers, and with no greater blemish upon his character than indiscretion. He soon proved himself a formidable ally, for what-

---

* *Ante*, pp. 93, 94.

ever his faults, his bitterest enemy—and he has many bitter enemies—cannot deny that Joseph Edouard Cauchon is a man of tremendous force, and that he was an awkward antagonist to encounter on the floor of the Assembly when he was in earnest. Unlike some of the most eminent of his contemporaries, he was never a diffident man, or one disposed to hide his intellectual light under a bushel. His great force, whether in journalism or political life, was instantly apparent, and on important occasions descended like an avalanche. His moods were variable, but when his least amiable fit was upon him there was a lurid light in his eyes, and he seemed to take delight in lashing his opponents to fury.

Pierre Joseph Olivier Chauveau, who had just defeated John Neilson in Quebec County, is a French Canadian of an altogether different stamp. He is a native of the city of Quebec, where he was born in 1820. He received his education and studied law in his native city. At the time of his first return to Parliament he was known as a rising young lawyer, as the author of several graceful poems, and as a contributor to *Le Canadien*. He disapproved of Sir Charles Metcalfe's policy, and was elected in the interest of the Opposition. He has since won a high reputation as a man of letters—a reputation not confined to his native land. He has also won a reputation as a public man, and is at the present time Sheriff of the district of Montreal.

Lewis Thomas Drummond, Mr. Aylwin's successor in the representation of Portneuf, is of Irish birth, but has lived in Canada from boyhood. After receiving his education at Nicolet College, he studied law. In 1836 he was called to the bar, and subsequently practised his profession with much success. He was a Liberal in politics, and a few months before the general election of 1844 he had been elected in that interest for the city of Montreal. When the general election came on, he had no difficulty about securing his election in Portneuf. He subsequently held office in several Administrations, and became one of the best known public men in Lower Canada. Later, he was elevated to the Bench, and now occupies the position of a retired Judge.

One name—beyond all comparison the most distinguished of the six—still remains to be mentioned.

During the election campaign of 1844, a young man, a member of the local bar, was brought forward by the Tories of Kingston as their candidate for that constituency. He was of Scottish birth and descent, having been born in Sutherlandshire in 1815. His father, with his family, had emigrated from Scotland to Upper Canada in 1820, and had settled in business at Kingston, where the boy received his education at the Royal Grammar School. Having chosen the law for a profession, he began his studies at fifteen, and was called to the bar of Upper Canada at twenty-one. He settled down to practise at Kingston, and had already won somewhat more than a local reputation when he was first returned to Parliament. He gained his election by a sweeping majority over his opponent, Mr. Manahan. He has sat in the Canadian Parliament ever since, and for at least a quarter of a century he has been one of the most conspicuous figures that ever had a place there. No public man known to our history has ever been able to command so large and enthusiastic a following, or has held the reins of power for so long a time. No man in British America has so entirely made politics his profession, or has been so loyally served by his adherents. No one has so completely identified himself with the country, or with the great party of which he has long been the universally-acknowledged head. No public man has so many personal friends, or so few personal enemies. Owing in part to the position which he has occupied, and in part to untoward circumstances, his conduct has evoked sharper and more vitriolic criticism than has been applied to that of any other Canadian statesman of his time; and—it would be affectation to mince the matter—the record of his career dis-

closes acts for which no valid or honest defence can be made. But
it is not by isolated acts that a man's life should be judged, and in
spite of all drawbacks; in spite of vehement and ceaseless assaults
from the Reform press; in spite of deplorable personal infirmities;
in spite of unforeseen quirks of diplomacy; in spite of jealous
rivals and powerful opponents, the man known to the present generation of Canadians as Sir John Alexander Macdonald has steadily
won his way to high and honourable rank; to far more than vice-regal power; and to a warm place in the hearts of a large element
in the national population. Few, if any, of those who assail him the
most bitterly have any personal dislike for him. On the contrary,
most of those who widely dissent from his political views admit the
magnetic influence of his personality, and the undoubted intellectual
power and earnestness which underlie the seeming ease and indifference of his nature. It is a simple fact that his graceful geniality,
his never-failing tact, his tenacity of purpose and general administrative ability have borne him through crises which would have
swamped any other statesman who has ever taken part in Canadian
affairs. But to say, as has frequently been said, that such a man is
merely a cunning politician and a clever manipulator of party wires,
is to talk foolishly. The same thing has been said, and with equal
truth, about the late Lord Beaconsfield, with whom he has often been
compared. No mere wire-puller ever won and retained the vast
influence which has long been wielded by Sir John Macdonald. No
selfish or inherently dishonest man ever made and kept so many
thousands of warm personal friends, or found himself, after nearly
forty years spent in the public service, a poorer man than when he
entered it. It is proverbially difficult to write impartially and
dispassionately of a very prominent man during his lifetime, and
this is more especially true when, as in the present instance, wide
diversity of opinion is all but inevitable. That his zeal for his country's welfare is on the whole sincere, albeit at times displayed in

dubious ways, must be conceded by every man whose eyes are not blinded by the prejudices of faction. We shall meet him often enough in the future to be able to form something like an accurate judgment of him, so far as his character has manifested itself in his public acts.

It was his misfortune to enter political life under auspices unfavourable to the speedy enlargement of his mind. He was returned as a supporter of the Government policy—a narrow and restricted policy which his maturer judgment most certainly would not have approved. That he was not enthusiastic in his support of old-fashioned Toryism may be inferred from the fact that he did not often intrude himself upon the attention of the Assembly during the early sessions of his public career. He redeemed his promise to his constituents, and upheld the ministerial policy by his votes, but it may well be doubted if his heart was in the struggle. It will hereafter be seen that he erelong outgrew the party-lines of his youth. It may almost be said that he originated a party of his own, for most assuredly Canadian Conservatism, as it exists to-day, would have been of a totally different complexion but for the hand of John Alexander Macdonald.

END OF VOL. I.

THE LAST FORTY YEARS.

CANADA since THE UNION OF 1841.

BY JOHN CHARLES DENT

GEO. VIRTUE
PUBLISHER
TORONTO

SIR SAMUEL LEONARD TILLEY.

ALEXANDRA COLLEGE, BELLEVILLE.

THE HON. SIR RICHARD J. CARTWRIGHT.

THE HON SIR ALEXANDER CAMPBELL.

THE LAST FORTY YEARS.

CHAPTER XIX.

BARON METCALFE OF FERN HILL.

"Lord Metcalfe ought not to have been sent to Canada. He was unfit to rule two millions of intelligent British subjects. He had been initiated in all the arts of Indian diplomacy, accustomed to the corruption and flattery, to the treachery and despotism of Eastern nabobs and rajahs, who are *everything*, and the mass of the people *nothing*. His experience had been gained in the wrong school, and he was too late in life to accommodate himself to the views and wishes of men as high-minded as himself. . . . Lord Metcalfe's administration is a beacon forever to his successors." Toronto *Globe*, December 2nd, 1845.

HE session of 1844-'45, inclusive of the adjournment for the Christmas holidays, lasted four months, and was throughout a most trying and arduous one for the party in power. As has been seen, the Government were able to command a majority of only three in favour of their candidate for the Speakership. At the conclusion of the debate on the Address in reply to the Speech from the Throne they had a majority of six, but even this was altogether too small a preponderance to enable them to feel safe, and it must be confessed that they were compelled to carry on the business of the country under great disadvantages. Various devices were from time to time resorted to for the purpose of strengthening the ministerial position; but in spite of all that could be done, that position was

never a secure one, and Sir Charles Metcalfe was continually harassed by the consciousness that his Administration was liable to drop to pieces upon any sudden emergency.

The business of the session, arduous as it was, was not productive of much important legislation, and need not detain us long. The Address in reply was moved in the Assembly by Rolland Macdonald, member for Cornwall, on the 4th of December, and was seconded by Eden Colville, the new member-elect for Beauharnois. Mr. Baldwin moved amendments expressive of regret that the summoning of Parliament had been so long delayed, and that the ministerial offices should have remained so long unfilled. The debate lasted three days. The division was forty-two to thirty-six in favour of the original motion, which may therefore be said to have fairly represented the strength—or weakness—of the Government. On the 20th of the month William Benjamin Robinson, member for Simcoe, a brother of Chief Justice Robinson, accepted office in the Ministry as Inspector-General, and on the 13th of the following January he was reëlected by his constituents. Mr. Draper, in the Legislative Council, defended the Governor's policy with all the subtlety at his command; but as the session proceeded it became apparent that the valuable services of the Attorney-General for Upper Canada were urgently needed in the Assembly. No member of the Government who had a seat in that body was capable of assuming the leadership. The Ministers disagreed among themselves, and appealed from decisions of the new Speaker who had just been elected under their own auspices. It was evident that they did not enjoy the entire confidence even of their own party. In a word, all was disorganization on the Government side in the Assembly, and it was certain that if the Ministry were to be kept together, some ruling mind must be placed over them. Mr. Draper was pressed to take upon himself the leadership. He accordingly resigned his seat in the Legislative Council at the end of January (1845), and offered himself as the representative of the town of London in the Assembly; the sitting member, Lawrence Lawrason, having resigned in his favour. He was returned on the 13th of February, and at once took his seat in the House, where he did his utmost to reduce the turbulent spirits to a state of subordination.

But in spite of all efforts the Government continued embarrassingly weak, and evidently held on to life by a very frail tenure. All through the session Sir Charles Metcalfe, for the first time in his long public career, found himself compelled to resort to party shifts and expedients which were inconceivably distasteful to him. "He was not," says his biographer, "by nature at all a tactician; and he had not been trained in the intricate manœuvres of party warfare. It was not, indeed, one of the least of his annoyances at this time that he was compelled to sanction a departure from that open, straightforward course of political conduct which he had all his life been steadfastly pursuing. He fell very slowly and reluctantly into the manœuvring ways common to party leaders. I do not mean that he did or sanctioned anything incompatible with public virtue as it is commonly understood—anything from which the most immaculate party leader in Europe would have shrunk. But he was out of his element as a manœuvrer. He felt that when he sanctioned a recourse even to the ordinary tactics of party, by which threatened defeats are converted into actual victories, he descended from the high position which he had previously occupied throughout nearly half a century of public service, and became, in his own estimation, something of a trickster."* A notable instance of this doubledealing is afforded by the Government's action on a matter which the French Canadian members had very much at heart. In a former chapter it has been seen that the official use of the French language had been practically proscribed by a clause in the Union

* Kaye, Vol. II., pp. 392, 393.

Act, and that this proscription had been keenly felt by the Lower Canadians of French origin.* At the opening of the session of 1844-'45, Mr. Lafontaine had it in contemplation to move an Address to the Throne, praying that the existing restrictions upon the use of the French language might be removed.† His intention having become known, the Government resolved to propitiate the favour of the French Canadian members by moving the Address as a ministerial measure. There were positive instructions from the Colonial Office to the effect that no such disingenuous proceedings should be resorted to by the Provincial Administration; but the Government's need of support was urgent, and, as Metcalfe's biographer naïvely remarks, "it was expedient to disarm the Opposition." Sir Charles gave his consent, and accordingly, on the 20th of December, Mr. Papineau, Commissioner of Crown Lands, to the great surprise of the Opposition, moved the Address. The motion was seconded by the Hon. George Moffatt, member for Montreal, an ultra-Tory. It was received with tumultuous applause by the Assembly, and the French Canadians, who knew nothing of the Government's tactics, were disposed to regard the motion as a genuine ebullition of patriotic zeal on the part of Mr. Papineau. The consideration of the question was postponed in order to give members time to deliberate upon it, but when it finally came before the House on the 31st of January it was carried by acclamation, and a select committee was appointed to prepare the Address, which was duly forwarded to the Colonial Office. There was no reluctance on the part of the Imperial Government to acquiesce, but before any action had been taken towards that end the question of the repeal of the Civil List established by the Union Act came before them. The latter was not an easy subject to deal with, and led to protracted negotiations. The Imperial Government did

---

* *Ante*, pp. 45, 46.

† He had moved an Address to a similar purport during the previous session.

not wish to go before Parliament a second time with amendments to the Union Act, but were desirous of embodying all requisite changes in one measure. Thus the question of the Address on the subject of the French language was for the time left in abeyance, and the restrictions were not actually removed until more than two years afterwards. Meanwhile, however, Mr. Papineau gained much credit with his compatriots for his motion, which did something to remove from their minds the effect produced by his vote on the Speakership.*

A good deal of important legislation was initiated during the session, but the Government were too weak to carry anything to a successful termination that was met by serious opposition. The status of the Ministry was most embarrassing, and all Mr. Draper's tact and ability were put forth to little purpose. Early in March he introduced his Bill for creating a university by the name and style of the University of Upper Canada. By this measure the proposed institution was to embrace three denominational colleges, viz., King's College, Toronto, for the Episcopalians; Queen's College, Kingston, for the Presbyterians; and Victoria College, Cobourg, for the Methodists. The Bill was very similar in its scope to a measure which had been introduced by Mr. Baldwin during the preceding session, the progress of which had been stopped by the resignation of the Ministry. Mr. Draper now declared that he and his colleagues had made up their minds to stand or fall by the measure. On the second reading it encountered such opposition that the mover was compelled to abandon it. Several Conservatives—Mr. Sherwood, Solicitor-General for Upper Canada, among the number—declared on the second reading that they voted for it only to prevent the Government from being defeated, and that if it came up for a third reading they would use all their influence against it.

---

* He had of course voted for the Government candidate, Sir Allan MacNab, and against his fellow-countryman, Mr. Morin.

Mr. Robinson, the new Inspector-General, could not tolerate some of the details of the Bill, and with a higher sense of his responsibilities as an adviser of the Governor than Mr. Sherwood seemed to entertain, he voted against the measure, and soon afterwards resigned his office. The other members of the Government, however, notwithstanding Mr. Draper's positive assurance on introducing the measure, clung to their places. They were badgered and baited as surely no Government in Canada ever were either before or since. And not without good and sufficient reason, for they lacked many of the qualifications by which a Government should be characterized. Their want of ability was not their only, or even their greatest, disqualification. It is to be feared that more than one of them had no proper idea of the moral responsibility which ought to attach to the position of a Minister of the Crown. Direct charges of attempts to corrupt members were made against Ministers across the floor of the House. Mr. Lafontaine declared, in so many words, that he was prepared to prove ministerial attempts at corruption of members. In support of the declaration, Mr. Louis Bertrand, member for Rimouski, asserted that both Mr. Daly and Mr. Papineau had declined to accede to a request preferred by him on behalf of his constituency, on the ground that he, Mr. Bertrand, did not support the Government. It was alleged that, so far as Mr. Daly was concerned, his ground for refusal might have been put forward merely by way of joke; though, sooth to say, a joke on such a subject was very uncomely in the mouth of a Cabinet Minister. It was not pretended, however, that Mr. Papineau had been jesting. He had expressly declined to do anything more for his compatriots, because they yielded him no Parliamentary support; and he had even gone so far as to add that if he received their support in future he might try what more could be done for them. Well might the member for Rimouski reply: "What! must we sell our consciences before we can obtain justice?"

While the session was in progress the Governor-General received an official intimation that Her Majesty, upon the recommendation of the Imperial Government, was about to raise him to the peerage, and he was asked to signify by what title he would wish to be called to the House of Lords. As the dignity to be conferred was a barony, he chose his surname for a title, and in due course became Baron Metcalfe of Fern Hill, in the county of Berks. It was doubtless felt that his long public services were deserving of recognition, and it was probably hoped that the honour thus bestowed upon him might impart some additional strength to his Canadian Government. The latter hope, if it had ever been really entertained, proved futile. The weakness of the Government was irremediable, and no honours conferred upon its head could galvanize it into even temporary vitality. As for the Governor himself, he was steadily sinking into his grave. His fearful malady had of late made rapid progress. Some months before this time a skilful surgeon had been specially sent out under the auspices of the Home Office to superintend the application of a strong preparation of chloride of zinc to the Governor's face. The application was made with all the skill which science could command, but the disorder had reached a stage when no treatment could be of much avail. To intense pain was now superadded a rapid destruction of tissue. One eye was totally destroyed, and the sight of the other, by force of sympathy, became greatly weakened. About the close of 1844 the sufferer found that he was no longer able to draft his despatches, as had always been his custom. He was unable to open his mouth to its full width, and had difficulty in masticating his food. Such was his unhappy condition when the intimation of a peerage reached him. The intimation was accompanied by the kindest of letters from Sir Robert Peel and Lord Stanley, and by an appreciative message from the Queen herself.

The announcement of the Governor's elevation to the peerage of course aroused much interest in Canada. The Legislative Council voted an unanimous Address of congratulation. The matter came up in the Assembly on the 25th of February, when a congratulatory Address was moved by Colonel Prince, and seconded by John P. Roblin, member for Prince Edward. It was strongly opposed by some members of the Opposition, and remarks were made during the ensuing discussion which reflected little credit upon the speakers. Mr. Aylwin expressed himself as being unable to congratulate either Sir Charles Metcalfe or the House of Lords. Sir Charles, he said, instead of having honours conferred upon him, ought to have been recalled and tried for high crimes and misdemeanors. Even Mr. Baldwin was betrayed into using expressions which were not characteristic of him. It is certainly to be borne in mind that the Reform party were placed in such a position that their leaders could hardly be expected to record a silent vote on such a motion. The Tory organs were unanimous in holding up his Excellency's conduct to unqualified admiration, and in trying to persuade the world that respectable Canadians of all classes approved of his policy. That Baldwin, Aylwin and others should have entered their protest against so false a showing was natural and right enough, but it is to be regretted that strict moderation of language was not preserved, and that the discussion should have been unnecessarily embittered. Of course the motion was carried, but out of seventy members no fewer than twenty-five voted for its rejection.

The weary, barren session came to an end at last. The prorogation took place on Saturday, the 29th of March. All things considered, the Government had little reason to congratulate itself on the work of the preceding four months. Of the many Acts passed, not one can be said to be of historical importance. The really important legislation which had been referred to by his Excellency at the opening of the session was still in the womb of time. The conduct

of business had been marked by chicanery and double-dealing. The
Conservatives, as a body, had not been loyal to the Government.
They had yielded their support in a grudging, half-hearted way,*
and some of them had stipulated for all sorts of personal advantages
as a condition of their support. Ministers never knew what a day
might bring forth. The Governor and Mr. Draper looked forward
to another session with the most gloomy forebodings. Without Mr.
Draper's advice and assistance the Governor must before this time
have given up the contest with the Assembly. Mr. Draper, however,
was chiefly valuable to the Governor by reason of his counsels, and
not at all by reason of his Parliamentary influence, which was very
small. The influence of the other members of the Government was
little if at all greater. Of these facts his Excellency was perfectly
conscious. "Mr. Draper," wrote the Governor to Lord Stanley,† "is
universally admitted to be the most talented man in either House
of the Legislature, and his presence in the Legislative Assembly was
deemed to be so essential that he resigned his seat in the Upper
House, sacrificing his own opinions in order that he might take the
lead in the Assembly; nevertheless, he is not popular with the party
that supports the Government, nor with any other, and I do not
know that, strictly speaking, he can be said to have a single follower.
The same may be remarked of every other member of the Executive
Council; and although I have much reason to be satisfied with them,
and have no expectation of finding others who would serve Her
Majesty better, still I do not perceive that any of them individually
have brought much strength to the Government." But notwithstanding the manifold difficulties of his position; notwithstanding the daily, almost hourly physical agony to which his malady

* "The Ministers wanted weight and influence; and therefore the supporters of the Government wanted union and stability."—Kaye, Vol. II., p. 393.

† See the despatch of May 13th, 1845, in "Selections from the Papers of Lord Metcalfe," p. 455.

subjected him, the Governor could not bear the idea of resignation. He seems to have honestly brought himself to the conclusion that his remaining at his post was essential to the welfare of the colony and the empire. By what process of reasoning he had arrived at such a state of mind it is difficult to conjecture. The Colonial Secretary seems to have shared the opinion, and to have repeatedly urged his Excellency to persevere in the course which he had adopted. Such was the light which illuminated the administration of the Colonial Office in the year of grace 1845.*

The late spring and early summer were marked by two conflagrations in the city of Quebec which were disastrous enough to be regarded as matters of national importance in Canada. The first took place on the 28th of May, the second a month later. By the former, 1650 dwellings, two churches, an extensive ship-yard, and several lumber yards and wharfs were consumed.† The later conflagration was more disastrous still. By these two terrible calamities a great portion of the old capital was reduced to ashes,‡ and more than 20,000 people were left houseless, penniless, and without food or clothing. The entire Province felt called upon to come forward for the relief of the sufferers. The Governor-General, with that large-hearted benevolence which always flowed

---

* "The Colonial Secretary believed he was guiding the ship into port when he was running her among the breakers."— *The Irishman in Canada*, p. 526.

† "No human power was of any avail to arrest the conflagration; so rapid was its advance that but little could be saved from the houses, and often life itself with difficulty; many were overtaken in their flight by the flames, and perished. Many who rose in the morning in possession of competence, or even of comparative wealth, the fruit of many years of industry and economy, found themselves in a state of destitution before night closed upon them. A million of money will not replace, in several years, the value of the property destroyed, nor can any correct estimate be now formed of the real extent of the calamity."—See the Address by the Corresponding Committee appointed in Quebec to procure aid for the sufferers by the fire.

‡ "As on the former occasion, a third part of the city has fallen a prey to the flames; and Quebec, on the landward side, is reduced to limits not much larger than it possessed when Wolfe fell before its walls."—Statement by the Bishops of Montreal and Quebec, published immediately after the disaster.

from him at any genuine tale of woe, personally set on foot a subscription list, and headed it himself by a munificent contribution of two thousand dollars. His good offices, however, were by no means confined to mere pecuniary assistance. He wrote urgent letters on the subject to friends in England, and in consequence of his representations several distinguished philanthropists there were induced to take the matter up. Queen Victoria herself set on foot a scheme of relief, and not only contributed liberally from her own private purse, but caused charity sermons to be preached throughout the United Kingdom. About half a million of dollars in all were subscribed and sent over from Great Britain to Canada. Nor were our brethren across the lines deaf to the call of humanity. Acting upon the principle that he gives twice who gives quickly, they promptly sent a shipload of food and clothing which went far to alleviate the untold miseries of the time. Boston, New York, Philadelphia, and other cities and towns of the republic opened subscription lists, and the national press preached effective charity sermons from day to day. Contributions amounting in the aggregate to more than a hundred thousand dollars came to the Quebec sufferers from the United States. Cynics of the London clubs, who had not forgotten the Ashburton Treaty, remarked that Brother Jonathan might not know how to be just, but that he certainly knew how to be generous.*

The rest of the summer glided uneventfully by. On the 6th of August Mr. William Cayley, then an unknown and untried man, accepted the vacant office of Inspector-General, with a seat in the Executive Council. The appointment gave umbrage to many ministerialists, and had a decidedly weakening effect upon the Government, which could ill endure any additional drafts upon its strength. Mr. Cayley did not find a seat in Parliament until more than six months had elapsed, when, in February, 1846, he was returned for the county

* See "The Talk of the Town," in *The Englishman* for October, 1845.

of Huron, where Dr. Dunlop had meanwhile resigned his seat. Within a fortnight after Mr. Cayley's appointment, Mr. Joseph Andrew Taschereau, a French Canadian lawyer of considerable learning and ability, was induced to accept the Solicitor-Generalship for Lower Canada without a seat in the Cabinet. His appointment was confirmed by his election for the county of Dorchester, but his acceptance of office did not conduce to his popularity among his compatriots generally.

About this time the French press of Lower Canada began to seriously advocate an idea which eventually came to be known as "the double-majority principle." The existing Government, ever since its formation, had been kept in power by a large Upper Canadian majority acting in concert with a small minority from Lower Canada. It was now proposed that it should be recognized as a vital principle of the constitution that a Government, in order to its continuance in power, must be sustained, not merely by a majority of votes in the entire Assembly, but by a majority of votes from each section of the Province. The object sought to be attained was to prevent either section of the Province from imposing unpalatable legislation upon the other. There were repeated attempts to apply this principle, but—contrary to what is asserted in most histories of Canada—it did not obtain general recognition until more than ten years subsequent to the date at which the narrative has arrived.* Even after it came into vogue its prevalence was of brief duration, and it was abandoned as impracticable. It was of course always considered desirable that a ministry should be able to command a majority from each section of the Province, but such a majority was not regarded as essential to the existence of an Administration. Out of this question, as will

---

* "Up to the time of my leaving Canada, in 1855, no political alliance was formed on the principle of securing majorities from the two Provinces."—*The Political History of Canada*, by the Hon. Sir Francis Hincks; p. 23.

hereafter be seen, the agitation on the subject of "Representation by Population" subsequently arose.

Both the Governor and Mr. Draper had long ceased to hope anything from Mr. Viger's efforts at conciliating his fellow-countrymen. It was, however, deemed absolutely necessary to gain increased French Canadian support. In the course of the summer of 1845 Mr. Draper opened a correspondence with the Hon. Réné Edouard Caron, Speaker of the Legislative Council, with that end in view. Mr. Caron seems to have been ready enough to act as an intermediary between the Government and the French Canadian leaders. The correspondence, which extended over several months, was communicated by him to Mr. Lafontaine, by whom it was again communicated to Mr. Morin. The Government were willing to sacrifice Mr. Viger and Mr. Papineau, but, so long as Lord Metcalfe remained at its head, it was impossible that Mr. Lafontaine could be admitted to the Cabinet, the differences between the latter and the Governor-General, ever since the resignation of the Lafontaine-Baldwin Ministry, having been of such a nature that no accommodation could reasonably be hoped for when their respective characters and positions were taken into consideration. Mr. Lafontaine, however, whatever his private inclinations may have been, determined not to stand in the way of any arrangement which might enure to the common weal of his fellow-countrymen. With the disinterestedness of a true patriot, he insisted on sinking his own claims, and thought only of the public good. But there was an insuperable difficulty in the way in the person of Mr. Daly. Mr. Caron, with the approval of Messieurs Lafontaine and Morin, required that the entire Lower Canadian section should be reconstructed, which would have involved Mr. Daly's retirement from office. This was more than Mr. Draper was authorized to consent to. Personally he would doubtless have been willing enough to let the Provincial Secretary go, but that gentleman had stood firmly by the Governor ever since the resignation of the Lafontaine-Baldwin Ministry, and his Excellency would not sacrifice him. The negotiations were accordingly hindered and postponed from time to time. In reading the later correspondence between Mr. Lafontaine and Mr. Caron, one cannot help being struck by the apparent fact that neither of these gentlemen entirely trusted the other. That the distrust was not entirely groundless was proved when, as erelong happened, the entire correspondence found its way to the public.* The negotiations were finally broken off by Lord Metcalfe's departure from Canada, having come to nothing. "The whole affair suddenly collapsed, and the only result was to intensify the political atmosphere, and aggravate the quarrel between a weak Government and a powerful Opposition."†

As for the Governor, his disorder was working frightful ravages upon him, and he was literally dying by inches. By the beginning of October his articulation began to be affected, and there was a hole through the cheek into the interior of the mouth. He was threatened with total loss of sight, and was in a condition of constant physical suffering, unless when under the influence of powerful narcotics. It was evident to himself, as well as to all about him, that "it must soon become physically impossible for him to administer successfully the affairs of the Government."‡ To persist any longer in his determination to "stick to the ship" was out of the question. On the 29th of the month he wrote to Lord Stanley, "I am unable to entertain company or to receive visitors, and my official business with public functionaries is transacted at my resi-

---

*For additional light on this somewhat curious correspondence, see a pamphlet published at Montreal in 1846, entitled "Correspondence between the Hon. W. H. Draper and the Hon. R. E. Caron; and between the Hon. R. E. Caron and the Honourables L. H. Lafontaine and A. N. Morin, referred to in a recent debate in the Legislative Assembly. Containing many Suppressed Letters."

†See Fennings Taylor's "Portraits of British Americans," Vol. I., p. 322.

‡Kaye, Vol. II., p. 418.

dence in the country instead of the apartment assigned for that purpose in the public buildings in town. I am consequently concious that I am inadequately performing the duties of my office, and if there were time to admit of my being relieved before the setting in of the winter, I should think that the period had arrived when I might, perfectly in consistence with public duty, solicit to be relieved; but as the doctors say that I cannot be removed with safety from this place during the winter, and as that season is fast approaching, it becomes a question whether I can best perform my duty to my country by working on at the head of the Government to the best of my ability until the spring, or by delivering over my charge to other hands, and remaining here as a private individual until the season may admit of my return to Europe with safety. In this dilemma I have hitherto abstained from submitting my formal resignation of my office; and shall continue to report by each successive mail as to my condition and capability of carrying on the duties of my post." He had written to his Lordship a fortnight before this date, acquainting him with his sad condition, and before his letter of the 29th reached its destination, the Imperial Government, "with a full and hearty recognition of his services," had determined upon relieving him from the cares of office. "I need hardly say," wrote Lord Stanley on the 2nd of November, "that your administration of affairs in Canada has more than realized the most sanguine expectations which I had ventured to form of it; and you will retire from it, whenever you retire, with the entire approval and the admiration of Her Majesty's Government; and, I may venture to add, of the Queen herself. . . I enclose you an official letter accepting your resignation, which you will understand me as authorizing you to make use of, or not, as and when you may see fit." He was authorized to hand over the Government provisionally to Earl Cathcart—who had succeeded Sir Richard Jackson* as Com-

---

* Sir Richard died at Montreal in the month of June, 1845.

mander-in-Chief of the forces in British North America—whenever he might think fit. He felt himself to be a dying man, but was loath to desert what he deemed to be his duty while life remained to him. He determined to be guided in the matter by the advice of his Council. During the third week in November, having received Lord Stanley's letter of the 2nd, he summoned the principal members of the Executive to a conference at Monklands. He explained his condition to them, and expressed his willingness to remain at his post if they deemed it advisable in the interests of the country. The Councillors, with strong traces of emotion on their cheeks, begged him to resign without further delay, and to take such rest as was possible to one in his maimed and suffering condition. He acted upon their advice, and made preparations for his immediate departure for England. Having demitted his functions to Earl Cathcart, he set out from Montreal at ten o'clock in the morning of Wednesday, the 26th of the month. His departure, as was fitting, considering his melancholy condition, was unaccompanied by any conspicuous public demonstrations, although a large deputation, consisting of the mayor, aldermen and council of Montreal and a large body of the citizens accompanied him to the place of his embarkation on board the Laprairie steamer *Prince Albert*. The municipal dignitaries presented him with an address, to which he briefly responded. He evidently felt much moved, and his emotion was reflected in many a countenance in the crowd. It was felt that loud cheers would be unseemly on such an occasion, and there was no open-mouthed valedictory. The streets were lined with the troops from the Haymarket to the wharf. His Excellency, accompanied by his military secretary and one of his aides, took what was then the usual route by way of St. John's and Lake Champlain to Boston, where, on the 4th of December, he embarked for Liverpool on board the Cunard steamer *Britannia*. It is sad to say it, but a large section of the Opposition press in Canada would not let him depart in peace. He was assailed in language which even such violations of the constitution as those of which he had been guilty did not wholly justify, and which certainly might far better have been left unsaid. There can be no doubt that Lord Metcalfe felt these parting shafts very keenly. When subsequently referring to them in a conversation with his sister, he remarked that they had cut so deeply as to leave him neither power nor will to strike back.[*]

His Lordship reached Liverpool on the 16th of December. He took up his quarters in London, where nothing that surgical science and friendly sympathy could do for him was wanting. All that could be done, however, was very little. The terrible bodily anguish he endured, and the inevitable doom that lay before him, did not deprive him of perfect self-control. Never in his life had the balance of his mental equanimity been more admirably preserved. Quacks pestered him with letters containing accounts of wonderful and never-failing specifics for the dreadful malady which held him in its grasp. Begging-letter-writers besieged his doors, and applications for contributions to all sorts of charities lay in wait for him at all hours of the day. With a wise and discriminating benevolence he caused inquiries to be instituted into the merits of all applicants, and to the deserving he gave from his abundance. As the weeks passed by, kindly-worded addresses came to him from beyond the Atlantic —from the colony which he had left only to die. He was also the recipient of addresses signed by almost every distinguished man in the kingdom who had been concerned in the administration of East Indian affairs. In April it was apparent that his strength was failing, and he quitted London to draw his last breath in the pure air of the country. Malshanger, a quiet country-house in the neighbour-

---

[*] See "Lord Metcalfe's Canadian Administration," by J. M. Towle; Toronto, 1847; p. 9.

hood of Basingstoke, Hampshire, was taken for him, and there, in the society of his sister, Mrs. Smythe, he lived out the five sad months of life that remained to him. Sad, but not altogether sad, for down to his last hour he remained perfect master of himself. As the summer drew to a close, and he felt his end to be rapidly approaching, he sent for little Mary Higginson—a child of seven years—the daughter of the secretary who has already been mentioned in these pages. "I think," he remarked to the child's father, "the termination of my sufferings must now be close at hand. I desire to see Mary before it comes. Hitherto, on her account, I have denied myself the gratification; but now—go and fetch her to me." Two days later the child arrived. She remained with him a week. Every day during that interval, as she sat by his bedside, she read aloud to him from the volume which has brought comfort to so many sore-stricken hearts. "He received the glad tidings of salvation as a little child," says his biographer.* Feeling that he had not many more days to live, he sent the child away with her father, in order that she might not have the pain of being present at his death. Before Captain Higginson's return the end had come. "His mind was unclouded to the last. The serene expression of his countenance indicated that he was in perfect peace. The last sounds which reached him were the sweet strains of his sister's harp, rising in a hymn of praise to the Great Father, into one of the many mansions of whose house he believed that he was about to enter. 'How sweet those sounds are,' he was heard to whisper almost with his dying breath. He sank very gently to rest. About 8 o'clock on the evening of the 5th of September, 1846, with a calm sweet smile on his long-tortured face, Charles Theophilus, first and last Lord Metcalfe, rendered up his soul to his Maker."†

He lies in the family vault of the Metcalfes, in the parish church

---

* Kaye, Vol. II., p. 443.   † Ib., 445.

of Winkfield, near the estate of Fern Hill, from which he derived his title. The well-known epitaph, composed by Macaulay, and carved on a marble tablet, may be seen against the wall in the body of the church.*

Having never married, he left no heir to his title, and the Metcalfe peerage became extinct at his death.

Enough has been said, it is hoped, to render any elaborate summing up of Lord Metcalfe's character unnecessary. The writer of these pages has not scrupled to comment upon the disastrous results of his Lordship's Canadian Administration, and to point out the defects of training which made him unfit to preside over the Government of such a colony as our own. That he was ever sent to Canada is a circumstance greatly to be deplored. In his private capacity it is impossible to do justice to Lord Metcalfe without employing language of almost unstinted praise. No man ever went through life with better intentions, or had a more disinterested zeal for his country's welfare. No man was ever less of a self-seeker. Throughout his career he never hesitated to spend himself and his means for the good of his fellow-creatures. During the two years and eight months which elapsed between the time of his arrival in Canada and his departure, scarcely a week elapsed which was not signalized by some liberal benefaction on his part. Said Egerton

---

*This epitaph cannot be silently passed over with due regard to historical truth. Monumental inscriptions are seldom to be implicitly depended upon, and this one is not more accurate than the common run of such productions. It is said that

"In Canada, not yet recovered from the calamities of civil war,
He reconciled contending factions
To each other, and to the mother country."

It is simple historic justice to say that he did nothing of the kind. On the contrary, he greatly embittered "contending factions" against each other. Upon his arrival he found party-feeling very much quieted down. The quieting process had been going on during the whole of Sir Charles Bagot's tenure of office. Metcalfe not only revived old hostilities, but brought about a ferocity of party-strife such as had never existed before his interference in Canadian affairs.

Ryerson, in one of the famous letters already referred to, "He is not a fortune-seeker, but a fortune-spender." He contributed to the building of churches, to the erection of almshouses, to innumerable public charities, and to every good enterprise which was submitted to him. He had not been a fortnight in Canada when he thus wrote home to his sister: "My establishment will be larger and more expensive than it was in Jamaica. My official income is less. And as there it was not sufficient without aid from my private fortune, I must of course expect the same will be the case here, to a larger extent. This, however, is a matter of little consequence; and I wish that all others could be as easily managed."* Upon this principle he acted throughout the whole term of his Administration. In numberless instances he did not his alms before men, and scarcely permitted his left hand to know what his right hand did. Scores of his private charities have never come to light. A notable instance of his generosity has been made public by the recipient himself. Students of Upper Canadian history are familiar with the name of Colonel James Fitz Gibbon, who rendered efficient services to Sir Francis Head during the rebellion, and who wearied successive Administrations by repeated applications for pecuniary aid. Upon Sir Charles Metcalfe's arrival he found a recent application from the Colonel, together with other papers bearing upon his claims. His Excellency at once inquired into the merits of the case. He found that Colonel Fitz Gibbon had indeed rendered valuable services, but that he had received considerable recompense in one shape and another, and that there was no special reason why Government should make further grants. Sir Charles found, however, that the Colonel was really a gallant and deserving man, who stood greatly in need of assistance, and he determined to grant him aid out of his own purse. "I received," says Colonel Fitz Gibbon, "a note from Mr. Secretary Higginson, saying that his Excellency

---

Kaye, Vol. II., p. 327.

desired to see me. On presenting myself he told me that he had submitted to the Executive Council my application for an advance, and that they declined to advise him to make it. 'But,' added his Excellency, 'name to me a sum of money sufficient to relieve you from your most pressing emergencies, and I will advance it to you out of my own funds.' Surprised at this offer—for his Excellency had arrived but a few days before, and was, as yet, a stranger in the Province—I paused and said, 'Your Excellency's offer is so unexpected that, for a moment, I know not what sum to name; but it humbles me to have to tell your Excellency that last week a baker stopped his issue of bread to my family because I could not make immediate payment;' and I stated another fact which I will not mention here because its publication would wound the too sensitive mind of the person to whom it referred. After another pause I continued, 'If your Excellency will advance me one hundred pounds, it may be enough to keep me from severe pressure until the next session.' Whereupon he said, 'From the view I have taken of your case I do not think that sum enough.' Still more surprised I again paused, and said, 'Then I will say two hundred pounds, but I will go no further;' and the following morning I received a cheque for two hundred pounds."[*] Such was Sir Charles Metcalfe's princely way of dispensing charity. To Captain Higginson, whose official salary was only three hundred pounds a year, he granted a thousand pounds a year additional out of his own resources. At least half a score of almost equally conspicuous private benefactions might be mentioned as having signalized his residence in Canada. In the face of such truths as these, one can readily accept the statement of his biographer that "they who approached him the most nearly, who lived in the most familiar intercourse with him, and were admitted the most intimately within the influence of the habitual tenderness of his

---

[*] See "An Appeal to the People of the late Province of Upper Canada," by James Fitz Gibbon," p. 50 (Montreal, 1847).

nature and playfulness of his spirit were those not only to lavish upon him the truest love, but to regard him with the most genuine admiration."* The faults of his Canadian Administration, after all, were faults for which it is scarcely fair to hold him deeply responsible, for the dispensing of Responsible Government was a thing foreign to his nature and training, and his instructions from the Home Office were of a kind rather to confuse than to assist him. It was not consciously that he struck so heavy a blow against freedom, and in apportioning the blame which attaches to the transaction it is simple justice to bear in mind that he believed himself to be acting, not only within his strict constitutional rights, but for the lasting peace and welfare of the colony and the empire. Taking even the least charitable view of the conduct which marked his administration of our affairs, it stands out as a solitary blot upon an otherwise fair and stainless escutcheon, and we may well say of him, as Prince Henry said of the brave Percy :

> "Thy ignomy sleep with thee in the grave,
> But not remember'd in thy epitaph."

---

* Kaye, Vol. II., p. 453.

CHAPTER XX.

EARL CATHCART.

"As a general thing, military governors are not wanted in Canada. Sir John Colborne and Sir Francis Head gave us two more than we needed. The peculiar circumstances of the present time, however, render a military governor of wisdom and experience, like Lord Cathcart, not only acceptable but desirable."—CANADIAN, in the *Morning Chronicle*.

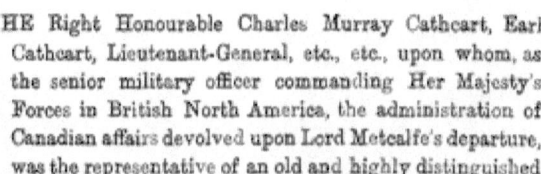HE Right Honourable Charles Murray Cathcart, Earl Cathcart, Lieutenant-General, etc., etc., upon whom, as the senior military officer commanding Her Majesty's Forces in British North America, the administration of Canadian affairs devolved upon Lord Metcalfe's departure, was the representative of an old and highly distinguished Scottish family. Sir Allan Cathcart, who bore the burden of the family honours in 1447, was ennobled in that year by King James the Second, who created him Baron Cathcart in the peerage of Scotland. The Baron's descendants have ever since been conspicuous members of the national aristocracy. One of them fell at Flodden in 1513; another on the field of Pinkie, in 1547. From the time of the union between England and Scotland down to the present there has been no important war involving the honour and arms of Great Britain in which a Cathcart has not borne a distinguished part. In 1807 the tenth Baron was Commander-in-Chief of the expedition to Copenhagen. Upon his return he was created Viscount Cathcart and Baron Greenock in the peerage of Great Britain. In 1814 he was advanced to an earldom. The future Governor-General of Canada was his second son, and was born at

Waltham, in the county of Essex, England, in 1783. As a boy he spent some time at Eton, but adopted the family profession of arms at an early age. It is no exaggeration to say of him that he added to the laurels of his ancestors. In 1799, when he was only fifteen, he formed part of the expedition to North Holland. He served under his father at Copenhagen in 1807, and subsequently fought his way all through the Peninsular War. At Barossa, Salamanca, Vittoria, and finally at Waterloo, he distinguished himself by deeds of valour, as well as by other high soldierly qualities, and stood high in the favour of the Great Duke. At Waterloo he had three horses shot under him, and on the same memorable day he bore the Marquis of Anglesea from the field in his arms when that nobleman received the wound which rendered necessary the amputation of his leg. He had by this time attained to the rank of a Colonel. For several years subsequent to the great battle he served with the army of occupation in France, and during that period received various honours and decorations, both British and foreign, including a Companionship of the Bath. There is no need for following him minutely through his subsequent career. Upon the death of his father, in 1843, he succeeded to the title as second Earl, his elder brother—known by courtesy as Lord Greenock—having died without issue during his father's lifetime. Upon the death of Sir Richard Jackson in the summer of 1845, Earl Cathcart, who had by this time attained the military rank of a Lieutenant-General, was appointed to succeed him, and came over to Canada accordingly. He had not been many months in the country ere Lord Metcalfe's departure compelled him to take upon himself the direction of affairs. He was sworn into office as Administrator, and assumed the reins of Government on the 26th of November, the day when Lord Metcalfe started on his homeward journey, as narrated in the last chapter.

It was at first supposed that Lord Cathcart's assumption of the

Administration was a mere temporary expedient until a successor to Lord Metcalfe should be appointed. The day of military governors was over, and it was not pretended that Lord Cathcart had any special fitness for discharging the functions of a civil administrator. Various rumours were afloat in Canadian political circles on the subject of Lord Metcalfe's successor. For a short time it was believed—apparently without any grounds whatever—that the Earl of St. Germans had solicited and obtained the appointment. Another equally well-founded report hailed Sir Henry Pottinger, whose civil experience, such as it was, had been gained at Hong Kong, as the coming man. The English mail which reached Canada about the end of January, however, brought definite intelligence on the subject of the Governor-Generalship. The appointment, in a word, was formally offered to Lord Cathcart, who at once signified his acceptance of it. Her Majesty's pleasure was conveyed to his Lordship in very complimentary terms, and he was officially assured that the uniting in his person of the civil and military authority was the result of no accidental combination of circumstances, but of a mature and deliberate conviction of his high qualifications for the administration of both. Notwithstanding this assurance, a belief began to gain ground that the Imperial Government had resolved to retain Lord Cathcart here in consequence of the relations between Great Britain and the United States having again become unsatisfactory. Rumours of war had once more become rife, and an unsettled, uncomfortable feeling pervaded the public mind. The causes which led to this ominous state of affairs will be explained in the following chapter. In the event of an actual rupture between the two nations it was of course highly desirable that one possessing the military knowledge and experience of Earl Cathcart should be at the head of affairs in Canada. That this was really the view taken by the authorities at home soon became evident enough. In the following April Earl Cathcart received his commission as Governor-

General.* Meanwhile, however, his Lordship, in his capacity of Administrator, summoned the Houses to meet on the 20th of March, on which day the second session of the Second Parliament accordingly assembled at Montreal for the despatch of business.

In the Speech from the Throne his Lordship informed the Houses that he had been designated as Her Majesty's future representative in the Province. Regret was expressed at the painful cause which had led to Lord Metcalfe's departure from Canada, and it was said that his Lordship had discharged the duties of his station with a zeal and ability that had on every occasion won for him " the highest approbation of his Sovereign, and the respect and gratitude of the people over whom he presided as her representative." The reorganization of the militia was strongly urged upon the consideration of the Houses, and they were informed that the unsettled state of the negotiations between the Imperial Government and the United States rendered such a reorganization imperative. "I feel," said his Excellency, "the most unbounded confidence that the loyalty and patriotism of every class of Her Majesty's subjects in Canada will be conspicuous, as they have been heretofore, should occasion call for their services to aid in the protection of their country; but a well-digested and uniform system is indispensable to give a fitting direction to the most zealous efforts. At the same time I feel warranted in assuring you that, while our gracious Sovereign will ever rely on the free and loyal attachment of her Canadian people for the defence of this Province and the maintenance of British connection, Her Majesty will be prepared, as her predecessors have always been, to provide with promptitude and energy corresponding with the power and resources of the Empire for the security of Her North American dominions." These very pertinent remarks were followed by a reference to the Civil List, as to which the Houses

---

* His commission bears date the 16th of March.

were recommended to make such provision as to justify the Imperial Parliament in making the requisite amendments to the Union Act. The recent change in the commercial policy of the empire was also glanced at, but only very briefly, as it was not yet known in Canada how much was involved in the change. The Corn Law Bill, then depending in the Imperial Parliament, had at this time passed its second reading only, and various opinions prevailed in Canada as to the merits of that measure, and as to how far the anti-protection feeling would go.

The resolutions in reply to the Speech were moved in the Legislative Council by the Hon. John Neilson, and seconded by the Hon. Barthelemi Joliette, on Monday, the 23rd. They were not permitted to pass without opposition. Mr. De Boucherville* declined to congratulate Earl Cathcart on his appointment, upon the ground that his Lordship was a member of the military profession, and that Lord Durham had recommended in his report that a civilian, and not a soldier, should have the direction of Canadian affairs. He further objected to the expressions of regret at the removal of Lord Metcalfe. The Hon. James Morris followed in the same strain. The Hon. Adam Ferrie took exception to the absence from the Speech of any reference to the subject of King's College. The resolutions, however, were finally put and passed seriatim, and the Address founded thereupon was reported and adopted. In the Assembly, the resolutions on which to found an Address in reply were moved by Colonel Prince and seconded by Mr. De Bleury. The Liberal party, as a whole, were of course unable to concur in the eulogistic remarks on Lord Metcalfe, and Mr. Baldwin moved an amendment in which those remarks were omitted, though no exception was taken to the expression of regret at the calamity which had been the direct cause of his Lordship's retirement. The motion was

---

* Mr. De Boucherville had been appointed to the Legislative Council just before the opening of the session of 1843.

seconded by Mr. Aylwin, who, in the course of his remarks, indulged in many caustic allusions to the President of the Council, Mr. Viger, whom he censured with much vehemence for retaining his seat in the Cabinet for so long a time without obtaining a seat in either branch of the Legislature. Mr. Viger replied at considerable length, his remarks being chiefly directed to indiscriminate eulogy of the character and policy of the late Governor. The debate lasted throughout the day, Messieurs Cauchon, Cameron, Gowan, Chauveau, Nelson, Boulton, John Sandfield Macdonald and others taking part in it. When the vote was taken the amendment was defeated by a majority of sixteen, the ayes being twenty-seven and the noes forty-three.

As the session advanced, however, it became evident that the vote on the Address afforded no indication of the actual strength of the Government. Several ministerial measures introduced at various times were actually defeated, and in one instance by a considerable majority. There was, however, no pretence of resignation on the part of the Ministry. They were afraid, as during the previous session, to introduce any legislation likely to arouse strong opposition, and only did so when such a course could not be avoided. Fortunately for them, several important measures introduced under ministerial auspices were of a character which commended them to the general approval of the Assembly. Such especially were the Militia Bill and the Act respecting the Civil List. The former was acceptable owing to the threatening aspect of affairs between the mother country and the United States. The latter was popular because it was a long step in the direction of Canadian self-government. The subject had already engaged the attention of the Canadian Parliament more than once since the Union, and the Act was the result of correspondence entered into between Sir Charles Metcalfe and the Secretary of State prior to the rupture between the former and his Government in 1843. The desirable object sought to be attained was the establishment of a permanent Civil List for the payment of public functionaries, in place of that imposed by the Imperial Parliament in the Union Act. The latter had provided a Civil List which, although in accordance with the conditions agreed to by the Upper Canadian Legislature and the Special Council of Lower Canada, was held by the Liberal party to be unconstitutional. It was finally agreed that the United Parliament should vote a Civil List. After considerable discussion as to matters of detail the Bill was passed, but it was of course reserved for the signification of Her Majesty's pleasure. The sequel may as well be told here. Owing to the repugnance between the Bill and the Act of Union, it was not competent for Her Majesty to assent to the former without the express authority of the Imperial Parliament. An Act was accordingly passed* in 1847 to enable her to assent, and the Canadian measure of 1846 became the law of the land. From that time forward the Provincial Parliament alone had authority to impose taxes upon the Canadian people.

During the third week of the session Mr. Lafontaine laid before the Assembly the correspondence already referred to as having taken place between Attorney-General Draper, the Hon. R. E. Caron, and himself. Mr. Caron had given a very reluctant consent to Mr. Lafontaine's making the circumstances public in this way, and he soon afterwards published the correspondence himself in pamphlet form, both in English and French.† The matter formed the subject of a very warm debate, and Mr. Lafontaine was strongly censured by the ministerialists for bringing the matter thus publicly before the country. The only effect of its introduction was to embarrass the Ministry, and to lead to doubts on the part of the

---

* See Imperial Statute 10 and 11 Vic., cap. 71, intituled "An Act to authorize Her Majesty to assent to a certain Bill of the Legislative Council and Assembly of Canada for granting a Civil List to Her Majesty, and to repeal certain parts of an Act for reuniting the Provinces of Upper and Lower Canada, and for the Government of Canada."

† Ante, p. 22, note.

French members as to Mr. Draper's sincerity in opening the correspondence. Mr. Viger felt his position very keenly,* though he claimed to have been cognizant of the proposed arrangement, and to have been willing to resign his office. There were references also to the Attorney-General for Lower Canada, and to the Commissioner of Crown Lands, which must have been far from palatable to those gentlemen.

As the weeks passed by, and as it became more and more evident that the Corn Law Bill would receive the sanction of the Imperial Parliament, a pretty general feeling of alarm and hostility to that measure was aroused in the bosom of the mercantile community in Canada. At public meetings held in Montreal and Quebec, "Cobden and the League" were denounced in no stinted terms. It was feared lest the proposed abolition of the differential duties on the importation of colonial and foreign grain into Great Britain would, if carried out, give a serious if not a fatal blow to Canadian prosperity. Canada, it was said, could not hope to compete with the United States if the British market was made equally free to both. The solicitude on this subject found expression in an address to the Queen, agreed to by the Assembly on the 12th of May, and forwarded to the Home Government by the next mail. It was received by the Colonial Secretary† while the debate on the famous Bill was actually in progress. The argument from the protectionist side was presented with remarkable clearness. "We cannot but fear," ran the Address, "that the abandonment of this protective principle, the very basis of the colonial commercial system, is not only calculated materially to retard the agricultural improvement

---

* One of Mr. Draper's letters to Mr. Caron contained a reference to Mr. Viger in the following language:—"I will not conceal from you . . that I have long viewed his [Mr. Viger's] retirement from the position he occupies as essential to the strengthening of the Government. The mode of effecting it is another consideration."—See letter of November 19th.

† Mr. Gladstone, who had succeeded Lord Stanley.

of the country, and check its hitherto rising prosperity, but seriously
to impair our ability to purchase the manufactured goods of Great
Britain; a result alike prejudicial to this colony and the parent
state. . . We respectfully represent to your Majesty that, situated
as Canada is, and with a climate so severe as to leave barely one-
half of the year open for intercourse by the St. Lawrence with the
mother country, the cost of transporting her products to market is
much greater than is paid by the inhabitants of the United States;
and that without a measure of protection, or some equivalent
advantage, we cannot successfully compete with that country." The
most gloomy consequences were foreshadowed in subsequent clauses,
and there can be no doubt that Canadian merchants generally were
thoroughly alarmed. Even those—and their number was very
small in the year 1846—who professed faith in the general principles
of free-trade, could not see how their interests could fail to suffer,
however greatly the British manufacturer might be benefited by
the change. Of course the obnoxious measure passed, and the
gloomy forebodings of the petitioners were not realized, but there
was for a time a very disturbed state of feeling in Canadian commercial circles, and perhaps a certain weakening of patriotic sentiment, even on the part of colonists who had always been conspicuous
for loyalty.

Among other important public measures passed during the session
were an Act to amend the Upper Canada School Act of 1843; an
Act amending an Act of the previous session respecting elementary education in Lower Canada; an Act to amend the Bankrupt
Laws; and an Act respecting improvements in the Gulf of St. Lawrence. The session extended over eleven weeks, and was brought
to a close on the 9th of June. Earl Cathcart, not only during
the sitting of Parliament, but throughout the entire term of his
Administration, displayed a wise discretion in interfering as little
as possible in civil affairs. He kept a watchful eye upon the

military forces, and introduced some important reforms among the troops. He kept entirely aloof from the disputes of the rival political parties, and confined himself to formally administering such functions as necessarily came within his province as Governor-General.

Six days after the close of the session all danger of immediate complications with the United States came to an end. On the 15th of June the Oregon Treaty was signed at Washington, and another vexed question was set at rest—for a time.

Chapter XXI.

THE OREGON BOUNDARY.

"By the Ashburton Treaty we gave up one-half of the territory in dispute, but by the next Treaty—the Oregon Treaty—we gave up the whole. In both cases, Canada reminds us of a rabbit or a dog in the hands of an experimental anatomist. Like animals doomed to vivisection for the benefit of science, she has been operated upon unsparingly for the good of the Empire. Diplomatic doctors, in constantly recurring succession, have given her up, and given her over. She has been the victim of an endless exhibition of Treaties, applied allopathically, and then, by force of counter-irritants, has been *treated* nigh unto death."—QUIRKS OF DIPLOMACY; a Paper read before the Literary and Scientific Society of Ottawa, January 22nd, 1874, by Lieut.-Col. Coffin.[*]

OF what precise nature was this cloud, considerably larger than a man's hand, which for some time prior to 1846 had gradually been overshadowing the diplomatic relations between Great Britain and the United States; which had several times seemed to be on the point of bursting, and thereby overwhelming Canada in an inundating and at least temporarily desolating flood?

In the tenth chapter of this work—a chapter devoted to an exposition of the Ashburton Treaty—it has been seen that the boundary between the British possessions and the United States to the west of the Rocky Mountains did not form a subject of negotiation between Lord Ashburton and Daniel Webster in 1842.[†] That boundary had long been a theme for diplomacy

---

[*] This paper, which was published at Montreal in pamphlet form in 1874, was reprinted, with some modifications, in the *Canadian Monthly* for May, 1876, under the title of "How Treaty-Making unmade Canada." See *ante*, p. 210, *note*.

[†] *Ante*, p. 205.

4

between the two nations directly concerned, and if wise counsels had prevailed it would have been settled once for all during the early years of the century. Twenty years before the signing of the Ashburton Treaty the Oregon boundary had produced so great a feeling of irritation in England that Lord Castlereagh had told Mr. Rush, the American Minister in London, that war could be produced by the holding up of a finger. Happily the occasion passed by without any elevation of the portentous finger, and the public in both countries were permitted for a brief season to forget or ignore the ground of dispute. From time to time, however, "the Oregon question" continued to disturb the harmony of international relations, and scarcely was the Ashburton Treaty ratified ere the clamour burst forth in the United States with greater vehemence than ever before. There was much swagger and loud talk, which might well be taken simply for what they were worth, but beneath and behind them were the exigencies of the Democratic party, and at the time of Lord Metcalfe's departure from Canada the alternative apparently lay between an immediate peaceful settlement and "grim-visag'd war." It is worth while to review the historical aspect of the question.

The country known at the present day by the name of Oregon is merely one of the Pacific States of the American Union, with an area of about 95,000 square miles. But at the period when "the Oregon territory" first became the subject of international dispute it consisted of an immense tract, embracing the entire region extending from the Rocky Mountains on the east to the Pacific Ocean on the west, and from a line adjacent to the Russian possessions on the north to 42° north latitude on the south. So far as can now be ascertained, the first European to set foot upon the territory enclosed within the limits above specified was that "bold discoverer in an unknown sea," Sir Francis Drake, who, in the year 1578, landed a short distance to the northward of the present site of

San Francisco. He took nominal possession in the name of his sovereign, Queen Elizabeth, and erected a pillar to commemorate that event. He christened the land New Albion, by which name it continued to be called by writers and geographers for considerably more than two hundred years.* So far, then, as priority of title can be conferred by priority of discovery, the title of England was perfect; for, although several enterprising Spanish navigators had preceded Sir Francis Drake into the Pacific Ocean, none of them had penetrated so far north as latitude 42°. How far Sir Francis sailed northward during this voyage has been disputed, but there seems good reason for believing that he coasted as far as 48°.† A succession of Spaniards, and other navigators in the Spanish service, followed in his track. It was at one time alleged on behalf of Spain that a mariner named Ferrelo had coasted to nearly the 43rd degree of latitude so early as 1543, but the account of his voyage is not well authenticated, and it is not even pretended that he went ashore. In any case, such rights of ownership as attach to early discovery were confined to England and Spain, no other nation having any shadow of claim whatever.

But discovery alone has been held not to confer a complete title in such a case. There must be something in the way of settlement before a claim can be set up which other nations are bound to

---

* "This barren sovereignty was soon forgotten, but the name of *New Albion* remained; and it was not till about 1832 that it began, as Mr. Greenhow tells us, to be called *Oregon*, from a name vaguely attributed by Carver, in his Travels (published 1778), to some 'Great River in the West,' which had been recently, and without any better authority that we can discover, applied to the Columbia." – *Quarterly Review*, Vol. LXXVII., p. 569. The Mr. Greenhow referred to was an American author who wrote several works relating to the Oregon territory.

† "There has been a vast deal of controversy raised by the Americans on this point; they insist that Drake reached no higher than 43°, instead of 48°; and this because one anonymous account of his voyage, interpolated into Hakluyt, says 43° by, probably, an error of the press or the copyist, while the authentic account published from the notes of Drake's chaplain, by his nephew, and repeated by all his companions and contemporaries, gives the true reading of 48°." *Quarterly Review*, Vol. LXXVII., p. 569.

respect; and neither Spain nor England took any steps towards settling the remote and savage land until more than two hundred years after Drake's discovery. There can be no doubt that any other nation might legitimately have settled and claimed it during the interval. As matter of fact, however, no such settlement or claim was made.

There is no authentic record of any voyage having been made by Spanish explorers between the years 1640 and 1774. In the year last named one Juan Perez, a Spaniard, sailed from San Blas, on the western coast of Mexico, and, standing out to sea, proceeded northward, and approached the land in latitude 55° north. It is presumed that he discovered the spot subsequently named by Captain Cook Nootka Sound. He did not go ashore, being prevented by tempestuous weather. No account of this voyage was given to the world until 1802, so that the Spanish Government " deprived itself of the means of establishing beyond question the claim of Perez to the discovery." * In 1775 the Spanish Government sent out an expedition consisting of two vessels, the *Santiago* and the *Senora*, under the command respectively of Don Bruno Heceta and one Ayala. After the expedition had started, Ayala was succeeded in the command by Don Juan Francisco de la Bodega y Quadra, and soon afterwards the two vessels parted company. Bodega proceeded as far north as 58°, and surveyed the coast of what is now Alaska. Heceta advanced as far north as 49° 30′, and then turned back. On the 15th of August, having, as he said, reached latitude 46° 17′, he noticed an opening in the coast, from which issued a current so strong as to prevent him from entering. Being convinced from this fact that the opening was the mouth of some great river, he set down his assumption on his chart, naming the supposed stream the Rio St.

---

* See "The History of Oregon and California, and the other Territories on the North-West Coast of America." By Robert Greenhow, Librarian to the Department of the United States. Boston, 1844. P. 117.

Roe. It was in reality the mouth of the Columbia river, and this, so far as is known, is the first intimation of its existence. Spain, however, being either timorous or jealous, preserved a rigid silence as to the voyages of Bodega and Heceta, as she had previously done with respect to the voyage of Perez. It is worth while to note that the correct latitude of the mouth of the Columbia is 46° 10′ and not 46° 17′, so that Heceta was somewhat out in his reckoning.

In 1778 Captain James Cook explored the west coast of North America on behalf of Great Britain, and made the first important survey of the shore of New Albion. He made the coast in latitude 44° north on the 7th of March. Proceeding northward he passed the mouth of the Columbia without perceiving it. He entered Nootka Sound, and bestowed upon it its name. It would be tedious and uninstructive to chronicle the subsequent voyages made by English and Spanish navigators along the Pacific coast. By degrees a certain amount of trade in furs and other commodities sprang up between English and Spanish merchants and the natives on the coast and on the neighbouring islands. Ten years after Captain Cook's visit Nootka Sound had become a sort of rendezvous for vessels engaged in trade hereabouts. The English were especially enterprising, and began to establish trading stations. This was displeasing to the Spanish Government, who determined to put a stop to British operations in that part of the world. Nootka Sound was farther north than Drake had penetrated, and Spain accordingly claimed authority over it by virtue of the alleged discovery by Perez in 1774. But, even admitting the discovery of Perez, it had not been proclaimed to the world, nor had it been followed by settlement. It was therefore no bar to the enterprise of other nations. Spain, however, appears to have entertained a contrary opinion. She carried matters with a high hand, and seized several British vessels at Nootka. Great Britain of course demanded restoration and reparation, and her demands were ultimately complied with. There is no necessity for pursuing the history of maritime exploration any farther, nor for discussing the rival claims of the two countries. Such rights as they possessed were settled by what is known as the Nootka Convention, the result of which was a treaty signed at the Escurial on the 28th of October, 1790. By the third article of this treaty it was agreed that the respective subjects of the contracting parties should not be molested in navigating or carrying on their fisheries in the Pacific Ocean or in the South Seas, or in landing on the coasts of those seas, in places not already occupied, for the purpose of conducting their commerce with the natives of the country, or of making settlements there. The right of the British Government to make settlements was thus established with sufficient distinctness,* and from that time forward Spain made no serious attempts at settlement within the limits of New Albion. It is therefore not extravagant to infer that the country was abandoned by Spain in favour of Great Britain.

So far, then, as to the respective claims of Spain and Great Britain. No other nation was interested in the question, or claimed any right to interfere in it.†

By the treaty ratified at Paris on the 3rd of September, 1783,

---

* "This convention was an admission of the right of the British Government to make settlements, and the right sanctioned is not to be distinguished from that of Russia to its settlements on the north-west coast. The admission of this right was not granted as a license, liable to be revoked or lost by a war—it was not made as a favour or concession. It is one of those agreements respecting territory—such, for instance, as the treaty of 1783, made between Great Britain and the United States—which a war does not revoke. The admission contained in the convention is of a principle to which the States of America, the colony of Canada and the State of Louisiana, owe their existence. No new doctrine was set up. An old-established rule was recognized, and a war would have been the result if it had continued to be contested."—See "The Oregon Question; or, A Statement of the British Claims to the Oregon Territory, in Opposition to the Pretensions of the Government of the United States of America ; with a Chronological Table and a Map of the Territory." By Thomas Falconer, Esq., Barrister-at-Law, of Lincoln's Inn, member of the Royal Geographical Society, etc. New York (reprint), 1845 ; p. 17.

† "As no other power then laid any claim to the territory, or protested against this mode of dividing it, their respective rights, thus limited and defined, were good against the world." *North American Review*, Vol. LXII., p. 237.

between Great Britain and the United States, whereby the independence of the latter was confirmed, the northwestern, western and southern boundary-line of "the new nation" was indicated as "a line through the middle of Lake Erie until it arrives at the water communication between that lake and Lake Huron; thence along the middle of the said water communication into the Lake Huron; thence through the middle of the said lake to the water communication between that lake and Lake Superior; thence through Lake Superior, northward of the Isles Royal and Philipeaux, to the Long Lake; thence through the middle of the Long Lake and the water between it and the Lake of the Woods, to the Lake of the Woods; thence through the said lake to the most northwestern point thereof; and from thence, on a due west course, to the River Mississippi; thence by a line drawn along the middle of the said River Mississippi, until it shall intersect the northernmost part of the 31st degree of north latitude—south, by a line to be drawn due east from the determination of the line last mentioned in the latitude 31 degrees north of the equator to the middle of River Apalachicola or Catahouche; thence along the middle thereof to its junction with the Flint River; thence straight to the head of the St. Mary's River, and thence along the middle of the St. Mary's River to the Atlantic Ocean."

No geographer of the present day needs to be informed that the boundary thus indicated was an impossible one, inasmuch as the head waters of the Mississippi River are south of the Lake of the Woods, and, consequently, a line carried due west from the lake would not touch the river. What was evidently intended, however, was that the boundary should lie at the place where the Mississippi, if it had had its rise farther to the north, would have been intersected by a line running due west from the Lake of the Woods.* The only concern we have with this erroneous boundary

---

* "But nothing west or north of this line was granted by Great Britain to the United

is to show that the United States acquired no rights over the Oregon territory by virtue of the treaty of 1783.

On the 6th of January, 1791, Captain Vancouver, a British officer, sailed from Deptford, in the *Discovery*, for the northwest coast of America, to take possession of Nootka Sound under the first article of the convention with Spain of the previous year. Having reached the west coast he proceeded very deliberately, making such surveys as he deemed advisable. On the 27th of April, 1792, he was off the mouth of what was afterwards called the Columbia river, but he had no idea of the proximity of a stream of such dimensions. He could perceive from the colour of the water that some stream entered the ocean there, but it did not appear to him to be large enough to admit of his entering it in a vessel of the size of the *Discovery*, so he continued his course to the northward. Two days later he encountered the United States ship *Columbia*, from Boston, commanded by Captain Robert Gray. The latter informed him that he, Gray, had been off the mouth of a river in latitude 46° 10′, "where the outset or reflux was so strong as to prevent his entering it for nine days." This was the mouth of the identical stream passed by the *Discovery* on the 27th. Vancouver was under special instructions to look out for "considerable inlets" and "large rivers,"* and ought to have had the wisdom to turn back on the strength of Captain Gray's information. He did not do so, however, but continued his course northward. On the 4th of June, having reached his original destination, he took possession, with the usual formalities, "of all that part of New Albion from the latitude 39° 20′ to the entrance of the inlet of the sea said to be the supposed Strait of Juan de Fuca, as also of all

---

States in 1783, and nothing north of the head waters of the Mississippi was retained by France under the treaty of 1763."—See "The Oregon Treaty," etc., *ubi supra*, p. 7.

* See "A Voyage of Discovery to the North Pacific Ocean and Round the World, in which the Coast of Northwest America has been carefully examined and accurately surveyed," etc., etc., by George Vancouver. London, 1798; Vol. I., p. 61.

the coasts, islands, etc., within the said strait and both its shores." Meanwhile Captain Gray had returned to the mouth of the great stream into which he had in vain essayed to find an entrance before. This time he was more successful. At daybreak on the 11th of May he ran his ship through the breakers, and ascended the estuary of the river about ten miles. This is almost certainly the first instance of that stream having been entered by civilized man.* He subsequently proceeded a few miles farther up the river, but "having taken the wrong channel," he could ascend no higher, and after a few days spent in filling his water-casks and trading with the natives he returned to the Pacific, having first bestowed upon the river the name of his vessel, which it has ever since borne.

Vancouver, with his vessel, returned to the spot in the following October, accompanied by Lieutenant Broughton, in the *Chatham*,† which was considerably smaller than the *Discovery*. The latter was unable to enter the river, but the *Chatham*, with Lieutenant Broughton, made her way in on the 20th of the month. In an interior angle of the harbour Broughton encountered the *Jenny*, of Bristol, under the command of Captain James Baker, who had been detained there by the state of the weather and the difficulties of exit for several weeks. Baker claimed to have been there earlier in the year. The pretence afterwards set up, however, that he had entered the mouth of the river before Captain Gray, has long since been given up. Lieutenant Broughton took his vessel considerably farther up stream than Gray had been, and then, finding the navigation intricate, anchored and took to his boats, wherein he ascended nearly a hundred miles farther. He "took possession" of the country in the name of his Sovereign, and "with the consent of the natives."

---

* See " The Oregon Question Examined, in respect to Facts and the Law of Nations ;" by Travers Twiss, D.C.L., F.R.S.; London, 1846; p. 136.

† Broughton, with the *Chatham*, had accompanied Vancouver from England, and formed part of the expedition.

It is thus clear that the discovery of the Columbia river was progressive. "Heceta noticed the discoloured water of the sea; . . Vancouver noticed the river outside the bar; Gray noticed the river within the bar; and Broughton explored both the bay and the river."*

So much for exploration from the sea-board. But there were also explorations from the landward side. In 1768, Captain Jonathan Carver, a native of Stillwater, Connecticut, and a British subject, explored the upper waters of the Missouri, and bestowed the Indian name of Oregon upon some great river in the west.† No very strong claim, however, can be established on the strength of Carver's expedition. In 1792-'93 Mr. (afterwards Sir) Alexander Mackenzie, a Scottish Canadian and an officer of the North-West Fur Company, made the first overland journey to the Pacific. He discovered the stream now called Fraser's river, and so far as can now be ascertained was the first white man to make any considerable exploration of the Oregon Territory. In 1800 Mr. David Thompson, of Montreal, a geological and geographical surveyor and astronomer in the employ of the Hudson's Bay Company, crossed the Rocky Mountains in latitude 51° north, and descended one of the great northern branches of the Columbia. Seven years later, having meanwhile transferred his services to the North-West Company, he established a fortified trading-post near the source of the Columbia; and within the next two or three years he established several other trading-posts on the main stream and some of its branches. One of the earliest and most important of the posts established by Thompson was on a sheet of water called Fraser's Lake.

The first overland expedition on the part of the United States was that of Captains Lewis and Clarke, who were commissioned in 1805 by President Jefferson "to explore the river Missouri, and its

---

* *Westminster Review*, Vol. XLV., p. 433. † *Ante*, p. 43, *note*.

principal branches, and then to seek and trace to its termination some stream, whether the Columbia, the Oregon, the Colorado, or any other which might offer the most direct water communication across the continent for the purpose of commerce." They crossed the Rocky Mountains, and in due course struck a branch of the Columbia, which they followed to its confluence with the main stream, and thence proceeded downward to the Pacific. In 1808 a Missouri Company established a post on one of the tributaries of the Columbia, but were soon compelled to abandon it, owing to the hostility of the Indians and the difficulty of obtaining supplies. In 1810 a great fur company was formed under the auspices of John Jacob Astor, of New York. During the following year they established a post at the mouth of the Columbia, on the south bank. In honour of Mr. Astor this post was named Astoria. The company consisted of ten persons, six of whom were subjects of Great Britain. The latter were assured by the British representative at Washington that they would be respected as British subjects and merchants in case of war. When David Thompson visited Astoria in July, 1811, he found the British flag flying there. In 1813 the company sold out to the (British) North-West Company, and towards the close of that year a British marine officer, acting under orders from his Government, took possession of the post in the name of the King, and hoisted the British ensign.*

In 1815, after the close of the war between Great Britain and the United States, application was made by the Government of the latter to that of the former for the restoration of Astoria under the first article of the Treaty of Ghent, by which it was agreed that all territory, places and possessions whatsoever taken by either party from the other during the war, except certain islands, should be restored without delay. To this demand Great Britain replied that

---

* Great Britain and the United States were then at war, and the sale of Astoria to British subjects was effected for the purpose of preventing it from being captured.

Astoria did not come within the article of the treaty, that post never having been captured. It had simply been sold to the North-West Company, and the vendors had vacated the place under a distinct agreement of sale. The post, however, was very foolishly surrendered to the United States, upon the understanding that the question of the title to the territory should be discussed in the negotiation on limits and other matters, which was soon to be commenced.*

On the question of discovery and occupation from overland, then, we find that "the expedition of Mackenzie was the first made by civilized men through the country west of the Rocky Mountains; and the settlement made by Thompson, on Fraser's Lake, was the first settlement or post of any kind made by British subjects, or by civilized men, west of the same mountains."† These explorations undoubtedly gave Great Britain a title to certain territory, but the difficulty was to know precisely *what* territory. To how much land could she lay claim? There is no precise rule as to definite limits where the land discovered and settled upon forms part of a vast continent. The question was doubtless an embarrassing one; but it was surely plain enough that Great Britain, by right of the explorations and settlements of Mackenzie and Thompson, could justly claim *some* title to the country watered by the Columbia river.

In 1803 the United States purchased Louisiana from France for the sum of $11,000,000. The territory so purchased included all lands "on the east side of the Mississippi River not then belonging to the United States, as far as the great chain of mountains which

---

* "Was ever such a position taken up by the Government of a nation having the least pretence to power or self-esteem? And how could it be wondered at that after this the Americans have really brought themselves to believe that they have a just and rightful claim to the territory in dispute."—"The Oregon Question: A Glance at the respective claims of Great Britain and the United States to the territory in dispute." By G. F. Ruxton, Esq.; London, 1846; p. 26.

† *Westminster Review*, Vol. XLV., p. 435.

divide the waters running into the Pacific and those falling into the Atlantic Ocean; and from the said chain of mountains to the Pacific Ocean, between the territory claimed by Great Britain on the one side and by Spain on the other."* There was no indication as to where the boundary-line from the chain of mountains was to begin, nor as to where the land "between the territory claimed by Great Britain on the one side and by Spain on the other" was to be found.†

By the Florida Treaty, signed at Washington on the 22nd of February, 1819, Spain ceded to the United States all her rights and claims to the country lying west of the Rocky Mountains. The western boundary was fixed at the River Sabine to the 32nd degree of latitude; thence due north to the Rio Roxo or the Red River of Nachitoches; thence westward along this river to the degree longitude 100 west from London (? Greenwich) and 23 from Washington; thence due north to the River Arkansas; thence to its source in 42° latitude; or if the source is north or south of latitude 42°, along a line due north or south until it meets the parallel of latitude 42°; and thence along this parallel to the Pacific. "Thus," says Mr. Falconer, "was the undefined line from the Rocky Mountains to the Pacific inserted in the agreement for the purchase of Louisiana converted into a defined line." ‡

Such, divested of a multitudinous array of more or less congruous facts, are the principal grounds upon which Great Britain and the United States respectively laid claim to the Oregon territory. It will be seen that the question was by no means free from ambiguity;

---

* "History of the Federal Government," by Alden Bradford, LL.D., Editor of the Massachusetts State Papers. Boston, 1840, p. 130.

† "France had nothing to sell but what constituted Louisiana after the cession made to Great Britain in 1763. There was nevertheless inserted in this treaty of sale a reference to a perfectly undefined line to the Pacific having no defined point of commencement, and referring to territory having no definable boundary either on the north, or the south, or the east."—See "The Oregon Question," by Thomas Falconer, ubi supra, p. 7.

‡ Ib., p. 8.

that neither party could lay claim to an absolute title to the whole, and that something approaching to a case might be made out for either or both. Each claimed the territory by right of prior discovery, and also by right of prior occupation. Britain's claim to discovery was by virtue of Drake's early explorations, and on the strength of those of Cook, Vancouver, Broughton, Mackenzie, Thompson and others. Her claim on the strength of prior occupation and settlement arose out of the posts established by the Hudson's Bay and North-West Company's officers. The United States answered these claims by alleging that Drake was a mere pirate, and that in any case his discovery was not followed by settlement; that at the time of the Nootka Convention Spain had at least equal rights with those of Great Britain in respect of the disputed territory; that she had retained those rights, and only admitted Great Britain's participation therein; that Spain had subsequently, by the Treaty of Florida, placed the United States in the same position as that in which she herself had previously been; that the explorations of Gray by seaboard and of Lewis and Clarke by land entitled them to claim by right of discovery on their own account, and that the founding of Astoria gave them a right by virtue of prior occupation. They also contended that their purchase of Louisiana from France gave them additional rights—although as simple matter of fact Louisiana had never extended beyond the Rocky Mountains. Some of the grounds of claim made on behalf of the United States were utterly absurd and inconsistent with each other.

The only thing standing out as a clear fact is that this Oregon question was essentially a matter for compromise. As such Great Britain was always prepared to regard it. Precisely how much of the territory, whether on the coast or inland, was to be apportioned to each claimant was manifestly not to be decided by any well-settled principles of international law. The settlement must evidently be arbitrary. Should it be by force of arms or by peaceable negotiation?

The latter method was repeatedly resorted to. On the 20th of October, 1818, a treaty was ratified between Great Britain and the United States whereby it was agreed that the 49th parallel of latitude should be the boundary from the Lake of the Woods to the Rocky Mountains, and that the country westward of the Rocky Mountains should be free and open for the term of ten years from the date of the convention to the vessels, citizens, and subjects of both powers, without prejudice to the claims of either country. The question by this time was practically narrowed down to the ownership of the territory lying between the mouth of the Columbia and the 49th parallel. Certain cantankerous citizens of the republic repudiated this curtailment of the ground of discussion, and denied the right of Great Britain to maintain any foothold whatever on this continent to the west of the Rocky Mountains; but the United States, as a nation, did not at that date endorse such an absurdity. As for Great Britain, she believed herself to be entitled to claim the territory as far south as latitude 42°, but did not deem it worth while to complicate the discussion by rigidly insisting upon the uttermost rood. The great river seemed to be a natural boundary, and it would give her all that was essential to the due maintenance of her sovereignty and prosperity on the Pacific. Actuated by this spirit of liberality, she in 1824 proposed "an equitable compromise"—viz., that the boundary between the two countries west of the Rocky Mountains should be the 49th parallel of latitude from the mountains to the north-eastern branch of the Columbia river, called in that part of its course McGillivray's river; thence along the middle of that stream to the main body of the Columbia; thence along the middle of the Columbia to the Pacific—the navigation of the river remaining perpetually free to both nations. "This proposition had the advantage of giving effect to the strongest local claims of both parties: it left to England the Upper Columbia, which she had first explored; it gave to the United States Clarke's and Lewis's rivers, which they had first explored; and it divided between them the Lower Columbia and the estuary, including Astoria, where Gray, and Broughton, and Thompson, and Lewis had all partial claims of discovery and exploration."[*] This proposal, though "it gave to the Americans the larger and richer half of the territory,"[†] was rejected, as it gave them no harbour. Two years later Britain improved on her former proposal, and paid due respect to the desire of the United States for a harbour. She submitted the following terms of accommodation: "That, considering that the possession of a safe and commodious post on the north-west coast of America, fitted for the reception of large ships, may be an object of great interest and importance to the United States, and that no such port is to be found between the 42nd degree of latitude and the Columbia river, Great Britain, in still adhering to that river as a basis, is willing so far to modify her former proposal as to concede, as far as she is concerned, to the United States the possession of Port Discovery, a most valuable harbour on the southern coast of De Fuca's inlet; and to annex thereto all that tract of country comprised within a line to be drawn from Cape Flattery along the southern shore of De Fuca's Inlet to Point Wilson, at the north-western extremity of Admiralty Inlet; from thence along the western shore of that inlet, across the entrance of Hood's Inlet, to the point of land forming the north-eastern extremity of the said inlet; from thence along the eastern shore of that inlet to the extremity of the same; from thence direct to the southern point of Gray's Harbour; from thence along the shore of the Pacific to Cape Flattery, as before mentioned." This proposal met with no better fate than its predecessor. It was briefly "declined with thanks."

---

[*] *Quarterly Review*, Vol. LXXVII., pp. 595, 596.
[†] "Quirks of Diplomacy," *ubi supra*, p. 15.

THE HON. ISAAC BURPEE.

SCENE ON THE RAT RIVER MENNONITE RESERVATION, MANITOBA.

From a Sketch by His Excellency the Earl of Dufferin.

SIR ALBERT J. SMITH.

KING'S COLLEGE, WINDSOR.

Negotiations were from time to time renewed, but no mutually satisfactory arrangement was arrived at. On the 6th of August, 1827, another treaty was concluded, whereby the period of ten years mentioned in the treaty of 1818 was indefinitely extended, with the stipulation that either party might terminate the arrangement by giving to the other twelve months' notice. Occasional attempts to bring the matter to a final settlement were still made, but nothing came of them. The Ashburton Treaty left the subject precisely where it was.

During the year 1843 a Bill for the occupation and military organization of Oregon was brought before the Congress of the United States, and it was therein set forth that "the title of the United States to the territory of Oregon is certain, and will not be abandoned." The Bill, after strong opposition, passed the Senate, but when it reached the House of Representatives it had to be abandoned for the time, owing to an adverse report of the Committee on Foreign Affairs. Meanwhile a considerable stream of emigration began to flow into the disputed territory from the Eastern States, and the national pretensions began to perceptibly enlarge. President Tyler, in his Message to Congress in December, 1843, laid claim, on behalf of the United States, to the entire territory on the Pacific lying between 42° and 54° 40′. In 1844, Mr. Pakenham, British Minister at Washington, had numerous conferences on the subject with John C. Calhoun, Secretary of State to the republic. A great deal of official correspondence passed between them, and the claims on each side were very fully stated, but no definite agreement could be arrived at. In August the following proposal was formally made by the British Minister:—"Whereas the proposals made on both sides in the course of the last negotiation have been mutually declined, Her Majesty's Government are prepared, in addition to what has already been offered on the part of Great Britain, and in proof of their earnest desire to arrive at an arrangement suitable to the interests and wishes of both parties, to undertake to make free to the United States any port or ports which the United States Government may desire either on the mainland, or on Vancouver's Island, south of latitude 49th degree." This was declined by Mr. Calhoun on the ground that "it would have the effect of restricting the possessions of the United States to limits far more circumscribed than their claims clearly entitle them to."

On the 4th of March, 1845, James K. Polk was "inaugurated" as President of the United States. Mr. Polk was a Democrat, and had simply been elected to do the bidding of his party. Among the most conspicuous planks in the platform of that party were the maintenance or extension of slavery and territorial aggrandisement. Texas had already been coerced into seeking admission into the Union, and the conquest of Mexico had been brought prominently forward by the "southern chivalry." They now clamoured loudly for Oregon, claiming the entire territory from 42° to 54° 40'. "They riled and they raged," says Colonel Coffin, "and gave vent to the national wrath in the fell alliteration of 'fifty-four forty or fight.'"* President Polk, in his inaugural address, declared that the title of the United States to the Oregon country was clear and unquestionable. "Already," he added, "are our people preparing to perfect that title by occupying it, with their wives and children." A short time after, in the course of a public speech, he declared that the republic knew what its rights were with respect to Oregon, and that it intended to maintain them, by force if necessary, against the arbitrary pretensions of Great Britain. Such a speech as this, from the mouth of the Chief Magistrate, and made entirely without provocation, was simply a diplomatic outrage. Sir Robert Peel referred to it in the House of Commons, and expressed his

---

* See "Quirks of Diplomacy," p. 13.

deep regret that such a reference should have been made in a tone and temper which were not likely to lead to an amicable and equitable settlement of the differences between the two countries. "We trust still to arrive at an amicable adjustment of the differences between ourselves and the United States," said Sir Robert; "but if, after having exhausted every effort to effect that settlement, our rights should be invaded, we are resolved and prepared to maintain them." *

By this time the party in power in the United States had thrown all suggestions of compromise to the winds, and coolly proposed that the boundary-line should be "54° 40' or nowhere." Mr. Polk, however—so Mr. Buchanan, the new Secretary of State, declared to the British Ministry—felt himself bound to some extent by the acts of his predecessors, otherwise he would have terminated the negotiations at once, and have *demanded* the entire country up to 54° 40'. As it was, Mr. Buchanan was authorized to offer the 49th parallel as a boundary from the Rocky Mountains to the Pacific. He at the same time offered to make free to Great Britain any port or ports on Vancouver Island which she might desire south of latitude 49°.

It was now Great Britain's turn to refuse, which she did in courtly and diplomatic language through the medium of Mr. Pakenham. The last proposal was then withdrawn, and it was understood that the President had finally made up his mind to claim the entire territory from California to the Russian possessions. Such was the state of affairs at the beginning of the year 1846.

The prospect was ominous indeed. Preliminary preparations were quietly made on both sides, and in both countries was there a strong war party. The national proclivities displayed themselves most characteristically. The amount of bombast and buncombe to which spread-eagle America gave utterance during the closing months of

---

* Hansard, Vol. LXXXI., Col. 199.

1845 and the early months of 1846 passed all calculation.* It seemed as though the lurid flames of war were inevitable. In Canada the solicitude was great, but not greater than was called for by the occasion. The wisdom displayed by the Imperial Government in retaining Earl Cathcart at the head of affairs in this country was now apparent. Military preparations were quietly made under his Excellency's auspices, and the efficiency of the local militia under the new Act was greatly increased.

In Her Majesty's Speech at the opening of the Imperial Parliament on the 22nd of January, 1846, there was an expression of regret that the conflicting claims of Great Britain and the United States in respect of the territory on the northwest coast of America still remained unsettled. It was added that no effort consistent with national honour should be wanting on the part of Her Majesty to bring the question to an early and peaceful termination. When the report of the Speech reached America the Congress of the United States was in session, and an almost interminable debate was the result. A resolution was finally passed by both Houses authorizing the President at his discretion to give notice to the British Government of the abrogation of the joint occupancy under the treaty of

---

* The following, taken from a report of the proceedings in the House of Representatives at Washington, will serve as a specimen. The "oratory" proceeded from Mr. Kennedy, of Indiana: "The march of your people is onward, and it is westward; that is their destiny. They are going onward to the Pacific; and if in the path which leads there the British lion shall lay him down, shall we on that account be craven to our duty and our destiny? No, never. The American eagle will stick his claws into the nose of the lion, and make his blood spout like a whale. This, too, is inevitable destiny. The British may make pretensions to Oregon, but rights they have none. Do we not want it? Yes, and we must have it. We want it to hold our people. Yes, Sir, and I will tell you another thing. The American multiplication table is at work. Go into our Western cabins, and you will find a young man of six feet, and all the rest of him in proportion, with a companion not much less than himself, and round their feet you will find a little company of twenty children. Ay, Sir, that is the American multiplication table. And now do you take our present numbers, and reckon twenty for every two, and where do you think we shall find hunting ground for them? I tell you we must have Oregon. The multitude of the West is demanding it at our hands, and they must have it."

1827. This resolution, had it been abrupt, and unaccompanied by any qualifying clause, might almost have been regarded as offensive by Great Britain. Fortunately, notwithstanding the oratory of General Cass and others who seemed determined to bring about war, the influence of the moderate party prevailed. The resolution was qualified by a preamble reciting that the step was taken in order that the attention of the Governments of both countries might be more earnestly directed to the adoption of all proper measures for the speedy and amicable adjustment of the dispute, "and that said territory may no longer than need be remain subject to the evil consequences of the divided allegiance of its American and British population, and of the confusion and conflict of national jurisdictions dangerous to the cherished peace and good understanding of the two countries." The tone of this preamble being mild, and even amicable, was responded to by Great Britain in a like mood. The Earl of Aberdeen, Secretary of State for Foreign Affairs, determined to make one more effort at a friendly compromise. Having matured a proposal he transmitted it to the British Minister at Washington, with instructions to submit it to the President without loss of time. Somewhat to the surprise of the British public, who had about made up their minds that the quarrel would have to be settled by the strong hand, the proposal was accepted by Mr. Polk and ratified by the Senate with very unusual alacrity. And well indeed it might be, for it yielded everything of importance for which Great Britain had been contending for nearly thirty years. The matter might have been settled on a similar basis long before, for the Government of the United States were never really disposed to seriously urge a claim to any territory north of the 49th parallel. The treaty, as has been seen, was signed on the 15th of June. By the first article it was agreed that "From the point on the 49th parallel of north latitude, where the boundary, laid down in existing treaties and conventions between Great Britain and the

United States, terminates, the line of boundary between the territories of Her Britannic Majesty and those of the United States shall be continued westward along the said 49th parallel of north latitude to the middle of the channel which separates the Continent from Vancouver Island, and thence, southerly, through the middle of the said channel and of Fuca's Straits to the Pacific Ocean. Provided, however, that the navigation of the whole of the said channel and straits, south of the 49th parallel of north latitude, remain free and open to both parties." By the second article the navigation of the Columbia and its great northern branch from the 49th parallel to the ocean was declared "free and open to the Hudson's Bay Company and to all British subjects trading with the same." By the third article the possessory rights of the Hudson's Bay Company and all other British subjects to land previously acquired by them south of the 49th parallel were preserved.

And this was all that Britain took under the treaty. The United States can hardly be blamed for accepting what was voluntarily offered to them; but there can be no sort of doubt that they had all along been demanding territory to which they had no claim, and that they now received more than an equitable arbitration would have awarded to them. Lord Aberdeen doubtless attached little importance to this wild land beyond the remote confines of civilization, as it was then regarded. He was desirous of settling the dispute on almost any terms before going out of office. A firmer diplomacy would have secured additional respect at Washington for British statesmanship, and would also have secured for Canada a more southerly boundary-line on the Pacific coast. For years afterwards American statesmen, with a jocular affectation of magnanimity, pretended to pique themselves on the national disinterestedness in waiving their claim to the extension of the 49th parallel across Vancouver Island.*

"In after discussions, the American Commissioner, Campbell, a man of shrewd wit

It was supposed that this long-contested boundary question, which had periodically disturbed the councils of the two nations for about thirty years, was finally adjusted. The hope was fallacious. A quarter of a century later another treaty became necessary, and the offices of the German Emperor had to be called into requisition. For the time, however, the vexed question was set at rest. The announcement of the concluding of the Oregon Treaty was made by Sir Robert Peel in the House of Commons, and by Lord Aberdeen in the Upper House, on the 29th of June. On the same day Sir Robert Peel's conversion to Free Trade principles sealed his political doom, and his Administration came to an end. A week later a Whig Ministry was formed under the auspices of Lord John Russell, with Earl Grey* as Colonial Secretary.

and sharp practice, dwelt loftily and long on the disinterestedness of America in this matter of 'swapping armour,'—the gold of Glaucus against the brass of Diomed—and about 270,750 square miles of the El Dorado of the Northern Pacific, compensated by a touch of Vancouver cement, laid on with a camel-hair paint brush."—See "Quirks of Diplomacy," p. 16.

*The eldest son and successor of the statesman whose name is identified with the Reform Bill of 1832, and who died in 1845.

Chapter XXII.

IRRESPONSIBLE GOVERNMENT.

"Perhaps the most instructive commentary on the part assumed by Lord Metcalfe in the controversy, and on the principle on which he sought to govern the Province, is found in the state of the Province since the accession of Mr. Draper to power. In some sense the country has, for the last two years, been without a Government. For nearly a year the affairs of nearly two millions of people were almost exclusively in the hands of a not very harmonious triumvirate. Since the dissolution of the Cabinet of which Mr. Baldwin was the head, the Government has never been in a state of complete and efficient organization. The Cabinet has been constructed and reconstructed, dismantled and patched up again, to the disgust of many in the Province, and to the amusement and edification of others. . . . With a Government in a state of virtual dismemberment, the affairs of the Province cannot be, as they are not, in a very promising condition. The Government remains in power without a party on which to rest." MONTREAL LETTER ON CANADIAN AFFAIRS, dated August 13th, 1846, and published in the London *Morning Chronicle* of September 1st.

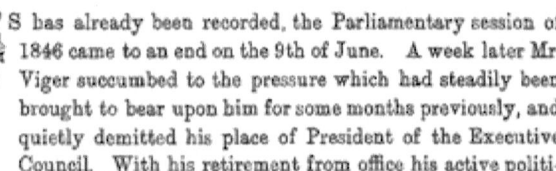

S has already been recorded, the Parliamentary session of 1846 came to an end on the 9th of June. A week later Mr. Viger succumbed to the pressure which had steadily been brought to bear upon him for some months previously, and quietly demitted his place of President of the Executive Council. With his retirement from office his active political career may be said to have ended, though he for some years afterwards continued to sit in the Legislative Council, and occasionally made his presence felt there. One cannot contemplate Mr. Viger's public life subsequent to the Union without regret. He had at one time been the idol of his fellow-countrymen, and had stood second only to Louis Joseph Papineau in their regards. His acceptance of office in Sir Charles Metcalfe's Administration was a great disappointment to the great body of French Canadians, and a serious political blunder on his own part. From that time forward his voice failed to charm, and his influence ceased to be of much account.* And while he did irreparable injury to himself, he altogether failed to impart any strength to the Government which he sought to serve. He had been accepted as a representative French Canadian, and it was soon apparent that he had ceased to be regarded in that light by his compatriots. He himself was the very last to acknowledge that his sceptre had departed from him, and that his name was no longer a conjuror's wand in his native Province. Long after he had ceased to exercise any appreciable influence over his compatriots he was wont to refer to that influence with a simple-hearted self-complacency which showed how utterly he failed to realize his true position. His defeat in Richelieu by Dr. Nelson was the first event which tended to open his eyes, and from that time he seems to have in great measure lost the mental elasticity which had always been characteristic of him. For some months prior to his resignation he gave but little attention to his official duties. The most important function appertaining to the Presidency—that of examining and reporting upon all matters laid before the Council—was discharged by Mr. Morris, the Receiver-General. As it will probably be unnecessary to make any further extended reference to Mr. Viger in the course of this work, the subsequent events of his life may as well be briefly noted here. After his retirement from the Ministry he continued to represent the town of Three Rivers until the close of the Second Parliament. In February, 1848, he was called by Lord Elgin to the Legislative Council. For some years

---

* "Loin d'avoir acquis de la gloire et de l'estime dans sa carrière ministérielle, M. Viger vit son prestige et son influence diminuer aux yeux de son ancien parti. . . On peut à peine comprendre qu' une conduite si contraire aux usages parlementaires ait été tenue par ce patriote qui avait rendu, avant l'Union, les services les plus éminents à son pays dans une carrière toute remplie d'honneur et de patriotisme."—*Le Canada Sous l'Union*, par Louis-P. Turcotte ; Première Partie, pp. 221, 222.

subsequent to that date he took his seat in the Upper House with more or less regularity, but he was by this time greatly advanced in life, and his health was precarious. As the years went by he became physically incapable of taking any part in the proceedings of the House, and finally he ceased to attend altogether. In March, 1858, amid general expressions of regret, his seat was declared vacant in consequence of his non-attendance for two successive sessions. He petitioned for a rescission of this proceeding, and a committee was appointed to consider the matter. The result of the committee's deliberations was a report to the effect that the House, in declaring Mr. Viger's seat vacant, had simply discharged an imperative duty imposed by the law of the land. The final clause of the report, however, shows the kindly feelings entertained by the committee towards the petitioner. Thus it runs: "Your Committee cannot close this report without expressing their deep regret that the physical sufferings of Mr. Viger have for so many years past deprived your Honourable House of his presence, and of his very valuable services as a Councillor and Legislator, and that the statute law of the land compelled your Honourable House to discharge the unpleasant duty of declaring that he was no longer one of its members. If it will be any consolation to Mr. Viger to know that this report is sincerely expressed by your Committee, they will feel that they may in some degree have mitigated the harshness with which Mr. Viger seems to think the law has operated in his particular case."[*] Mr. Viger survived nearly three years longer, and died at his home in Montreal, in his eighty-seventh year, on the 13th of February, 1861.

After Mr. Viger's resignation Mr. Morris continued to discharge the functions of President of the Council, in addition to his duties as Receiver-General, though he was not actually installed into the

---

[*] See Journals of the Legislative Council of the Province of Canada, Vol. XVI. (1858), pp. 43, 44.

former office until the following year. It was anticipated that Mr. Sherwood would resign his post of Solicitor-General for Upper Canada at the close of the session of 1846. He had come into frequent collision with the members of the Cabinet during the progress of the session, and they had ceased to have any political confidence in him. The causes of divergence were numerous, and as he openly professed to reciprocate the hostility entertained towards him, his demission of office was regarded as a foregone conclusion. He had ceased to give the Government a cordial or consistent support, and did not think it necessary to dissemble his views when called to account for his conduct. He had more than once expressed his dissatisfaction at the ministerial method of carrying on the Administration, and had made no secret of his disapproval of some of the ministerial measures. He had repeatedly absented himself from important divisions, and this had occurred so often that his doing so could not be treated as accidental. He found fault with the Ministry for not having redeemed their pledges with respect to the University Bill. Whatever merit there may have been in this censure, considered in the abstract, it certainly came with ambiguous grace from a gentleman who had voted *for* the measure in one session and *against* it in another.* When the Draper-Caron correspondence was made public, Mr. Sherwood became aware for the first time of the negotiations which had been carried on, and he made this another cause of offence against the Government. He spoke roundly on the subject, and declared that it was in the highest degree unseemly and improper that Mr. Draper should have offered to dispose of the offices of some of his colleagues without their knowledge and consent. If Mr.

---

* "Ill-natured people might say that he gave his first vote to secure his place, and his second to gratify his animosities. But we abhor scandal. As Mr. Sherwood says he has the measure so profoundly at heart, we are bound to believe him." *Montreal Gazette*, August 4th, 1846.

Draper really did so, his conduct certainly merited condemnation, but the persons aggrieved thereby were primarily entitled to pronounce judgment upon it, and Mr. Sherwood was not of their number. He was not a member of the Cabinet, and had neither responsibility for nor direct interest in the Attorney-General's act.* And here was the root of the whole matter. Mr. Sherwood's ambition prompted him to aspire to a seat in the Executive Council. He considered that his office should be made a Cabinet one, and felt bitterly towards Mr. Draper because that gentleman could not be brought to assent to such a proposition. Mr. Draper undoubtedly had his share of political sins to answer for, but this cannot be ranked among them. When Mr. Sherwood accepted the Solicitor-Generalship he did so with full knowledge that a seat in the Cabinet was not attached to that office. No promise, direct or indirect, was made to him that the privileges then appurtenant to the office would be increased or enlarged. As simple matter of fact, Mr. Draper had never implicitly trusted Mr. Sherwood, and would not under any circumstances have admitted him to his inmost counsels. Of this Mr. Sherwood sooner or later became aware, and he henceforward cherished a feeling of hostility towards the Attorney-General. The latter suspected the Solicitor-General of intriguing against the Government, and determined to be rid of him. When the end of the session arrived, and the latter manifested no disposition to resign, an official intimation that his resignation would be acceptable was conveyed to him by the Provincial-Secretary, acting on behalf of the Governor-General. Nothing could have more clearly indicated the unsatisfactory and unfriendly nature of Mr. Sherwood's relations

---

* "What had Mr. Sherwood to do with the matter? *His* place was not menaced, nor could easily be involved in a settlement for Lower Canada. . . He was not compromised, and was free to resign his office if he did not like his principals. Yet he 'felt strongly,' nor were 'his feelings and views kept a secret.' It would have been much more proper, we think, if he had kept them a secret, at least while he retained his office. The secret he does not explain is what he had to do with the matter at all."—*Montreal Gazette*, August 4th, 1846.

with the Government. The sending of such an intimation was
indicative of a desire to humiliate him ; for it would have been easy
enough to convey an indirect and unofficial hint which would have
afforded him an opportunity for voluntary resignation. The course
resorted to was tantamount to a dismissal, and as such was regarded
by Mr. Sherwood, who promptly handed in his resignation.* He
published an explanatory letter in the Toronto *Colonist*, wherein he
entered very fully into the facts, but he did no particular harm to
the Administration thereby, and certainly did not add to the esteem
in which he himself was held by the country at large, for his
letter was replied to by the organs of the Government, and the
weakness of his position was very clearly demonstrated.

He was succeeded in the Solicitor-Generalship by Mr. John
Hillyard Cameron, a young man who had only just entered upon
his thirtieth year, who had already attained to a foremost position at
the Upper Canadian bar, and who had made his influence felt in the
ranks of the Conservative party, although he had not up to this
time aspired to a seat in Parliament. A constituency was soon found
for him. Rolland Macdonald, who represented the town of Cornwall,
resigned his seat, and on the 17th of August Mr. Cameron was
returned in his stead. The fact of his being selected to fill such a
position before he had obtained a seat in the Legislature was in
itself sufficient evidence of the respect in which his abilities were
held ; but it was also evidence that the Conservative lawyers in the
House were not rated as of much account by the Government.
There was one exception. Mr. John A. Macdonald, the young
member for Kingston, was doubtless fully equal to the position, and
was spoken of in connection with it, but local jealousies stood in his
way, and he was compelled to bide his time. Similar causes prevented him from assuming the Commissionership of Crown Lands,†

---

* He ceased to hold office on the last day of June.
† Mr. Macdonald, as mentioned at the close of Vol. I., "did not often intrude himself
upon the attention of the Assembly during the early sessions of his public career ; " but

a post which Mr. Papineau professed his willingness to resign. W. B. Robinson, who had resigned the Inspector-Generalship more than a year before, now accepted the Chief Commissionership of Public Works, and upon returning to his constituents in Simcoe he was reëlected without opposition.

It cannot be said, however, that any of these changes did much to strengthen the Administration, and in the course of the summer and autumn of 1846 there were manifest indications of a Liberal reaction. Mr. Baldwin's consistent and straightforward course ever since his resignation of office had extorted respect, and even admiration, from persons of all shades of political opinion. On the other hand, the weakness and consequent vacillation of the Government had alienated or rendered lukewarm many persons who had once been among their firmest supporters. Mr. Draper came in for a formidable share of animadversion, and he was held responsible at the bar of public opinion for most of the ministerial shortcomings. To speak sooth, Mr. Draper's path, since his re-entry into the Assembly, had not been strewn with roses. He had all along been compelled to fight a hopeless battle, and he now found himself taken to task because he had not been able to achieve a victory. He had set out by professing his adherence to the doctrine of Executive responsibility, and had repeatedly violated that doctrine in the face of Parliament and the country. He had declared that he and his colleagues would hold office only so long as they were supported by a Parliamentary majority. The small majority which he had at first been able to com-

---

he was not long in making his individuality felt in the House. Soon after the close of the session of 1846, when it was rumoured that he was to be appointed Commissioner of Crown Lands, a leading Conservative newspaper which was not a mere Government organ referred to him in this wise : "The appointment of Mr. Macdonald, if confirmed, will, we believe, give universal satisfaction. A liberal, able, and clear-headed man, of sound Conservative principles, and of unpretending demeanour, he will be an accession to any Ministry, and bring energy and business habits into a department of which there have been for many years, under the present, and still more under preceding managements, many complaints."—See *Montreal Gazette*, June 16th, 1846.

mand had soon failed him, and he had sustained defeat after defeat. On one occasion his policy had been condemned by the Assembly twice in the course of a single night. Instead of acting up to his professed principles by a prompt resignation, he had clung to office with a tenacity which surprised his own colleagues. Reconstruction, remonstrance, conciliation—all had been tried in vain. The present was dark and lowering, the future seemed hopeless. He felt that he had tempted his fate to its utmost limit. He was weary of the ceaseless turmoil and bickering of public life, and longed for the comparative repose of the judicial bench. He was only restrained from gratifying his desire by the fact that the party to which he belonged could not agree among themselves as to who should succeed him as their leader, and he would not leave them altogether in the lurch. With him at the head of affairs, the Government, though weak and unstable as water, was still a Government. Without him the ministerial machine would probably have collapsed altogether. Ministers found themselves unable to count upon cordial support from any party, while the Opposition belaboured them without stint. They were discredited by outsiders, and suspicious of each other. Even such conspicuous Tories as Ogle R. Gowan and the Hon. George Moffatt made no secret of their distrust. Mr. Sherwood and his friends lost no opportunity of attacking the Government through the newspapers. The Toronto *Globe* regaled its readers with column after column of extracts from Conservative journals, all condemnatory of the ministerial no-policy, and all conceived in a spirit of the most unmistakable hostility and contempt. Messrs. Cayley and Robinson, both of whom had accepted office for no other purpose than to prevent the Liberals from succeeding to power, could not conceal their antipathy to Mr. Draper. Still, there was no word of resignation. Such was the state of affairs within the ministerial precincts during the summer and autumn of the year 1846.

The Liberals, meanwhile, did not neglect to avail themselves of
the tide which was evidently turning in their favour. They held
meetings in various parts of the Province, and did much to increase
the efficiency of their party organization. They prepared an elaborate platform which, while it embodied little or nothing that had not
been advocated by them ever since the Union, seemed wondrously
effective when marshalled into a comprehensive and harmonious
whole. A primary axiom was that the Provincial Government was
practically as well as theoretically a Parliamentary Government,
and that no Ministry should under any circumstances continue in
power after it failed to command a Legislative majority. Should
an appeal to the country be deemed advisable, resignation might
be deferred until the result of the elections could be known; whereupon, should the vote be adverse to the Ministry, resignation must
immediately follow. These principles, of course, were merely what
had all along been contended for by the Liberal party, and—at any
rate latterly—conceded by their opponents, but they had been so
repeatedly violated during the last two or three years that there
seemed to be a peculiar fitness in bringing them conspicuously
before the public eye at this juncture of affairs.

The mutual responsibility of the Governor-General and the Provincial Ministry to each other, and the duties of both to the Sovereign,
were also reduced to something like a tabulated system in the Liberal
programme. The Queen's representative, it was said, should not
assume that he degrades the Crown by following in a colony, with
a constitutional Government, the example of the Crown at home.
Responsible Government had been conceded to Canada, and should be
attended, in its workings, with all the consequences of Responsible
Government in the mother country. "What the Queen cannot do in
England," said the Canadian Liberals, "the Governor should not be
permitted to do in Canada. In making Imperial appointments she
is bound to consult her Cabinet; in making Provincial appoint-

ments, the Governor should be bound to do the same. Lord Metcalfe found himself surrounded by the leaders of a large Parliamentary majority, and, in making appointments, refused to consult them. By such conduct he brought himself and the Sovereign whom he represented into direct antagonism with the local Parliament. To say, as he said, that it would be derogatory to the dignity of the Crown that he should act in harmony with the views of the majority in Parliament, when those views were insisted upon as the proper construction of a system of Government which had been conceded to them by the Crown of England, was but to throw the Crown into collision with the people of Canada. It made the Crown more or less a party to an infringement of the Provincial constitution. Nay more, it tended to inculcate the pernicious doctrine that the proper maintenance of the dignity of the Crown is incompatible with the inviolability of the constitution guaranteed to the Province. The Canadian people will never consent to having their constitution but partially enforced, and it is the extreme of folly in those who assume to be the peculiar conservators of Provincial loyalty to bring the Crown into antagonism with the people, by making an invasion of their rights a necessary condition to the maintenance of its dignity. We, the Canadian Liberals, see nothing in Responsible Parliamentary Government at war with any of the great prerogatives of the Crown. To maintain the contrary is, in our estimation, to convert the Crown from being the Executive head of a constitutional Government, into a repository of ancient prerogative, inconsistent with the spirit of the age, and incompatible with the liberty of the subject. It is not the wish of the Liberals here to take any such view of the Imperial Executive. Instead of being an antagonist with which, in the working of their Government, they are constantly called upon to cope, they wish to regard it, as they wish it to be, through its representative in the Province, as an harmonious component of their local constitution." *

---

* See *Morning Chronicle*, September 1st, 1846.

The Liberal platform also condemned in the strongest manner the identification by a Governor of himself with either or any of the political parties in the Province. The Governor of Canada, it was said, should bear in mind that the purpose of his mission to the Province is not to secure the ascendency of any faction, but to administer his Government for the good of the colony. The colonists themselves are the best judges of all matters of local concern. To their judgment he should defer. Their views and wishes are indicated by the political complexion of their majorities in their local Parliament. The majority for the time being embodies the views of the country for the time being, and so long as these views continue unchanged, he should throw no obstacles in the way of their fulfilment, provided they do not clash with Imperial interests. When these views change, it is for him to modify his course; but he has no right to assume in any case, as was recently done, that the triumph of a party is but temporary and accidental; and on such assumption, and in the hope that a change will soon take place, refuse to move from his party intrenchments, and keep his Executive in antagonism with the popular branch of the Government. He may see every reason to believe that a revolution in the position of parties may be but temporary, but he has no right to act on such a supposition, or to lend the aid of Executive influence for the purpose of expediting the return of the defeated faction to power.*

The Liberals, moreover, would not sanction continual references by the Governor to the Home Office as to matters which were of purely local application. It was insisted that the dependence of the Governor of the Province should be upon the local Parliament, and not on the Home Government, as regarded the proper management of the affairs of the colony. "It will not do," said the Liberals, "that we shall be told, in reference to measures of a

---

* See *Morning Chronicle*, September 1st, 1846.

purely local character, to look to England for redress if we consider ourselves aggrieved by the conduct of the Executive. We battled long for the establishment among us of Representative Government, with all its legitimate consequences. To look to England for redress in matters of mere local interest would be only to countenance a representative system utterly inefficient, so far as local matters are concerned; and as the complete control of local affairs has always been the great aim of all organized agitation in Canada, such a course would be but to sanction the rendering our representative system inoperative in reference to the great object for which it was coveted and obtained. This we cannot and will not consent to do. We see no reason in such cases to make any appeal whatever to England, inasmuch as we conceive the Provincial constitution, if properly carried out, adequate for every emergency. We deny the right of the Governor to set Parliament at defiance, on the ground that the people have a remedy in appeal. It is his duty to act with a Ministry having the confidence of Parliament, or to appeal to the people of the Province, should he differ with his Cabinet and the Parliamentary majority which supports it. If the popular decision is then against him, he should succumb or retire; he should, at all events, refrain from acting, in any case, in opposition to a Parliamentary majority, and then looking to England for a ratification of his conduct. In the management of affairs exclusively local the people of the Province are averse, in all cases, to a submission, direct or implied, to any extraneous tribunal. To Canadians alone must the Governor look for ratification and approval of his conduct in the management of their domestic affairs; to the Imperial Government alone is he to render an account of his stewardship in the conservation of Imperial interests. The Canadians have entire faith, so far as Provincial matters are concerned, in the adequacy and efficiency of Responsible Government. If anything goes wrong, in the system itself are found all the essential elements of cure. In the free and unfettered working of the ocean lies the secret of the purity of its waters; and so to the untrammelled operation of Responsible Government do the Canadians now look for the correction of abuses and the extirpation of wrong. What they want, and what they have long struggled to obtain, is a self-adjusting constitution. In 1841 they conceived that the Imperial Government recognized it as their right, and guaranteed it to them as an inalienable possession. Tranquillity was at once restored to the Province, and a loyalty which previous events had a little shaken recovered its wonted place in the sympathies and affections of the people. They secured, as they believed, a system of Government in itself sufficient for all the local wants of the Province. To deny that the constitution of 1841 is sufficient would be the signal for renewed agitation. It is the *sine qua non* of Canadian tranquillity. It is impolitic to teach them, by word or deed, that they have been cheated in supposing that they had acquired it—in other words, that their contests with England are not yet over; that there is still something indispensable to their rights as British subjects of which they are deprived, and which they must yet struggle with the mother country to obtain."[*]

But the foregoing sentiments were not to be construed as indicating any want of loyalty on the part of the Canadian Liberals. They claimed that their loyalty was based, not upon a mere sentiment, but upon reason and logic. "Treat us fairly," they said, in effect, "and you will find us easy to manage. Oppress us, and we will offer a constitutional resistance." They justly complained of the persistent misrepresentation to which they had been subjected. As a party, they were commonly regarded in Great Britain as disaffected or disloyal "They look upon this," said the Liberals, speaking of themselves in the third person, "as a great barrier to the harmony and tranquillity of the Province, inasmuch as it tends to place every Governor in a false position

---

[*] See *Morning Chronicle*, September 1st, 1846.

as regards them, at the very outset of his career. If he shares in the impression too prevalent in this respect, he commences his administration of affairs on the supposition that he is called upon to suspect them, and to act more or less against them. They are the popular party here; they are numerically the stronger party, and were no sinister influences brought to bear upon the elections, could command at any time a large majority in the representation. How can the Provincial Government be equitably and satisfactorily administered, if the aim of the Governor's policy is to maintain with this party a constant and an unremitting struggle? It is the policy of the Executive, in all free countries at least, to act in all cases, if possible, in harmony with the people, instead of placing itself in systematic opposition to them. And yet this latter is the position which Canadian Governors too frequently assume towards the popular party here. They look upon the preservation of the connection of the Province with the mother country as the great object of their administration, and are too apt to fall into the error of supposing that this can only be effected by systematically checking the popular party. By the acts of the local Executive, the Crown and the Liberals are thus, with but little interruption, kept in antagonism to each other. The conviction is thus forced upon the latter by their daily experience that their great political antagonist is not the rival domestic party, but the Imperial Government. If anything could tend to impair their loyalty it would be this. Unmerited suspicion very often begets the very evil which it fancies to exist. The Canadian Liberals regard the Colonial Office as more or less imbued with the opinions in this respect prevalent out of doors. They fear that it acts under the erroneous impression that party warfare in the Province has a view to objects beyond its legitimate range. The colony, they conceive, is set down at home as divided into the British and anti-British parties; and they fear that its successive Governors are deputed, with instructions more or less direct, to co-operate with the one party for the suppression of the other. There is at present no anti-British party in Canada, and nothing but the grossest mismanagement and the most systematic disregard of the interests of the Province can create one. There is as much loyalty in the ranks of the one party as in those of the other. The object of the Provincial Government should be to perpetuate the existing loyalty among all classes, instead of to check the disloyalty which it too frequently assumes to characterize a particular party."[*]

Such is a brief exposition of the leading planks in the Liberal platform. Regarded as a whole, it had the great merit of being consistent with itself, as well as of being logically deducible from the fact that the mother country recognized Canada as a colony possessed of a constitution. The time was approaching when the doctrines so propounded were to receive general assent, and when Responsible Government should be defended by the Governor-General as strenuously as it had ever been by its promoters. And it is worthy of remark that the Governor who was destined to take this stand was one who had inherited Tory traditions, and had been cradled in the lap of old-world Conservatism.

With the signing of the Oregon Treaty all present danger of serious embroilment between Great Britain and the United States passed by. It was no longer either necessary or desirable that a soldier, whatever his personal or professional merits, should be at the head of Canadian affairs. The situation was one calling for the exercise of qualities such as are possessed by few, and which a military training cannot be expected to bestow. What was needed was "a person possessing an intimate knowledge of the principles and practice of the constitution of England, some experience of popular assemblies, and considerable familiarity with the political questions of the day."[†] Where was such a man to be found? Again,

---

[*] See *Morning Chronicle*, September 1st, 1846.
[†] See "The Colonial Policy of Lord John Russell's Administration," by Earl Grey, Vol. I., p. 207.

as on the contemplated retirement of Lord Metcalfe, there were various rumours as to who would be sent out to succeed Lord Cathcart. Among other high dignitaries to whom the post was absurdly assigned was the Duke of Bedford. Early in September all doubt on the subject was set at rest. Definite intelligence arrived by the English mail that Lord Elgin, who had succeeded Sir Charles Metcalfe as Governor of Jamaica, was to be the next representative of Her Majesty in Canada. Very little was known about him here, but that little was in his favour. It was known that he was the representative of an old and honourable Scottish family; that he had been trained to political duties; and that he had administered the Government of Jamaica to the satisfaction of the colonists, as well as to that of the Imperial authorities. It was also known that he had been a Conservative in Home politics, but that circumstance was not regarded as a disqualification. That it should not be so regarded by the Conservatives was a matter of course; but even among Reformers there was no dissatisfaction on that score. It was remembered that Sir Charles Bagot had been a Conservative, and that he had sunk his native and inherited proclivities on this side of the Atlantic: that he had honestly endeavoured to carry on the colonial Government according to the constitution, and that Liberal principles had been in the ascendant throughout the whole term of his Administration. It was also remembered that Sir Charles Metcalfe had been heralded as a Liberal of the most pronounced cast; that he had allied himself with the party of obstruction, and that he had brought the country to the verge of ruin. It was therefore not strange that but little account was taken of Lord Elgin's domestic politics. "Lord Elgin is said to be a Tory," wrote Mr. Hincks, in the Montreal *Pilot,* " and there is no doubt that he is of a Tory family. We look upon his bias as an English politician with the most perfect indifference. We do not think it matters one straw to us Canadians whether our Governor is a Tory or a Whig, more especially a Tory of the Peel school. We have to rely on ourselves, not on the Governor; and if we are true to ourselves, the private opinions of the Governor will be of very little importance." The history of the next few years proved most indubitably that Mr. Hincks's view of the matter was sound, and that Canadians had nothing to fear from either the public or private opinions of this, the most enlightened and statesmanlike of Canadian Governors since the Union.

CHAPTER XXIII.

LORD ELGIN.

"The reactionary policy of Lord Metcalfe had clearly demonstrated that the concession of so great a boon as free Parliamentary rule was in itself of little avail, unless some man thoroughly imbued with its spirit were called upon to preside over its practical operation. So long as theorists in high places could, at pleasure, set at nought its plainest axioms, the security for Canadian liberty must necessarily be precarious. The hour had now come when the controversy was to be settled at once and forever; and with it appeared the man."—THE SCOT IN BRITISH NORTH AMERICA, *by W. J. Rattray, B.A.*; Vol. II., p. 607.

JAMES BRUCE, eighth Earl of Elgin and twelfth Earl of Kincardine, in the peerage of Scotland: afterwards first Baron Elgin, of Elgin, in the peerage of the United Kingdom: enjoyed the distinction of having sprung from one of the royal houses of Scotland—the historic house which numbers among its representatives the hero of Bannockburn. The chronicles of the Bruces in early and mediæval times abound with thrilling and romantic incidents, and form some of the most memorable passages of Scottish history. For centuries before the period to which this work relates the family had been settled in Fifeshire, and during the greater part of that time had been more or less connected with the diplomatic service. The father of the future Governor-General of Canada was that well-known despoiler of the Parthenon who was so mercilessly, and at the same time so unjustifiably, pilloried by Lord Byron in "The Curse of Minerva,"* for removing the Elgin marbles, as they are now called, from Athens to England. The archæological extrava-

---

* See also "Childe Harold's Pilgrimage," Canto II., stanzas xi–xv.

gances of this nobleman did much to impoverish the family estate. He had a numerous progeny, for most of whom he was able to make but slender provision. The member of his family with whom we in this country are more immediately concerned was born in London, on the 20th of July, 1811. Being a second son, and having no expectation of succeeding to the title and estates, he was from an early age taught to regard himself as one who must largely depend upon himself for his future position in life. As a boy he spent some time at Eton, whence he passed to Christ Church, Oxford, where he won a well-deserved reputation for diligence, and was accredited with the possession of a shrewdness and native sagacity beyond his years. During his University career he had for his friends and contemporaries many young men who afterwards became eminent in political and professional life. Among the number were William Ewart Gladstone, Roundell Palmer (now Lord Selborne), James Ramsay (afterwards Lord Dalhousie), Sidney Herbert (afterwards Lord Herbert of Lea), Robert Lowe (now Lord Sherbrooke), and the young gentleman who subsequently became Duke of Newcastle, and who at a much more mature phase of his existence accompanied the Prince of Wales to Canada as his friend and guardian in 1860. It was something to shine in such a galaxy, and young James Bruce fully held his own with the brightest of his compeers at the Union debating club.*

Illness, induced by overstudy, prevented him from competing for double honours, but he obtained a first-class in classics at the Michaelmas Examination of 1832, and was currently spoken of as "the best first of his year." He was soon after elected to a fellow-

---

* One of the brightest of them all, writing of Lord Elgin after intelligence of that nobleman's death reached England in 1863, thus referred to his old friend of college days : "I well remember placing him, as to the natural gift of eloquence, at the head of all those I knew, either at Eton or at the University."—See extract from letter of Mr. Gladstone, quoted in Walrond's "Letters and Journals of James, Eighth Earl of Elgin ;" p. 3, note.

ship of Merton College. In June, 1835, he entered himself as a student at Lincoln's Inn, but does not seem to have had any serious idea of devoting himself to the legal profession. He gave much attention to politics, and published one or two pamphlets on important public questions. As became one of his lineage and training, he was attached to the Conservative side, but his Conservatism was of a most liberal complexion, and had nothing in common with the old-fashioned Toryism in which he had been bred. In 1837 he was an unsuccessful candidate for the representation of Fifeshire in the House of Commons. He had made very insufficient preparation for his candidature, which was suddenly determined upon in consequence of an unexpected vacancy in the representation of the shire, combined with the injudicious importunities of some of his friends. As a consequence he was defeated by a large majority. He made no further attempt to obtain a seat in Parliament until 1841, when he was returned in the Conservative interest for the borough of Southampton. In the course of a speech made by him at this time he laid down his political platform with sufficient clearness, as well as with much eloquence. "I am a Conservative," said he—"not upon principles of exclusionism; not from narrowness of view, or illiberality of sentiment; but because I believe that our admirable constitution, on principles more exalted and under sanctions more holy than those which Owenism or Socialism can boast, proclaims between men of all classes and degrees in the body politic a sacred bond of brotherhood in the recognition of a common warfare here, and a common hope hereafter. I am a Conservative, not because I am adverse to improvement, not because I am unwilling to repair what is wasted, or to supply what is defective in the political fabric, but because I am satisfied that, in order to improve effectually, you must be resolved most religiously to preserve."

His party were then in Opposition, Lord Melbourne's Whig Government being still in power. To him was assigned the duty of seconding the amendment to the Address. His speech on the occasion, in the course of which he professed himself a friend to Free Trade, was replete with promise, and foreshadowed the broad and just-minded statesman of later times. The amendment was carried by a large majority, and Lord Melbourne's Government gave place to that of Sir Robert Peel. The new Ministry was formed early in September. It of course received cordial support from young Bruce, but he was not destined to remain long enough in the House of Commons to make his presence strongly felt there. On the 14th of November he succeeded, on the death of his father, to the family honours and estates, his elder brother having died about two years before. A Parliamentary career thus seemed to be closed to him, a Scottish peer being, according to the generally received opinion, ineligible for a seat in the Commons. But a new field for the exercise of his talents soon presented itself. In March, 1842, the important post of Governor of Jamaica was offered to him. He accepted it, and in doing so decided his vocation in life.

In April of the previous year he had married Elizabeth Mary, daughter of Mr. C. L. Cumming Bruce, of Roseisle. Accompanied by his wife, he set sail for Jamaica within a month from the date of his appointment. The vessel was wrecked on the voyage, and though no lives were lost, Lady Elgin's system received a shock from which it never entirely recovered. She died in the summer of the following year, having meanwhile given birth to a daughter, the present Baroness Thurlow. Lord Elgin spent somewhat more than four years in Jamaica, during which he fully justified the good opinion of the Government to which he owed his appointment. His moderation, eloquence, and high sense of justice commended him to the goodwill of all classes. He did much to promote the education and general welfare of the emancipated negroes, and his administration of affairs was marked by considerable moral and social progress in the colony. He left for Great Britain in the spring of 1846, and, though he had merely obtained leave of absence, it was understood that he was not to be asked to return.

Upon the change of Government in the summer of 1846, as has been seen, Lord Grey became Secretary of State for the Colonies. His politics were opposed to those of Lord Elgin, but he was wise and just enough to recognize merit wherever he found it. Before the summer came to an end Lord Elgin received at his hands an offer of the Governor-Generalship of British North America. The offer was accepted; "not," says Lord Elgin's biographer, "in the spirit of mere selfish ambition, but with a deep sense of the responsibilities attached to it."[*] It was arranged that his Lordship should leave for Canada early in the following year. How the news of the appointment was received in this country has already been narrated.

Two months before departing for the seat of his Government Lord Elgin married his second wife—Lady Mary Louisa Lambton, daughter of the first Earl of Durham, whose connection with Canadian affairs has been outlined in the first chapter of this work. Leaving his bride behind in England, to follow him across the sea at a less inclement season, his Lordship set out from Liverpool early in January, 1847, in the Cunard steamship *Hibernia*. The vessel encountered unusually rough weather, even for that time of year, and the voyage was a most uncomfortable one. Having reached Halifax on the 20th of the month, the Governor disembarked and spent a few hours as the guest of Sir John Harvey, Lieutenant-Governor of Nova Scotia. It had been Lord Elgin's intention to pass some days in the Maritime Provinces, and then to proceed to Montreal by way of Fredericton, but he now learned that the condition of the roads was not suited to such an undertaking; so, after receiving and replying to addresses from the Legislative

---

[*] Walrond, p. 29.

Council and Assembly of the Province,* he re-embarked on board the *Hibernia*, and proceeded to Boston, whither he arrived on the 25th. On the morning of the following day he set out for Montreal. He reached his destination on the 29th, and took up his abode at Monklands. On the 30th he made his public entry into the city, and was sworn into office at the Government House, in the presence of Earl Cathcart, the members of the Executive Council, and other public functionaries. The enthusiastic addresses usual to such an occasion were received and replied to by his Excellency, who made a most favourable impression on the French Canadian population by replying to them extemporaneously in their own language. The impression made by his Lordship upon all classes, indeed, was most favourable. His manners and his power of utterance proclaimed him to be no mere office-holder, but a cultured and polished statesman, imbued with a high sense of the responsibilities of his position. "I am sensible," said he, in reply to an address from the inhabitants of Montreal, "that I shall best maintain the prerogative of the Crown, and most effectually carry out the instructions with which Her Majesty has honoured me, by manifesting a due regard for the wishes and feelings of the people and by seeking the advice and assistance of those who enjoy their confidence." So that there was at least no seeming probability of his foundering upon the rock upon which Lord Metcalfe had been wrecked.

Earl Cathcart's administration of Canadian affairs having come to an end, that nobleman soon afterwards returned to Great Britain,

---

* The Halifax papers of the period contain very full accounts of Lord Elgin's flying visit. The *Morning Post* has the following reference to his personal appearance:—"The Governor-General is a man of middle stature, with an open and prepossessing countenance, over which an expression of innate benevolence beamed as he read his reply to the addresses. His forehead is one exhibiting great capacity, and in his action and utterance, as well as in the sentiments of his address, one could not help being struck with a remarkable evidence of strong common sense, and ready talents for business."

where he was appointed to the military command of the northern and midland district of England, a position which he retained until 1854. He lived for about twelve years after his departure from Canada, and died at St. Leonard's-on-Sea, Sussex, England, on the 16th of July, 1859.

For some months after Lord Elgin's assumption of office there seemed to be a lull in public affairs. The Draper Ministry still held office, but it was tottering to its fall. The fact is that, as Lord Elgin's biographer remarks, "there was no real political life; only that pale and distorted reflection of it which is apt to exist in a colony before it has learned to look within itself for the centre of power."* Parties were formed, "not on broad issues of principle, but with reference to petty local and personal interests; and when they sought the support of a more widespread sentiment they fell back on those antipathies of race which it was the main object of every wise Governor to extinguish."† As for Lord Elgin himself he grew in favour day by day. Physically, as well as mentally, he furnished a marked contrast to his immediate predecessors. He was young, and enjoyed vigorous health. He could upon occasion work eighteen hours a day, and felt himself entirely independent of the state of the weather. If his presence was needed at a public meeting, the howling blasts and keen frosts of a Canadian winter offered no obstacle to him. He possessed an admirable temper, and always displayed a pleasant demeanour before the public eye. He did not consider it derogatory to his dignity to walk to church, instead of being conveyed thither in his carriage. He was ever ready to respond impromptu to any address which might be presented to him, and, like Lord Dufferin in more recent times, he always contrived to say something appropriate to the occasion. It was soon discovered that he was the most effective speaker in the Province. His marriage to the daughter of Lord Durham was an additional

---

* Walrond, p. 37.   † Ib.

recommendation in the eyes of most Canadians, who regarded his Lordship's memory with the respect due to one who had fought and suffered in their cause.*

The Governor-General had been carefully instructed by Lord Grey before his departure from England as to the policy to be pursued by him in carrying on his Canadian Administration. The instructions were of a liberal and enlightened character, but they implied a certain amount of subservience on the part of the Legislature, and Lord Elgin improved upon them. He had made himself thoroughly familiar with Lord Durham's views on colonial questions, and those views had fully commended themselves to his judgment. He saw his way to yielding a full measure of Responsible Government without in any degree curtailing the power and prerogative of the Crown. He refused to embroil himself in the bickerings of faction. He acted harmoniously with the Ministry, but did not attempt to conceal from them that he would, if necessary, work with their opponents with equal cordiality should the necessity for doing so arise. About this time he wrote to Lady Elgin expressing his opinion that the real and effectual vindication of her illustrious father's memory and proceedings would be the success of a Governor-General of Canada who should work out Lord Durham's views of Government fairly. "Depend upon it," wrote his Excellency, "if this country is governed for a few years satisfactorily, Lord Durham's reputation as a statesman will be raised beyond the reach of cavil. I do not indeed know whether I am to be the instrument to carry out this work, or be destined, like others who have gone before me, to break down in the attempt; but I am still of opinion that the thing may be done, though it requires some good-fortune, and some qualities not of the lowest order."† Happily, as the event proved, the diffidence displayed in the above extract did not proceed from conscious weakness. It was reserved for Lord Elgin to see Respon-

---

* Walrond, p. 36.   † Ib., p. 41.

sible Government established in Canada on a firm and permanent basis, and from that time down to the present day there has been no successful endeavour on the part of any public man to undermine it. True, there have at odd times been arbitrary pretensions on the part of one or two of Lord Elgin's successors, but there has been no deliberate attempt to force the will of a minority upon a free people, nor to assert the prerogatives of the Crown as an excuse for One-Man Government. There is surely no intelligent Canadian of the present day, to whichsoever side of politics he may belong, who would be satisfied with the old system of Executive irresponsibility, or who cannot distinguish between disloyalty to the Sovereign and loyalty to Canada.

During the spring of the year there was a repetition of former attempts to reinforce the Ministry by inducing some of the French Canadian leaders to join it. The advances at this time were made to Mr. Caron by Mr. Cayley. As on former occasions, the attempt utterly failed. The stumbling-block, as before, was Mr. Daly, who would not resign, and who could not well be dismissed.* Then followed several important ministerial changes. On the 22nd of April Mr. Smith, Attorney-General for Lower Canada, resigned his place, and on the following day was appointed a Judge of the Court of Queen's Bench in his native Province. He was succeeded by the Hon. William Badgley, who had long been a conspicuous member of the British party in the Lower Province, and who had recently filled the office of a circuit judge and commissioner in bankruptcy. Mr. Taschereau, the Solicitor-General for Lower Canada, took umbrage at Mr. Badgley's accession to an office to which he considered that he himself had a prior claim. He resigned the Solicitor-Generalship,

---

* "Les prétentions de M. Daly s'opposaient à un arrangement acceptable. Le ministère était prêt à céder trois portefeuilles aux libéraux ; mais il refusait de sacrifier M. Daly qui se croyait inamovible dans son poste de secrétaire provincial."—*Le Canada Sous l'Union*, Deuxième Partie, p. 11.

and announced his intention of going into Opposition ; a contingency which the Ministry avoided by appointing him to a circuit judgeship. In May Mr. John A. Macdonald joined the Ministry, and became Receiver-General, Mr. Morris succeeding to the Presidency of the Council. Mr. Draper having by this time completed arrangements for retiring from political life, the portfolio of Attorney-General for Upper Canada, together with the leadership of the Government in the Assembly, were offered to Mr. John Hillyard Cameron. That gentleman was willing enough to accept those dignities, but as Mr. Henry Sherwood pressed his own claims with much fervour, and threatened to bring all his influence to bear against the Ministry upon the opening of the approaching session if his pretensions were disallowed, the Government yielded, and upon Mr. Draper's retirement from office on the 28th of May, Mr. Sherwood accordingly succeeded to the place to which he had so long aspired—that of Attorney-General and Prime Minister. Mr. Cameron, however, as a mark of special respect, was admitted to a seat in the Cabinet on the strength of his Solicitor-Generalship. On the last day of the month Mr. Peter McGill became Speaker of the Legislative Council, with a seat in the Cabinet. Mr. Caron, the last Speaker, had been displaced about a fortnight before. The Ministry, being unable to persuade that gentleman to join hands with them, or to induce any of his compatriots to do so, determined to remove him from office. He was officially informed by Mr. Daly that the office of Speaker of the Legislative Council would for the future be a ministerial one, and that his Excellency had accordingly found it necessary to direct the revocation of his, Mr. Caron's, commission. This proceeding, as will readily be conceived, did not tend to make the Government more popular than it had previously been with the French Canadian population. As for Mr. Caron, as will in due course be seen, he was out of office only about ten months, when he was called upon to resume his former place, with the added dignity of a seat in the Cabinet.

The Ministry, as reconstructed in the month of May, 1847, is known to our history as the Sherwood-Daly Ministry. It contained but one French Canadian member—Mr. Papineau—and there seemed to be no possibility of inducing any other of that nationality to enrol himself in its ranks. Mr. Draper, though he had resigned his place in the Cabinet, was still a member of Parliament, and took his seat on the independent benches in the Assembly at the beginning of the session. On the opening day, in order that no time might be lost in providing for the future representation of London, he gave notice of his intention to resign his seat for that place.

The opening took place on the 2nd of June. The Speech from the Throne was of a somewhat non-committal character, but announced several concessions on the part of the Imperial Government, including the control of the Post Office Department, and authority to repeal the differential duties in favour of British manufactures. The amendment, which was moved by Mr. Baldwin on the 8th, afforded that gentleman an opportunity of making a vigorous attack upon the Ministry. The ensuing debate lasted until the 12th, when a vote was taken, and the amendment negatived by a majority of two. A division was then taken on each clause of the Government Address in Reply, and the result was the same throughout. Mr. Draper voted with the Ministry, and this was the last vote recorded by him within the walls of Parliament. In the course of his speech, which wound up the debate, he took his farewell of the House and of public life. He stated that that was probably the last time he should ever address a political assembly, and that he was anxious to retire on terms of amity with every member of the House. He then entered upon what he intended as a defence of his own career as First Minister of the Crown. He referred the House back to the period when Sir Charles Metcalfe dissolved the Administration of Messieurs Lafontaine and Baldwin, and reminded them of the difficult task he had undertaken in endeavouring to carry on a Government with a large majority in Parliament against him. So painful had the task been, he alleged, that had he anticipated what he had since suffered, he would never have accepted the responsibility. When he had taken office, he had felt that to attempt to carry on the Government on the old system would be absurd. He had desired to lay the basis of a larger party than had ever before been seen in Canada—a party which would at once have the confidence of the country, and be efficient in the conduct of public affairs. He had laboured with all his energy and in all honesty for this one object, and he felt that the days and nights of pain which he had devoted to the cause had been but ill requited by those with whom he had acted. (Here the honourable gentleman wept.) He did not wish to reproach any one, but he would say that his exertions in the Conservative cause had been ill repaid. It was easy for people to find fault: to say that the Government should have done this or that: but he could tell them, and the honourable gentlemen opposite he knew would corroborate it, that to conduct the affairs of the country, with the material which could be procured, was a most difficult undertaking. The present system of Government had been in operation only five or six years; the people were yet unused to it; and it was too much to expect that heaven-born statesmen would spring up in a day. The entire speech from first to last, as was to be expected, was listened to with close attention by the Assembly. In the course of his remarks Mr. Draper declared, to the huge astonishment of most of his hearers, that Responsible Government was the only system on which Canada could be governed, and he declared that on that principle he had accepted and held office under Lord Metcalfe. He admitted that Government patronage should be employed for strengthening the hands of the Administration of the day; that for all appointments the Ministry are responsible, and that had any appointment been made without his advice, he would have resigned office. Such was the last deliverance of the Honourable William Henry Draper on the floor of the Assembly. He immediately afterwards accepted the place of a puisné Judge of the Court of Queen's Bench for Upper Canada, as successor to Mr. Justice Hagerman, deceased. Nine years later he succeeded Sir James Macaulay as Chief Justice of the Court of Common Pleas, a position which he retained till July, 1863, when he succeeded the Hon. Archibald McLean as Chief Justice of Upper Canada. In February, 1869, he attained the highest dignity known to the judicial bench of the Province—that of President of the Court of Error and Appeal. This position he retained until his death in November, 1877. As has been remarked elsewhere,[*] whatever differences of opinion may be entertained as to his political career, there can be but one verdict upon his long judicial life. It extended over more than thirty years. It was marked by unflagging industry, and by the higher attributes of great learning and stainless honour. His judgments will long be regarded by the profession with the respect due to great legal acquirements, wonderful power of analysis, and a mind of broad and firm intellectual grasp.

The session lasted eight weeks, during which some useful laws were enacted, and a fair share of business was despatched. The weakness of the Ministry, however, was made manifest from day to day, and there was no chance for them to carry any measure as to which there was serious divergence of opinion. They were repeatedly defeated, and there were again indications of internal disorganization. Still they would not demit their power, though they professed to be sanguine as to the result in case of a general election. The session was brought to a close on the 28th of July, and the rest of the year was largely devoted by both parties to active preparations for an election campaign.

There was another subject, however, which engaged public atten-

[*] *Ante*, Vol. I., p. 71.

tion to a large extent. The year was marked by a very large immigration to Canada from Ireland. As a rule, it is to the interest of colonies to promote immigration to their shores, but the rule is subject to modification by circumstances. In 1847 the exodus from Ireland was chiefly due to the failure of the potato crop, and the famine which ensued therefrom. The immigrants to Canada were for the most part from the poor and indigent classes. Many of them were enfeebled in health by poverty, starvation, and suffering. Owing to their unhealthy condition, and to the insufficient accommodation provided for such immense numbers on the vessels which conveyed them across the ocean, a malignant form of ship-fever broke out among them. Many died on the way out, and of those who reached our shores alive a large percentage were fit only for the hospitals. Some idea of the extent of the misery which prevailed may be formed when it is known that nearly 100,000 immigrants were landed at Quebec during the year, and that the number confined in the hospitals at one time was not far short of 10,000. The mortality was very great among persons of all ages, and though children suffered equally with adults, nearly 1,000 immigrant orphans were left destitute at Montreal alone. Other Canadian cities and towns underwent similar inflictions. Children and adults alike were compelled to depend upon public and private charity. "Army after army of sick and suffering people, fleeing from famine in their native land to be stricken down by death in the valley of the St. Lawrence, stopped in rapid succession at Grosse Isle, and then, leaving numbers of their dead behind, pushed upwards towards the lakes in overcrowded steamers, to burden the inhabitants of the western towns and villages."[*] It is worthy of being recorded to the lasting honour of our people that, irrespective of politics, nationality or colour, they responded to the demands thus made upon their philanthropy, not only with readiness, but even with

---

[*] See MacMullen's History of Canada, p. 504.

generous eagerness. Their grumblings at the burdens imposed upon them did not make themselves heard until the crisis was over, and until the gaunt wolf had been driven from the door. Relief committees were formed all over the Province, not merely on behalf of the sufferers who had arrived in Canada, but also on behalf of those who remained in Ireland. The wealthy gave from their abundance ; the poor from such store as they could command. The Indians of Caughnawaga, of the Credit, of the Grand River, of Munceytown, and of the Bay of Quinté, contributed their respective mites to relieve the sufferings of their white brethren. The coloured inhabitants, not a few of whom were escaped slaves from the Southern States, and who, as was to be expected, were almost all in poor worldly circumstances themselves, proved that they appreciated the blessings of manhood and of freedom, and that they could practise self-denial for a season to relieve the pressing needs of their more indigent fellow-creatures.

The necessities of the time were indeed imperative. The official mind ceased, for the nonce, to concern itself with party questions. Government awoke to the urgency of the occasion. The duty of making public provision for the sick and destitute was apparent, and the task of doing so was practically withdrawn from the Civil Secretary's Department, and assumed by the Administration as a whole. Immigrant sheds and temporary hospitals were erected in the principal cities, and such professional assistance as could be obtained was pressed into the public service. In spite of all that could be done, thousands of the starved and fever-stricken victims died from disease and exposure. Many Canadians who volunteered as physicians or nurses fell victims to contagion, and died by the side of their suffering patients. The Roman Catholic priesthood and the Sisters of Charity, as is their wont in such emergencies, displayed a courage and self-sacrifice which awoke general admiration. Early in the season they repaired in considerable numbers to

Grosse Isle, the quarantine station, about thirty miles below Quebec, in the middle of the St. Lawrence, where thousands of the sufferers were disembarked. A vast majority of the latter professed the Roman Catholic faith, and as such had special claims upon the Roman Catholic clergy. So numerous were the patients, and so foul was the disorder from which they suffered, that the island was for some time a mass of putrescent loathsomeness. The atmosphere was as deadly as that of the fabled valley of Java through which the upas was said to send forth its fatal exhalations. So malignant was the poison that in some instances healthy persons, landing on the island to minister to the wants of the sufferers, were struck down by the pestilence and lay dead within a few hours. It will hardly be denied that the courage which enables a human being to encounter such dangers as these is at least as worthy of emulation as that more demonstrative heroism which impels to such achievements as the charge of the Light Brigade. The priesthood and sisterhood of Rome descended upon Grosse Isle like angels of mercy. If it cannot be said that at their control "Despair and anguish fled the struggling soul," it is at least true that they did what in them lay to cool the parched tongue, to lighten the pangs of dissolution, and to prepare the mind of the sufferer for the great change before him. They ministered to the temporal comforts of the living, and held the crucifix before the fading eyes of the dying. They had indeed the courage begotten of that implicit faith which removes mountains. It mattered not to them that the air was laden with pestilence; that the next breath which they drew might be charged with germs as fatal to human life as was the death-dealing draught of the Borgias. They felt that in alleviating human suffering they were carrying out the injunctions of the Founder of all Christian faiths, and that neither pestilence, poison, nor any other deadly thing had power to harm them without their Master's leave.

With the advent of autumn and cool weather the virulence of the disease showed signs of abatement, and then the voice of the Canadian people began to make itself heard. They had nobly responded to the call of charity, and had spent both themselves and their substance in the cause of suffering humanity. Now they began to inquire why they should have been called upon to do so. They had been put to great expense to provide for the starving and helpless poor of Great Britain, who, as it seemed, had been inflicted upon the Canadians merely because Britain herself wished to be rid of them. Canada, they said, had been made a scapegoat. It seemed only fair that the mother-country should at least recompense them for the outlay which had been imposed upon them. "It is enough," said they, "that our houses should be made a receptacle of this mass of want and misery; it cannot surely be intended that we are to be mulcted in heavy pecuniary damages besides."* As the season advanced, and the extent of the pecuniary infliction came to be more definitely known, the feeling of dissatisfaction towards the mother-country began to make itself more manifest. The French population had never been favourable to British immigration to Canada, and the events of the year had not tended to reconcile them to it. The Opposition, as usual under such circumstances, sought to make political capital out of the calamities of the time by holding the Government to some extent responsible therefor. The republican element in the population had an opportunity of contrasting the immigration arrangements of the United States with our own, and the contrast was not to our advantage. At New York, no sooner did the character of the year's immigration become known than the laws were rigidly enforced against shipowners who violated their bonds by landing destitute and indigent persons; and this had the effect of diverting such persons to our own shores. In a word, there were abundant grounds for dissatisfaction on the part of Canadians, and they

---

* See Lord Elgin's letter to Lord Grey, quoted in Walrond, p. 43.

waxed moody and angry. The climax was reached just as the season's navigation closed, when, in spite of the remonstrances against further inflictions which had been sent across the Atlantic, a shipload of emigrants from Lord Palmerston's Irish estates were landed at Quebec. Now, Lord Palmerston was Secretary for Foreign Affairs in the existing Home Government, and this depletion from his estates was looked upon in this country as a wilful and quasi-official disregard of our representations. Some of the newspapers indulged in much plainness of language. Lord Elgin himself wrote to Earl Grey urging the claims of Canada to recompense for her pecuniary loss, and it was not till his Excellency was able to assure the public that his arguments had produced the desired effect, and that England would herself bear the expense to which the colony had been subjected, that the public pulse quieted down.

Towards the end of September the Governor visited Quebec, and early in October he started on a western tour, in the course of which he visited the chief towns on Lake Ontario. He won the hearts of the people wherever he went. In Lower Canada he delighted the French by talking to them in their native tongue. In Upper Canada his replies to the innumerable addresses which awaited him were characterized by a combined statesmanship and good-fellowship which produced a very palpable effect upon public opinion. As the year drew to its close it was rumoured that there was to be an immediate dissolution. The rumour was followed by its fulfilment on the 6th of December, and from that date until the 24th of January following the Province was in the throes of a general election campaign. On the 8th of December some changes occurred in the composition of the Ministry. Mr. Papineau resigned his place as Commissioner of Crown Lands, and was succeeded by Mr. John A. Macdonald, who was succeeded in the post of Receiver-General by the Hon. F. P. Bruneau, a member of the Legislative Council

At the same time the Hon. J. E. Turcotte accepted the Solicitor-Generalship for Lower Canada, a post which had been vacant ever since Mr. Taschereau's resignation, already noted, more than six months previously.

There was of course great activity and excitement all through the election campaign, but the result was from the first a foregone conclusion. The reaction had fairly set in, and when all the returns had been made it was found that the Government were in a hopeless minority. The Reformers swept the constituencies like a broom in both sections of the Province. All the leading members of their party were returned, and it was evident that if they judiciously availed themselves of their opportunities a long lease of power was before them. The Government recognized their defeat, and it was a question with them whether they should forthwith tender their resignations or wait until the meeting of Parliament. The latter course was finally decided upon, as the day of assembling was near at hand.

Chapter XXIV.

LAFONTAINE—BALDWIN.

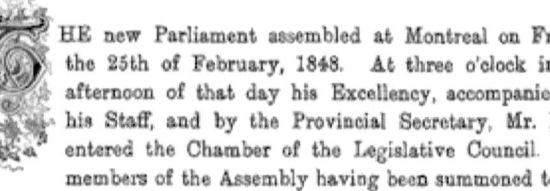

"Remember that the first care of a Governor in a free colony is to shun the reproach of being a party man. Give all parties, and all the Ministries formed, the fairest play. . . . After all, men are governed as much by the heart as by the head. Evident sympathy in the progress of the colony; traits of kindness, generosity, devoted energy, where required for the public weal; a pure exercise of patronage; an utter absence of vindictiveness or spite; the fairness that belongs to magnanimity—these are the qualities that make Governors powerful, while men merely sharp and clever may be weak and detested."— Sir Edward Bulwer Lytton to Sir George Bowen, quoted in Todd's *Parliamentary Government in the British Colonies*, p. 575.

THE new Parliament assembled at Montreal on Friday, the 25th of February, 1848. At three o'clock in the afternoon of that day his Excellency, accompanied by his Staff, and by the Provincial Secretary, Mr. Daly, entered the Chamber of the Legislative Council. The members of the Assembly having been summoned to the bar, Mr. McGill, Speaker of the Legislative Council, announced that his Excellency did not think fit to declare the causes for summoning the present Parliament until a Speaker to the Assembly should be elected, according to law. Monday, the 28th, being named for the delivery of the Speech from the Throne, the members of the Lower House retired to their own Chamber, and proceeded to the election of a Speaker.

The strength of parties was soon put to the test. The proceedings in the Assembly were commenced by Mr. Cayley, Inspector-General in the moribund Ministry, who proposed that Sir Allan

MacNab, the late incumbent of the office, should be Speaker. The motion was seconded by Colonel Prince, who highly complimented Sir Allan on the manner in which he had discharged his official duties during the last Parliament. Mr. Baldwin then rose and moved that the Hon. A. N. Morin should be Speaker. He admitted that Sir Allan had usually discharged the duties pertaining to the office as efficiently as was possible in a gentleman unacquainted with the French language, but he submitted that in a House where so many members were French, and some of whom were unable to speak or understand English, it was a practical necessity that the Speaker should have a knowledge of both languages. Mr. Morin's familiarity with both French and English, combined with his dignity, knowledge of Parliamentary law, and general urbanity of manner, were referred to by Mr. Baldwin as preëminently fitting him for the Speaker's office. The motion was seconded by Mr. Lafontaine. A vote was then taken, and Sir Allan's candidature was defeated by a vote of fifty-four to nineteen.* Mr. Morin was then elected by acclamation, and conducted to his seat amid loud cheering from all parts of the Chamber. The vote on the Speakership afforded a plain indication of the weakness of the Ministry. And here it is worth while to note the most important changes brought about by the recent elections.

To begin with the ministerial side: three members of the Government—Messieurs Morris, McGill and Bruneau—were members of the Legislative Council, and had no need to appeal to the suffrages of the people. The other six Executive Councillors had all been returned for their old constituencies, viz.: Mr. Sherwood for Toronto, Mr. Cayley for Huron, Mr. Badgley for Missisquoi, John A. Macdonald for Kingston, John Hillyard Cameron for Cornwall,†

---

* There were seventy-five members present, but the candidates themselves refrained from voting.

† The Solicitor-General for Upper Canada also contested the county of Kent with Mr. Malcolm Cameron, but was defeated by a majority of more than 500.

and the never-failing Mr. Daly for Megantic. Mr. Turcotte, the new Solicitor-General East, had been defeated in St. Maurice, and it had not been deemed worth while to find another constituency for him, as the Ministry well knew that their reign was at an end, and that they would be unable to hold office after the vote on the Address. Sir Allan MacNab had again been returned for Hamilton, W. B. Robinson for Simcoe, and George Sherwood for Brockville. These were all the conspicuous ministerialists in the House, for there had been no important new accessions on that side as a result of the elections. It was significant, too, that some of the ministerial candidates, and even some of the Ministers themselves, had been returned by narrow majorities.

Turning to the side of the Reformers, a very different state of affairs was disclosed. Not only had all the most conspicuous of the old members been returned by considerable majorities, but there were several important additions to their ranks. In Upper Canada Messieurs Baldwin and Price had swept the North and South Divisions of York respectively, against the Government candidates, Messieurs Gamble and Scobie. John Sandfield Macdonald, who now acted with the Reform party, and was commonly classed as a Reformer, had again been elected for Glengarry. Lincoln had again returned W. H. Merritt, and Malcolm Cameron had been elected for Kent. Five Upper Canadian constituencies had been wrested by Reformers from their opponents, one of the most important victories of the five being in Leeds, where no less a personage than the Grand Master, Mr. Ogle R. Gowan, had been defeated by a sound and prosperous lawyer of Brockville, named William Buell Richards, as to whom more hereafter. Mr. Gowan's public services were for the time lost to his party, and he did not again sit in Parliament until about ten years afterwards. Mr. Hincks, after more than four years' absence from public life, enjoyed the honour of being returned for his old constituency of Oxford, although he was himself out of the country at the time, and unable to take part in the canvass. Several months before the dissolution he had temporarily consigned the editorship of the *Pilot* to other hands, and had crossed the Atlantic on a visit to the home of his boyhood. In anticipation of a general election, he had before leaving Canada made provision for such a contingency, by consigning to trustworthy hands a declaration of qualification, as required by the statute in that behalf. The precaution was wise, as the election for Oxford came on at the end of December, 1847, at which time Mr. Hincks was still absent from Canada, and could not legally have been a candidate unless the statutory declaration had been forthcoming. His interests would seem to have been well taken care of in his absence, as he was returned by a majority of 335 votes over his opponent, a local candidate named Peter Carroll. The returning officer, however, Mr. John George Vansittart, was a strong partisan on the Tory side, and was guilty of most culpable partiality. Before the voting began an elector demanded the production of Mr. Hincks's declaration of qualification. The document was handed to the returning officer by Mr. Hincks's agent, and the former at once perceived that it bore a date prior to that of the writ of election. This was owing to its having been signed and dated by Mr. Hincks before his departure, when it was not even known for certain that an election would take place during the winter. The returning officer made no objection at the time, but allowed the election to proceed. When the result was known, however, he announced that he would treat Mr. Hincks's return as a nullity, the declaration being dated before the writ of election, and Mr. Hincks not having furnished any legal declaration of qualification. He accordingly made a return to the effect that Mr. Carroll had been duly elected, and at the opening of the session that gentleman actually took his seat for Oxford, and voted on the

Speakership in favour of the ministerial candidate, Sir Allan MacNab. This gross injustice to Mr. Hincks and to the electors was speedily remedied by the Assembly, which amended the return, declared Mr. Hincks duly elected, and reprimanded Mr. Vansittart at the bar of the House. Owing to Mr. Hincks's prominent position the affair made a great deal of noise throughout the Province, and aroused an amount of discussion altogether out of proportion to the magnitude of the event itself. Mr. Hincks returned to Canada in time to take his seat on the 1st of March, at which date Mr. Carroll's name was erased from the return, and Mr. Hincks's substituted therefor.*

Among the new Upper Canadian members returned in the interests of the Opposition, several deserve somewhat more than mere mention.

Reference has already been made to William Buell Richards, the new member for Leeds. Mr. Richards, who is still living, is well known throughout the Dominion, more especially throughout that part of it now called Ontario, where his life has been passed. Though he was for more than a quarter of a century an occupant of the judicial bench, and is now retired to private life, he is not yet an old man, and many years of health and usefulness, it is to be hoped, may yet be in store for him. He was born in 1815, at Brockville, in what was then the Johnstown District. His father, Mr. Stephen Richards, was a well-known resident of Brockville, where he for many years exerted a strong political influence on the Reform side, and where he was highly respected for his sterling integrity and shrewdness of judgment. The son studied law, and was called to the bar of Upper Canada in 1837. He settled down to practice in his native town, and was soon known as a successful lawyer. From an early age he had taken a warm interest in politics. He espoused Reform views, and during the

---

* See Legislative Assembly Journals for 1848, p. 11.

www.ingramcontent.com/pod-product-compliance
Lightning Source LLC
Chambersburg PA
CBHW021227300426
44111CB00007B/455